P9-CLC-694

Cooking Light

COOKBOOK 1992

Cooking Light
COOKBOOK 1992

Oxmoor House

Copyright 1991 by Oxmoor House, Inc.
Book Division of Southern Progress Corporation
P.O. Box 2463, Birmingham, Alabama 35201

All rights reserved. No part of this book may be reproduced in any form or by any means without the prior written permission of the Publisher, excepting brief quotes in connection with reviews written specifically for inclusion in a magazine or newspaper.

Library of Congress Catalog Number: 87-61020
ISBN: 0-8487-1068-1
ISSN: 1043-7061

Manufactured in the United States of America
First Printing 1991

Executive Editor: Ann H. Harvey
Director of Manufacturing: Jerry R. Higdon
Production Manager: Rick Litton
Art Director: James Boone

Cooking Light® Cookbook 1992

Editor: Cathy A. Wesler, R.D.
Copy Editor: Diane Lewis Swords
Editorial Assistants: Sue L. Killingsworth, Carole Cain, Kelly E. Hooper, Whitney Wheeler
Director, Test Kitchens: Vanessa Taylor Johnson
Assistant Director, Test Kitchens: Gayle Hays Sadler
Test Kitchen Home Economists: L. Michele Brown, Caroline Grant, R.D.,
    Elizabeth Luckett, Angie Neskaug, Christina A. Pieroni, Kathleen Royal, Jan A. Smith
Senior Photographer: Jim Bathie
Photographer: Ralph Anderson
Senior Photo Stylist: Kay E. Clarke
Photo Stylist: Virginia R. Cravens
Designer: Faith Nance
Associate Production Manager: Theresa L. Beste
Production Assistant: Pam Beasley Bullock
Recipe and Menu Developers: Patricia Coker, Marilyn Wyrick Ingram, Trish Leveret,
    OTT Communications, Inc., Jane Ingrassia Reinsel, Elizabeth J. Taliaferro
Exercise Model: Judith A. Mason

Consultants: Maureen Callahan, M.S., R.D.; University of Alabama School of Medicine in
    Birmingham: Julius Linn, M.D.; Susan Brown, Assistant Editor

Cover: *Cranberry-Topped Chocolate Squares (page 243)*
Back cover: *Fruit en Papillote (page 215)*
Page 2: *Caramel-Peach Trifle (page 229)*

To subscribe to *Cooking Light* magazine, write to *Cooking Light,* P.O. Box C-549,
    Birmingham, Alabama 35283.

Contents

Living Well Is The Best Reward

There is no better time to enjoy life than right now. And as you do so, enjoy a relaxing brunch consisting of Spinach Soufflé Roll served on Peppery Fennel Sauce (page 144), a fresh fruit cup, and chilled orange juice.

Living healthy, living well. Let *Cooking Light Cookbook 1992* help you do both as you take the path toward better health. Along with recipes, menus, a calorie-nutrient chart, and a weekly meal plan, *Cooking Light* offers an abundance of information on nutrition and fitness. And within these pages, you'll learn how nutrition and exercise work together to bring about a healthier lifestyle.

To develop an exercise program, follow our fitness guides, and include muscle strengthening and toning in your workout schedule. This type of exercise can reduce body fat, tone and firm your body (regardless of age), increase motivation and concentration, and improve health and overall physical fitness.

For many, an exercise program includes walking. In fact, 66 million Americans are walking for fitness, according to the National Sporting Goods Association. Walking is particularly suited to today's philosophy of moderate exercise for everyone, and it's less likely to cause injuries than more vigorous activities such as running or jogging.

A recent Gallup Poll showed that people who are committed to taking charge of their health have an increased sense of well-being. They feel confident in their appearance and overall are more satisfied with their lives. With these benefits in mind, take charge of your health—with *Cooking Light*.

Update '92

At the beginning of the century, an American could expect to live about 47 years. Now Americans have a better-than-average chance of reaching age 75. And national health experts are targeting factors that will improve health even more as year 2000 approaches. Although there is a way to go, Americans have begun to get the message that they need to eat better, stay active, stop smoking, and consume less alcohol to prevent premature deaths and improve health during those added years.

If everyone in the U.S. quit using tobacco, 390,000 lives would be lengthened each year. If all Americans ate less fat and walked just 30 minutes a day, a similar number might be spared a premature death.

A recent study suggested that eating less fat would extend an average American's life only a few months. Don't be mislead by this analysis. The study considered neither the benefits to people predisposed to heart disease or cancer, nor the benefits of living life free of heart disease that comes, in part, from eating less fat.

More Fruit, Less Fat

Health authorities from the American Cancer Society and the American Dietetic Association say the best way to cut fat in the diet and from the waistline is to eat more cereals, grains, fruits, and vegetables, and fewer high-fat meats, snacks, and fried foods.

Even though nutritionists give fruits and vegetables high marks, Americans are still not eating enough of these foods to get all the health benefits they offer. The second National Health and Nutrition Examination Survey (NHANES II) asked people what they had eaten on a given day. Researchers found that 45 percent of the population had consumed no servings of fruit or juice; 22 percent had eaten no vegetables. A whopping 91 percent had failed to eat three servings of vegetables and two or more fruits—the five-a-day recommended allotment by the U.S. Department of Agriculture (USDA).

Less Cancer

Health authorities note that as deaths from heart disease decline, cancer rates are rising. The good news, however, is that scientists are finding that what you eat and how you live can limit cancer risks.

Eating more fruits and vegetables gives you a rich selection of vitamins and minerals, such as beta carotene, which studies suggest lowers the incidence of lung, skin, and digestive tract cancers. Foods with beta carotene, such as cabbage, carrots, cauliflower, and broccoli, protect the body from substances that damage cells and alter genes leading to cancerous changes.

By eating diets lower in fat and richer in fiber, Americans may decrease their risk of breast, colon, and prostate cancers. The National Cancer Institute estimates that if by the year 2000, all Americans ate a low-fat, high-fiber diet, colon and rectal cancer rates would drop 50 percent, and breast cancer 25 percent.

Less Protein

The average American diet contains 91 grams of protein a day, two to three times what the body needs. To see what eating less protein and more grains and vegetables can do, consider the rural Chinese. They take in one-third less protein than Americans do—only one-tenth of which comes from animal products. They get most of their calories (as much as 77 percent) from complex carbohydrates found in rice, other grains, and vegetables, with only 15 percent coming from fat.

Although they're taking in 20 percent more calories than Americans, the Chinese are 20 percent thinner. Because their cholesterol levels are much lower, only four in 100,000 Chinese men die of heart disease, compared to 67 out of 100,000 American men. No one is proposing that we adopt the diet of the Chinese, but these differences do underscore the need for adding more fruits, vegetables, and grains in the place of too many fatty meats.

Less Vessel-Clogging Plaque

Americans' heart disease rates continue to fall, due in large part to lifestyle changes—eating less fat, exercising more, giving up cigarettes, losing weight, and limiting stress. Scientists no longer doubt that high blood cholesterol levels contribute to heart and blood vessel diseases, and that lowering cholesterol levels plays a major role in halting the process.

Now scientists are finding that lowering cholesterol also can reverse atherosclerosis. In a study of men with coronary artery disease, University of Washington researchers used intensive drug therapy to lower cholesterol levels. This therapy halved the progression of coronary artery lesions and tripled the disappearance of vessel-clogging plaque.

Although most people don't need drug therapy, this research proves once again that lowering blood cholesterol can reverse the plaque buildup inside vessel walls and thus prevent heart attacks and strokes. These studies add weight to last year's landmark study that showed that better diets, more exercise, and less stress can reverse plaque buildup.

Most studies on the benefits of lowering cholesterol have focused on middle-aged men—the group with the highest incidence of heart disease. But studies last year showed that women and older men also benefit from lowering cholesterol levels. Finding that just as many women die of heart disease as do men emphasizes the importance of women keeping cholesterol levels under control.

Oat bran's ability to lower cholesterol gained further support this year.

By comparing people who ate the same amounts of fat, Chicago researchers proved eating soluble fiber from oat bran or oatmeal every day lowered total cholesterol and low-density lipoprotein (LDL) cholesterol, the type that increases heart disease risk. Be aware, however, that there's nothing magical about oat bran. Other sources of soluble fiber, such as dried or canned beans, achieve the same results.

Children and Cholesterol

The cholesterol message is not limited to adults. The National Heart, Lung, and Blood Institute recommends that children over the age of two limit saturated fat to 10 percent of total calories and total fat to 30 percent, the same as its recommendations for adults. The reason: Studies show the process that leads to heart disease begins in childhood.

Researchers found that American children have higher cholesterol levels than do children in countries where heart disease is less of a problem. Scientists also say that young children with high cholesterol tend to carry the problem into adolescence and adulthood.

In addition to substituting tasty fruit and vegetable choices for high-fat snacks, keeping children away from the television may help lower their cholesterol levels. Recent studies from the University of California, Irvine, School of Medicine showed that children who watched at least two hours of television a day were twice as likely to have high cholesterol levels as those children who watched less television.

Losing Extra Pounds

Shedding pounds is an obsession for the more than 34 million Americans who are overweight. Keeping the weight off proves an even greater frustration, and this problem is becoming an increasingly important part of any weight-loss program.

Losing weight only to put it back on may be as dangerous as staying overweight, according to a Yale University study analyzing the effects of yo-yo dieting. It found that men who lost more than 25 pounds only to regain it had nearly twice the risk of dying from heart disease as those who remained overweight. This research emphasizes the importance of selecting a weight-loss program that teaches you nutritionally sound eating habits that you can follow for a lifetime.

Additional information from the University of Pennsylvania School of Medicine emphasizes the importance of exercise in any weight-loss program. The study of overweight women showed that exercise overcomes the natural slow-down in metabolic rate that accompanies cutbacks in calories.

Encouraging studies from Cornell University nutritionists revealed that people on low-fat diets lost weight even when they didn't restrict calories. Those who ate the low-fat way sustained weight loss for months without cutting calories, suffering hunger pangs, craving foods, or slipping into depression. The women in the study lost about a half pound a week, which is a reasonable amount that encourages slow, but sure and sustained, weight loss.

Putting It All Together

The government's new dietary guidelines are designed to help Americans put into practice today's health advice. The guidelines, last issued in 1985, were revised in 1990. The new ones give recommendations on how much to eat per day—3 to 5 servings of vegetables; 2 to 4 of fruit; 6 to 11 of grains; 2 to 3 of milk, yogurt, or cheese; and 2 to 3 servings of meat, poultry, fish, dried beans and peas, eggs, or nuts.

In 1985, the advice was to avoid too much fat and cholesterol. The 1990 recommendations say to limit fat intake to no more than 30 percent of total calories with no more than 10 percent from saturated fat.

Couched in more positive terms, the new version says to use sugars only in moderation and to eat sparingly of sugar-laden foods high in calories and low in nutrients. Moderation is the key for sodium and alcohol intake as well. The advisory committee that developed the new guidelines concludes that the central message of 1985 remains sound, but the new version is more specific.

Vitamins and Minerals

Today's vitamin research underscores the wisdom of eating a variety of foods to get the proper vitamins and minerals. A study from the University of Edinburgh found that men with higher levels of vitamins C, E, and beta carotene had significantly less pain from coronary artery disease. Of the three, vitamin E showed the strongest relationship. In addition,

a Swiss study showed men in 16 countries with the highest levels of vitamin E intake had the lowest chances of dying from heart disease.

Eating plenty of foods rich in vitamins A, C, and beta carotene also may keep precancerous lesions from developing into cancerous ones. And it may cut your chances of getting cataracts. A study by the Human Nutrition Center on Aging at Tufts University found that people between the ages of 40 and 70 who consumed less than 1½ servings of fruit or juice a day or less than 2 servings of vegetables were 3½ times more likely to have cataracts.

Women six or more years past menopause can reduce bone loss (an effect of aging) by getting adequate calcium. The Tufts University study showed those who got less than 400 milligrams of calcium a day lost 2 to 3 percent of bone density, while those who added a 500 milligram supplement lost 1 percent or less. But calcium supplements didn't slow bone loss in women in the years just after menopause when bone loss is greatest. Women of all ages should make sure they get the Recommended Dietary Allowance (RDA) for calcium.

More Activity, Less Intensity

When exercise experts plotted fitness objectives for the nation 10 years ago, they emphasized vigorous physical conditioning and exercise.

Now the government is trying to get the message out that moderate exercise for everyone is the goal. The Department of Health and Human Service's *Healthy People 2000* objectives have set the goal of getting at

least 30 percent of people to increase moderate daily activity. The second and more sweeping physical fitness goal seeks to reduce by 38 percent the number of people who don't exercise.

If you can't find an hour to exercise, take heart. Shorter, more frequent aerobic exercise sessions can strengthen the heart and burn calories. Women in one study ran on a treadmill either in one 50-minute or two 25-minute sessions. Those who exercised twice burned slightly more calories because their metabolisms remained elevated for 30 minutes after each exercise session.

A Stanford University study confirmed the benefits of even shorter sessions. Thirty-six healthy men jogged five days a week for eight weeks; half did three 10-minute bouts of jogging daily separated by 4 hours; the other group did one 30-minute session a day. Men in both groups significantly improved their physical fitness.

Exercise Boosts Immunity

In addition to the familiar benefits of exercise on the heart, blood pressure, stress, diabetes, and general fitness, it also may boost the body's immune defense systems—at least when done in moderation. Loma Linda University researchers found that marathoners running at their fastest pace actually slowed their immune systems' natural killer cells, making the runners more vulnerable to bacterial and viral infections.

In a subsequent study, the researchers found that a brisk 45-minute walk five days a week boosted killer cells' germ-fighting potential. Exercisers in this study suffered cold and flu symptoms half as often as did a group that didn't exercise.

Exercising Employees

The government's physical fitness objectives for 1990 included getting one-fourth of the companies with more than 500 employees to offer company fitness programs. Reaching that goal could certainly pay off. A study of employees from 35 U.S. corporations showed that the more fit people are, the less time they miss from work. Employees in the excellent fitness category had a 37 percent lower absentee rate than those in the poor fitness group.

Underscoring today's philosophy that lower-intensity exercise can promote good health is the finding that golfers who walk the course can lower their cholesterol levels. The New Hampshire Heart Institute studied golfers who played 18 holes three times a week, either pulling a cart or carrying a light bag. They walked a total of 14 miles a week. The golfers lowered total cholesterol by an average of 17 milligrams, and their LDL cholesterols by 13 milligrams—and they lost weight.

Children and Fitness

Even though adults may be exercising more, children seem to be exercising less. The President's Council on Physical Fitness says the fitness level of American school kids hasn't improved in the past 10 years. As a result, one-third of all children under

12 have high cholesterol levels and 40 percent are obese.

Confirming these findings is a 10-year Columbia University study that looked at 216 inner-city children. Researchers concluded that even at the age of five or six, blood pressure levels were linked to fatness and fitness. They found the more fit a child was, the lower the blood pressure; the fatter the child, the higher the blood pressure.

Regular exercise could lower their blood pressure and risks of developing heart disease. The government's goal is to have 50 percent of American children and teens involved in daily school physical education by the year 2000.

The Melpomene Institute for Women's Health Research found that one-fifth of children under 13 were not very active. One-third were only moderately active; nearly half were fairly active. The biggest influence on children's exercise habits was their parents' exercise patterns.

Data from the Framingham Children's Study confirmed that active children have active parents. Children with physically active mothers were twice as likely to be active as children of sedentary mothers. Children with two parents who exercised were almost six times as likely to be active as children with two inactive parents.

More Benefits

Don't worry about exercise making you hungry—even if you eat some extra calories, you'll burn them and more with a regular program. Washington University School of Medicine

researchers measured the number of calories eaten by active men and women of normal weight. They found that physical activity didn't increase the women's calorie intake. And although the men ate 200 more calories a day, they burned 600, so they still lost 400 calories—enough to burn almost a pound of fat a week.

While eating right and exercising regularly can lead to a longer, healthier life, don't forget the benefits of simple relaxation. Learning to relax a few minutes each day can help allay the stress and anxiety that accompany modern life. Harvard University studies have shown that taking a few minutes each day for total relaxation can provide your body many of the same benefits you get from sleeping. During relaxation, heart rate, blood pressure, and breathing rate drop. You experience feelings of peace and tranquility while soothing alpha waves wash across the circuitry of your brain.

Simplify and Enjoy

Fresh produce doesn't require the fancy packaging that processed foods do. So eating fresh foods means you'll be making less garbage—an important step toward saving the earth for future generations.

Simplifying your exercise program is just as easy; you don't need fancy equipment to go on a brisk walk every day.

Stay committed and active, and enjoy a stress-relieving activity such as gardening. That way, you can grow the fresh produce that's such an important part of a *Cooking Light* lifestyle.

The Food
& Fitness
Connection

The right amount of aerobic exercise combined with a balanced diet is the key to feeling great and looking good. To accomplish this, relax by the pool after a late morning swim, and enjoy a refreshing lunch. Vegetable Cheese Burritos (page 191) served atop shredded lettuce and Hurry Up Chocolate Cake (page 243) are perfect pool-side pleasers. Accompany them with California Lemonade (page 59).

In the third and latest edition of the U.S. Dietary Guidelines, the Department of Agriculture and the Department of Health and Human Services have joined together to issue a framework for healthful eating that requires minimal effort. And to assist you in following these guidelines, *Cooking Light* continues to show that variety, balance, and moderation are important in meal planning.

Along with healthful eating comes exercise. Although many people begin an exercise program, few stick with it—as many as 80 percent drop out soon after starting. If you fall into this group, take note of what some Montreal researchers discovered. They found that people who developed a regular exercise program liked the activity they chose and had a realistic perception of how hard they were exercising. The regular exercisers' lives weren't centered on exercise but rather on work or family. They also felt exercise gave them energy rather than making them tired.

As you use these principles to form an exercise plan, be sure to include strength training. In 1990, the American College of Sports Medicine added strength training to its exercise recommendations. Although the suggestions were made over a year ago, the push is only now trickling down to health professionals and health club personnel. Adding muscle strengthening and toning exercises to your fitness program can give you a fit, toned body.

To start you on your way to healthier eating, turn to the *Cooking Light* Kitchen for ways to trim fat and calories from recipes while still attaining great-tasting results. And let Marketplace walk you through the grocery store with helpful information for purchasing foods low in fat.

Throughout *Cooking Light,* you will find nutrition and fitness guidelines that make for a healthy lifestyle. Share these tips with your family and friends, and you will encourage even the heartiest eater to become more health conscious. You'll find the guidelines flagged with the following symbols:

NUTRITION · FITNESS

Nutrition Basics for *Cooking Light*

It's not hard to figure out what's good for you when it comes to basic nutrition: fresh fruits, vegetables, whole grains, the leanest cuts of meat, the dairy products lowest in fat. And most of the time, it takes little effort to highlight these foods at a meal. To be sure, supermarkets now offer many more lean food items. There's an even wider selection of foods that are naturally low in fat such as whole grain products, legumes, and fresh produce. More meats are now available that come trimmed of all but a pencil-thin layer of fat. And reduced-fat versions of old favorites such as cheese and luncheon meats are multiplying at a rapid pace. In fact, everything from margarine to sour cream to snack foods has seen the "light."

Of course, having the healthiest of foods right at your fingertips doesn't automatically ensure good nutrition—particularly if your idea of what constitutes a balanced diet is somewhat skewed. Experts give kudos to Americans for shunning all of these fatty meats, greasy fried foods, and high-fat sauces. However, they worry that many let their penchants for chocolate, premium ice cream, and high-fat cheeses negate all of these fat savings. In other words, many Americans overindulge in some areas while cutting back in others.

The key to good eating is to strive for moderation and balance. It takes no high-tech planning or mathematical combinations to focus on a healthy eating style. All it takes are some commonsense practices. In the third and latest edition of the U.S. Dietary Guidelines, the Department of Agriculture and the Department of Health and Human Services joined together to issue a framework for healthful eating that requires only minimal effort.

Scientists' knowledge about how diet affects health enables them to make specific suggestions about how people need to eat. It's not that food alone will keep disease at bay. But laying the framework for a healthy eating pattern is a good hedge for preventing problems such as heart disease, obesity, diabetes, and cancer.

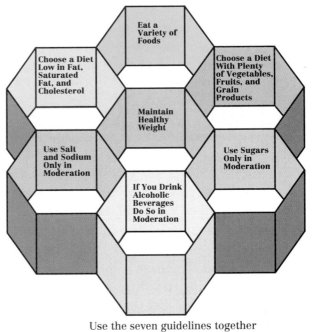

Use the seven guidelines together
as you choose a healthful and enjoyable diet.

RULES TO EAT BY

As the first step toward healthy eating, the newest seven U.S. dietary guidelines encourage Americans to keep food choices varied. Eating a variety of foods lessens the chance that any one essential nutrient will be lacking. If you're a headline reader, you may have read that eating beta carotene-rich foods such as cantaloupe, spinach, and carrots may lessen the risk for cancer and possibly heart disease. However, singling out one food as a means of disease prevention or health promotion is not a smart strategy in the game of good nutrition. Variety is the better bet.

One guideline that many Americans find particularly troublesome encourages people to keep weight at a healthy level. Eating too much and exercising too little can jeopardize health; it's that simple. That's why the guidelines also encourage moderation when it comes to sugar, salt, and alcohol. None of these are dietary villains, but in excess all three can negatively influence health.

Another guideline highlights the importance of choosing more fresh fruits, vegetables, and whole grains to boost the amount of carbohydrate and fiber in the diet. Since these foods generally contain very little fat, this guideline works in tandem with the final rule: Choose a diet low in fat, saturated fat, and cholesterol. Because fat has twice the calories of carbohydrate or protein, eating foods containing generous amounts of fat is thought to be at the crux of this country's weight problems.

FOCUS ON FAT

Aside from being calorie-dense, fat is a nutrient that, if overdone, can contribute to a multitude of health problems including heart disease, obesity, diabetes, and cancer. If people could make only one nutritional change in their eating habits, experts unanimously agree that trimming fat intake would be the most important goal. Currently, people in the U.S. consume about 37 percent of their calories each day as fat. Some of the fat is from obvious sources such as butter, margarine, or vegetable oils. Other fats are not so visible. They come hidden in luncheon meats or snack foods. For health purposes, experts recommend reducing fat calories to less than 30 percent of total calorie intake.

Over the last few years, emphasis has been placed on the quantity of various types of fat that people eat—saturated animal fats, polyunsaturated vegetable fats, and monounsaturated fats. Saturated fats pose the biggest health risk. Studies find that eating too much of this fat may increase risk for heart disease and certain types of cancer. Nevertheless, the amount of fat you eat may be an even bigger issue than saturated fat. Scientists feel that if people would concentrate just on cutting back on total fat, levels of each of the three types might fall naturally into place.

PORTION CONTROL

Keeping tabs on total fat intake requires paying attention to how much you eat or the size of the servings. Think about cafeteria-style dining for a minute. Every dish of green beans, mashed potatoes, and macaroni is exactly the same size. Restaurants dish up servings with ice cream-style scoops to keep food costs in line. Since some foods do pack large amounts of fat and calories, the art of measuring

serving sizes can't hurt on the home kitchen front. If you have some idea what constitutes a reasonable portion size, it will be easier to eat your fill yet not fill up on the wrong foods.

In the new dietary guidelines, 6 ounces of lean meat is considered a reasonable meat or protein food allotment for the entire day. Unless you're a butcher or have trained yourself on portion sizes, it's not easy to estimate them. Nutritionists describe 6 ounces as roughly the size of two decks of playing cards: one deck of playing cards at lunch, and one at supper. Because more than half the fat Americans eat comes from animal sources, learning portion control for meats is very important. Kitchen scales can help you learn to judge portion size. That's how trained chefs can look at a piece of meat or a bunch of broccoli and know how many servings it will make.

The whole idea behind learning serving sizes is to know what foods you can eat larger portions of (fruits, vegetables, and whole grains) and what foods you need to eat in smaller quantities (high-fat items, such as ice cream, ground beef, and high-fat dairy foods). If you're still hungry at a meal, a high carbohydrate side dish such as potatoes, rice, bread, or fruit is much better than a second helping of meat or a high-fat dessert.

In other countries, carbohydrate-rich grains are the focus of the meal. Studies seem to show that a carbohydrate-rich diet may help promote good health and protect the body against diseases.

ETHNIC DIVERSITY

What Americans can learn from ethnic cuisine is that it focuses on grains and complex carbohydrate foods instead of large quantities of meat and high-fat animal foods. When legumes such as lentils or black beans are combined with a grain such as rice, the combination provides a high-quality protein that is just as nutritious as meat. Throughout the pages of *Cooking Light*, you will find a mixture of the best and tastiest of American and ethnic foods. Recipes combine good nutrition with flavors that range from old-fashioned to exotic. Whatever foods you are in the mood for, chances are that *Cooking Light* has a good-tasting, good-for-your-health version.

Computing Nutrition

Your Daily Needs

To estimate your daily calorie requirement, multiply your current weight by 15. Remember that this is only a rough guide because calorie requirements vary according to age, body size, and level of activity. If a change of weight is desired, add or subtract 500 calories per day to allow for weight gain or loss of 1 pound a week. However, a diet of less than 1,200 calories a day is not recommended unless medically supervised. For more information concerning your requirements, consult a registered dietitian.

Implement the *Cooking Light* 50-20-30 guidelines (page 30) by calculating the amount of carbohydrate, protein, and fat for optimal health. Multiply your calorie requirement by the percentages 50, 20, and 30 to give the calories from each nutrient. Divide the carbohydrate and protein calories by 4 (4 calories per gram) and the fat by 9 (9 calories per gram) to determine how many grams of each nutrient you need.

For example, here's how to calculate the distribution of a 2,000-calorie diet:

50% carbohydrate = 1,000 calories ÷ 4 = 250 grams carbohydrate

20% protein = 400 calories ÷ 4 = 100 grams protein

30% fat = 600 calories ÷ 9 = 67 grams fat

Therefore, for a person eating 2,000 calories a day, 1,000 calories would meet the 50 percent carbohydrate guideline, while no more than 400 calories and 600 calories would be from protein and fat, respectively.

When planning your meals, refer to the daily amounts of nutrients to help you make the most of the nutrient values that follow *Cooking Light* recipes. Although there is no Recommended Dietary Allowance (RDA) for sodium or cholesterol, suggested intake is listed below along with the RDA for iron and calcium.

Iron 15 milligrams
Calcium 800 milligrams
Sodium 3,300 milligrams or less
Cholesterol 300 milligrams or less

Every Recipe Analyzed

Calories and a nutrient breakdown per serving accompany every recipe. The nutrients listed include grams of carbohydrate, protein, and fat along with milligrams of cholesterol, calcium, iron, and sodium.

Determining Calorie Percentages

Use *Cooking Light* nutrient breakdowns to calculate the percentage of calories contributed by carbohydrate, protein, and fat. Let's say you are looking at the recipe for Cilantro-Stuffed Baked Potatoes (complete recipe on page 143), and you want to determine the percentage of fat in one serving.

First, find the number of grams of fat per serving. This is calculated in the analysis to be 3.7 grams. To find the percentage of calories from fat, multiply grams of fat by 9 (the number of calories per gram of fat) to get fat calories per serving. Then divide this quantity by the total calories. You'll find that fat contributes about 10 percent of the calories.

Cilantro-Stuffed Baked Potatoes

PROTEIN 16.6 FAT 3.7 CARBOHYDRATE 62.9 CHOLESTEROL 12
IRON 3.8 SODIUM 304 CALCIUM 244

To calculate the calories contributed by carbohydrate and protein, multiply grams of carbohydrate or protein per serving by 4 (the number of calories per gram of carbohydrate or protein). Divide the quantity by total calories.

Menus and Menu Plans Meet 50-20-30 Guidelines

All recipes will not fall so neatly within the guidelines. When this occurs, effort should be made to combine these foods with other foods to meet the recommended percentages: more than 50 percent carbohydrate, about 20 percent protein, and no more than 30 percent fat. The goal is to achieve the recommended balance of nutrients on a daily basis, taking into consideration three meals and a snack.

How the Recipes Are Analyzed

The recipes are developed for people interested in lowering their intake of calories, sodium, fat, and/or cholesterol to maintain healthy eating patterns. If you are following a medically prescribed diet, consult a registered dietitian to see how *Cooking Light* recipes can fit into your specific meal plan.

The calorie and nutrient breakdown of each recipe is derived from computer analysis, based primarily on information from the U.S. Department of Agriculture. The values are as accurate as possible and are based on these assumptions:

- All nutrient breakdowns are listed per serving.
- All meats are trimmed of fat and skin before cooking.
- When a range is given for an ingredient (for example, 3 to 3½ cups flour), the lesser amount is calculated.
- A percentage of alcohol calories evaporates when heated, and this reduction is reflected in the calculations.
- When a marinade is used, only the amount of marinade used (not discarded) is calculated.
- Garnishes and other optional ingredient items are not calculated.
- Fruits and vegetables listed in the ingredients are not peeled unless otherwise specified.

Exercise—The Perfect Partner

Unfortunately, many Americans have lost sight of the long list of health benefits that come with regular activity. That may explain why more than 34 million adults in this country, ages 20 to 72, are obese by medical standards. One out of four people has a blood cholesterol level above 200, a factor which puts them at high risk for heart disease. To make matters worse, these unhealthy habits are being passed on to the children. Youngsters are joining the ranks of the clinically fat in such alarming numbers that one healthcare expert proclaims we are raising a nation of butterballs.

Forty percent of American children between the ages of five and eight are inactive, obese, or have at least one of the risk factors for developing heart disease (either an elevated cholesterol level or high blood pressure). Sadly, physical education, which could possibly bring down these numbers, is no longer required in most grade schools. Only 36 percent of American children in grades 1 through 12 are enrolled in a daily physical education class. Indeed, the country is full of sedentary children and adults who have turned off activity.

PERSONAL TRAINERS

The solution for these people may be found in personal fitness training. Movie stars, professional athletes, and business executives fork over large sums of money to have individual trainers put them through rigorous exercise routines. But you don't need lots of money to gain the benefits of a personal trainer. Fitness experts say that with a little effort, you can tailor-make a program that suits your lifestyle and exercise preferences, all without spending a cent. The key is to discover what type of activities or sports make you feel good. Start by trying several activities, some by yourself and some in groups.

Once you decide on your favorites, build an exercise routine. Many people pursue fitness arbitrarily, but exercising needs commitment to yield healthy long-term results. For the best training program, think of what you would like to accomplish—be it preventing illness, toning the body, relieving stress, or losing weight. That's exactly what paid trainers do when they first sit down with clients; they start by discussing long-term goals. Take time to record your long-term goals, and then easier short-term goals, such as how many times you will exercise per week, can be determined.

Learn to read your body lingo to discover what time of the day is the best to exercise. People peak mentally and physically at different times during the day. "Early birds" seem to stick with fitness plans that emphasize early morning workouts; "night owls" do better with evening pursuits.

MUSCLES LARGE AND SMALL

Every movement of the body uses a muscle or groups of muscles, and each movement requires energy. The reason some exercises and sports burn more energy than others has to do primarily with the muscle groups being used.

Larger muscles—those that move the legs, hips, and arms—require more oxygen and energy to be worked. Working these larger muscle groups not only burns more energy (calories) but it also works the cardiovascular system. Smaller muscles, while they don't require as much energy or heart effort, still need to be kept in shape. Therefore, working the large and small muscles is very important for overall fitness.

Basically, three types of exercise are needed to work all the muscles: warm-up, conditioning, and circulatory (cardiovascular). Use warm-up exercises such as light side-to-side movements to limber up muscles and to prevent injury from the other types of exercises.

Conditioning or strength exercises are those that tone the muscles through repetitive movements. Either hand-held weights or a weight machine can be used to shape and define the muscles. But the most crucial exercises are those that work the heart and circulatory system. Running, walking, jumping rope, swimming, and aerobic dancing use major muscle groups, burn fat, and help keep the heart working efficiently.

REVISED RECOMMENDATIONS

The American College of Sports Medicine (ACSM) has updated its guidelines on the quantity and quality of exercise needed to achieve and maintain fitness. But the ACSM guidelines still include recommendations on frequency, intensity, and duration of exercise.

While the suggested duration of the workout is 20 to 60 minutes, it is dependent upon the intensity of the exercise. Thus, less intense exercises should be done longer than intense ones to achieve the same fitness benefits. And lower to moderately intense exercises coupled with longer duration is the preferred method to prevent injury and enhance fitness for the nonathletic adult.

For the first time, ACSM has included resistance training in its fitness guidelines. Recommendations include completing one set of 8 to 12 repetitions for 8 to 10 exercises that utilize the major muscle groups. These workouts should be done at least two days a week to develop and maintain body muscle. Because muscles are metabolically more active than fat, strength training enhances your metabolic rate. So as an added benefit to having a toned, firm body, this type of regimen will enable you to burn more calories.

COUNTING THE BEATS

To determine your heart rate, locate your radial artery (on the thumb side of your wrist) and take your pulse during your exercise session. Take your pulse count for 10 seconds and then multiply that number by 6 to get your actual heart rate. If that number is above your target heart rate (THR) zone, slow down. If the number is below the zone, step up the pace.

AGE	PREDICTED MAXIMUM HEART RATE	TARGET HEART RATE ZONE		NUMBER OF HEARTBEATS IN 10 SECONDS	
	(in minutes)	60%	- 90%	60%	- 90%
20	200	120	180	20	30
25	195	117	176	20	29
30	190	114	171	19	29
35	185	111	167	19	28
40	180	108	162	18	27
45	175	105	158	18	26
50	170	102	153	17	26
55	165	99	149	17	25
60	160	96	144	16	24

MATHEMATICAL FORMULA
Maximum Heart Rate (MHR) = 220 minus age
MHR x 60% and 90% = THR in minutes

ONE FOOT FORWARD

You don't have to take up the latest exercise craze to become fit. Instead, you can forge your own path at your own pace and in your own direction with walking. The frequency, intensity, and duration of your walking workouts influence the extent of the health benefits you reap. Slow walking, a pace 1 to 3 miles per hour, is not vigorous enough to give you much of a cardiovascular workout. But just covering the distance, no matter what the pace, does give the muscles a workout.

Increase the pace to 3 to 5 miles per hour and the heart gets a workout; race walking, a pace of about 6 to 9 miles per hour, provides the same cardiovascular benefits, but the energy required to move the body at a faster speed is greater. Race walking and brisk walking are the same for cardiovascular purposes; the difference between the two is the amount of energy expended. Race walking burns similar amounts of energy as compared with jogging.

As you continue to engage in these aerobic activities, your heart will beat stronger and steadier, breathing will become easier and deeper, and your blood circulation will improve. Ignore these activities and you may suffer the consequences. An inactive body is one that loses efficiency. Use exercise to keep your body at peak efficiency. With the proper care and feeding, anybody can improve his health.

Muscle Strengthening and Toning

Strength training shapes and tones the muscles, thus providing an energy-burning benefit. Muscles are metabolically more active than fat, which means that they burn calories and keep the metabolic rate at a higher level. Sedentary people, and even those who engage only in aerobic exercise, begin losing muscle mass in their mid-twenties—up to a half pound of muscle per year. As the muscle mass decreases, the resting metabolic rate decreases. Building or maintaining muscle mass with strength training helps keep the metabolic rate from decreasing.

Strength training, if done properly, can slenderize the waist, hips, and buttocks. It also can reduce body fat, tone and firm the body (regardless of age), increase motivation and concentration, and improve health and overall physical fitness.

While body builders emphasize the amount of weight lifted, strength training focuses on the number of times a weight is lifted (repetitions). So instead of bulking up, muscles become sleek, toned, and much more efficient.

Start by using 1-pound dumbbells for the upper-body exercises and increase to 3-pound weights when comfortable with the routine; add 1-pound ankle weights for resistance during lower-body calisthenics. Be sure to move the muscles through their full range of motion, using a slow, fully controlled movement in both directions. Don't forget to breathe; exhale during the lift or push, and inhale during the release or return.

Warm up—Stand with feet shoulder-width apart and knees slightly bent. Extend arms out to the sides. Gently twist to the right, swinging arms as you turn. Lift left heel to fully extend left leg. Repeat on opposite side. Continue for 2 to 3 minutes.

Triceps (back of arm)—Bend both knees slightly and rest one arm on thigh for support. With a dumbbell in hand, hold arm at a 90-degree angle, and then straighten it backward. Start with 15 to 20 repetitions per arm.

Biceps (front of arm)—Stand with feet shoulder-width apart, arms straight down at sides, and a dumbbell in each hand with palms facing forward. Keep your elbows and upper arms close to your body. Curl both dumbbells upward until you cannot curl any higher. Apply resistance as you lower arms to starting position. Repeat 12 to 18 times.

Shoulders, back, and upper arms—Stand with feet shoulder-width apart, arms at 90-degree angles, and a dumbbell in each hand with palms facing forward. Raise both arms above head. Pull arms down until elbows are at shoulder height, keeping elbows bent at 90-degree angles. Return arms to starting position. Repeat 12 to 18 times.

Quadriceps (front thighs), hips, and buttocks—Stand up straight with a dumbbell in each hand. Step forward with left foot, bending right knee toward ground. Slowly rise straight up to starting position. Step forward with right foot, repeating movements. Do 10 to 15 steps with each leg.

Abdominals—Lie on your back with knees bent and feet flat on floor. Hold a 3-pound dumbbell against chest. Exhale while slowly curling up, keeping the lower back pressed against the floor. Inhale while slowly lowering to starting position. Repeat 8 to 12 times.

Outer thigh—Lie on side with torso raised and weight resting on forearm. Flex feet and slowly raise top leg. Slowly lower leg, using resistance. Start with 15 to 20 lifts per side.

Abdominals—Lie on floor with lower back pressed toward floor and weight on arms for support. Extend legs in air with feet flexed. Alternately raise and lower legs, bending at knees. Repeat 12 to 18 times.

Calves, quadriceps, hamstrings, and buttocks—Place feet on stairclimber and rest hands on side bars. Follow manufacturer's instructions for equipment operation. Adjust level of intensity according to your level of fitness. Start with a 5-minute workout and increase to 15 to 20 minutes for a vigorous cardiovascular workout. If a stairclimber isn't available, climbing ordinary stairs can provide the same benefits.

ALPINE LIFE SPORTS

Set Yourself Up for Success

If you could change anything about yourself, what would it be? If you said size and shape, you're not alone. Many are sure they are too fat—they lament about bulging middles, heavy thighs, or wide hips, worrying mostly about cosmetics. But wanting to weigh less for the sake of appearance only is not a good reason.

When scientists and health professionals met recently to issue the latest edition of the U.S. Dietary Guidelines, they debated about shifting weight preoccupation in a more constructive direction. Health, they felt, should be the top priority.

HEALTHY VERSUS DESIRABLE

Along with some carefully worded advice regarding weight, the latest dietary guidelines suggest that you maintain a "healthy" weight. Old advice was to keep a "desirable" weight. It might not seem like a big change, but the one-word difference speaks volumes.

Research shows that the number of pounds necessary for good health is not necessarily the number that will transform you into a thin, sleek model. In fact, a few extra pounds don't always contribute to ill health, particularly as people get older. Furthermore, health professionals now realize that the total weight picture encompasses more than one number on a chart. Other important numbers to consider include blood pressure, cholesterol, and blood sugar level. Moreover, frame size, where the extra pounds are located, and genetics all influence the healthiness of an individual.

WORKING CHARTS AND BLUEPRINTS

If statisticians were to plot the heights and weights of a group of people on a bell curve, like teachers plot test scores, the dots would be littered all over the curve. Some people would fall on the left of the curve, some people would dot the lines along the center, and others would end up on the far right. So why do so many want to fall to the far left of the curve in one small area that denotes model thinness, and perhaps even the eating disorder anorexia?

Unrealistic weight expectations are the reason, say health experts.

If you look at the new weight charts, it's obvious that what is considered a "healthy" weight range is more generous than previous weight charts, particularly once a person passes the age of 35. And rather than focus on men and women separately, the new charts break healthy weights into age categories.

SUGGESTED WEIGHTS FOR ADULTS

Keep in mind the following chart is for height without shoes, weight without clothing, and that the higher weights in each range generally are for males. The lower weights more often apply to females, who have less muscle and bone.

HEIGHT	WEIGHT IN POUNDS	
	19 TO 34 YEARS	35 YEARS AND OVER
5'0"	97—128	108—138
5'1"	101—132	111—143
5'2"	104—137	115—148
5'3"	107—141	119—152
5'4"	111—146	122—157
5'5"	114—150	126—162
5'6"	118—155	130—167
5'7"	121—160	134—172
5'8"	125—164	138—178
5'9"	129—169	142—183
5'10"	132—174	146—188
5'11"	136—179	151—194
6'0"	140—184	155—199
6'1"	144—189	159—205
6'2"	148—195	164—210
6'3"	152—200	168—216
6'4"	156—205	173—222
6'5"	160—211	177—228
6'6"	164—216	182—234

Source: National Research Council, 1989.

WHERE'S THE FAT?

The location and the percentage of weight that's stored as fat play critical roles in health. Of course, weight ranges are rough estimates of healthy weight; the top of the range refers mainly to men or those with muscular athletic bodies, since muscle weighs more than fat. But it's not only the muscle-to-fat ratio that makes a difference in the health value of a certain weight. If you have extra weight, consider where that fat is located.

Extra pounds around the waist or midsection are linked to a higher risk of heart disease and diabetes. Pudgy thighs, however, don't appear to be detrimental to health.

SETTING THE PACE

If, after looking at the new weight guidelines, you fit into an unhealthy category, experts have another piece of good advice. As you set weight-loss goals, keep in mind realistic expectations and time limits. Believe it or not, the slower you take extra pounds off, the more likely they are to stay off. The newest recommendations set a reasonable pace for weight loss— ½ to 1 pound per week.

To lose 1 pound a week, cut back or burn 250 to 500 calories per day (3,500 calories equal 1 pound). You could burn 250 calories a day by simply walking briskly for 30 to 40 minutes. Combine walking with some cutbacks in fat and calories, and the result is gradual weight loss. This illustrates the new message about managing weight: Eat smart and stay active to keep your weight at a healthy level.

Researchers have pinpointed four factors common to people who lose weight and keep it off. First, those who win at the losing game exercise regularly—90 percent exercise at least three times a week for 30 minutes. Second, they change their eating habits, eating less fat and sugar and more fruits and vegetables. Instead of severely restricting food intake, they eat enough, including some of their favorite foods, so they don't feel deprived. Third, they feel good about their bodies. And finally, they confront their problems directly and seek help, whether from friends, family, or professionals.

THINK SLIM, TRIM, AND HEALTHY

- Make a list of all the health reasons for losing weight. Periodically review these goals so that your attitude toward weight shifts toward a healthful focus rather than a cosmetic one.
- Limit high-calorie foods you love, but don't eliminate them. Just eat small portions, less often. Don't deprive yourself and then binge.
- Dish up a single serving at meals and immediately refrigerate leftovers—no second helpings.
- Avoid the starve-all-day, stuff-yourself-at-night attitude. Space food out over the course of the day; eat at least three main meals, to help keep appetite under control.
- Keep a food diary to find out what triggers you to overeat or eat erratically. Once you figure out why, it's easier to change unhealthy habits.
- Instead of eating an extra helping or snack, take a walk or do something active. Contrary to popular belief, exercise doesn't induce hunger; it's a fat burner.
- Start thinking of eating as a balancing act. If you indulge on occasion, make up for it at the following meal or the next day.
- Make small portions of food look larger by serving them on salad plates instead of dinner plates.
- Rethink the clean-your-plate mentality. It's better to throw out the last few bites than to consume extra calories when you're not really hungry.
- Park the car a block away from your destination and walk the remaining distance.
- Learn the fat content of your favorite foods—read food labels or look in a nutrition guide. Hidden fats sabotage weight control and health strategies.
- If a bad habit resurfaces, visualize health goals. The long-term rewards of a fit, healthy body hold strong appeal when compared with a few minutes of indulgence.

The *Cooking Light* Kitchen

Most traditional recipes can easily be lightened in fat and calories by making a few changes in the ingredient list. When developing *Cooking Light*'s Creamy Chocolate Cheesecake (complete recipe, page 246), just a few of these changes in ingredients have allowed over 500 calories to be shaved from each serving. This cheesecake recipe is a perfect example of how to prepare flavorful food without being guilt-ridden about the calories, fat, and cholesterol. Each serving of *Cooking Light's* cheesecake contains 76 percent fewer calories, 84 percent less fat, and 82 percent less cholesterol than the traditional version.

Part-skim ricotta cheese and Neufchâtel cheese are combined to form the base of the *Cooking Light* cheesecake. These two ingredients alone offer a savings of nearly 150 calories per serving when substituted for the cream cheese used in the traditional version. The eggs in the traditional recipe are replaced with a commercial egg substitute, and

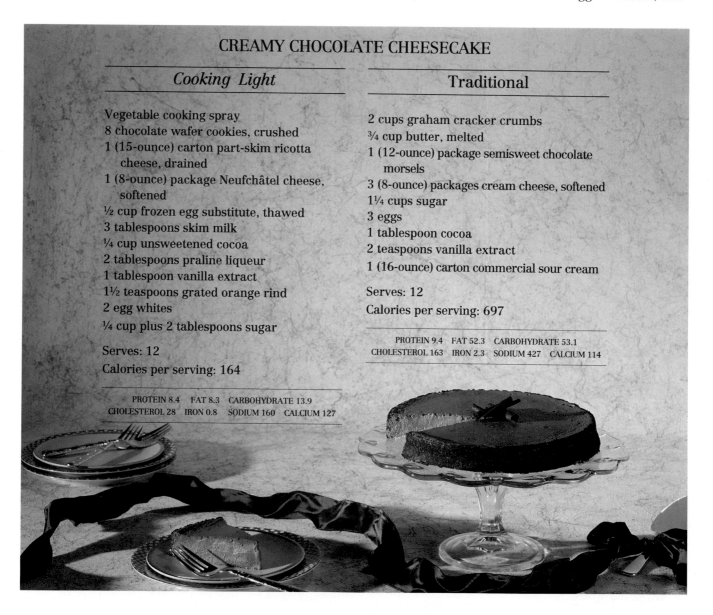

CREAMY CHOCOLATE CHEESECAKE

Cooking Light

Vegetable cooking spray
8 chocolate wafer cookies, crushed
1 (15-ounce) carton part-skim ricotta cheese, drained
1 (8-ounce) package Neufchâtel cheese, softened
½ cup frozen egg substitute, thawed
3 tablespoons skim milk
¼ cup unsweetened cocoa
2 tablespoons praline liqueur
1 tablespoon vanilla extract
1½ teaspoons grated orange rind
2 egg whites
¼ cup plus 2 tablespoons sugar

Serves: 12
Calories per serving: 164

PROTEIN 8.4   FAT 8.3   CARBOHYDRATE 13.9
CHOLESTEROL 28   IRON 0.8   SODIUM 160   CALCIUM 127

Traditional

2 cups graham cracker crumbs
¾ cup butter, melted
1 (12-ounce) package semisweet chocolate morsels
3 (8-ounce) packages cream cheese, softened
1¼ cups sugar
3 eggs
1 tablespoon cocoa
2 teaspoons vanilla extract
1 (16-ounce) carton commercial sour cream

Serves: 12
Calories per serving: 697

PROTEIN 9.4   FAT 52.3   CARBOHYDRATE 53.1
CHOLESTEROL 163   IRON 2.3   SODIUM 427   CALCIUM 114

egg whites are beaten and folded in for additional volume.

These techniques make it possible for even the most inexperienced cook to modify family favorites without sacrificing one morsel of flavor.

TESTED FOR ASSURANCE

Feel confident as you prepare *Cooking Light* recipes and menus. Each has been developed and tested by a staff of home economists to meet strict standards for sound nutrition, excellent flavor, and visual appeal. And to add to the visual appeal, garnishing and serving suggestions have been provided to help you create great-looking, great-tasting meals.

As you cook the low-fat way, use *Cooking Light* ideas to add additional flavor to your meals. And feel good knowing that you are making nutritious meals an enjoyable, pleasant experience.

KEEP IT LIGHT AND KEEP THE FLAVOR

Low-sugar jams and jellies and all-fruit spreads can add a fresh fruit flavor without the excess sugar contained in their higher calorie counterparts. They can be purchased commercially or made from scratch, such as Raspberry Refrigerator Jam (right, page 33).

Mild mustards or the hot and spicy varieties can be low-fat condiments for sandwiches—but watch out for sodium. Prepared mustard has only 12 calories and less than 1 gram of fat per tablespoon, but it contains 196 milligrams of sodium.

Salt-free herb seasonings add flavor and zest to grilled meats and poultry, steamed vegetables, soups, and sauces. While a variety of seasonings are available in the supermarket, Caribbean Spice Mix (page 203) can be made at home and kept as a staple on your spice rack.

Salsa, the Mexican word for sauce, is made mainly of diced ingredients that are cooked or left raw. Fresh or commercial salsas can be purchased in supermarkets or you can make your own. Try Tomatillo Salsa (right, page 204) or Black Bean Salsa (left, page 205).

New nonfat dairy products are arriving on the grocery store shelves. A sampling of these items includes (clockwise from top left) nonfat sour cream (10 calories per tablespoon), nonfat mayonnaise (12 calories per tablespoon), and nonfat cottage cheese (90 calories per ½ cup).

When combined with herbs, fruits, and spices, vinegar takes on intense flavors that add spark to soups, salads, and side dishes. These infused vinegars can be purchased in gourmet food shops or you can make them yourself. Start with Garlic-Herb Vinegar (page 203).

What's New In The Marketplace?

Supermarket shopping in the nineties is becoming an exercise in high-tech wizardry. And the emphasis is on health. Grocers are stocking shelves with low-fat and nonfat snacks, sauces, desserts, and meals. At the same time, they're also testing state-of-the-art gadgets designed to simplify shopping for health items. One of the latest is a computer-programmed shopping screen that sits on the grocery cart. As you amble down the store aisles, the screen lights up with pictures, nutrition profiles, sale information, or food preparation tips.

Other high-tech advances include computers that accept bank or automated teller machine (ATM) cards as payment for groceries, computer information kiosks that dispense coupons, recipes, and nutrition information at the point of purchase, and electronic shelf tags that list the most up-to-date prices. At this rate, it's possible that by the year 2000, clipping coupons, paying with cash, and standing in long check-out lines may become obsolete. Ditto for worrying about purchasing foods high in fat.

Considering the abundance of lightened and lean food products, it might not take long to achieve recommended fat contributions of 30 percent of calories or less. Here's a brief aisle-by-aisle guide of some of the new selections. Keep in mind, of course, that all fresh fruits and vegetables (except coconuts and avocados) are naturally lean and low in calories. Primarily, it is the dairy, meat, and convenience food aisles that are filled with a number of fat-reduced items.

UP AND DOWN THE AISLES

Several manufacturers produce reduced-calorie sour cream in which the fat content is often half that of the regular variety. And many versions of sour cream substitutes, yogurt, and cottage cheese which already were available in low-fat versions are now also being offered in nonfat varieties. Block cheeses, such as Cheddar, Swiss, and colby, now come in reduced-fat versions. While fat levels may vary, manufacturers continuously try to get below 5 grams of fat per ounce instead of the 8 to 10 grams of fat normally found in these cheeses.

Try using low-fat dairy products in place of their high-fat counterparts. They work well in casseroles, coffee cakes, and other recipes without harming the texture or flavor of the foods.

With the focus on reducing fat, most meats come trimmed of most or all of the visible fat. Newest debuts in the meat case include ground turkey and ground chicken. These can be substituted for the high-fat meats commonly called for in meat loaves, soups, and casseroles.

Be sure to read the labels, as these products vary in fat content. Fresh ground poultry without the skin is available, but poultry typically is ground with some of the skin. Still, most turkey and chicken products such as turkey sausage, turkey bacon, and turkey or chicken frankfurters carry less fat and calories than their beef and pork counterparts. But when compared to other choices, these lower-fat products may still be high in fat. Take chicken franks, for example. They contain less fat than regular hot dogs (an average of 11 grams of fat instead of 13), but they are still a high-fat choice when compared to broiled or baked skinned chicken.

The same goes for deli meats and sausage. Labels may trumpet the product as being 85 to 90 percent fat free. But the companies are measuring fat by weight, not calories. So while lean bologna is 85 percent fat free or a turkey bacon or turkey sausage is 90 percent fat free, fat still comprises more than half of their calories. Better lean selections include deli turkey, lean baked ham, Canadian bacon, and lean roast beef.

While a cholesterol-free label makes a vegetable oil sound healthier, remember that all vegetable oils are free of cholesterol. Although the new fat-free or oil-free salad dressings are not a bad addition to the pantry, be sure to look closely at the serving sizes. Most companies list the serving size as one tablespoon, and many people use much more than that. If you multiply the fat and calories per serving by a more realistic portion, you will have a better idea of how light a dressing is. So rather than worry over the type of oil or dressing you use, focus on the amount. The best way to lighten up on fats is to use less of them.

Thin-sliced and reduced-calorie breads with 40 calories or less per slice have quadrupled over the last few years. Extra fiber and a generous dose of water are usually what lightens the loaf. The same holds true for light pasta noodles and light bread mixes. When cereal manufacturers mention healthfulness, they usually are referring to a lower quantity of sugar and a higher amount of fiber. However, don't be swayed by cereal labels boasting that the product is low in fat because most cereals contain little or no fat. The exception would be a granola cereal which contains nuts or coconut.

Convenience foods definitely have seen the "light." But be careful when making selections in this area. Currently, "light" has no legal definition, so it can mean a lighter texture, color, or flavor. Your best bet is to compare leaner versions with a similar size serving of the original product. A light fried fish product might just mean a lighter breading, not less fat. Since the fat added to convenience food can't be removed (except by manufacturers), be sure to pay close attention to the amount of fat per serving. Sometimes you can lighten mixes such as macaroni and cheese by adding less fat or oil than the box instructions call for.

Potato chips, corn chips, peanuts, and popcorn now come in lighter versions that carry one-third to one-half less fat. The savings are good but don't forget snacks that are naturally low in fat—pretzels, air-popped corn, and saltine crackers. No matter how much potato chips are lightened, they will still contain more fat and calories than these low-fat choices.

Low-fat, low-calorie cake mixes, frostings, cookies, coffee cakes, and frozen desserts are other new by-products of the fat conscious nineties. Fat-free frozen desserts typically use fat substitutes or gums and stabilizers to provide the taste and texture of ice cream. Even though these frozen desserts are fat free, they do contain some calories. In fact, most of these products are similar to ice milks, sherbets, and sorbets in fat and calorie content.

The secret to many of the low-fat baked treats is a combination of a little less fat and a skimpier portion size. Some companies suggest one ounce as a serving size for pound cake or coffee cake, which is a very thin slice.

FITNESS FUN

The fitness marketplace is growing at a fast pace, and blading is becoming the most popular of all fitness-fun activities. The primary equipment needed is in-line skates, but safety equipment such as knee pads and wrist braces are also recommended.

In-line skates are a combination of roller skates and ice skates with wheels down the middle of each skate instead of a blade. In-line skates can provide transportation as well as good exercise. For years, hockey players and  cross-country skiers have used these skates to keep in shape and train during the off-season. In addition to being a good workout for the legs, blading is a good overall exercise. By swinging the arms while moving on the skates, more energy is expended and the heart pumps harder, yielding a good cardiovascular workout.

Healthy American Meals

Pepper-Crusted Crown Roast of Pork is the star of the Holiday Dinner Party menu. Accompany this impressive entrée with Savory Mushroom Pilaf, Seasoned Broccoli, Festive Spinach Salad, and Poppy Seed Crescents. (Menu begins on page 83.)

Each menu has been carefully developed for your enjoyment, and each meets the *Cooking Light* guidelines for healthy eating. No more than 50 percent of the total calories of the menu are derived from carbohydrate, 20 percent from protein, and less than 30 percent are contributed by fat. Use this 50-20-30 ratio as a guide when planning your own menus.

The four menu chapters reflect the growing interest in nutrition and health along with a desire for freshness and simple elegance. Regional and ethnic flavor adds to the variety. Whether you need ideas for a quick-to-prepare breakfast, a last-minute lunch, or a special meal to entertain friends, look to these sections for your menu needs.

Breakfast and Brunch. You'll find plenty of recipes here to help start your day. For a nutritious coffee break, prepare English muffins or bagels (either can be topped with fruit spread) and serve with a glass of skim milk. For more leisurely dining, try Autumn Celebration Breakfast, Brunch on a Deck, or Family Fun Breakfast, complete with Pigs in Blankets.

Quick and Easy. Fast, wholesome meals can be a real challenge. But From the Pantry allows you to prepare a quick meal that is only a kitchen cupboard away. For a festive south-of-the-border dinner, try Make It Mexican. Or if holiday leftovers seem to have multiplied, let Holiday Encore show you how to transform them into a meal that no one can complain about.

Microwave It Light. How about a fresh Supper from the Garden? The microwave oven can assist you in putting this nutritious meal on the table for family and friends. For a taste of native New England, try New England Sampler with its fresh fish, clams, maple syrup, and cranberries. If you want a meal that's close to home, Picnic on the Porch includes favorites such as chicken, corn-on-the-cob, and lemonade.

That's Entertaining. Dinner parties are back in style and what better way to entertain than with a Holiday Dinner Party? Pepper-Crusted Crown Roast of Pork is an impressive entrée. Or, for more casual entertaining, transform your backyard into an island paradise. Fresh tropical flowers and tiki lights will set the mood for Tropical Beef Kabobs, Pit-Roasted Corn-On-The-Cob, Mamey-Spinach Salad, and Hawaiian Wine Cooler. Whatever the occasion, your family and friends will enjoy being entertained with *Cooking Light* menus.

Cornmeal-Cheddar English Muffins, Strawberry Yogurt Spread, and Raspberry Refrigerator Jam can be packed for a quick breakfast on the go. (Menu begins on page 32.)

Breakfast & Brunch

Coffee Break

Cornmeal-Cheddar
English Muffins
Basic Bagels
Strawberry Yogurt Spread
Raspberry Refrigerator Jam

When you don't have time for breakfast at home and have to resort to a portable meal, try these filling English muffins and bagels; they are the perfect eat-at-your-desk choice. Either one can easily be topped with the delicious, fruit-flavored strawberry spread or raspberry jam, both of which are low-fat, heart-healthy choices.

The breads can be frozen and reheated in a microwave or toaster oven. Stop the coffee cart for a carton of skim milk to round out the meal.

Try Cornmeal-Cheddar English Muffins topped with Raspberry Refrigerator Jam for a low-fat snack.

CORNMEAL-CHEDDAR ENGLISH MUFFINS

1 package dry yeast
1 cup water (105° to 115°)
3 cups all-purpose flour, divided
¼ cup plus 2½ tablespoons cornmeal, divided
2 tablespoons honey
2 tablespoons unsalted margarine, melted
½ teaspoon salt
¼ teaspoon ground red pepper
½ cup (2 ounces) finely shredded 40% less-fat
   Cheddar cheese
1 tablespoon all-purpose flour

Dissolve yeast in warm water in a large bowl; let stand 5 minutes. Add 2 cups flour, ¼ cup cornmeal, and next 4 ingredients; stir well. Stir in enough of the remaining 1 cup flour to make a soft dough. Gently knead in cheese.

Sprinkle 1 tablespoon flour evenly over work surface. Turn dough out onto floured surface. Roll dough to ½-inch thickness; cut with a 3-inch biscuit cutter. Sprinkle 3 baking sheets evenly with 1½ tablespoons cornmeal. Transfer rounds to baking sheets, placing 2 inches apart. Sprinkle remaining 1 tablespoon cornmeal over tops of dough rounds. Cover and let rise in a warm place (85°), free from drafts, 1 hour or until doubled in bulk.

Heat an electric skillet at medium heat (350°) until hot. Using a wide spatula, transfer 5 muffins to skillet. Cook, partially covered, 3 to 5 minutes or until golden on bottom. Turn muffins over. Cook, partially covered, an additional 5 to 7 minutes or until golden on bottom. Remove from skillet, and let cool on wire racks. Repeat procedure with remaining muffins. Yield: 20 muffins (106 calories each).

PROTEIN 3.2   FAT 2.2   CARBOHYDRATE 18.4   CHOLESTEROL 2
IRON 1.0   SODIUM 104   CALCIUM 42

BASIC BAGELS

3¼ to 3½ cups all-purpose flour,
    divided
3 tablespoons sugar
2 packages dry yeast
½ teaspoon salt
1 cup warm water (120° to 130°)
1 tablespoon all-purpose flour
Vegetable cooking spray
3½ quarts water
1 tablespoon sugar
1 teaspoon salt
1 egg white
1 tablespoon water

Combine 1½ cups all-purpose flour, 3 tablespoons sugar, dry yeast, and ½ teaspoon salt in a large bowl, stirring well. Add warm water. Beat mixture at medium speed of an electric mixer 2 minutes. Gradually stir in enough of the remaining 2 cups all-purpose flour to make a stiff dough.

Sprinkle 1 tablespoon flour over work surface. Turn dough out onto floured surface, and knead until smooth and elastic (8 to 10 minutes). Place dough in a large bowl coated with cooking spray, turning to coat top. Cover and let rise in a warm place (85°), free from drafts, 1 hour or until doubled in bulk.

Punch down dough; cover and let rest 15 minutes. Divide dough into 15 equal portions. Shape each portion into a ball. Punch a hole through each ball, using a floured finger.

Bring 3½ quarts water, 1 tablespoon sugar, and 1 teaspoon salt to a boil in a large Dutch oven. Reduce heat. Drop bagels, a few at a time, into gently boiling water. Simmer 1 minute on each side. Drain on paper towels.

Place bagels on a baking sheet coated with cooking spray. Combine egg white and 1 tablespoon water, stirring well; brush over bagels. Bake at 375° for 25 minutes or until golden. Yield: 15 bagels (106 calories each).

PROTEIN 3.0 FAT 0.3 CARBOHYDRATE 22.4 CHOLESTEROL 0
IRON 1.3 SODIUM 119 CALCIUM 5

STRAWBERRY YOGURT SPREAD

2 (8-ounce) cartons strawberry
    low-fat yogurt

Line a colander or sieve with a double layer of cheesecloth that has been rinsed out and squeezed dry; allow cheesecloth to overlap side of colander.

Stir yogurt until smooth; pour into colander, and fold edges of cheesecloth over to cover yogurt. Place colander in a large bowl; refrigerate 12 to 24 hours. Remove yogurt from colander, and discard liquid. Cover and chill. Yield: 1¾ cups (16 calories per tablespoon).

PROTEIN 0.6 FAT 0.2 CARBOHYDRATE 3.0 CHOLESTEROL 1
IRON 0.0 SODIUM 9 CALCIUM 22

RASPBERRY REFRIGERATOR JAM

1½ teaspoons unflavored gelatin
3 tablespoons frozen unsweetened grape juice
    concentrate, thawed and undiluted
3 cups fresh raspberries
¼ cup plus 1 tablespoon sugar

Sprinkle gelatin over grape juice concentrate in a medium saucepan; let stand 1 minute. Add raspberries and sugar; cook over low heat until gelatin and sugar dissolve and berries are crushed, stirring occasionally. Cool to room temperature. Transfer jam to an airtight jar; cover and chill overnight. Store in refrigerator. Yield: 2 cups (18 calories per tablespoon).

PROTEIN 0.2 FAT 0.1 CARBOHYDRATE 4.3 CHOLESTEROL 0
IRON 0.1 SODIUM 0 CALCIUM 3

Family Fun Breakfast

Pigs in Blankets
Oven Hash Browns
Overnight Vanilla Fruit Cup
Skim Milk

SERVES 6
TOTAL CALORIES PER SERVING: 466

Children can be finicky eaters, especially at breakfast. Get your children to eat a nutritious breakfast by tempting them with this hands-on menu. Finger foods and children are a natural combination.

Pancakes never tasted so good as when they are wrapped around sausage links. Let the children shape the pork mixture into links, and mix up the pancake batter themselves.

Hash browns may be Mom and Dad's favorite, but the children will also enjoy these crisp potato treats. With a little supervision, they can grate the potatoes and assemble the casserole.

By making the fruit cup the night before, breakfast will be even one step easier to get ready.

Menu calories include 1 cup skim milk per person.

There's something for everyone to enjoy when Pigs in Blankets, Oven Hash Browns, and Overnight Vanilla Fruit Cup are on the menu.

PIGS IN BLANKETS

½ cup self-rising flour
2 tablespoons cornmeal
2 tablespoons wheat germ
½ teaspoon baking soda
1 egg white, beaten
¾ cup nonfat buttermilk
1 tablespoon vegetable
  oil
Vegetable cooking spray
Spicy Sausage Links

Combine first 4 ingredients in a large bowl; make a well in center of mixture. Combine egg white, buttermilk, and oil; add to dry ingredients, stirring just until dry ingredients are moistened.

For each pancake, pour ¼ cup batter onto a hot griddle coated with cooking spray, spreading to a 4-inch circle. Turn pancakes when tops are covered with bubbles and edges look cooked. Place 1 Spicy Sausage Link on each pancake, and roll to enclose. Yield: 6 servings (218 calories per serving).

Spicy Sausage Links

⅓ cup warm unsweetened apple juice
¼ teaspoon beef-flavored bouillon granules
¾ pound lean ground pork
3 tablespoons fine, dry breadcrumbs
¾ teaspoon fennel seeds, crushed
¼ teaspoon cracked pepper
¼ teaspoon crushed red pepper
⅛ teaspoon salt
Vegetable cooking spray

Combine apple juice and bouillon granules in a large bowl; stir until granules dissolve. Add pork and next 5 ingredients; stir well. Shape mixture into 6 (6-inch) links.

Coat a nonstick skillet with cooking spray; place over medium heat until hot. Place links in skillet; cover and cook over medium-low heat 15 to 20 minutes or until browned, turning frequently. Drain well on paper towels. Yield: 6 links.

PROTEIN 15.9 FAT 10.1 CARBOHYDRATE 15.1 CHOLESTEROL 43
IRON 1.3 SODIUM 301 CALCIUM 61

OVEN HASH BROWNS

3 medium-size baking potatoes (about 1½ pounds)
4 cups water
½ cup skim milk
½ cup frozen egg substitute, thawed
½ teaspoon dried whole thyme
¼ teaspoon garlic powder
¼ teaspoon salt
¼ teaspoon freshly ground pepper
½ cup chopped onion
½ cup chopped green pepper
Vegetable cooking spray
½ teaspoon paprika
Apple slices (optional)

Peel and shred potatoes. Transfer to a bowl, and cover with water. Let stand 5 minutes.

Remove ¼ cup water from potatoes. Place in a small saucepan with milk. Cook just until hot (do not boil); remove from heat, and set aside.

Combine egg substitute, thyme, garlic powder, salt, and pepper; beat well. Gradually add milk mixture, beating constantly.

Drain potatoes, and press out excess liquid with paper towels. Combine potatoes, onion, green pepper, and egg substitute mixture in a large bowl, stirring well. Spoon into a 13- x 9- x 2-inch baking dish coated with cooking spray; sprinkle with paprika. Bake, uncovered, at 350° for 1 hour or until set in center and edges are browned and crispy. Cut into 12 triangles. Garnish with apple slices, if desired. Yield: 6 servings (94 calories per serving).

PROTEIN 5.0 FAT 0.3 CARBOHYDRATE 18.5 CHOLESTEROL 0
IRON 1.9 SODIUM 146 CALCIUM 50

OVERNIGHT VANILLA FRUIT CUP

¼ cup unsweetened orange juice
3 tablespoons sugar
2 tablespoons water
1½ tablespoons lemon juice
2 teaspoons brown sugar
½ teaspoon vanilla extract
1½ cups fresh strawberries
1 cup peeled, sliced fresh peaches
1 cup honeydew melon balls

Combine first 5 ingredients in a medium saucepan; stir well. Bring to a boil; reduce heat, and simmer 3 minutes. Remove from heat, and stir in vanilla. Combine strawberries, peaches and honeydew in a nonaluminum bowl; pour orange juice mixture over fruit, and toss gently. Cover and refrigerate at least 8 hours. Yield: 6 servings (68 calories per ½-cup serving).

PROTEIN 0.6 FAT 0.2 CARBOHYDRATE 17.0 CHOLESTEROL 0
IRON 0.2 SODIUM 3 CALCIUM 10

Fiesta Breakfast For Two

Mexican-Style Breakfast
Cups
Avocado Sauce
Banana-Coffee Biscuits
Strawberries with Lime
Mexican Orange Juice

SERVES 2
TOTAL CALORIES PER SERVING: 404

With this Mexican-inspired breakfast, you can whip up a batch of biscuits flavored with banana and coffee and freeze the leftovers to enjoy later. Menu calories include 1 biscuit and ¼ cup Avocado Sauce per person.

The breakfast cups, colorful strawberries, and flavorful juice complete the meal.

With such do-ahead convenience, you'll have time to enjoy your fiesta!

Mexican-Style Breakfast Cups, Avocado Sauce, Banana-Coffee Biscuits, Strawberries with Lime, and Mexican Orange Juice add to this morning fiesta.

MEXICAN-STYLE BREAKFAST CUPS

2 large tomatoes (about 1 pound)
Vegetable cooking spray
½ cup frozen egg substitute, thawed
¼ teaspoon ground cumin
2 tablespoons (½ ounce) shredded reduced-fat
  Monterey Jack cheese
1½ tablespoons crushed unsalted tortilla chips
1 tablespoon minced fresh parsley

Cut tomatoes in half, and scoop out pulp, leaving shells intact. Chop pulp, and set aside. Invert tomato shells on paper towels to drain.

Place shells in a shallow baking dish coated with cooking spray, cut side up. Bake, uncovered, at 400° for 5 minutes. Remove shells from oven, and set aside.

Combine chopped pulp, egg substitute, and cumin in top of a double boiler; bring water to a boil. Reduce heat to low; cook until egg substitute mixture is firm but still moist, stirring frequently. Spoon into shells. Top with cheese, crushed chips, and parsley. Bake, uncovered, at 400° for 5 minutes or until cheese melts and tomato is thoroughly heated. Serve immediately. Yield: 2 servings (124 calories per serving).

PROTEIN 10.5   FAT 3.5   CARBOHYDRATE 14.6   CHOLESTEROL 5
IRON 2.5   SODIUM 161   CALCIUM 93

AVOCADO SAUCE

½ small avocado, peeled and coarsely chopped
¼ cup plain nonfat yogurt
1 tablespoon minced green onions
2 teaspoons minced fresh cilantro
2 teaspoons lemon juice
¼ teaspoon cracked pepper
Dash of hot sauce

Combine all ingredients in container of an electric blender or food processor; top with cover, and process until smooth. Cover and chill thoroughly. Serve with Mexican-Style Breakfast Cups. Yield: ½ cup (18 calories per tablespoon).

PROTEIN 0.6 FAT 1.3 CARBOHYDRATE 1.4 CHOLESTEROL 0
IRON 0.1 SODIUM 7 CALCIUM 16

BANANA-COFFEE BISCUITS

1 cup all-purpose flour
1 cup whole wheat flour
1 tablespoon baking powder
¼ teaspoon salt
¼ cup sugar
½ teaspoon ground cinnamon
¼ teaspoon ground nutmeg
⅓ cup margarine
½ cup mashed ripe banana
¼ cup strong cold coffee
1½ tablespoons skim milk
1 tablespoon all-purpose flour
Vegetable cooking spray

Combine first 7 ingredients in a medium bowl; cut in margarine with a pastry blender until mixture resembles coarse meal. Combine banana, coffee, and milk; stir well. Add to flour mixture, stirring just until dry ingredients are moistened.
Sprinkle 1 tablespoon flour over work surface. Turn dough out onto floured surface, and knead

3 or 4 times. Roll dough to ½-inch thickness; cut with a 2-inch biscuit cutter. Transfer to a baking sheet coated with cooking spray. Bake at 425° for 8 to 10 minutes or until lightly browned. Yield: 18 biscuits (95 calories each).

PROTEIN 1.8 FAT 3.6 CARBOHYDRATE 14.4 CHOLESTEROL 0
IRON 0.6 SODIUM 123 CALCIUM 40

STRAWBERRIES WITH LIME

1 cup sliced fresh strawberries
2 Bibb lettuce leaves
2 teaspoons honey
¼ teaspoon grated lime rind
2 teaspoons fresh lime juice

Arrange strawberries over lettuce leaves on individual salad plates.
Combine honey, lime rind, and lime juice; stir well with a wire whisk. Drizzle over fruit. Yield: 2 servings (47 calories per ½-cup serving).

PROTEIN 0.6 FAT 0.3 CARBOHYDRATE 11.9 CHOLESTEROL 0
IRON 0.4 SODIUM 2 CALCIUM 12

MEXICAN ORANGE JUICE

1 cup unsweetened orange juice
2 tablespoons grenadine syrup
¾ cup plus 2 tablespoons orange-flavored
   sparkling mineral water, chilled

Combine orange juice and syrup; stir well. Chill thoroughly. Just before serving, stir in mineral water. Yield: 2 cups (66 calories per 1-cup serving).

PROTEIN 0.8 FAT 0.1 CARBOHYDRATE 16.2 CHOLESTEROL 0
IRON 0.1 SODIUM 24 CALCIUM 11

Grits Soufflé Roll, Honey-Dijon Vegetables (page 40), Fig-Orange Muffins (page 40), and Coffee Bracer (page 40) bring warmth to a chilly autumn morning.

Autumn Celebration Breakfast

Grits Soufflé Roll
Honey-Dijon Vegetables
Fig-Orange Muffins
Coffee Bracer

SERVES 8
TOTAL CALORIES PER SERVING: 312

Autumn is the time to get out and enjoy the crisp air and beautiful blue skies. Whether you're off for a brisk walk amid the spectacular foliage or out for a morning of antiquing across the countryside, this menu is a perfect way to start the day.

The soufflé roll can be easily made ahead to save time. Simply reheat it as everyone is arriving. The muffins can also be made in advance. Serve warm Coffee Bracer for just the right complement to this autumn celebration.

GRITS SOUFFLÉ ROLL

Vegetable cooking spray
½ cup skim milk
½ cup plain nonfat yogurt
¼ cup quick-cooking grits, uncooked
½ cup (2 ounces) shredded reduced-fat
   Monterey Jack cheese
½ teaspoon hot sauce
3 eggs, separated
3 egg whites
Spinach-Mushroom Filling
Tomato roses (optional)

Coat a 15- x 10- x 1-inch jellyroll pan with cooking spray. Line pan with wax paper, allowing paper to extend beyond ends of the pan. Coat wax paper with cooking spray; set aside.

Place milk in a large saucepan; bring to a boil. Stir in yogurt and grits (mixture will look curdled). Cover, reduce heat, and simmer 5 minutes or until thickened. Remove from heat, and stir in cheese and hot sauce.

Beat 3 egg yolks until thick and lemon colored. Gradually stir about one-fourth of hot mixture into yolks. Add to remaining hot mixture, stirring well.

Beat 6 egg whites (at room temperature) at high speed of an electric mixer until stiff peaks form. Fold one-third of egg whites into grits mixture; carefully fold in remaining egg whites. Pour grits mixture into prepared pan, spreading evenly. Bake at 350° for 15 to 20 minutes or until puffed and lightly browned. Loosen edges of soufflé with a metal spatula.

Turn soufflé out onto a double layer of wax paper. Carefully peel off top layer of wax paper. Spread Spinach-Mushroom Filling evenly over soufflé. Starting with wide side and using wax paper for support, carefully roll soufflé, jellyroll fashion. Cut into slices, and serve warm. Garnish with tomato roses, if desired. Yield: 8 servings (114 calories per serving).

Spinach-Mushroom Filling

1 (10-ounce) package frozen chopped spinach
Vegetable cooking spray
2 cups diced fresh mushrooms
½ cup finely chopped onion
2 cloves garlic, minced
⅓ cup nonfat sour cream
½ teaspoon dried whole thyme
¼ teaspoon ground white pepper
¼ teaspoon lemon juice

Cook spinach according to package directions, omitting salt and fat. Drain well; press between paper towels to remove excess moisture.

Coat a large nonstick skillet with cooking spray; place over medium-high heat until hot. Add mushrooms, onion, and garlic; sauté until tender. Stir in spinach, sour cream, and remaining ingredients. Cook over low heat, stirring constantly, until thoroughly heated (do not boil). Yield: 1¾ cups.

PROTEIN 9.8 FAT 3.8 CARBOHYDRATE 10.5 CHOLESTEROL 85
IRON 1.6 SODIUM 138 CALCIUM 165

 ON THE SURFACE
The type of surface you exercise on makes a big difference in safety. Runners do best with soft, spongy surfaces that cushion impact. Grass or an open field is fine, as long as the terrain is smooth. Other good choices for running include a composition track, cinder track, or dirt road.

Aerobic dancers also need flooring surfaces that cushion against high impact. Hardwood floors are typically built with a cushion of air or sometimes with a spring base and a cushion of air. These floors work well because they have some give on impact.

Not-so-good choices for running or aerobics include carpeting or tile over concrete or brick floors, plain concrete, or blacktop. None of these surfaces have much give, and so the likelihood for injury is increased.

HONEY-DIJON VEGETABLES

1 pound fresh brussels sprouts
1 cup water
1½ cups diagonally sliced carrot
1½ cups cauliflower flowerets
2 tablespoons reduced-calorie margarine
2 tablespoons minced onion
2 tablespoons all-purpose flour
½ cup canned no-salt-added chicken broth, undiluted
½ cup skim milk
1½ tablespoons Dijon mustard
1 tablespoon honey
¼ teaspoon hot sauce

Wash brussels sprouts; remove discolored leaves. Cut off stem ends; slash bottoms with a shallow X.

Bring water to a boil in a large saucepan. Add brussels sprouts; return to a boil. Cover, reduce heat, and simmer 5 minutes. Add carrot and cauliflower; cover and simmer 10 minutes or until vegetables are crisp-tender. Drain; transfer to a serving bowl, and keep warm.

Melt margarine in a small skillet over medium heat; add onion, and sauté until tender. Add flour; cook 1 minute, stirring constantly. Add chicken broth and remaining ingredients; cook 2 to 3 minutes or until thickened and bubbly. Pour over vegetable mixture, and toss gently to coat. Yield: 8 servings (78 calories per ½-cup serving).

PROTEIN 3.2 FAT 2.4 CARBOHYDRATE 12.6 CHOLESTEROL 0
IRON 1.0 SODIUM 153 CALCIUM 53

FIG-ORANGE MUFFINS

2 large fresh figs, finely chopped
1 cup plus 2 tablespoons all-purpose flour, divided
1 cup unprocessed oat bran
1 tablespoon baking powder
¼ teaspoon salt
2 teaspoons grated orange rind
1 teaspoon ground cinnamon
1 cup skim milk
2 egg whites, lightly beaten
¼ cup firmly packed brown sugar
¼ cup margarine, melted
Vegetable cooking spray

Dredge figs in 2 tablespoons flour, tossing lightly.

Combine remaining 1 cup flour and next 5 ingredients in a bowl; make a well in center of mixture. Combine milk, egg whites, brown sugar, and margarine; add to dry ingredients, stirring just until dry ingredients are moistened. Fold in figs. Spoon batter into muffin pans coated with cooking spray, filling two-thirds full. Bake at 450° for 15 minutes or until golden. Remove from pans, and serve warm. Yield: 14 muffins (113 calories each).

PROTEIN 2.7 FAT 4.2 CARBOHYDRATE 16.9 CHOLESTEROL 0
IRON 1.1 SODIUM 156 CALCIUM 77

COFFEE BRACER

½ cup ground coffee
2 tablespoons grated orange rind
2 teaspoons ground cinnamon
7½ cups water
2 teaspoons brown sugar
½ teaspoon brandy extract

Combine first 3 ingredients in basket of a drip coffee maker or electric percolator. Fill pot with water. Prepare coffee according to manufacturer's instructions. Stir in brown sugar and extract. Yield: 6 cups (7 calories per ¾-cup serving).

PROTEIN 0.0 FAT 0.0 CARBOHYDRATE 1.6 CHOLESTEROL 0
IRON 0.3 SODIUM 0 CALCIUM 10

Brunch On A Deck

Canadian Bacon and Cheese
Sandwiches
Tropical Fruit Kabobs
Scented Sugar Cookies
Berry Cider Fizz

SERVES 4
TOTAL CALORIES PER SERVING: 491

Start your day outdoors with a
nutritious brunch on the deck.
Make the Canadian bacon and
Cheddar cheese breakfast sandwiches in a waffle iron for extra
appeal.

Skewer ripe, fresh strawberries, pineapple, and kiwifruit for
the colorful fruit kabobs and
serve them with the creamy pineapple sauce.

The Berry Cider Fizz is a
delicious sparkling beverage and a
pleasing accompaniment to this
brunch.

And for the perfect ending,
serve the delightfully tangy lemon
sugar cookies—they are sure to
please all of your guests. Menu
calories are calculated to include
2 cookies per person.

*Assemble the family on the deck for Canadian Bacon and Cheese Sand-
wiches, Tropical Fruit Kabobs, Scented Sugar Cookies, and Berry Cider Fizz.*

CANADIAN BACON AND CHEESE SANDWICHES

3 tablespoons reduced-calorie mayonnaise
2 teaspoons Dijon mustard
1 teaspoon honey
8 (¾-ounce) slices reduced-calorie whole
    wheat bread
4 (¾-ounce) slices Canadian bacon
4 (¾-ounce) slices low-fat process Cheddar
    cheese
4 thin tomato slices
Butter-flavored vegetable cooking
    spray

Combine first 3 ingredients; stir well. Spread
mixture evenly over 4 slices of bread. Top each
with 1 slice of Canadian bacon, cheese, and tomato. Top with remaining bread slices.

Transfer sandwiches to a hot waffle iron or
griddle coated with cooking spray. Cook until
bread is lightly browned and cheese melts. Yield:
4 servings (191 calories per serving).

PROTEIN 13.6   FAT 8.3   CARBOHYDRATE 17.7   CHOLESTEROL 14
IRON 1.6   SODIUM 985   CALCIUM 189

TROPICAL FRUIT KABOBS

8 medium-size fresh strawberries, hulled
8 canned pineapple chunks in juice, drained
2 kiwifruit, peeled and cut into 8 slices
Tropical Sauce

Alternately thread strawberries, pineapple chunks, and kiwifruit on 4 (8-inch) skewers. Serve with Tropical Sauce. Yield: 4 servings (67 calories per serving).

Tropical Sauce

3 tablespoons crushed pineapple in juice
¼ cup plus 1 tablespoon vanilla low-fat yogurt
⅛ teaspoon coconut extract

Place pineapple in container of an electric blender; top with cover, and process until smooth. Combine pineapple and remaining ingredients in a small bowl; stir well. Yield: ½ cup.

PROTEIN 1.7   FAT 0.7   CARBOHYDRATE 14.0   CHOLESTEROL 1
IRON 0.4   SODIUM 13   CALCIUM 48

SCENTED SUGAR COOKIES

½ cup reduced-calorie margarine,
  softened
¼ cup sugar
¼ cup sifted powdered sugar
1 egg white
½ teaspoon lemon extract
¼ teaspoon anise extract
2¼ cups all-purpose flour
1 tablespoon plus 1½ teaspoons grated
  lemon rind, divided
½ teaspoon baking soda
½ teaspoon cream of tartar
⅛ teaspoon salt
Vegetable cooking spray
2 tablespoons sugar

Cream margarine in a medium bowl; gradually add ¼ cup sugar and powdered sugar, beating at medium speed of an electric mixer until light and fluffy. Add egg white and flavorings, beating well.

Combine flour, 1½ teaspoons lemon rind, and next 3 ingredients, stirring well. Gradually add flour mixture to creamed mixture, beating at low speed of an electric mixer until well blended. Divide dough in half. Shape each half into a ball, and wrap in wax paper; chill 1 hour.

Shape each half into 20 (1-inch) balls. Place on cookie sheets coated with cooking spray. Flatten each cookie with a fork to a 1½-inch circle. Combine 2 tablespoons sugar and remaining 1 tablespoon lemon rind; sprinkle over cookies. Bake at 375° for 8 minutes or until lightly browned. Cool on wire racks. Yield: 40 cookies (47 calories each).

PROTEIN 0.8   FAT 1.5   CARBOHYDRATE 7.6   CHOLESTEROL 0
IRON 0.3   SODIUM 44   CALCIUM 3

BERRY CIDER FIZZ

1 (10-ounce) package frozen raspberries in
  light syrup, thawed
2⅔ cups sparkling apple cider, chilled
½ cup club soda, chilled

Place raspberries with syrup in container of an electric blender or food processor; top with cover, and process until smooth. Strain raspberry puree; discard seeds.

Combine puree, cider, and club soda in a large pitcher; stir gently. Serve immediately. Yield: 4 cups (139 calories per 1-cup serving).

PROTEIN 0.5   FAT 0.3   CARBOHYDRATE 34.8   CHOLESTEROL 0
IRON 1.0   SODIUM 11   CALCIUM 22

Southwestern cooking offers color and variety to menu possibilities. Enjoy Citrus Carne Asada, Jalapeño Hominy, and Mexican Café au Lait. (Menu begins on page 48.)

Toasted Vegetable-Cheese Sandwiches and Cranberry-Mint Tea combine flavor and familiar ingredients for a simple lunch.

Drop By For Lunch

Creamy Broccoli-Ham Soup
Toasted Vegetable-Cheese Sandwiches
Graham Cracker Quickies
Cranberry-Mint Tea

SERVES 2
TOTAL CALORIES PER SERVING: 521

Renew friendships and spirits—invite someone to stop by for lunch. And the simpler and more casual the meal, the easier it will be to put together.

Soup and sandwiches are a good choice. Creamy Broccoli-Ham Soup cooks in only 8 minutes, and then it's pureed in an electric blender or food processor. Yogurt is folded in for additional creaminess.

The hearty sandwich is composed of mushrooms, zucchini, and carrots piled on slices of whole wheat toast. The sandwich is topped with mozzarella cheese and broiled just until the cheese melts.

Graham Cracker Quickies are a sweet bite-sized way to end a meal. Menu calories are calculated to include 4 cookies per person.

CREAMY BROCCOLI-HAM SOUP

1¼ cups water
1 (10-ounce) package frozen chopped broccoli, thawed
½ teaspoon chicken-flavored bouillon granules
1 clove garlic, sliced
½ teaspoon dried whole marjoram
¼ teaspoon dried whole basil
⅓ cup chopped lean cooked ham
¼ cup plain nonfat yogurt
¼ cup nonfat sour cream

Bring water to a boil in a saucepan. Add broccoli and next 4 ingredients; cover, reduce heat, and simmer 8 to 10 minutes or until broccoli is tender.

Transfer mixture to container of an electric blender or food processor; top with cover, and process until smooth. Gently stir in ham, yogurt, and sour cream. Serve immediately. (If soup is made ahead and reheated, do not boil.) Yield: 2 servings (143 calories per 1½-cup serving).

PROTEIN 12.7   FAT 5.6   CARBOHYDRATE 11.8   CHOLESTEROL 15
IRON 1.6   SODIUM 649   CALCIUM 146

TOASTED VEGETABLE-CHEESE SANDWICHES

1 cup sliced fresh mushrooms
2 tablespoons shredded zucchini
2 tablespoons shredded carrot
2 tablespoons water
½ teaspoon lemon juice
⅛ teaspoon garlic powder
2 tomato slices
2 slices whole wheat bread, toasted
2 (1-ounce) slices part-skim mozzarella cheese, cut into fourths

Combine first 6 ingredients in a small skillet; sauté over medium heat until crisp-tender. Drain. Place tomato slices on toast; spoon mushroom mixture over tomatoes. Top each with 4 cheese pieces. Broil 5½ inches from heat 2 to 3 minutes or until cheese melts. Serve immediately. Yield: 2 servings (159 calories per serving).

PROTEIN 10.9   FAT 5.6   CARBOHYDRATE 18.1   CHOLESTEROL 17
IRON 1.3   SODIUM 288   CALCIUM 217

GRAHAM CRACKER QUICKIES

2 whole graham crackers
2 tablespoons evaporated skimmed milk
1 tablespoon brown sugar
1½ teaspoons reduced-calorie margarine
2 tablespoons toasted wheat germ
1 tablespoon unsweetened coconut
⅛ teaspoon ground cinnamon

Separate graham crackers into fourths, dividing along lines. Place in a single layer on an ungreased cookie sheet.

Combine milk, brown sugar, and margarine in a small saucepan. Bring to a boil, stirring until smooth. Boil 1 minute. Stir in wheat germ, coconut, and cinnamon. Spread evenly over graham crackers. Bake at 350° for 7 to 8 minutes or until golden. Cool completely. Yield: 8 cookies (36 calories each).

PROTEIN 0.9   FAT 1.3   CARBOHYDRATE 5.3   CHOLESTEROL 0
IRON 0.3   SODIUM 37   CALCIUM 14

CRANBERRY-MINT TEA

2 mint-flavored tea bags
1 cup boiling water
1 cup cranberry juice cocktail

Combine tea bags and water; steep 5 minutes. Remove and discard tea bags; let cool. Stir in cranberry juice. Serve over ice. Yield: 2 cups (75 calories per 1-cup serving).

PROTEIN 0.0   FAT 0.1   CARBOHYDRATE 19.2   CHOLESTEROL 0
IRON 0.2   SODIUM 5   CALCIUM 4

From The Pantry

Oriental Tuna Patties
Tangy Snow Peas and Peaches
Sesame-Onion Toast
Orange Parfaits

SERVES 4
TOTAL CALORIES PER SERVING: 505

If you have had a frenzied day and planning a dinner menu has been at the bottom of your list of things to do, relax. Here is a nutritious meal that is only a kitchen cupboard away.

With just a few selected pantry and freezer items, dinner can be a snap to pull together. Canned tuna easily becomes an entrée when just a few spices and vegetables are added.

Frozen snow peas and canned sliced peaches add both color and flavor to the meal. Add Orange Parfaits, a last-minute dessert, for a refreshing and satisfying conclusion to the meal.

Orange sherbet and low-fat yogurt are two convenience products used in easy-to-make Orange Parfaits.

ORIENTAL TUNA PATTIES

Vegetable cooking spray
⅓ cup sliced green onions
⅓ cup chopped celery
2 cloves garlic, minced
1 (12½-ounce) can chunk white tuna in spring
  water, well drained
¼ cup fine, dry breadcrumbs
¼ cup frozen egg substitute, thawed
2 tablespoons low-sodium soy sauce
½ teaspoon grated fresh ginger
¼ teaspoon prepared horseradish

Coat a large nonstick skillet with cooking spray; place over medium-high heat until hot. Add green onions, celery, and garlic; sauté until tender.

Combine sautéed vegetables, tuna, and remaining ingredients in a large bowl; stir well. Cover and chill 15 minutes. Shape mixture into 4 patties.

Coat skillet with cooking spray, and place over medium-high heat until hot. Add patties, and cook 3 minutes on each side or until lightly browned. Yield: 4 servings (152 calories per serving).

PROTEIN 23.5 FAT 2.4 CARBOHYDRATE 6.9 CHOLESTEROL 33
IRON 1.2 SODIUM 583 CALCIUM 25

TANGY SNOW PEAS AND PEACHES

1 (8¾-ounce) can peach slices in juice, undrained
1 (10-ounce) package frozen snow pea pods
¾ teaspoon Dijon mustard
⅛ teaspoon pepper

Drain peaches, reserving 2 tablespoons juice.

Cook snow peas according to package directions, omitting salt and fat. Drain. Combine reserved 2 tablespoons juice, mustard, and pepper; pour over peas. Add reserved peaches; cook until thoroughly heated. Yield: 4 servings (56 calories per serving).

PROTEIN 2.3 FAT 0.2 CARBOHYDRATE 12.0 CHOLESTEROL 0
IRON 1.6 SODIUM 33 CALCIUM 34

SESAME-ONION TOAST

1 tablespoon plus 1 teaspoon reduced-calorie
  margarine
1 teaspoon cider vinegar
4 (1-ounce) slices French bread
1 teaspoon sesame seeds
1 teaspoon instant minced onion
¼ teaspoon garlic powder
¼ teaspoon ground ginger
⅛ teaspoon sugar
⅛ teaspoon crushed red pepper

Combine margarine and vinegar in a small saucepan; cook over low heat until margarine is melted. Brush top side of each bread slice lightly with margarine mixture. Combine sesame seeds and remaining ingredients; sprinkle evenly over bread slices. Bake at 350° for 5 to 10 minutes or until bread slices are lightly browned. Yield: 4 servings (110 calories per serving).

PROTEIN 2.8 FAT 3.4 CARBOHYDRATE 16.7 CHOLESTEROL 1
IRON 0.8 SODIUM 202 CALCIUM 21

ORANGE PARFAITS

2 cups orange sherbet
¼ cup low-sugar orange marmalade
1 (8-ounce) carton vanilla low-fat yogurt
2 teaspoons grated orange rind

Scoop ½ cup sherbet into each of 4 parfait glasses; top each with 1 tablespoon marmalade. Spoon yogurt evenly over each; sprinkle ½ teaspoon orange rind over each parfait. Serve immediately. Yield: 4 servings (187 calories per serving).

PROTEIN 4.0 FAT 2.6 CARBOHYDRATE 38.3 CHOLESTEROL 10
IRON 0.2 SODIUM 85 CALCIUM 158

A short list of select ingredients makes Kiwifruit-Blueberry Salad easy to prepare and attractive to serve.

Make It Mexican

Citrus Carne Asada
Commercial Flour Tortillas
Jalapeño Hominy
Kiwifruit-Blueberry Salad
Mexican Café au Lait

SERVES 4
TOTAL CALORIES PER SERVING: 485

Chili powder, cilantro, cumin, and onions join together to create this typical Mexican dinner.

Select lean tenderloin steaks for Citrus Carne Asada. Serve them topped with a fresh salsa made with tomatillos, purple onion, jicama, cilantro, and fresh oranges. Accompany the steaks with flour tortillas; menu calories include 1 per person.

Yellow hominy gets in the south-of-the-border spirit when chopped jalapeño pepper is added. Be sure to remove the seeds of the pepper, for that is where much of the fire is. Low-fat sour cream adds a rich creaminess with a minimum of fat.

Kiwifruit-Blueberry Salad is simple, but when artfully arranged on leaf lettuce, it can become the star of the meal.

For a pleasant ending to this Mexican meal, wrap your hands around steaming mugs of Mexican Café au Lait. To add extra flavor, start with vanilla-flavored coffee, then add Kahlúa for additional flavor, and smooth it out with milk.

CITRUS CARNE ASADA

2 tablespoons diced tomatillos
2 tablespoons peeled, chopped fresh orange
2 tablespoons diced jicama
1 tablespoon minced purple onion
1 tablespoon minced cilantro
¼ teaspoon chili powder
⅛ teaspoon ground cumin
3 tablespoons lime juice
1 tablespoon unsweetened orange juice
4 (4-ounce) beef tenderloin steaks (1 inch thick)
Vegetable cooking spray

Combine first 9 ingredients; cover and set aside.
Trim fat from steaks. Coat a nonstick skillet with cooking spray, and place over medium-high heat until hot. Add steaks, and cook 2 minutes on each side to sear. Transfer to rack of a broiler pan coated with cooking spray. Broil 5½ inches from heat 4 minutes on each side or to desired degree of doneness. Place steaks on a serving platter; top with tomatillo salsa. Yield: 4 servings (145 calories per serving).

PROTEIN 18.1   FAT 6.0   CARBOHYDRATE 3.9   CHOLESTEROL 53
IRON 2.6   SODIUM 49   CALCIUM 14

JALAPEÑO HOMINY

2 cups canned yellow hominy, drained
¼ cup water
1½ teaspoons seeded, minced jalapeño pepper
1 (2-ounce) jar diced pimiento, drained
1 clove garlic, minced
3 tablespoons low-fat sour cream
¼ teaspoon ground cumin

Combine first 5 ingredients in a saucepan; bring to a boil. Cover, reduce heat, and simmer 10 minutes; drain. Stir in sour cream and cumin. Yield: 4 servings (73 calories per ½-cup serving).

PROTEIN 1.5   FAT 1.7   CARBOHYDRATE 12.9   CHOLESTEROL 4
IRON 0.7   SODIUM 6   CALCIUM 15

KIWIFRUIT-BLUEBERRY SALAD

4 Boston lettuce leaves
4 kiwifruit, peeled and quartered
½ cup fresh blueberries
2 tablespoons reduced-calorie mayonnaise
2 tablespoons unsweetened orange juice
½ teaspoon sugar
½ teaspoon poppy seeds
4 fresh strawberries, halved

Place lettuce on 4 individual serving plates. Arrange kiwifruit on lettuce. Top evenly with blueberries. Combine mayonnaise and next 3 ingredients; stir well with a wire whisk. Drizzle evenly over salads. Top with strawberries, and serve immediately. Yield: 4 servings (97 calories per serving).

PROTEIN 1.6   FAT 2.9   CARBOHYDRATE 16.8   CHOLESTEROL 2
IRON 0.6   SODIUM 58   CALCIUM 32

MEXICAN CAFÉ AU LAIT

1 cup plus 2 tablespoons skim milk
¼ cup Kahlúa or other coffee-flavored liqueur
1½ cups plus 2 tablespoons strong, hot brewed
    vanilla-flavored coffee
⅛ to ¼ teaspoon ground cinnamon

Combine milk and liqueur in a saucepan; cook over low heat until very warm. Stir in hot coffee. Divide mixture evenly among 4 coffee cups. Sprinkle with cinnamon, and serve immediately. Yield: 3 cups (59 calories per ¾-cup serving).

PROTEIN 2.5   FAT 0.2   CARBOHYDRATE 12.0   CHOLESTEROL 1
IRON 0.5   SODIUM 39   CALCIUM 89

Holiday Encore

Sliced Turkey with
Pumpkin Chutney
Steamed Potatoes
Garlic Green Beans
Easy Green Salad
Sweet Potato Gingerbread
Hot Tea

SERVES 4
TOTAL CALORIES PER SERVING: 459

One theory about holiday dinners is that leftovers seem to multiply in the refrigerator. Sure, there was a little turkey left, but you didn't realize it was half the bird. And where do all of the mashed sweet potatoes keep coming from?

With this easy Holiday Encore menu, these leftovers can be transformed into an entire meal without anyone moaning about having to eat turkey "one more time." Slices of turkey are accented with that

dab of pumpkin that was also leftover. But this time, the pumpkin is teamed with apples, raisins, and red pepper for a robust chutney.

Green beans, tossed with browned margarine, and a crisp green salad complete the main part of the meal. And for a special ending, transform leftover sweet potatoes into a wonderful dessert by preparing Sweet Potato Gingerbread, which can be enjoyed with a cup of warm tea.

SLICED TURKEY WITH PUMPKIN CHUTNEY

2 tablespoons brown sugar
2 tablespoons cider vinegar
2 tablespoons unsweetened apple
  juice
¼ cup chopped apple
1 tablespoon raisins
1 tablespoon chopped onion
1 teaspoon finely grated lemon rind
Dash of ground red pepper
2 tablespoons cooked, mashed pumpkin
Vegetable cooking spray
8 (1½-ounce) slices cooked skinned turkey
  breast

Combine sugar, vinegar, and apple juice in a large nonstick skillet. Add apple and next 4 ingredients. Cook 3 to 5 minutes or until apple is tender. Stir in pumpkin. Remove chutney from skillet; set aside, and keep warm.

Coat skillet with cooking spray; place skillet over medium-high heat until hot. Add turkey, and cook 5 to 6 minutes or until thoroughly heated, turning once. Serve with pumpkin chutney. Yield: 4 servings (170 calories per serving).

PROTEIN 25.9 FAT 0.9 CARBOHYDRATE 14.0 CHOLESTEROL 71
IRON 1.8 SODIUM 47 CALCIUM 23

Sliced Turkey with Pumpkin Chutney, steamed potatoes, Garlic Green Beans (page 52), Easy Green Salad (page 52), and warm tea create an enjoyable meal.

GARLIC GREEN BEANS

2 cups frozen cut green beans
2 tablespoons reduced-calorie margarine
⅛ teaspoon garlic powder
⅛ teaspoon salt

Cook green beans according to package directions, omitting salt and fat. Drain; set aside, and keep warm.

Melt margarine in a small saucepan; cook over medium heat until browned. Pour over beans; sprinkle with garlic powder and salt. Toss gently to coat. Yield: 4 servings (53 calories per ½-cup serving).

PROTEIN 1.3　FAT 3.8　CARBOHYDRATE 5.0　CHOLESTEROL 0
IRON 1.0　SODIUM 141　CALCIUM 29

EASY GREEN SALAD

1 cup torn Bibb lettuce
1 cup torn Boston leaf lettuce
1 cup torn green leaf lettuce
1 cup shredded red cabbage
¼ cup commercial oil-free Italian
　dressing
½ cup alfalfa sprouts

Combine first 5 ingredients in a large bowl; toss well. Arrange on individual salad plates, and top with sprouts. Yield: 4 servings (20 calories per 1-cup serving).

PROTEIN 1.1　FAT 0.2　CARBOHYDRATES 4.0　CHOLESTEROL 0
IRON 0.3　SODIUM 141　CALCIUM 17

SWEET POTATO GINGERBREAD

Vegetable cooking spray
2 eggs
½ cup sugar
¾ cup cooked, mashed sweet potato
2 tablespoons molasses
1 teaspoon vanilla extract
¾ cup all-purpose flour
1 teaspoon baking powder
1 teaspoon ground cinnamon
1 teaspoon ground ginger
¼ teaspoon ground cloves
1 teaspoon powdered sugar

Coat a 9-inch square baking pan with cooking spray. Line bottom of pan with wax paper; coat with cooking spray, and set aside.

Beat eggs at high speed of an electric mixer 2 minutes in a large bowl. Add sugar, 1 tablespoon at a time, beating well. Add mashed sweet potato, molasses, and vanilla; beat at medium speed 2 minutes.

Combine flour and next 4 ingredients; stir well. Add flour mixture to sweet potato mixture; stir well. Spoon batter into prepared pan. Bake at 375° for 20 minutes or until wooden pick inserted in center comes out clean. Let cool 5 minutes in pan; remove from pan. Peel off wax paper. Sift powdered sugar over gingerbread, and serve warm. Yield: 8 servings (149 calories per serving).

PROTEIN 3.1　FAT 1.6　CARBOHYDRATE 30.5　CHOLESTEROL 53
IRON 1.3　SODIUM 59　CALCIUM 55

Shrimp and Scallop Kabobs and Spinach-Laced Barley join together for an easy weeknight dinner.

Respite After Work

Shrimp and Scallop Kabobs
Spinach-Laced Barley
Commercial Dinner Rolls
Lemon Sorbet with Summer Fruits

SERVES 2
TOTAL CALORIES PER SERVING: 487

When it's only midweek and you feel in need of a weekend, sit back and have a relaxing dinner to rejuvenate. This respite is just what you need to allow the midweek tension to slip away and be replaced by a sense of calm.

The menu is a feast for both your eyes and palate, yet it requires very little effort. Shrimp and Scallop Kabobs is an elegant entrée that marinates and cooks in less than 30 minutes. Menu calories include 1 dinner roll per person.

Quick-cooking barley is a new product that trims almost 40 minutes off the cooking time.

End the evening with a luscious bounty of summer fruits topped with refreshing lemon sorbet.

SHRIMP AND SCALLOP KABOBS

½ cup Chablis or other dry white wine
2 tablespoons lemon juice
1 tablespoon Creole mustard
1 teaspoon vegetable oil
¼ teaspoon dried whole dillweed
⅛ teaspoon hot sauce
¼ pound fresh sea scallops
¼ pound medium-size fresh shrimp, peeled and
  deveined
4 frozen artichoke hearts, thawed and halved
4 pitted ripe olives
Vegetable cooking spray

Combine first 6 ingredients in a shallow dish. Add scallops, shrimp, and artichoke hearts; toss gently. Cover and marinate in refrigerator 15 minutes.

Remove scallops, shrimp, and artichokes from marinade, reserving marinade; place marinade in a saucepan. Bring to a boil over medium-high heat; boil 2 minutes. Remove from heat; set aside.

Thread scallops, shrimp, artichokes, and olives alternately on 4 (10-inch) skewers. Place kabobs on rack of a broiler pan coated with cooking spray. Broil 5½ inches from heat for 6 minutes or until scallops are opaque and shrimp is done, turning once and basting with reserved marinade. Yield: 2 servings (159 calories per serving).

PROTEIN 19.4 FAT 5.0 CARBOHYDRATE 10.5 CHOLESTEROL 98
IRON 2.4 SODIUM 348 CALCIUM 57

SPINACH-LACED BARLEY

½ cup water
3 tablespoons quick-cooking barley, uncooked
Vegetable cooking spray
2 tablespoons minced onion
1 clove garlic, minced
1 cup thinly sliced fresh spinach leaves
2 cherry tomatoes, quartered
⅛ teaspoon salt
Dash of pepper

Bring water to a boil in a saucepan; add barley. Cover, reduce heat, and simmer 10 to 12 minutes or until barley is tender. Remove from heat; let stand 5 minutes.

Coat a small nonstick skillet with cooking spray; place over medium-high heat until hot. Add onion and garlic; sauté until tender. Stir in cooked barley, spinach, tomato, salt, and pepper. Cook 1 to 3 minutes or until spinach wilts and tomato is thoroughly heated. Yield: 2 servings (67 calories per ½-cup serving).

PROTEIN 2.6 FAT 0.5 CARBOHYDRATE 15.1 CHOLESTEROL 0
IRON 0.8 SODIUM 171 CALCIUM 29

LEMON SORBET WITH SUMMER FRUITS

2 fresh apricots, seeded and quartered
½ cup fresh raspberries
½ cup chopped fresh pineapple
½ cup cubed honeydew melon
1 cup lemon sorbet

Arrange fruits on 2 individual dessert plates or in shallow bowls. Scoop sorbet onto fruit, and serve immediately. Yield: 2 servings (189 calories per serving).

PROTEIN 1.2 FAT 0.6 CARBOHYDRATE 26.4 CHOLESTEROL 0
IRON 0.8 SODIUM 8 CALCIUM 21

With the growing interest in American cuisine comes an appreciation for regional differences in our vast culinary landscape. The New England dinner showcases Spinach-Flounder Pinwheels, Maple-Glazed Carrots, and Green Salad with Cranberry Vinaigrette. (Menu begins on page 63.)

Microwave It Light

Simple Summer Supper

Chicken and Ham Medley
Lemon Asparagus Spears
Red Berries and Cream
Citrus Sours

SERVES 6
TOTAL CALORIES PER SERVING: 627

Start the meal with creamy Chicken and Ham Medley. The microwave oven is ideal for making the sauce because the need for constant stirring is eliminated. Accompany the hearty entrée with Lemon Asparagus Spears and Citrus Sours. Remember to place the delicate tips toward the center of the dish for more even cooking.

Bring this summer supper to a satisfying conclusion with Red Berries and Cream.

Simplicity prevails when Chicken and Ham Medley, Lemon Asparagus Spears, and Citrus Sours are on the menu.

CHICKEN AND HAM MEDLEY

½ cup sliced fresh mushrooms
¼ cup chopped onion
¼ cup chopped sweet red pepper
1 teaspoon reduced-calorie margarine
1 cup skim milk, divided
3 tablespoons cornstarch
3 tablespoons Chablis or other dry white wine
½ cup water
½ teaspoon chicken-flavored bouillon granules
½ teaspoon dried whole thyme
¼ teaspoon ground white pepper
¼ teaspoon dried whole rosemary
1 cup diced cooked chicken breast
1 cup diced cooked lean ham
½ cup (2 ounces) shredded reduced-fat Swiss cheese
3 (4-ounce) plain bagels, split and toasted
Chopped fresh chives (optional)

Place mushrooms, onion, sweet red pepper, and margarine in a 2-quart casserole. Cover with heavy-duty plastic wrap and vent. Microwave at HIGH 2 to 3 minutes or until crisp-tender.

Combine ¼ cup milk and cornstarch. Add cornstarch mixture, remaining ¾ cup milk, wine, and next 5 ingredients to vegetable mixture; stir well. Microwave, uncovered, at HIGH 2 minutes; stir well. Microwave at HIGH 3 to 4 minutes or until thickened, stirring after every minute. Stir in chicken, ham, and cheese. Microwave at HIGH 30 seconds or until cheese melts. Spoon mixture over bagel halves; sprinkle with chives, if desired. Yield: 6 servings (334 calories per serving).

PROTEIN 24.8 FAT 7.9 CARBOHYDRATE 39.7 CHOLESTEROL 47
IRON 2.5 SODIUM 709 CALCIUM 198

LEMON ASPARAGUS SPEARS

1½ pounds fresh asparagus spears
¼ cup water
2 tablespoons reduced-calorie margarine
1 teaspoon grated lemon rind
1 tablespoon lemon juice
¼ teaspoon salt-free lemon-pepper seasoning
1 tablespoon finely chopped toasted hazelnuts
Lemon rind curls (optional)

Snap off tough ends of asparagus. Remove scales from spears with a knife or vegetable peeler, if desired. Place spears in an 11- x 7- x 2-inch baking dish with stem ends toward outside of dish; add water. Cover with heavy-duty plastic wrap and vent. Microwave at HIGH 6 to 7 minutes or until crisp-tender; drain.

Place margarine in a 1-cup glass measure. Microwave at HIGH 15 to 20 seconds or until melted. Stir in lemon rind, lemon juice, and lemon-pepper seasoning. Pour over asparagus.

Arrange asparagus on individual serving plates, and sprinkle with nuts. Garnish with lemon curls, if desired. Yield: 6 servings (48 calories per serving).

PROTEIN 2.7 FAT 3.6 CARBOHYDRATE 3.5 CHOLESTEROL 0
IRON 0.6 SODIUM 38 CALCIUM 22

RED BERRIES AND CREAM

2 cups skim milk
3 tablespoons sugar
1 tablespoon plus 2 teaspoons cornstarch
¼ teaspoon ground mace
½ teaspoon almond extract
½ teaspoon vanilla extract
1½ cups sliced strawberries
1½ cups fresh raspberries
1 tablespoon grated semisweet chocolate
Fresh mint sprigs (optional)

Combine first 4 ingredients in a 1-quart casserole, stirring well. Microwave, uncovered, at HIGH 5 to 6 minutes or until slightly thickened, stirring every 2 minutes. Stir in flavorings. Cover and chill thoroughly.

Combine strawberries and raspberries in a medium bowl, stirring gently. Place ½ cup berry mixture in each of 6 individual dessert bowls. Pour ⅓ cup cream mixture over each serving. Sprinkle evenly with grated chocolate. Garnish with fresh mint sprigs, if desired. Yield: 6 servings (100 calories per serving).

PROTEIN 3.4 FAT 1.1 CARBOHYDRATE 19.9 CHOLESTEROL 2
IRON 0.4 SODIUM 43 CALCIUM 114

CITRUS SOURS

1 (6-ounce) can frozen lemonade concentrate,
    thawed and undiluted
1 (6-ounce) can frozen orange juice
    concentrate, thawed and undiluted
1 cup unsweetened apple juice
⅓ cup bourbon
3⅓ cups club soda, chilled

Combine first 4 ingredients in a large pitcher; stir well. Cover and chill thoroughly. Just before serving, stir in club soda, and serve over ice. Yield: 6 cups (145 calories per 1-cup serving).

PROTEIN 0.8 FAT 0.2 CARBOHYDRATE 29.0 CHOLESTEROL 0
IRON 0.5 SODIUM 30 CALCIUM 20

Picnic On The Porch

Chicken with
Fresh Herbs
Seasoned Corn-on-the-Cob
Striped Salad Platter
Midori Melon Balls
California Lemonade

SERVES 6
TOTAL CALORIES PER SERVING: 515

Plan this menu around Chicken with Fresh Herbs. This is a health-conscious version of an all-time picnic favorite, fried chicken, and boasts a savory coating of crushed wheat cereal and fresh summer herbs. The lemonade is a refreshing accompaniment to this entrée.

Corn-on-the-cob retains its garden-fresh flavor when microwaved. To enhance this flavor, the recipe features a seasoned margarine mixture that's added before cooking.

Shredded cabbage, carrot, yellow squash, and beets are drizzled with a celery seed dressing for an unusual salad presentation. For dessert, offer melon balls sprinkled with mint and tossed with a special dressing.

Arrange shredded vegetables on a pretty plate for Striped Salad Platter.

CHICKEN WITH FRESH HERBS

1¼ cups shredded whole wheat cereal biscuits,
  crushed
1 tablespoon chopped fresh parsley
2 teaspoons chopped fresh tarragon
1 teaspoon chopped fresh summer savory or
  ¼ teaspoon dried summer savory
½ teaspoon paprika
¼ teaspoon salt
¼ teaspoon ground white pepper
6 (4-ounce) skinned, boned chicken breast
  halves
2 tablespoons skim milk

Combine first 7 ingredients in a shallow dish; stir well. Dip each chicken breast in milk; dredge in cereal mixture.

Place chicken in an 11- x 7- x 2-inch baking dish with thickest portions toward outside of dish. Cover with wax paper, and microwave at HIGH 10 to 12 minutes or until chicken is tender, rotating a half-turn every 4 minutes. Yield: 6 servings (173 calories per serving).

PROTEIN 27.9 FAT 1.8 CARBOHYDRATE 10.5 CHOLESTEROL 66
IRON 1.8 SODIUM 176 CALCIUM 38

SEASONED CORN-ON-THE-COB

6 ears fresh corn
2 tablespoons reduced-calorie margarine
½ teaspoon onion powder
½ teaspoon dried whole sage
¼ teaspoon pepper

Remove husks and silks from corn; set aside.

Place margarine in a 1-cup glass measure; microwave, uncovered, at MEDIUM (50% power) 20 to 30 seconds or until melted. Stir in onion powder, sage, and pepper.

Brush margarine mixture on each ear of corn. Wrap each ear in a 12-inch sheet of heavy-duty plastic wrap, twisting ends to seal. Arrange corn on paper towels in microwave oven. Microwave at HIGH 16 minutes, rearranging corn after 8 minutes. Let stand 5 minutes. Yield: 6 servings (102 calories per serving).

PROTEIN 2.5 FAT 3.3 CARBOHYDRATE 19.0 CHOLESTEROL 0
IRON 0.6 SODIUM 50 CALCIUM 4

STRIPED SALAD PLATTER

1½ cups finely shredded cabbage
1 cup shredded carrot
1 cup shredded yellow squash
1 (15-ounce) can whole beets, drained and
    shredded
½ cup chopped fresh parsley
⅓ cup white wine vinegar
1 tablespoon water
2 teaspoons vegetable oil
2 teaspoons sugar
¼ teaspoon salt
¼ teaspoon celery seeds
¼ teaspoon pepper
1 clove garlic, crushed

Arrange cabbage, carrot, squash, and beets in rows on a serving platter, separating rows with parsley. Combine white wine vinegar and remaining ingredients in a small bowl, stirring

well. Drizzle over vegetables. Serve immediately. Yield: 6 servings (56 calories per serving).

PROTEIN 1.3 FAT 1.7 CARBOHYDRATE 9.6 CHOLESTEROL 0
IRON 1.0 SODIUM 212 CALCIUM 37

MIDORI MELON BALLS

¼ cup unsweetened orange juice
1 tablespoon sugar
2 tablespoons Midori
1 tablespoon lemon juice
1 teaspoon grated fresh ginger
1 cup watermelon balls
1 cup honeydew melon balls
1 cup cantaloupe balls
2 tablespoons chopped fresh mint

Combine first 5 ingredients in a 2-cup glass measure. Cover with heavy-duty plastic wrap and vent. Microwave mixture at HIGH 1 to 2 minutes or until sugar dissolves; let cool.

Combine melon balls and mint in a large bowl. Pour orange juice mixture over melon balls, and toss gently. Chill at least 2 hours. Yield: 6 servings (49 calories per ½-cup serving).

PROTEIN 0.7 FAT 0.2 CARBOHYDRATE 10.9 CHOLESTEROL 0
IRON 0.2 SODIUM 7 CALCIUM 9

CALIFORNIA LEMONADE

3 cups white grape juice, chilled
1 (6-ounce) can frozen lemonade concentrate,
    thawed and undiluted
2¼ cups club soda, chilled
Lemon slices (optional)

Combine first 3 ingredients in a 2-quart pitcher. Serve over ice; garnish with lemon slices, if desired. Yield: 6 cups (135 calories per 1-cup serving).

PROTEIN 0.1 FAT 0.1 CARBOHYDRATE 34.9 CHOLESTEROL 0
IRON 0.6 SODIUM 24 CALCIUM 23

For a sure taste of summer, try Garden Corn Soup and Zucchini Bread (page 62), that blend fresh vegetables hand-picked from the garden or produce department.

Supper From The Garden

Garden Corn Soup
Beef and Summer Vegetable Ragoût
Zucchini Bread
Peaches Rosé

SERVES 8
TOTAL CALORIES PER SERVING: 553

Plan supper around the bountiful selection of fresh vegetables from your garden or favorite produce market. The meal begins with rich, golden Garden Corn Soup, featuring fresh corn and tomatoes.

Beef and Summer Vegetable Ragoût is hearty and satisfying, yet void of excess calories and fat. It cooks quickly in the microwave oven, guaranteeing

perfect texture, bright color, and of course, full nutritional value.

Mix up a batch of spicy Zucchini Bread for a moist, tasty accompaniment. Use a microwave-safe ring mold to ensure best results.

Peaches Rosé is a delicious finale for this fresh and flavorful summer supper.

GARDEN CORN SOUP

1 cup chopped onion
1 cup chopped green pepper
2 cloves garlic, minced
1 teaspoon vegetable oil
4 cups fresh or frozen corn kernels
3½ cups water
1⅓ cups peeled, seeded, and chopped tomato
    (about 2 medium)
1 teaspoon chicken-flavored bouillon granules
½ teaspoon dried whole marjoram
¼ teaspoon dried whole thyme
¼ teaspoon dry mustard
¼ teaspoon ground white pepper
1 tablespoon cornstarch
1 tablespoon water
¼ cup chopped fresh parsley

Combine onion, green pepper, garlic, and oil in a 3-quart casserole. Cover with heavy-duty plastic wrap and vent. Microwave at HIGH 3 to 4 minutes or until crisp-tender. Drain vegetables, and pat dry with a paper towel. Wipe drippings from casserole with a paper towel.

Return onion mixture to casserole; add corn and next 7 ingredients. Combine cornstarch and 1 tablespoon water, stirring well. Add to vegetable mixture; cover and vent. Microwave at HIGH 9 to 10 minutes or until thoroughly heated. Stir in parsley, and ladle soup into individual bowls. Yield: 8 servings (86 calories per 1-cup serving).

PROTEIN 2.7 FAT 1.4 CARBOHYDRATE 18.5 CHOLESTEROL 0
IRON 0.8 SODIUM 108 CALCIUM 12

BEEF AND SUMMER VEGETABLE RAGOÛT

1½ pounds lean round steak (½ inch thick)
1 cup thinly sliced onion (about 1 medium)
2 cloves garlic, minced
1 teaspoon vegetable oil
1 cup water
1 (14½-ounce) can no-salt-added whole
    tomatoes, undrained and coarsely chopped
½ cup thinly sliced carrot (about 1 medium)
½ teaspoon beef-flavored bouillon granules
½ teaspoon dried whole basil
½ teaspoon dried whole thyme
¼ teaspoon pepper
3¾ cups peeled, cubed eggplant (about 1 small)
1½ cups cut fresh green beans
1 cup cubed yellow squash (about 1 small)
1 cup julienne-cut sweet red pepper (about 1
    medium-size)
4 cups cooked medium egg noodles (cooked
    without salt or fat)

Trim fat from steak; cut steak into ½-inch pieces. Combine steak, onion, garlic, and oil in a 3-quart casserole. Cover with wax paper, and microwave at HIGH 10 to 12 minutes or until meat is no longer pink, stirring every 2 minutes. Drain and pat dry with a paper towel. Wipe drippings from casserole with a paper towel.

Return meat mixture to casserole; stir in water and next 6 ingredients. Cover with heavy-duty plastic wrap and vent. Microwave at MEDIUM HIGH (70% power) 45 minutes, stirring 3 times. Add eggplant, green beans, squash, and sweet red pepper. Cover and vent. Microwave at MEDIUM HIGH 20 minutes or until meat and vegetables are tender. Serve over noodles. Yield: 8 servings (284 calories per serving).

PROTEIN 26.5 FAT 6.1 CARBOHYDRATE 30.9 CHOLESTEROL 81
IRON 4.3 SODIUM 119 CALCIUM 70

ZUCCHINI BREAD

Vegetable cooking spray
1 tablespoon fine, dry breadcrumbs
¾ cup all-purpose flour
¾ cup whole wheat flour
½ cup sugar
1 teaspoon baking soda
1 teaspoon ground cinnamon
½ teaspoon ground nutmeg
⅛ teaspoon salt
½ cup skim milk
½ cup unsalted margarine, softened
½ cup frozen egg substitute, thawed
½ teaspoon vanilla extract
1½ cups shredded zucchini, well
    drained

Coat a 6-cup microwave-safe ring mold with cooking spray; dust with breadcrumbs.

Combine all-purpose flour and next 10 ingredients in a medium bowl. Blend at low speed of an electric mixer until moistened. Beat 2 minutes at medium speed; stir in zucchini. Pour into prepared ring mold. Microwave, uncovered, at MEDIUM HIGH (70% power) 10 to 12 minutes or until a wooden pick inserted near center comes out clean, rotating mold a quarter-turn every 4 minutes. Let stand 5 minutes. Invert onto serving plate. Yield: 16 servings (126 calories per serving).

PROTEIN 2.6 FAT 6.0 CARBOHYDRATE 16.1 CHOLESTEROL 0
IRON 0.7 SODIUM 92 CALCIUM 31

PEACHES ROSÉ

½ cup rosé wine
½ cup unsweetened orange juice
2 tablespoons sugar
2 teaspoons grated orange rind
¼ teaspoon ground cinnamon
⅛ teaspoon ground cardamom
3½ cups sliced fresh peaches
½ cup fresh blueberries

Combine wine, orange juice, sugar, orange rind, cinnamon, and cardamom in a 2-cup glass measure.

Microwave at HIGH 1½ to 2 minutes or until sugar dissolves; let cool.

Combine wine mixture and peaches in a medium bowl, stirring gently. Cover and chill 2 hours. Spoon peaches evenly into individual dessert bowls, using a slotted spoon. Top peaches evenly with blueberries. Yield: 8 servings (57 calories per serving).

PROTEIN 0.7 FAT 0.1 CARBOHYDRATE 14.7 CHOLESTEROL 0
IRON 0.2 SODIUM 2 CALCIUM 9

ROPING IN FITNESS GAINS

Jumping rope, which used to be only a kid-sized sport, is rapidly gaining adult participants. One of the major reasons for its new-found popularity with adults is that the list of health benefits is lengthy. For starters, jumping rope is aerobic, giving the heart a good workout. In addition, twirling the rope and moving the body in different directions help strengthen muscles and build endurance for both the upper and lower body. Here are a few things for you to consider.

• Make sure to use a rope long enough to match your height. Stand on the rope's center; handles should fit snugly under armpits.
• Keep the body erect and the head up. Ankles and knees need to stay together, and upper arms should remain close to the body as you swing the rope. Turn the rope by making small circles with the hands.
• Land on the balls of feet with knees slightly bent. Keep jumps low—about 1 or 2 inches off the floor. Vary your jumps to keep the routine challenging and fun.

Crinkle-cut slices of carrot, cucumber, and yellow squash add color to Seaside Clam Spread (page 64).

New England Sampler

Seaside Clam Spread
Raw Vegetables
Spinach-Flounder Pinwheels
Maple-Glazed Carrots
Green Salad with Cranberry Vinaigrette
Commercial Hard Rolls
Individual Blueberry-Topped Cheesecakes

SERVES 4
TOTAL CALORIES PER SERVING: 579

New England cooking showcases native foods which were present when the first settlers arrived.

Begin with Seaside Clam Spread—menu calories allow 3 tablespoons spread and ½ cup vegetables per person.

Arrange flounder pinwheels and carrots on individual plates, and serve with 1 dinner roll.

The salad and dessert spotlight two fruits native to New England—cranberries and fresh blueberries.

SEASIDE CLAM SPREAD

1 (8-ounce) carton plain nonfat yogurt
¼ cup (1-ounce) shredded 40% less-fat Cheddar
  cheese
1 tablespoon skim milk
1 tablespoon finely chopped green pepper
1 tablespoon grated onion
1 teaspoon low-sodium Worcestershire sauce
2 tablespoons canned minced clams, rinsed and
  drained

Line a colander or sieve with a double layer of cheesecloth that has been rinsed out and squeezed dry. Allow cheesecloth to extend over edge of colander. Stir yogurt until well blended. Pour yogurt into colander and fold edges of cheese cloth over to cover yogurt. Place colander in a large bowl to drain; cover and chill at least 8 hours. Remove yogurt from colander, and discard liquid in bowl. Remove yogurt from cheesecloth.

Combine drained yogurt, Cheddar cheese, and next 4 ingredients; stir well. Stir in clams. Serve clam spread on fresh vegetable slices. Yield: ¾ cup (19 calories per tablespoon).

PROTEIN 1.7   FAT 0.4   CARBOHYDRATE 2.3   CHOLESTEROL 1
IRON 0.2   SODIUM 18   CALCIUM 56

SPINACH-FLOUNDER PINWHEELS

½ cup frozen chopped spinach, thawed
  and well drained
⅓ cup soft whole wheat breadcrumbs
1 (2-ounce) jar sliced pimiento, drained
2 tablespoons grated onion
1 tablespoon finely chopped pecans
1 teaspoon lemon juice
¼ teaspoon dried whole marjoram
¼ teaspoon salt
¼ teaspoon pepper
4 (4-ounce) flounder fillets
¼ cup Chablis or other dry white
  wine
1 teaspoon grated lemon rind
Fresh spinach leaves (optional)
Lemon wedges (optional)

Combine first 9 ingredients in a medium bowl; stir well. Spoon 3 tablespoons spinach mixture in center of each fillet; roll up, jellyroll fashion, beginning at narrow end. Secure with a wooden pick.

Place rolls, seam side down, in an 11- x 7- x 2-inch baking dish. Combine wine and lemon rind; pour over rolls. Cover with heavy-duty plastic wrap and vent. Microwave at HIGH 5 to 7 minutes or until fish flakes easily when tested with a fork. Let stand 1 minute. Remove and discard wooden picks. Slice rolls, and transfer to serving plates. If desired, garnish with spinach and lemon wedges. Yield: 4 servings (126 calories per serving).

PROTEIN 22.1   FAT 2.7   CARBOHYDRATE 2.7   CHOLESTEROL 54
IRON 0.9   SODIUM 256   CALCIUM 36

FIBER FACTS
Fiber, an important component of fruits, grains, and vegetables, may decrease colon cancer risks, but less than one-fourth of the people in a survey conducted at the University of Utah knew the daily amount the National Cancer Institute recommends—25 to 35 grams. And just over half of the participants in the study knew which foods had the most fiber.

MAPLE-GLAZED CARROTS

1 pound baby carrots, scraped
¼ cup water
¼ teaspoon salt
2 tablespoons reduced-calorie maple syrup
1 teaspoon reduced-calorie margarine, melted
1 teaspoon grated orange rind

Combine carrots, water, and salt in a 1½-quart casserole. Cover with heavy-duty plastic wrap and vent. Microwave carrot mixture at HIGH 6 minutes; drain.

Combine syrup, margarine, and orange rind; pour over carrots. Cover and vent. Microwave at HIGH 2 to 3 minutes or until carrots are crisp-tender. Yield: 4 servings (51 calories per serving).

PROTEIN 1.0 FAT 0.8 CARBOHYDRATE 11.2 CHOLESTEROL 0
IRON 0.5 SODIUM 192 CALCIUM 29

GREEN SALAD WITH CRANBERRY VINAIGRETTE

3 tablespoons cranberry juice
  cocktail
2 tablespoons cider vinegar
1 teaspoon Dijon mustard
1 teaspoon vegetable oil
¼ teaspoon ground ginger
1 cup torn romaine lettuce
1 cup torn Boston lettuce
¼ cup sliced green onions
½ cup coarsely chopped apple

Combine first 5 ingredients in a jar. Cover tightly, and shake vigorously .

Combine salad greens and green onions. Arrange ½ cup mixture on each of 4 individual salad plates. Drizzle each with cranberry juice mixture. Top each serving with 2 tablespoons chopped apple. Yield: 4 servings (32 calories per serving).

PROTEIN 0.4 FAT 1.3 CARBOHYDRATE 5.2 CHOLESTEROL 0
IRON 0.3 SODIUM 39 CALCIUM 8

INDIVIDUAL BLUEBERRY-TOPPED CHEESECAKES

4 vanilla wafers
¼ cup plus 2 tablespoons 1% low-fat
  cottage cheese
½ (8-ounce) package Neufchâtel cheese,
  softened
¼ cup sugar
1 egg
2 teaspoons lemon juice
½ teaspoon vanilla extract
½ teaspoon grated lemon rind
¼ cup vanilla low-fat yogurt
⅓ cup fresh blueberries
Fresh mint sprigs (optional)

Line 4 muffin pans with paper baking cups. Place 1 wafer in the bottom of each baking cup.

Combine cottage cheese and next 5 ingredients in container of an electric blender; top with cover, and process until smooth. Pour cottage cheese mixture into a 1-quart casserole; stir in grated lemon rind. Microwave cottage cheese mixture at HIGH 6 minutes, stirring after every minute. Spoon cottage cheese mixture evenly into prepared muffin cups. Cover and chill at least 8 hours.

Remove cheesecakes from pans; spread yogurt evenly over cheesecakes, and top with blueberries. Garnish with mint sprigs, if desired. Serve immediately. Yield: 4 servings (195 calories per serving).

PROTEIN 8.0 FAT 9.2 CARBOHYDRATE 20.4 CHOLESTEROL 76
IRON 0.4 SODIUM 241 CALCIUM 67

Entertain on a weeknight by serving Thai Shrimp and Rice, Asian Fruit Salad (page 68), and Bangkok Cocktail (page 68).

Taste Of Thailand Dinner

Kiss of Lemon Soup
Thai Shrimp and Rice
Asian Fruit Salad
Banana-Pineapple Delight
Bangkok Cocktail

SERVES 6
TOTAL CALORIES PER SERVING: 595

Thai cuisine is an exotic blend of several Asian cultures. A typical dinner includes rice, spicy hot curry, a subtly seasoned soup, and fresh vegetables or fruit. Set the mood for this Thai dinner with Kiss of Lemon Soup. Then serve Thai Shrimp and Rice accompanied by Asian Fruit Salad, an unusual combination of apple, onion, and chopped mango topped with honey-ginger dressing.

Cool the palate with Banana-Pineapple Delight for dessert.

KISS OF LEMON SOUP

3 stalks lemon grass
2 cups water
2 cups canned low-sodium chicken broth, undiluted
½ cup Chablis or other dry white wine
¼ cup lemon juice
1 teaspoon grated lemon rind
1 clove garlic, minced
1 (15-ounce) can straw mushrooms, drained
½ cup shredded carrot
½ cup thinly sliced celery
¼ cup finely chopped onion
¼ teaspoon crushed red pepper

Remove tough outer leaves from lemon grass stalks. Cut a 2-inch length from bottom of each stalk; mince. Bruise remaining part of leaves with meat mallet. Combine minced and bruised lemon grass, water, and next 5 ingredients in a 2½-quart casserole. Cover with heavy-duty plastic wrap and vent. Microwave at HIGH 8 minutes. Strain, reserving liquid; discard solids.

Return reserved liquid to casserole. Stir in mushrooms, shredded carrot, sliced celery, chopped onion, and crushed red pepper. Cover and vent. Microwave at MEDIUM (50% power) 7 to 8 minutes or until vegetables are crisp-tender. Ladle soup into individual bowls. Yield: 6 cups (28 calories per 1-cup serving).

PROTEIN 1.2 FAT 0.2 CARBOHYDRATE 5.5 CHOLESTEROL 0
IRON 0.5 SODIUM 13 CALCIUM 10

THAI SHRIMP AND RICE

½ cup sliced green onions
½ cup fresh bean sprouts
2 cloves garlic, minced
1 teaspoon vegetable oil
1 pound medium-size fresh shrimp, peeled and deveined
2 tablespoons brown sugar
2 tablespoons no-salt-added tomato sauce
1 tablespoon low-sodium soy sauce
1 tablespoon fish sauce
1 teaspoon ground cumin
½ teaspoon ground coriander
½ teaspoon crushed red pepper
3 cups cooked long-grain rice (cooked without salt or fat)
¼ cup chopped, peeled cucumber
¼ cup sliced green onions

Combine ½ cup green onions, bean sprouts, garlic, and oil in a 3-quart casserole. Cover with heavy-duty plastic wrap and vent. Microwave at HIGH 2 to 3 minutes or until vegetables are crisp-tender. Drain; pat dry with a paper towel.

Return vegetables to casserole; stir in shrimp and next 7 ingredients. Cover and vent. Microwave at HIGH 5 to 7 minutes or until shrimp turn pink, stirring once. Stir in rice; microwave at HIGH 1 minute or until thoroughly heated. Sprinkle with cucumber and ¼ cup green onions. Yield: 6 servings (217 calories per serving).

PROTEIN 14.9 FAT 2.1 CARBOHYDRATE 32.9 CHOLESTEROL 86
IRON 3.1 SODIUM 272 CALCIUM 58

SOUPER BOWL

Some inexpensive but appetizing advice for those watching their weight is to start the meal with a bowl of hot soup. Studies done on more than 1,000 dieters found that weight watchers who started meals with hot soup ate fewer calories than those who skipped the soup course. Researchers theorize that this drop in intake may have to do with the time it takes to eat hot soup. Sipping on soup may slow the pace of the whole meal. Moreover, eating slowly usually means eating fewer calories than when you gobble down food. In addition, most soups—unless they are the rich, creamy variety—have less than 200 calories per bowl.

ASIAN FRUIT SALAD

¼ cup rice wine vinegar
1 tablespoon honey
2 teaspoons low-sodium soy sauce
1 teaspoon grated fresh ginger
1 teaspoon vegetable oil
⅛ teaspoon hot pepper sauce
6 curly lettuce leaves
1 large Granny Smith apple, thinly sliced
1 cup coarsely chopped mango
½ cup thinly sliced purple onion
¼ cup chopped unsalted peanuts

Combine first 6 ingredients in a jar. Cover tightly, and shake vigorously. Chill thoroughly.

Place lettuce leaves on individual salad plates. Arrange sliced apple, mango, and onion evenly over lettuce. Shake vinegar mixture, and drizzle evenly over salads. Sprinkle with chopped peanuts. Yield: 6 servings (105 calories per serving).

PROTEIN 2.4 FAT 4.5 CARBOHYDRATE 15.8 CHOLESTEROL 0
IRON 0.4 SODIUM 48 CALCIUM 18

BANANA-PINEAPPLE DELIGHT

2 tablespoons brown sugar
1 tablespoon reduced-calorie margarine
1 tablespoon Triple Sec or other
   orange-flavored liqueur
1 tablespoon rum
1 teaspoon grated lime rind
2 teaspoons lime juice
3 medium bananas, peeled and cut in half
   lengthwise, then crosswise
2 cups pineapple sherbet
2 tablespoons unsweetened coconut, toasted

Combine first 6 ingredients in a 2-quart casserole. Cover with heavy-duty plastic wrap and vent. Microwave at MEDIUM HIGH (70% power) 3 to 4 minutes or until sugar dissolves, stirring once. Add bananas, stirring gently to coat each piece. Microwave at HIGH 1 to 2 minutes or until hot.

Place 2 banana pieces on each individual dessert plate, and pour syrup mixture evenly over bananas. Top each with ⅓ cup pineapple sherbet, and sprinkle with coconut. Serve immediately. Yield: 6 servings (153 calories per serving).

PROTEIN 1.3 FAT 3.5 CARBOHYDRATE 31.2 CHOLESTEROL 0
IRON 0.4 SODIUM 65 CALCIUM 32

BANGKOK COCKTAIL

2 cups unsweetened pineapple juice
1 cup water
1 (6-ounce) can frozen orange juice
   concentrate, thawed and undiluted
¼ cup gin
3 tablespoons lime juice
2 teaspoons rum extract
1 teaspoon coconut extract
12 ice cubes
Fresh mint sprigs (optional)

Combine first 7 ingredients, stirring well. Transfer mixture in batches into container of an electric blender; top with cover, and process until smooth. Add ice cubes, and process until blended. Garnish with fresh mint sprigs, if desired. Serve immediately. Yield: 6 cups (92 calories per ¾-cup serving).

PROTEIN 0.7 FAT 0.1 CARBOHYDRATE 17.2 CHOLESTEROL 0
IRON 0.2 SODIUM 1 CALCIUM 18

Transform your backyard into an island paradise. Fresh tropical flowers and tiki lights will set the mood for Tropical Beef Kabobs, Pit-Roasted Corn-on-the-Cob, Mamey-Spinach Salad, and Hawaiian Wine Cooler. (Menu begins on page 73.)

That's Entertaining

Chicken and Shrimp Jambalaya with Creole Sauce, Strawberry Salad Cups (page 72), and Parsley-Dijon French Bread (page 72) combine to create a flavorful Cajun celebration.

A Cajun Celebration

Chicken and Shrimp Jambalaya
Creole Sauce
Strawberry Salad Cups
Parsley-Dijon French Bread
Spirited Cinnamon Cream

SERVES 8
TOTAL CALORIES PER SERVING: 705

Bayou country cuisine offers its own unique identity. This Cajun celebration can be presented buffet-style, beginning with jambalaya. Similar to a hearty pilaf, it can be packed into cups while hot and then unmolded moments later onto a large platter for a distinctive presentation. Let each of your guests spoon ¼ cup Creole Sauce over the rice mounds.

The menu strikes real harmony with the supporting recipes. Parsley-Dijon French Bread can be assembled up to one day in advance. Strawberry Salad Cups can be prepared early in the day.

Spirited Cinnamon Cream will surely bring smiles to every face, as no Cajun party would be complete without the popular flavor of sweet, creamy pralines.

CHICKEN AND SHRIMP JAMBALAYA

1½ teaspoons dried whole thyme
1 teaspoon ground red pepper
½ teaspoon ground white pepper
½ teaspoon pepper
½ teaspoon rubbed sage
¼ teaspoon salt
4 bay leaves
Vegetable cooking spray
1 tablespoon vegetable oil
8 ounces lean cooked ham, chopped
2 (4-ounce) skinned, boned chicken breast
    halves, cut into 1-inch pieces
1½ cups chopped onion
1½ cups chopped celery
1½ cups chopped green pepper
4 cloves garlic, minced
1 cup no-salt-added tomato sauce
2 cups peeled, chopped fresh tomato
2½ cups canned no-salt-added chicken
    broth, undiluted
1½ cups long-grain rice, uncooked
½ pound medium-size fresh shrimp,
    peeled and deveined

Combine first 7 ingredients in a small bowl; stir well. Set aside.

Coat a Dutch oven with cooking spray; add oil. Place over medium-high heat until hot. Add ham, and sauté 3 minutes or until lightly browned. Add chicken, and sauté 5 to 7 minutes or until chicken is browned, stirring constantly. Stir in thyme mixture, chopped onion, celery, green pepper, and minced garlic; sauté 5 to 7 minutes or until vegetables are tender.

Stir in tomato sauce; bring to a boil. Remove from heat, and stir in chopped tomato, chicken broth, rice, and shrimp. Place mixture in a 3-quart baking dish coated with cooking spray. Cover and bake at 350° for 45 minutes or until rice is tender and liquid is absorbed. Remove from oven, and stir well. Remove and discard bay leaves. Cover and let stand 5 minutes. Mold rice mixture into 8 (10-ounce) custard cups; let stand 5 minutes. Invert custard cups onto a large serving platter. Yield: 8 servings (283 calories per serving).

PROTEIN 20.8 FAT 5.1 CARBOHYDRATE 37.6 CHOLESTEROL 66
IRON 3.5 SODIUM 599 CALCIUM 54

CREOLE SAUCE

¾ teaspoon dried whole oregano
½ teaspoon dried whole thyme
½ teaspoon dried whole basil
¼ teaspoon salt
¼ teaspoon pepper
¼ teaspoon ground red pepper
¼ teaspoon paprika
⅛ teaspoon ground white pepper
2 bay leaves
Vegetable cooking spray
2 teaspoons reduced-calorie
    margarine
¾ cup chopped onion
¾ cup chopped celery
¾ cup chopped green pepper
2 cloves garlic, minced
1 cup peeled, chopped tomato
¾ cup canned no-salt-added chicken
    broth, undiluted
¾ cup no-salt-added tomato
    sauce
1 teaspoon sugar

Combine first 9 ingredients in a small bowl; stir well. Set aside.

Coat a saucepan with cooking spray; add margarine. Place over medium-high heat until margarine melts. Add onion, celery, green pepper, and garlic; sauté until tender. Stir in oregano mixture, tomato, broth, tomato sauce, and sugar. Bring to a boil; reduce heat, and simmer 50 minutes. Remove from heat. Remove and discard bay leaves. Serve with jambalaya. Yield: 2 cups (9 calories per tablespoon).

PROTEIN 0.3 FAT 0.3 CARBOHYDRATE 1.5 CHOLESTEROL 0
IRON 0.1 SODIUM 28 CALCIUM 4

STRAWBERRY SALAD CUPS

4 heads Bibb lettuce
2⅔ cups halved fresh strawberries
Honey-Peanut Vinaigrette

Cut lettuce heads in half lengthwise. Remove and discard core and innermost leaves. Place lettuce on a large serving platter. Fill each half with ⅓ cup strawberries. Place Honey-Peanut Vinaigrette in center of platter. To serve, drizzle vinaigrette evenly over salads. Yield: 8 servings (93 calories per serving).

Honey-Peanut Vinaigrette

¼ cup plus 1 tablespoon honey
¼ cup white wine vinegar
3 tablespoons water
1 tablespoon Dijon mustard
3 tablespoons chopped unsalted roasted
  peanuts
2 tablespoons chopped green onions

Combine first 4 ingredients in container of an electric blender; top with cover, and process until smooth. Stir in peanuts and green onions. Transfer mixture to a small bowl. Cover and refrigerate at least 1 hour. Yield: 1 cup.

PROTEIN 2.2 FAT 2.6 CARBOHYDRATE 17.0 CHOLESTEROL 0
IRON 0.5 SODIUM 61 CALCIUM 14

PARSLEY-DIJON FRENCH BREAD

½ (16-ounce) loaf French bread
2 tablespoons reduced-calorie margarine
1½ tablespoons Dijon mustard
1 tablespoon minced fresh parsley
⅛ teaspoon pepper

Slice bread in half lengthwise, leaving one side attached. Open bread, butterfly fashion; set aside.
Combine margarine, mustard, parsley, and pepper in a small bowl; stir well. Spread mixture over cut sides of bread. Reassemble loaf, and wrap tightly in aluminum foil. Bake at 350° for 15 minutes or until thoroughly heated. Cut bread into 8 (1-inch) slices. Serve warm. Yield: 8 servings (101 calories per serving).

PROTEIN 2.6 FAT 2.6 CARBOHYDRATE 15.9 CHOLESTEROL 1
IRON 0.7 SODIUM 276 CALCIUM 13

SPIRITED CINNAMON CREAM

3 tablespoons cognac
3½ cups vanilla nonfat frozen yogurt, softened
¼ teaspoon ground cinnamon
Vegetable cooking spray
1 medium cooking apple, peeled, cored, and
  thinly sliced
1 tablespoon lemon juice
½ cup unsweetened apple juice
3 tablespoons hot water
8 pitted whole dates, chopped
4 caramel candies, chopped
8 pecan halves, toasted

Place cognac in a small saucepan; bring to a boil. Remove from heat, and let cool.
Combine cognac, frozen yogurt, and cinnamon; stir until well blended. Spoon mixture into a 7-inch springform pan coated with cooking spray. Cover and freeze until firm.
Place apple slices in a medium bowl; add lemon juice, and toss well. Combine apple slices and apple juice in a nonstick skillet. Bring to a boil; reduce heat, and simmer 6 minutes or until tender. Remove apple with a slotted spoon; set aside. Add water, dates, and caramels to apple juice; cook over low heat until caramels melt and mixture is smooth, stirring constantly. Add reserved apple slices, and toss to coat. Let cool.
Arrange apple slices and pecan halves over frozen yogurt mixture. Cover and freeze at least 8 hours. Yield: 8 servings (192 calories per serving).

PROTEIN 3.5 FAT 5.1 CARBOHYDRATE 34.7 CHOLESTEROL 0
IRON 0.4 SODIUM 68 CALCIUM 359

Pipe Coconut-Pineapple Sherbet (page 75) into baby pineapple shells for a satisfying conclusion to your luau.

Hawaiian Luau

Smoked Turkey and Melon Rolls
Tropical Beef Kabobs
Pit-Roasted Corn-On-The-Cob
Mamey-Spinach Salad
Coconut-Pineapple Sherbet
Hawaiian Wine Cooler

SERVES 8
TOTAL CALORIES PER SERVING: 715

Invite your family and friends over for a taste of paradise. Fresh tropical flowers, candlelit tables, and comfortable, casual attire set the mood for traditional island fare.

Just the aroma of food cooking on the grill enhances this menu. Tropical Beef Kabobs star in this exotic feast. Mingle the flavors of steak, sweet red pepper, and onions in a gingery sweet-and-sour marinade before sizzling them on the grill.

Mamey, a tropical fruit, is showcased in the spinach salad. After peeling, mamey reveals a deep red-orange flesh and a sweet but nutty flavor.

The most popular flavor of the islands is juicy fresh pineapple. Using fresh pineapple is the key to Coconut-Pineapple Sherbet's uncompromising taste.

For a change of pace to a plain wine cooler, serve Hawaiian Wine Cooler chilled over crushed ice. It tastes ideal with the appetizer or the meal.

SMOKED TURKEY AND MELON ROLLS

½ medium-size ripe cantaloupe, seeded
1 tablespoon plus 1 teaspoon Dijon mustard
4 (1-ounce) slices smoked turkey, cut in half
　　lengthwise
Dash of pepper

Cut cantaloupe into 8 thin lengthwise slices.
Remove rind from each slice, using a sharp knife.

Spread mustard evenly over one side of each turkey slice. Wrap one slice of turkey around each melon wedge. Place on a serving platter, and sprinkle with pepper. Chill. Yield: 8 servings (41 calories per serving).

PROTEIN 3.8　FAT 1.1　CARBOHYDRATE 4.3　CHOLESTEROL 8
IRON 0.5　SODIUM 176　CALCIUM 7

TROPICAL BEEF KABOBS

2 pounds lean boneless beef sirloin steak
½ cup honey
¼ cup white wine vinegar
2 tablespoons Dijon mustard
1 tablespoon minced fresh ginger
1 tablespoon low-sodium soy sauce
¼ teaspoon garlic powder
¼ teaspoon pepper
¼ pound fresh snow pea pods
2 large sweet red peppers, seeded and cut into
　　1-inch pieces
2 large yellow onions, cut into 1-inch pieces
Vegetable cooking spray

Trim fat from steak; cut steak into 1-inch pieces, and place in a shallow dish. Combine honey and

next 6 ingredients; pour over steak. Cover and marinate in refrigerator at least 2 hours, stirring occasionally.

Remove steak from marinade; place marinade in a small saucepan. Bring to a boil; reduce heat, and simmer 3 minutes.

Thread steak, snow peas, sweet red pepper, and onion alternately on 8 (12-inch) skewers. Coat grill rack with cooking spray, and place on grill over medium-hot coals. Place kabobs on rack, and cook 12 minutes or to desired degree of doneness, turning and basting frequently with marinade. Yield: 8 servings (285 calories per serving).

PROTEIN 27.4　FAT 8.0　CARBOHYDRATE 25.7　CHOLESTEROL 76
IRON 3.9　SODIUM 248　CALCIUM 31

PIT-ROASTED CORN-ON-THE-COB

8 ears fresh corn in husks
⅓ cup commercial oil-free Italian dressing
2½ tablespoons water
1 tablespoon chili powder
⅛ teaspoon ground red pepper

Carefully peel back husks, exposing corn. Leave husks attached. Remove and discard silks. Combine Italian dressing and remaining ingredients

in a small bowl; stir well. Brush liberally over corn. Return husks to original position, and tie the tips with wire twist-ties. Grill corn over medium-hot coals 30 minutes or until corn is tender, turning corn every 5 minutes. Yield: 8 servings (88 calories per serving).

PROTEIN 2.6　FAT 1.1　CARBOHYDRATE 20.3　CHOLESTEROL 0
IRON 0.7　SODIUM 112　CALCIUM 6

MAMEY-SPINACH SALAD

1 (1½-pound) mamey, peeled
8 cups torn spinach
⅓ cup chopped green onions
Almond and Chutney Dressing

Cut mamey in half lengthwise; remove and discard seed. Cut mamey into thin slices. Place spinach in a large salad bowl. Arrange mamey and green onions over spinach. Cover and chill.

Just before serving, shake Almond and Chutney Dressing, and drizzle over salad. Yield: 8 servings (99 calories per serving).

Almond and Chutney Dressing

½ cup commercial chutney
3 tablespoons chopped toasted almonds
2 tablespoons water
1 tablespoon white wine vinegar
1 tablespoon lemon juice
1 tablespoon Dijon mustard
Dash of pepper

Combine all ingredients in a small jar; cover tightly, and shake vigorously. Chill at least 1 hour. Yield: 1 cup.

PROTEIN 2.2 FAT 1.7 CARBOHYDRATE 19.5 CHOLESTEROL 0
IRON 0.9 SODIUM 109 CALCIUM 34

COCONUT-PINEAPPLE SHERBET

3 cups cubed fresh pineapple
¼ cup sugar
1 teaspoon lime juice
1⅓ cups nonfat buttermilk
½ teaspoon coconut flavoring
Fresh pineapple shells (optional)

Combine first 3 ingredients in container of an electric blender; top with cover, and process until smooth. With processor running, gradually add buttermilk and coconut flavoring. Process until blended.

Pour mixture into freezer can of a 2-quart hand-turned or electric freezer. Freeze according to manufacturer's instructions. Let ripen 1 hour, if desired. Scoop sherbet into pineapple shells, if desired. Serve immediately. Yield: 4 cups (71 calories per ½-cup serving).

PROTEIN 1.7 FAT 0.4 CARBOHYDRATE 16.2 CHOLESTEROL 0
IRON 0.2 SODIUM 43 CALCIUM 5

HAWAIIAN WINE COOLER

3¾ cups fresh orange juice, chilled
2½ cups cranberry juice cocktail, chilled
1½ cups Chablis or other dry white wine, chilled
¼ cup fresh lime juice, chilled

Combine all ingredients in a tall pitcher; stir well. Serve over crushed ice. Yield: 8 servings (131 calories per 1-cup serving).

PROTEIN 0.9 FAT 0.1 CARBOHYDRATE 25.6 CHOLESTEROL 0
IRON 0.5 SODIUM 6 CALCIUM 18

NUTTY COMPARISONS

Eating nuts out of hand can add up to dangerously high amounts of calories. High fat content is the reason. In small quantities, however, a few chopped nuts sprinkled over a salad or pasta dish can add more flavor than fat.

TYPE	AMOUNT (1 ounce)	CALORIES	FAT (grams)
Almonds	22	176	16.4
Cashews	18	163	13.7
Chestnuts	4	70	0.6
Filberts	16	187	18.1
Macadamias	11	204	21.7
Peanuts	40	165	14.0
Pecans	8	195	20.2
Pine nuts	86	146	14.4
Walnuts	7	182	17.6

Serve an ensemble of classic French recipes that include Coq au Vin (page 78), steamed baby carrots, Provençal-Style Tomatoes (page 78), and Salad Verte with Fresh Raspberries (page 79).

Classic French Cuisine Goes Light

Braised Artichokes with Sauce Béarnaise
Coq au Vin
Steamed Baby Carrots
Provençal-Style Tomatoes
Salad Verte with Fresh Raspberries
Commercial French Bread
Almond Floating Islands
Blush Wine

SERVES 6
TOTAL CALORIES PER SERVING: 692

Our ensemble of classic French recipes includes Coq au Vin served with a broiled tomato half and ½ cup steamed baby carrots for a visually striking and delicious dinner plate.

The dessert is Almond Floating Islands, mounds of meringue atop a pool of chilled vanilla custard. Menu calories include a 6-ounce glass of wine and a 1-ounce slice of French bread per person.

BRAISED ARTICHOKES WITH SAUCE BÉARNAISE

1¼ cups plain nonfat yogurt
2 tablespoons reduced-calorie mayonnaise
3 tablespoons white wine vinegar
1 tablespoon minced green onions
2 cloves garlic, minced
¼ teaspoon pepper
1½ teaspoons minced fresh tarragon
6 medium artichokes (about 2¼ pounds)
Lemon wedge
1 large sweet yellow pepper, cut into julienne strips

Line a colander or sieve with a double layer of cheesecloth that has been rinsed out and squeezed dry; extend over edge of colander.

Stir yogurt until well blended. Pour into colander, and fold edges of cheesecloth over to cover yogurt. Place colander in a bowl to drain; chill 8 hours. Remove yogurt from colander; discard liquid in bowl. Remove yogurt from cheesecloth.

Combine drained yogurt and mayonnaise; set aside. Combine vinegar and next 3 ingredients in a saucepan; bring to a boil. Reduce heat, and simmer until mixture is reduced by half. Strain, reserving liquid; cool. Combine yogurt mixture, vinegar mixture, and tarragon; cover and chill.

Wash artichokes by plunging up and down in cold water. Cut off stem end; trim about ½ inch from top of each artichoke. Remove any loose bottom leaves. With scissors, trim away about one-fourth of each outer leaf. Rub top and edges with a lemon wedge to prevent discoloration.

Place artichokes in a Dutch oven; add water to a depth of 1 inch. Bring to a boil; cover, reduce heat, and simmer 25 minutes or until almost tender. Drain; let cool. Spread leaves apart; scrape out the fuzzy thistle center (choke) with a spoon.

Place artichokes on serving plates. Arrange pepper strips on plates. Serve with chilled yogurt sauce. Yield: 6 servings (82 calories per serving).

PROTEIN 4.9 FAT 1.7 CARBOHYDRATE 13.5 CHOLESTEROL 3
IRON 1.5 SODIUM 129 CALCIUM 135

COQ AU VIN

6 (6-ounce) skinned chicken breast halves
3 tablespoons all-purpose flour
24 small pearl onions
Vegetable cooking spray
24 small fresh mushrooms
1 tablespoon olive oil
2 tablespoons cognac
3 ounces lean cooked ham, cut into julienne
   strips
2 cups Pinot Noir or other dry red wine
1 cup water
2 cloves garlic, minced
1 teaspoon sugar
1 teaspoon beef-flavored bouillon granules
¼ teaspoon pepper
⅛ teaspoon freshly grated nutmeg
Bouquet Garni

Dredge chicken in flour; set aside.

Blanch onions in boiling water 1 minute; drain and pat dry with paper towels. Coat a large Dutch oven with cooking spray; place over medium-high heat until hot. Add blanched onions and mushrooms; sauté until tender. Remove from pan; set mixture aside.

Coat pan with cooking spray; add oil. Place over medium-high heat until hot. Add chicken; cook 4 minutes on each side or until chicken is browned. Pour cognac over chicken; ignite with a long-stemmed match. When flames die, stir in ham and next 8 ingredients. Bring to a boil; reduce heat, and simmer 30 minutes.

Add reserved onions and mushrooms; simmer an additional 30 minutes or until chicken is tender. Transfer chicken to a serving platter, using a slotted spoon. Discard Bouquet Garni. Cook sauce mixture over high heat 15 minutes or until reduced to a glaze; spoon over chicken. Yield: 6 servings (207 calories per serving).

Bouquet Garni

6 fresh parsley sprigs
6 fresh thyme sprigs
2 fresh rosemary sprigs
2 (4-inch) pieces celery

Place half of herbs in hollow of each celery piece. Place celery pieces together, hollow side in, and secure with cotton string. Yield: 1 Bouquet Garni.

PROTEIN 30.3 FAT 5.0 CARBOHYDRATE 9.3 CHOLESTEROL 74
IRON 1.8 SODIUM 442 CALCIUM 37

PROVENÇAL-STYLE TOMATOES

3 medium tomatoes, halved crosswise
1 teaspoon olive oil
Vegetable cooking spray
3 cloves garlic, minced
¼ cup fine, dry breadcrumbs
2 tablespoons chopped fresh parsley
1 teaspoon chopped fresh thyme
1 teaspoon sugar
¼ teaspoon salt
¼ teaspoon pepper

Place tomatoes, cut side up, on an ungreased baking sheet. Brush cut side of tomatoes with olive oil; set aside.

Coat a small nonstick skillet with cooking spray; place over medium-high heat until hot. Add garlic, and sauté until tender. Stir in breadcrumbs and remaining ingredients. Sprinkle breadcrumb mixture evenly over tomatoes. Broil 3 inches from heat 3 to 4 minutes or until lightly browned. Serve immediately. Yield: 6 servings (49 calories per serving).

PROTEIN 1.5 FAT 1.3 CARBOHYDRATE 8.8 CHOLESTEROL 0
IRON 1.0 SODIUM 138 CALCIUM 20

SALAD VERTE WITH FRESH RASPBERRIES

¼ cup raspberry vinegar
2 tablespoons balsamic vinegar
2½ tablespoons reduced-calorie mayonnaise
2 teaspoons white wine Worcestershire
   sauce
2 cups torn curly endive
2 cups torn Boston or Bibb lettuce
2 cups torn romaine lettuce
1 cup fresh raspberries

Combine first 4 ingredients in a small bowl; stir with a wire whisk until blended. Set aside.

Combine salad greens in a large bowl; add vinegar mixture, and toss well. Add raspberries; toss lightly. Arrange on individual salad plates. Yield: 6 servings (36 calories per 1-cup serving).

PROTEIN 0.8 FAT 1.9 CARBOHYDRATE 4.9 CHOLESTEROL 2
IRON 0.4 SODIUM 67 CALCIUM 17

ALMOND FLOATING ISLANDS

3 cups skim milk
2 eggs, lightly beaten
½ cup sugar, divided
2 tablespoons plus 1
   teaspoon cornstarch
1 teaspoon almond extract
2 egg whites
2 tablespoons finely chopped toasted almonds

Heat milk in a medium saucepan to simmering; set aside.

Combine eggs, ¼ cup plus 2 tablespoons sugar, and cornstarch in top of a double boiler; beat with a wire whisk until blended. Gradually stir about one-fourth of hot milk into egg mixture; add remaining hot milk, stirring constantly.

Bring water to a boil; reduce heat to low, and cook 12 to 15 minutes or until mixture coats a metal spoon, stirring constantly. Remove from

heat, and stir in almond extract. Let cool; cover and chill thoroughly.

Beat egg whites (at room temperature) at high speed of an electric mixer until soft peaks form. Gradually add remaining 2 tablespoons sugar, 1 tablespoon at a time, beating until stiff peaks form. Fold in almonds.

Pour boiling water into a 13- x 9- x 2-inch baking pan to a depth of 1 inch. Drop egg white mixture in 6 equal portions into boiling water. Bake at 350° for 15 to 18 minutes or until lightly browned. Carefully remove islands with a slotted spoon; drain on paper towels. Chill until ready to serve.

Spoon custard mixture into 6 individual dessert dishes; top each with an island. Serve immediately. Yield: 6 servings (165 calories per serving).

PROTEIN 7.9 FAT 3.1 CARBOHYDRATE 26.2 CHOLESTEROL 73
IRON 0.4 SODIUM 103 CALCIUM 166

 SNEAKY STEPS TOWARD FITNESS

Planned exercise workouts—aerobic class, a morning jog, an evening swim—are obvious routes toward achieving fitness. But don't forget that it's easy to sneak activity into your everyday schedule, too. If you take the stairs to the second floor of the library or park the car at the outskirts of the supermarket parking lot, you will burn a few more calories by walking the extra steps.

Once you start taking the active approach to daily life, those small calorie losses will begin to add up. Other ideas for sneaking in fitness include riding your bicycle to work once in a while, walking to the supermarket, and running in place or up and down the stairs for 5 minutes as part of your work break. Make it automatic to search out the most active way to approach daily errands and tasks.

Invite friends over for a feast of She Crab Soup, Crab Cake Sandwiches, Tangy Horseradish Coleslaw (page 82), chilled watermelon wedges, and Spiced Blueberry Tart (page 82).

Chesapeake Crab Feast

She Crab Soup
Crab Cake Sandwiches
Tangy Horseradish Coleslaw
Watermelon Wedges
Spiced Blueberry Tart

SERVES 8
TOTAL CALORIES PER SERVING: 696

The Chesapeake Bay offers a harvest of seafood, especially hard-shell crabs. Fortunately, crab is available at most seafood counters, so you don't have to venture to the Eastern Shore to satisfy your craving.

Crab Cake Sandwiches anchor the meal along with She Crab Soup, providing your guests with a double dose of bay favorites. Add the crab to the soup just 5 minutes before serving. And for easier

handling, after shaping the crab cakes, refrigerate them for 15 minutes.

The coleslaw is a bright combination of vegetables tossed with a zesty dressing. Accompany this feast with chilled wedges of watermelon; menu calories include 1 cup per person. And the tart is the perfect ending for this meal. It can be prepared early in the day, and served at room temperature.

SHE CRAB SOUP

Butter-flavored vegetable cooking spray
⅔ cup chopped leek
½ cup chopped celery
2¾ cups evaporated skimmed milk
2½ cups peeled, diced red potato
1 cup canned no-salt-added chicken broth, undiluted
¼ teaspoon salt
⅛ teaspoon ground white pepper
2 tablespoons dry sherry
½ pound fresh lump crabmeat, drained

Coat a medium saucepan with cooking spray; place over medium-high heat until hot. Add leek and celery; sauté until tender. Stir in milk and next 4 ingredients. Bring to a boil; reduce heat, and simmer 20 minutes or until potato is tender. Cool slightly.

Transfer mixture in batches to container of an electric blender or food processor; top with cover, and process until smooth.

Return mixture to saucepan; stir in sherry and crabmeat. Cook over medium heat 5 minutes or until thoroughly heated. Yield: 8 cups (137 calories per 1-cup serving).

PROTEIN 13.5 FAT 1.1 CARBOHYDRATE 17.8 CHOLESTEROL 32
IRON 1.0 SODIUM 281 CALCIUM 295

CRAB CAKE SANDWICHES

Vegetable cooking spray
⅓ cup chopped onion
⅓ cup chopped celery
1½ pounds fresh lump crabmeat, drained
1 cup soft breadcrumbs
⅓ cup frozen egg substitute, thawed
2 tablespoons reduced-calorie mayonnaise
2 teaspoons Dijon mustard
2 teaspoons reduced-sodium Worcestershire sauce
½ teaspoon Old Bay seasoning
¼ teaspoon ground red pepper
2 tablespoons plus 2 teaspoons reduced-calorie mayonnaise
8 (1½-ounce) reduced-calorie whole wheat hamburger buns
8 curly leaf lettuce leaves
8 (¼-inch-thick) tomato slices
Dash of freshly ground pepper

Coat a small nonstick skillet with cooking spray; place over medium-high heat until hot. Add onion and celery; sauté until tender. Combine sautéed vegetables, crabmeat, and next 7 ingredients in a medium bowl; stir gently until blended. Shape crabmeat mixture into 8 (1-inch-thick) patties. Place on a baking sheet; cover and chill at least 15 minutes.

Coat a large nonstick skillet with cooking spray; place over medium heat until hot. Add crab cakes, in batches, and cook 4 minutes on each side or until lightly browned.

Spread 1 teaspoon mayonnaise on one side of each hamburger bun, and top with 1 crab cake. Top each with a lettuce leaf, tomato slice, ground pepper, and remaining half of hamburger bun. Serve hot. Yield: 8 servings (240 calories per serving).

PROTEIN 22.1 FAT 5.0 CARBOHYDRATE 24.8 CHOLESTEROL 76
IRON 1.4 SODIUM 690 CALCIUM 107

TANGY HORSERADISH COLESLAW

4 cups coarsely shredded cabbage
2 cups seeded, chopped tomato
1½ cups frozen whole kernel corn, thawed
1 cup coarsely shredded red cabbage
1 cup chopped green pepper
½ cup plain nonfat yogurt
½ cup low-fat sour cream
2 tablespoons Dijon mustard
1 tablespoon plus 1 teaspoon prepared
    horseradish
¼ teaspoon salt
¼ teaspoon hot sauce
¼ cup (1 ounce) shredded 40% less-fat Cheddar
    cheese

Combine cabbage, chopped tomato, corn, red cabbage, and green pepper in a large bowl, and toss gently.

Combine yogurt, sour cream, mustard, horseradish, salt, and hot sauce, stirring well. Add to cabbage mixture, and toss gently. Cover and chill at least 1 hour.

Just before serving, add Cheddar cheese to cabbage mixture, stirring well to combine. Yield: 8 servings (95 calories per 1-cup serving).

PROTEIN 3.9   FAT 3.1   CARBOHYDRATE 14.8   CHOLESTEROL 6
IRON 0.9   SODIUM 219   CALCIUM 94

SPICED BLUEBERRY TART

1 cup all-purpose flour
¼ cup cold margarine
2 to 3 tablespoons cold water
½ cup low-fat sour cream
3 tablespoons sugar
1 egg, lightly beaten
1 teaspoon vanilla extract
1⅔ cups fresh blueberries
¼ teaspoon ground cinnamon
1 tablespoon reduced-calorie
    maple syrup
Fresh mint sprigs (optional)

Place flour in a bowl, and cut in margarine with a pastry blender until flour mixture resembles coarse meal. Sprinkle cold water, 1 tablespoon at a time, evenly over surface; stir with a fork just until dry ingredients are moistened. Shape flour mixture into a ball.

Gently press dough between 2 sheets of heavy-duty plastic wrap to a 4-inch circle. Chill 15 minutes. Roll dough to an 11-inch circle. Remove plastic wrap. Fit dough into an ungreased 9-inch tart pan. Prick bottom and sides of pastry with a fork. Bake at 375° for 15 minutes or until lightly browned.

Combine sour cream, sugar, egg, and vanilla; stir well. Pour sour cream mixture into prepared pastry shell. Arrange blueberries over tart. Sprinkle with cinnamon. Bake at 375° for 30 minutes or until mixture is set. Drizzle syrup over tart. Let cool. Garnish with fresh mint sprigs, if desired. Yield: 8 servings (173 calories per serving).

PROTEIN 3.0   FAT 8.4   CARBOHYDRATE 21.7   CHOLESTEROL 32
IRON 0.9   SODIUM 84   CALCIUM 26

 CORPORATE FITNESS
Many companies are implementing corporate fitness or wellness programs. The success of these programs has been measured in three ways. One is improved health and fitness levels. Second is the positive effect on job performance, work satisfaction, and lack of absenteeism. And, finally, the bottom line is the amount of money saved by decreased health care costs and absenteeism.

Many companies are finding that the best way to keep health care costs down and keep profits up is to keep their employees healthy through exercise, weight loss, smoking cessation, stress management, and nutrition education. In return for the employee's participation in these corporate fitness programs, companies often give employees flexibility in their work schedule and offer incentives for motivation.

Holiday Dinner Party

Pepper-Crusted Crown
Roast of Pork
Savory Mushroom Pilaf
Seasoned Broccoli
Festive Spinach Salad
Poppy Seed
Crescents
Strawberry-Champagne
Sorbet with Spring Fruits

SERVES 12
TOTAL CALORIES PER SERVING: 647

Even a formal affair takes little effort with appropriate planning. These recipes will appeal to all of your guests and some can be assembled the day before the party, leaving only last-minute cooking.

Plan for the pork crown roast to come out of the oven moments before guests arrive, as it needs to stand at least 15 to 20 minutes before carving.

Dinner parties are back in style. And what entrée could be more spectacular than Pepper-Crusted Crown Roast of Pork.

PEPPER-CRUSTED CROWN ROAST OF PORK

1½ tablespoons crushed green
   peppercorns
1 tablespoon lemon juice
1 teaspoon poultry seasoning
½ teaspoon garlic powder
½ teaspoon cracked black pepper
½ teaspoon crushed red pepper
½ teaspoon ground nutmeg
1 (12-rib) crown roast of pork, well
   trimmed (about 4½ pounds)
Curly endive (optional)
Red grape clusters (optional)

Combine first 7 ingredients; rub pepper mixture over inside of roast. Place roast, bone ends up, on a rack in a roasting pan. Cut a piece of foil long enough to fit around ribs; fold foil lengthwise into thirds. Wrap foil around ribs, and fold over tips of ribs. Insert meat thermometer into roast without touching bone or fat.

Place roast in a 450° oven; reduce heat to 325°. Bake for 2½ to 3 hours or until meat thermometer reaches 160°. Remove from oven, and let stand 15 minutes. Transfer to a large serving platter. If desired, garnish with curly endive, and red grape clusters. Yield: 12 servings (202 calories per serving).

PROTEIN 23.8 FAT 10.9 CARBOHYDRATE 0.7 CHOLESTEROL 76
IRON 1.1 SODIUM 58 CALCIUM 9

SAVORY MUSHROOM PILAF

Vegetable cooking spray
1 tablespoon all-purpose flour
1 tablespoon vegetable oil
2½ cups sliced fresh mushrooms
½ cup chopped onion
2¼ cups canned no-salt-added chicken
    broth, undiluted
1½ cups water
½ teaspoon salt
¾ teaspoon dried whole thyme
½ teaspoon garlic powder
¼ teaspoon ground red pepper
1 (14-ounce package) instant brown rice, uncooked
2 tablespoons currants
¼ cup chopped sweet red pepper

Coat a large saucepan with cooking spray; add flour and oil, stirring until blended. Place over medium heat, and cook until mixture is lightly browned, stirring constantly. Add mushrooms and onion; cook until tender, stirring constantly.

Stir in broth and next 5 ingredients; bring to a boil. Add rice; cover, reduce heat, and simmer 8 to 10 minutes or until rice is tender and liquid is absorbed. Remove from heat; add currants and sweet red pepper, tossing gently. Cover and let stand 5 minutes. Yield: 12 servings (155 calories per ½-cup serving).

PROTEIN 4.0 FAT 2.7 CARBOHYDRATE 30.1 CHOLESTEROL 0
IRON 0.5 SODIUM 179 CALCIUM 8

SEASONED BROCCOLI

3 pounds fresh broccoli
¼ cup white wine vinegar
3 tablespoons water
2 teaspoons dark sesame oil
¼ teaspoon salt
¼ teaspoon pepper

Trim off large leaves and tough ends of broccoli. Wash broccoli, and separate into spears. Arrange broccoli in a vegetable steamer over boiling water. Cover and steam 6 minutes or until crisp-tender. Place on serving platter, and keep warm.

Combine vinegar and remaining ingredients in a small bowl, stirring well. Drizzle over broccoli, and serve immediately. Yield: 12 servings (30 calories per serving).

PROTEIN 2.3 FAT 1.4 CARBOHYDRATE 4.1 CHOLESTEROL 0
IRON 0.7 SODIUM 95 CALCIUM 38

FESTIVE SPINACH SALAD

9¾ cups torn fresh spinach
2¼ cups fresh strawberries, hulled
    and sliced
¼ cup plus 2 tablespoons sugar
1½ tablespoons sesame seeds
2¼ teaspoons poppy seeds
1½ teaspoons minced onion
¼ teaspoon paprika
½ teaspoon low-sodium Worcestershire
    sauce
¼ cup plus 2 tablespoons cider
    vinegar
1½ tablespoons vegetable oil
1½ tablespoons water

Combine spinach and strawberries in a large bowl; toss gently. Cover and chill.

Combine sugar and remaining ingredients in container of an electric blender; top with cover, and process at low speed for 30 seconds. Drizzle over spinach mixture; toss gently. Serve spinach salad immediately. Yield: 12 cups (68 calories per 1-cup serving).

PROTEIN 1.6 FAT 2.8 CARBOHYDRATE 10.7 CHOLESTEROL 0
IRON 1.4 SODIUM 31 CALCIUM 62

POPPY SEED CRESCENTS

3¼ cups all-purpose flour, divided
2 cups whole wheat flour
2 packages dry yeast
1½ teaspoons salt
1¼ cups skim milk
½ cup water
½ cup 1% low-fat cottage cheese
¼ cup honey
3 tablespoons margarine
3 tablespoons plus 1 teaspoon all-purpose
  flour
Butter-flavored vegetable cooking spray
1 tablespoon poppy seeds

Combine 1 cup all-purpose flour, whole wheat flour, yeast, and salt in a large mixing bowl, stirring well.

Combine skim milk and next 4 ingredients in a small saucepan; cook over medium heat until margarine melts, stirring occasionally. Cool to 120° to 130°.

Gradually add liquid mixture to flour mixture beating well at high speed of an electric mixer. Beat an additional 3 minutes at medium speed. Gradually add remaining 2¼ cups all-purpose flour to make a firm dough.

Sprinkle 3 tablespoons flour evenly over work surface. Turn dough out onto floured surface, and knead until smooth and elastic (about 5 to 8 minutes). Place dough in a large bowl coated with cooking spray, turning to coat top. Cover and let rise in a warm place (85°), free from drafts, 1 hour or until doubled in bulk.

Sprinkle remaining 1 teaspoon flour over work surface. Punch dough down; turn onto floured surface, and knead lightly 4 or 5 times. Divide dough into thirds. Cover and let rise 10 minutes. Roll each portion to a 12-inch circle (¼-inch thick). Coat surface of dough with cooking spray; cut each circle into 12 wedges. Roll up wedges, beginning at the wide end. Place, point side down, on a baking sheet coated with cooking spray. Sprinkle with poppy seeds. Curve rolls into crescent shapes. Cover and let rise in a warm place, free from drafts, 1 hour or until doubled in bulk.

Bake at 375° for 8 to 10 minutes or until golden. Yield: 3 dozen (87 calories each).

PROTEIN 2.9   FAT 1.4   CARBOHYDRATE 15.9   CHOLESTEROL 0
IRON 0.9   SODIUM 127   CALCIUM 21

STRAWBERRY-CHAMPAGNE SORBET WITH SPRING FRUITS

1½ cups champagne
¾ cup sugar
6 cups ripe fresh strawberries, hulled
1½ teaspoons lemon juice
1½ cups fresh strawberries
¾ cup fresh blueberries
¾ cup fresh raspberries

Combine champagne and sugar in a nonaluminum saucepan. Bring to a boil over medium heat; cook until sugar dissolves, stirring occasionally. Boil 3 minutes without stirring. Remove from heat, and let champagne mixture cool.

Combine 6 cups strawberries and lemon juice in container of an electric blender; top with cover, and process until smooth. Stir strawberry puree into champagne mixture. Pour into freezer can of a 2-quart hand-turned or electric freezer. Freeze according to manufacturer's instructions. Let ripen 1 hour, if desired. Scoop sorbet into individual dessert bowls, and top with fresh berries. Serve immediately. Yield: 12 servings (105 calories per ½-cup serving).

PROTEIN 0.7   FAT 0.4   CARBOHYDRATE 21.0   CHOLESTEROL 0
IRON 0.5   SODIUM 3   CALCIUM 15

Light
Recipes

Light and healthy eating does not have to mean less flavor or variety. You'll find these light recipes taste as good as they are nutritious: (from left) Caramel-Peach Trifle (page 229), Raspberry Cream Bombe (page 232), and Strawberry Lemonade (page 99).

Cooking Light's attention to presentation and flavor will invite success as you plan light meals. Remember that appearance counts, especially when introducing new foods to family and guests. Enhance the visual appeal of your meal by including items of contrasting color and texture.

When putting together a menu, note that of the total calories provided, at least 50 percent should be from carbohydrate, 20 percent from protein, and no more than 30 percent from fat. By keeping this 50-20-30 ratio in mind, you can create nutritionally balanced meals for optimal health.

Attention to these principles will give you confidence as a cook. But even more important, you will have the satisfaction of serving your family and friends the healthiest, freshest, and most attractive meals possible.

Whether you are having an intimate fireside dinner, a backyard gathering, a holiday celebration, or a last-minute lunch, you will find many ideas in the following recipe sections to help you create exciting meals that meet today's high standards in nutrition.

In "Light Recipes," you will discover recipes that capture the best flavors of fresh, wholesome foods. From entrées of beef, pork, fish, poultry, and meatless main dishes to accompaniments of pasta, grains, salads, fruits, and vegetables, your family is sure to enjoy the variety that *Cooking Light* offers. And there is no better way to top off a meal than by including a *Cooking Light* dessert. Use our recipes for baked fruit, cookies, cheesecake, or luscious tarts, and no one will guess that each has less than 200 calories per serving!

Dazzle your guests when you serve Steamed Chicken Medaillons in Raspberry Sauce (page 96), an elegant appetizer.

Appetizers & Beverages

JICAMA-ZUCCHINI DIP

1 cup shredded zucchini
¾ cup shredded jicama
2 cloves garlic, crushed
¼ teaspoon salt
½ cup plain nonfat yogurt

Combine first 4 ingredients in a small bowl; stir well. Let stand 30 minutes at room temperature. Press mixture between paper towels to remove excess moisture. Combine zucchini mixture and yogurt, stirring well. Cover and chill at least 1 hour. Serve with fresh raw vegetables. Yield: 1 cup (10 calories per tablespoon).

PROTEIN 0.7   FAT 0.0   CARBOHYDRATE 1.6   CHOLESTEROL 0
IRON 0.1   SODIUM 45   CALCIUM 22

ROASTED YELLOW PEPPER DIP

4 large sweet yellow peppers (about 1½ pounds)
Vegetable cooking spray
½ cup chopped onion
2 cloves garlic, minced
2 tablespoons chopped fresh basil
¼ cup reduced-calorie mayonnaise

Place peppers on a baking sheet. Broil 5½ inches from heat, turning with tongs as peppers blister and turn dark on all sides. Place peppers in a paper bag; seal and let stand 10 minutes to loosen skins. Peel and discard skins; remove and discard seeds from peppers. Set peppers aside.

Coat a small nonstick skillet with cooking spray; place over medium-high heat until hot. Add onion and garlic; sauté until tender.

Position knife blade in food processor bowl; add peppers, sautéed onion and garlic, and basil. Process until smooth. Stir in mayonnaise. Serve with fresh raw vegetables. Yield: 2 cups (10 calories per tablespoon).

PROTEIN 0.2   FAT 0.6   CARBOHYDRATE 1.2   CHOLESTEROL 1
IRON 0.3   SODIUM 14   CALCIUM 11

PEACHES-AND-CREAM SPREAD

1⅓ cups finely chopped peeled peaches,
    divided (about 3 medium)
½ (8-ounce) package Neufchâtel cheese, cubed
½ cup (2 ounces) shredded 40% less-fat
    Cheddar cheese
1 teaspoon Dijon mustard
1 tablespoon minced fresh chives
1 tablespoon finely chopped walnuts
⅛ teaspoon paprika

Position knife blade in food processor bowl; add ½ cup peaches, Neufchâtel, Cheddar cheese, and mustard. Process until smooth. Transfer to a bowl; stir in remaining peaches, chives, walnuts, and paprika. Serve with melba rounds. Yield: 1½ cups (37 calories per tablespoon).

PROTEIN 1.5   FAT 2.7   CARBOHYDRATE 2.1   CHOLESTEROL 8
IRON 0.1   SODIUM 56   CALCIUM 24

HERBED TOMATO SPREAD

1 quart plain nonfat yogurt
2 tablespoons minced fresh chives
2 tablespoons minced fresh dillweed
2 cloves garlic, crushed
⅛ teaspoon salt
2 large ripe tomatoes (about 1 pound), peeled,
    seeded, and diced

Line a colander or sieve with a double layer of cheesecloth that has been rinsed out and squeezed dry; allow cheesecloth to overlap side of colander.

Stir yogurt until smooth; pour into colander. Fold cheesecloth over to cover yogurt. Place colander in a bowl; refrigerate 12 to 24 hours. Remove yogurt from colander; discard liquid.

Combine drained yogurt, chives, dillweed, garlic, and salt; fold in tomato. Serve with melba rounds. Yield: 3 cups (12 calories per tablespoon).

PROTEIN 1.2   FAT 0.0   CARBOHYDRATE 1.8   CHOLESTEROL 0
IRON 0.1   SODIUM 21   CALCIUM 39

SOUTHWESTERN TUNA PÂTÉ

2 (6½-ounce) cans white tuna in
  spring water, drained
3 tablespoons reduced-calorie
  mayonnaise
¼ cup minced fresh chives
¼ cup minced fresh cilantro
2 tablespoons lime juice
2 tablespoons tequila
¼ teaspoon crushed red pepper
Fresh cilantro sprigs (optional)
Jalapeño pepper slices (optional)

Combine tuna and mayonnaise in a small bowl; stir well. Add chives, cilantro, lime juice, tequila, and crushed red pepper. Transfer mixture to a small crock or bowl. Cover and chill at least 1 hour. If desired, garnish with fresh cilantro sprigs and jalapeño pepper slices. Serve pâté with cucumber slices or melba rounds. Yield: 1½ cups (26 calories per tablespoon).

PROTEIN 3.5 FAT 0.8 CARBOHYDRATE 0.3 CHOLESTEROL 6
IRON 0.1 SODIUM 65 CALCIUM 1

WATER-CRISPED TORTILLA CHIPS

12 (6-inch) corn tortillas
¼ teaspoon garlic powder
¼ teaspoon salt

Fill a shallow baking dish with water. Dip tortillas, one at a time, into water for 2 seconds. Drain; cut each tortilla into 6 wedges. Place half of wedges on an ungreased baking sheet.

Combine garlic powder and salt, stirring well. Sprinkle half of garlic powder mixture evenly over tortilla wedges. Bake at 500° for 4 minutes. Turn wedges; bake an additional 3 minutes or until crisp. Repeat procedure with remaining wedges and garlic mixture. Yield: 6 dozen (8 calories each).

PROTEIN 0.3 FAT 0.1 CARBOHYDRATE 1.6 CHOLESTEROL 0
IRON 0.2 SODIUM 15 CALCIUM 5

SESAME CRISPS WITH TOMATO VINAIGRETTE

10 egg roll wrappers
Vegetable cooking spray
2½ teaspoons sesame oil
2 teaspoons low-sodium soy sauce
½ teaspoon water
¼ teaspoon ground cumin
1 tablespoon sesame seeds
Tomato Vinaigrette

Cut each egg roll wrapper lengthwise into 4 strips. Place strips on baking sheets coated with cooking spray.

Combine sesame oil, soy sauce, water, and cumin; brush evenly over strips. Sprinkle evenly with sesame seeds. Bake at 375° for 5 to 7 minutes or until golden. Remove from baking sheets, and let cool on wire racks. Serve with Tomato Vinaigrette. Yield: 40 appetizer servings (18 calories per strip and 2½ teaspoons sauce).

Tomato Vinaigrette

1 pound tomatoes, quartered
1½ cups peeled, seeded, and chopped
  tomato
1 tablespoon white wine vinegar
1 teaspoon sesame oil
1 teaspoon sugar
¼ teaspoon salt
½ teaspoon ground cumin
½ teaspoon hot sauce

Place tomato quarters in a medium saucepan, and cook over medium-low heat 25 to 30 minutes or until thick, stirring frequently. Let cool slightly. Pour into container of an electric blender or food processor; top with cover, and process until smooth. Strain tomato puree; discard skin and seeds.

Combine strained tomato puree, chopped tomato, and remaining ingredients in a small bowl; stir well. Yield: 2 cups.

PROTEIN 0.5 FAT 0.8 CARBOHYDRATE 2.2 CHOLESTEROL 7
IRON 0.2 SODIUM 40 CALCIUM 6

FRUIT AND CHEESE KABOBS

32 fresh pineapple chunks (about 1 pound)
32 small strawberries (about 3 cups)
32 honeydew melon balls (about 3 cups)
¼ cup rum
8 ounces light Havarti cheese, cut into 32 cubes
2 (8-ounce) cartons strawberry low-fat yogurt
½ teaspoon ground cardamom

Combine first 4 ingredients; toss gently to coat. Cover and chill 4 hours, stirring occasionally.

Thread fruit and cheese onto 32 (6-inch) wooden skewers. Combine yogurt and cardamom; stir well. Serve kabobs with yogurt dip. Yield: 32 appetizers (49 calories per kabob and 1 tablespoon yogurt dip).

PROTEIN 2.5 FAT 1.5 CARBOHYDRATE 6.1 CHOLESTEROL 5
IRON 0.1 SODIUM 51 CALCIUM 71

MARINATED ANTIPASTO KABOBS

1 (4-ounce) package lean baked ham slices
1 (20-ounce) can pineapple chunks in juice
18 pimiento-stuffed olives
18 medium-size fresh mushrooms
1 large sweet red or yellow pepper, seeded and
    cut into 18 (1-inch) squares
1 (14-ounce) can artichoke hearts, drained and
    sliced in half
1 (8-ounce) bottle commercial oil-free Italian
    dressing

Cut each ham slice into 4 strips. Combine ham strips and remaining ingredients in a large zip-top heavy-duty plastic bag. Marinate in refrigerator 8 hours. Drain.

Thread ham strips, pineapple, olives, mushrooms, pepper, and artichokes onto 18 (8-inch) wooden skewers. Serve chilled or at room temperature. Yield: 18 appetizers (37 calories each).

PROTEIN 2.0 FAT 0.9 CARBOHYDRATE 6.2 CHOLESTEROL 4
IRON 0.6 SODIUM 402 CALCIUM 10

MARINATED MOZZARELLA APPETIZERS

8 ounces part-skim mozzarella cheese, diced
1 (7-ounce) jar roasted red peppers in water,
    drained and coarsely chopped
2 tablespoons minced fresh oregano
½ teaspoon freshly ground pepper
1½ tablespoons lemon juice
2 teaspoons olive oil
16 endive leaves
16 small radicchio leaves
Fresh oregano leaves (optional)

Combine first 6 ingredients in a medium bowl; stir well. Cover and chill at least 6 hours.

Spoon 1 tablespoon cheese mixture onto each endive and radicchio leaf. Arrange endive and radicchio on a serving platter. Cover and refrigerate up to 2 hours, if desired. Garnish with fresh oregano leaves, if desired. Yield: 32 appetizers (23 calories each).

PROTEIN 1.9 FAT 1.4 CARBOHYDRATE 0.8 CHOLESTEROL 4
IRON 0.1 SODIUM 108 CALCIUM 51

ROASTED SWEET PEPPER AND EGGPLANT TERRINE

4 large sweet red peppers
Vegetable cooking spray
2 (1-pound) eggplants, peeled and cut into
    ½-inch slices
½ teaspoon freshly ground pepper
¼ teaspoon salt
¾ cup packed basil leaves, divided
1 tablespoon olive oil, divided
Fresh basil leaves (optional)

Cut peppers in half lengthwise; remove and discard seeds and membrane. Place peppers, skin side up, on a baking sheet; flatten with palm of hand. Broil 5½ inches from heat 15 to 20 minutes or until charred. Remove peppers from baking sheet, reserving liquid; place peppers in a large

Garnish individual slices of Roasted Sweet Pepper and Eggplant Terrine with fresh basil leaves for a spectacular start to your meal.

bowl, and cover with plastic wrap. Let peppers cool completely. Remove peppers, reserving liquid; peel and discard skins. Set peppers aside.

Coat a large nonstick skillet with cooking spray; place over medium-high heat until hot. Add eggplant, in batches, and sauté 2 to 3 minutes on each side or until tender.

Line an 8½- x 4½- x 3-inch loafpan with heavy-duty plastic wrap. Arrange one-third of eggplant slices in bottom of pan. Combine reserved liquid from red peppers, ground popper, and salt. Drizzle 2 teaspoons liquid mixture over eggplant slices. Arrange one-third of basil over eggplant, and top

with one-third of peppers. Drizzle 1 teaspoon olive oil over peppers. Repeat layers twice using remaining ingredients. Cover loafpan with heavy-duty plastic wrap. Place a heavy object (2 to 3 pounds) on top layer of loafpan. Refrigerate terrine 24 hours.

Invert terrine onto a serving platter; remove plastic wrap. Slice terrine with an electric knife. Garnish with fresh basil leaves, if desired. Yield: 8 appetizer servings (78 calories per serving).

PROTEIN 2.6   FAT 2.6   CARBOHYDRATE 14.1   CHOLESTEROL 0
IRON 4.3   SODIUM 82   CALCIUM 173

PEPPER TRIANGLES WITH TOMATO-OLIVE SALAD

3 large sweet red peppers
2 large green peppers
1½ cups seeded, chopped tomato
1 (4¼-ounce) can chopped ripe olives, drained
3 tablespoons minced celery
3 tablespoons minced fresh parsley
1 tablespoon minced fresh basil
2 teaspoons olive oil
½ teaspoon freshly ground pepper

Cut red peppers and green peppers in half lengthwise; remove and discard seeds and stems. Cut each pepper half into 4 triangular wedges, and set wedges aside.

Combine tomato and remaining ingredients in a small bowl; mix well. Spoon tomato mixture evenly into pepper wedges, and arrange on a serving platter. Cover and chill. Yield: 40 appetizers (12 calories each).

PROTEIN 0.3 FAT 0.6 CARBOHYDRATE 1.5 CHOLESTEROL 0
IRON 0.4 SODIUM 28 CALCIUM 5

HERBED EGGPLANT AND GOAT CHEESE ROLLS

1 (1-pound) eggplant
Olive oil-flavored vegetable cooking spray
½ cup minced fresh thyme or basil
3 ounces goat cheese, softened
40 sprigs fresh watercress

Cut eggplant lengthwise into ¼-inch-thick slices; cut each slice in half lengthwise. Arrange slices in a single layer in two 15- x 10- x 1-inch jellyroll pans coated with cooking spray. Lightly spray eggplant with cooking spray. Bake, uncovered, at 450° for 8 minutes. Carefully turn eggplant slices, and lightly spray slices with cooking spray; sprinkle evenly with thyme. Bake an additional 5 minutes or until eggplant is tender. Remove from oven, and cool in pans.

Place ½ teaspoon cheese at one end of each eggplant slice. Top each with 2 sprigs watercress, allowing some leaves to hang over edges. Roll up, and secure with wooden picks. Serve immediately, or refrigerate and serve chilled. Yield: 20 appetizers (20 calories each).

PROTEIN 0.9 FAT 1.1 CARBOHYDRATE 1.7 CHOLESTEROL 4
IRON 0.2 SODIUM 50 CALCIUM 33

VEGETABLE SALSA ON POTATO ROUNDS

2 medium baking potatoes (about 18 ounces),
  cut into ¼-inch slices
Vegetable cooking spray
¼ teaspoon garlic powder
10 red or yellow cherry tomatoes
⅓ cup minced sweet red pepper
⅓ cup minced sweet yellow pepper
¼ cup grated carrot
1 serrano chile, seeded and minced
2 tablespoons minced fresh cilantro
1½ tablespoons fresh lime juice
1 clove garlic, minced
¼ teaspoon salt
Fresh cilantro sprigs (optional)

Arrange potato slices in a single layer on a baking sheet coated with cooking spray. Spray potatoes with cooking spray. Turn potatoes, and spray again; sprinkle evenly with garlic powder. Bake at 400° for 10 minutes or until potato slices are tender; let cool completely.

Position knife blade in food processor bowl; add tomatoes. Pulse 7 times or until tomatoes are minced. Add red pepper and next 7 ingredients; pulse 5 times or just until mixture is combined.

Arrange potato slices on a serving platter. Spoon 2 teaspoons tomato mixture on each slice, using a slotted spoon. Garnish each with a cilantro sprig, if desired. Yield: 30 appetizers (17 calories each).

PROTEIN 0.5 FAT 0.1 CARBOHYDRATE 3.6 CHOLESTEROL 0
IRON 0.3 SODIUM 22 CALCIUM 4

SQUASH WITH HERBED EGG SALAD

12 small yellow squash (about 3½ inches long),
  untrimmed
4 hard-cooked eggs
½ cup minced celery
2 tablespoons minced fresh basil
1 tablespoon minced fresh dillweed
3 tablespoons diced pimiento
2 tablespoons reduced-calorie mayonnaise
¼ teaspoon salt
¼ teaspoon ground red pepper

Cut squash in half lengthwise; remove and discard pulp. Blanch squash halves by submerging in boiling water for 12 seconds. Plunge squash halves in ice water to stop the cooking process. Drain well; pat dry with paper towels.

Slice eggs in half lengthwise, and carefully remove yolks. Reserve 2 yolks for other uses. Finely chop egg whites and remaining 2 yolks.

Combine celery, basil, dillweed, pimiento, mayonnaise, salt, and red pepper in a small bowl; stir well. Add chopped egg whites and yolks; stir gently. Spoon egg mixture evenly into squash halves. Cover and chill thoroughly. Yield: 24 appetizers (20 calories each).

PROTEIN 1.3 FAT 0.8 CARBOHYDRATE 2.2 CHOLESTEROL 17
IRON 0.3 SODIUM 47 CALCIUM 14

BLUE CHEESE-STUFFED CHERRY TOMATOES

20 cherry tomatoes (about 1 pint)
4 ounces blue cheese, crumbled
¼ cup plain nonfat yogurt
2 tablespoons minced fresh dillweed
½ teaspoon freshly ground pepper
Fresh dillweed sprigs (optional)

Cut top off each tomato; scoop out pulp, reserving for other uses. Invert tomatoes on paper towels, and let stand 30 minutes. Combine blue cheese, nonfat yogurt, minced dillweed, and pepper in a small bowl; stir well. Spoon blue cheese mixture evenly into tomato shells. Garnish with fresh dillweed sprigs, if desired. Yield: 20 appetizers (25 calories each).

PROTEIN 1.6 FAT 1.7 CARBOHYDRATE 1.0 CHOLESTEROL 4
IRON 0.1 SODIUM 83 CALCIUM 41

HORSERADISH BEEF ROLL-UPS

¾ cup 1% low-fat cottage cheese
¼ cup prepared horseradish, drained
1 tablespoon Dijon mustard
¼ cup reduced-calorie mayonnaise
18 thin slices lean roast beef (1 pound)
2⅓ cups alfalfa sprouts

Combine first 3 ingredients in container of an electric blender or food processor; top with cover, and process until smooth. Stir in mayonnaise.

Spread about 1 tablespoon cottage cheese mixture on each roast beef slice. Divide sprouts evenly on each slice. Roll up each slice, jellyroll fashion, starting with short side.

Arrange roll-ups on a large serving platter. Cover and chill thoroughly. Yield: 18 appetizers (68 calories each).

PROTEIN 9.5 FAT 2.7 CARBOHYDRATE 1.1 CHOLESTEROL 23
IRON 0.8 SODIUM 107 CALCIUM 12

BAKED CHICKEN AND VEGETABLE EGG ROLLS

2 (4-ounce) skinned, boned chicken breast
　halves, cut into small pieces
1 (10-ounce) package frozen chopped broccoli,
　thawed and well drained
½ cup chopped water chestnuts
¼ cup sliced green onions
2 cloves garlic, minced
¼ cup low-sodium soy sauce, divided
Vegetable cooking spray
1 egg white
12 egg roll wrappers
¼ cup canned low-sodium chicken broth,
　undiluted
2 tablespoons minced green onions
1 teaspoon sesame oil

Position knife blade in food processor bowl; add chicken, broccoli, water chestnuts, ¼ cup green onions, garlic, and 1 tablespoon soy sauce. Process 5 seconds.

Coat a large nonstick skillet with cooking spray, and place over medium-high heat until hot. Add chicken mixture, and cook 5 to 6 minutes or until chicken is done. Remove from heat, and let cool. Stir in egg white.

Mound 2 heaping tablespoons of chicken mixture in center of each egg roll wrapper. Fold top corner of each wrapper over filling; then fold left and right corners over filling. Lightly brush exposed corner of wrappers with water. Tightly roll filled end of wrapper toward exposed corner; gently press the corner to seal securely. Coat both sides of egg roll with cooking spray.

Place egg rolls on a baking sheet coated with cooking spray. Bake at 450° for 6 to 7 minutes on each side or until golden brown.

Combine remaining 3 tablespoons soy sauce, chicken broth, 2 tablespoons green onions, and oil in a small bowl; stir well. Serve with egg rolls. Yield: 12 appetizers (76 calories per egg roll and 1½ teaspoons sauce).

PROTEIN 6.7　FAT 1.8　CARBOHYDRATE 7.7　CHOLESTEROL 36
IRON 0.7　SODIUM 215　CALCIUM 24

STEAMED CHICKEN MEDAILLONS IN RASPBERRY SAUCE

4 (4-ounce) skinned, boned chicken breast
　halves
12 large fresh spinach leaves
¼ cup (1 ounce) shredded part-skim farmer
　cheese
¼ cup minced green onions
3 cups fresh raspberries
1 teaspoon Dijon mustard

Place chicken between 2 sheets of heavy-duty plastic wrap, and flatten to ¼-inch thickness, using a meat mallet or rolling pin. Arrange 3 spinach leaves on each chicken breast.

Combine farmer cheese and minced green onions, stirring well. Sprinkle cheese mixture evenly over chicken breasts. Roll up chicken lengthwise, tucking ends under. Secure chicken breast rolls with wooden picks.

Arrange rolls in a vegetable steamer over boiling water. Cover and steam 15 minutes or until chicken is done. Let cool slightly.

Position knife blade in food processor bowl; add raspberries, and process until smooth. Strain raspberry puree, and discard seeds. Combine puree and mustard, stirring well.

To serve, spoon raspberry mixture onto a large serving platter. Cut chicken into ½-inch slices, and arrange over raspberry mixture. Yield: 24 appetizer servings (34 calories per serving).

PROTEIN 4.8　FAT 0.9　CARBOHYDRATE 1.7　CHOLESTEROL 13
IRON 0.3　SODIUM 28　CALCIUM 16

MINIATURE CRAB CAKES

3 egg whites
2 tablespoons reduced-calorie mayonnaise
1½ teaspoons dry mustard
½ teaspoon freshly ground pepper
1 pound fresh lump crabmeat, drained
¾ cup soft whole wheat breadcrumbs
3 tablespoons minced fresh cilantro
3 tablespoons diced pimiento
Vegetable cooking spray
Creole Mustard Sauce

Combine first 4 ingredients in a medium bowl; stir well. Add crabmeat, breadcrumbs, cilantro, and pimiento, stirring well. Shape mixture into 24 (2-inch-round) patties. Cover and chill at least 30 minutes.

Coat a large nonstick skillet with cooking spray; place over medium-high heat until hot. Add crab cakes, in batches, and cook 3 to 4 minutes on each side or until golden. Serve with Creole Mustard Sauce. Yield: 24 appetizer servings (47 calories per crab cake and 2¾ teaspoons sauce).

Creole Mustard Sauce

½ cup creole mustard
½ cup reduced-calorie mayonnaise
3 tablespoons minced fresh cilantro
2 tablespoons minced green onion
2 tablespoons minced celery
2 tablespoons minced sweet red pepper

Combine all ingredients in a small bowl, stirring well. Cover and chill at least 2 hours. Yield: 1⅓ cups.

PROTEIN 4.5   FAT 2.4   CARBOHYDRATE 1.8   CHOLESTEROL 19
IRON 0.3   SODIUM 158   CALCIUM 22

SHRIMP WITH TART DIPPING SAUCE

32 medium-size fresh shrimp (about 1½ pounds)
4½ cups water
32 (4½-inch) fresh chives
¼ cup Chablis or other dry white wine
¼ cup raspberry wine vinegar
1 tablespoon minced shallots
1 tablespoon minced chives
½ teaspoon freshly ground pepper

Peel and devein shrimp, leaving tails intact. Bring water to a boil; add shrimp, and cook 3 to 5 minutes. Drain well; rinse with cold water. Tie a chive around each shrimp. Chill.

Combine wine, vinegar, and shallots in a small saucepan. Bring to a boil, and cook 1 minute. Remove from heat, and stir in minced chives and pepper. Let cool to room temperature.

Arrange shrimp on a serving platter. Serve with sauce. Yield: 32 appetizers (19 calories each).

PROTEIN 3.3   FAT 0.3   CARBOHYDRATE 0.4   CHOLESTEROL 24
IRON 0.4   SODIUM 24   CALCIUM 9

CANTALOUPE COOLER

2 cups chopped ripe cantaloupe
2 cups skim milk
1 (8-ounce) carton vanilla low-fat yogurt
2 teaspoons lime juice

Place cantaloupe in a single layer on a baking sheet; cover and freeze until firm. Combine frozen cantaloupe and milk in container of an electric blender; top with cover, and blend until smooth. Add yogurt and lime juice; blend just until mixed. Serve immediately. Yield: 5½ cups (43 calories per ½-cup serving).

PROTEIN 2.8   FAT 0.4   CARBOHYDRATE 7.5   CHOLESTEROL 2
IRON 0.1   SODIUM 39   CALCIUM 93

Greet your guests with sparkling Midori Spritzer served from a decorated sideboard.

BANANA-BERRY SLUSH

4 cups unsweetened frozen strawberries
2 cups peeled, sliced banana (about 2 large
  bananas)
¼ cup plus 1 tablespoon crème de bananes
3 cups ice cubes
5 fresh strawberries
Lime curls (optional)

Combine frozen strawberries, sliced banana, and liqueur in container of an electric blender; top with cover, and process until smooth. Add ice cubes; process until slushy.

Place a strawberry on each of 5 (6-inch) wooden skewers. Garnish skewers with lime curls, if desired. Pour beverage into glasses, and add strawberry skewers. Serve immediately. Yield: 5 cups (126 calories per 1-cup serving).

PROTEIN 1.5   FAT 2.6   CARBOHYDRATE 26.9   CHOLESTEROL 0
IRON 1.1   SODIUM 16   CALCIUM 25

STRAWBERRY LEMONADE

1 quart fresh strawberries, washed
  and hulled
¾ cup fresh lemon juice
⅓ cup superfine sugar
3¼ cups club soda, chilled
Fresh strawberries (optional)

Place 1 quart strawberries in container of an electric blender or food processor; top with cover, and process until smooth.

Combine lemon juice and sugar in a pitcher; stir until sugar dissolves. Add strawberry puree, stirring well. Stir in club soda just before serving. Serve over ice. Garnish each glass with a fresh strawberry, if desired. Yield: 7 cups (70 calories per 1-cup serving).

PROTEIN 0.6   FAT 0.3   CARBOHYDRATE 18.0   CHOLESTEROL 0
IRON 0.4   SODIUM 23   CALCIUM 20

PEACH MELBA SMOOTHIE

1 (16-ounce) package frozen unsweetened
  sliced peaches
2 cups cranberry-raspberry juice cocktail,
  chilled
1 (8-ounce) carton raspberry low-fat yogurt

Position knife blade in food processor bowl; add half of all ingredients. Process until smooth. Repeat with remaining ingredients. Yield: 5 cups (144 calories per 1-cup serving).

PROTEIN 2.5   FAT 0.6   CARBOHYDRATE 33.9   CHOLESTEROL 2
IRON 0.3   SODIUM 28   CALCIUM 70

CITRUS SQUIRT

2 cups fresh orange juice (about 4 oranges)
1 cup fresh grapefruit juice (about 1 grapefruit)
½ cup fresh lemon juice (about 2 lemons)
2 tablespoons light corn syrup
2½ cups seltzer water, chilled

Combine juices and corn syrup in a large pitcher; stir well. Chill thoroughly. Just before serving, stir in seltzer water. Serve over ice. Yield: 6 cups (78 calories per 1-cup serving).

PROTEIN 0.8   FAT 0.1   CARBOHYDRATE 19.5   CHOLESTEROL 0
IRON 1.2   SODIUM 26   CALCIUM 20

MIDORI SPRITZER

1¾ cups Chablis or other dry white wine,
  chilled
1 cup plus 3 tablespoons club soda, chilled
1 tablespoon Midori

Combine all ingredients in a small pitcher; stir well. Yield: 3 cups (72 calories per ¾-cup serving).

PROTEIN 0.1   FAT 0.0   CARBOHYDRATE 0.8   CHOLESTEROL 0
IRON 0.5   SODIUM 19   CALCIUM 13

LEMON CHABLIS COOLER

1 cup water
⅓ cup sugar
1 tablespoon grated lemon rind
4 cups Chablis or other dry white wine
⅓ cup fresh lemon juice
1 sprig fresh lemon verbena
3 cups sparkling mineral water
1 small lemon, thinly sliced

Combine first 3 ingredients in a small saucepan; cook over medium heat until water comes to a boil. Remove from heat, and let stand 15 minutes. Strain mixture, discarding lemon rind.

Combine sugar mixture, wine, lemon juice, and lemon verbena, stirring well. Cover and chill 1 hour. Remove and discard lemon verbena. Pour mixture into a pitcher; add mineral water and lemon slices, stirring well. Serve over crushed ice. Yield: 8 cups (109 calories per 1-cup serving).

PROTEIN 0.2   FAT 0.0   CARBOHYDRATE 9.9   CHOLESTEROL 0
IRON 0.6   SODIUM 23   CALCIUM 12

HOT SPICED CHOCOLATE

3 cups 2% low-fat chocolate milk
1½ cups skim milk
4 (3-inch) sticks cinnamon
Dash of ground nutmeg
Dash of ground cloves
1½ teaspoons vanilla extract
36 miniature marshmallows
Ground cinnamon (optional)
6 (3-inch) sticks cinnamon (optional)

Combine first 5 ingredients in a large saucepan; stir with a wire whisk. Cook over low heat until thoroughly heated (do not boil). Remove and discard cinnamon sticks; stir in vanilla. Pour into individual mugs, and top each with 6 marshmallows. If desired, sprinkle with ground cinnamon, and garnish with cinnamon sticks. Yield: 4½ cups (125 calories per ¾-cup serving).

PROTEIN 6.1   FAT 2.6   CARBOHYDRATE 18.5   CHOLESTEROL 10
IRON 0.3   SODIUM 108   CALCIUM 219

COFFEE PRALINE PUNCH

2 quarts strong brewed coffee
⅓ cup firmly packed brown sugar
3½ cups skim milk
2 cups vanilla ice milk, softened
½ cup praline liqueur
2 teaspoons vanilla extract
⅛ teaspoon ground cinnamon

Combine coffee and sugar in a large pitcher, stirring well. Chill thoroughly.

To serve, transfer chilled coffee mixture to a large punch bowl. Stir in milk, ice milk, praline liqueur, and vanilla. Sprinkle punch with cinnamon, and serve immediately. Yield: 14½ cups (49 calories per ½-cup serving).

PROTEIN 1.4   FAT 0.5   CARBOHYDRATE 7.9   CHOLESTEROL 2
IRON 0.4   SODIUM 25   CALCIUM 52

BLACKBERRY CIDER

3 cups boiling water
6 decaffeinated blackberry tea bags
3 cups unsweetened apple cider
1 tablespoon brown sugar

Pour boiling water over tea bags; cover and steep 5 minutes. Remove and discard tea bags. Combine tea, cider, and brown sugar in a medium saucepan; stir well. Cook over medium heat until thoroughly heated (do not boil). Serve immediately. Yield: 6 cups (64 calories per 1-cup serving).

PROTEIN 0.1   FAT 0.1   CARBOHYDRATE 15.9   CHOLESTEROL 0
IRON 0.5   SODIUM 4   CALCIUM 10

Wake your family with the aroma of (from top) warm Overnight Sour Cream-Cinnamon Rolls (page 112) and Raspberry Pinwheels (page 106).

PEANUT BUTTER GRAHAM CRACKERS

1½ cups whole wheat flour
¾ cup all-purpose flour
½ teaspoon baking powder
½ teaspoon baking soda
¼ cup unsalted margarine, softened
¼ cup creamy peanut butter
¼ cup mashed, ripe banana
¼ cup honey, divided
2 tablespoons molasses
⅓ cup nonfat buttermilk
1 teaspoon vanilla extract
¾ teaspoon ground cinnamon

Combine first 4 ingredients in a small bowl, stirring well; set aside.

Combine margarine and peanut butter in a large bowl; beat at medium speed of an electric mixer until smooth. Add banana, 2 tablespoons honey, and molasses; beat well. Combine buttermilk and vanilla; add to creamed mixture alternately with flour mixture, beginning and ending with flour mixture. Mix well after each addition. Cover and let dough rest 10 minutes.

Divide dough into 4 equal portions. Roll each portion to 15- x 5-inch rectangle between 2 sheets of heavy-duty plastic wrap. Remove plastic wrap, and cut each portion into six 5- x 2½-inch rectangles. Lightly score each rectangle in half forming 2 squares, using the dull side of a knife. Prick surface of each square in 3 parallel rows, using a fork. Place rectangles 1 inch apart on ungreased baking sheets.

Combine remaining 2 tablespoons honey and cinnamon; brush lightly over rectangles. Bake at 350° for 12 minutes or until browned. Remove from baking sheets; cool completely on wire racks. Yield: 4 dozen crackers (47 calories each).

PROTEIN 1.2   FAT 1.7   CARBOHYDRATE 7.1   CHOLESTEROL 0
IRON 0.3   SODIUM 21   CALCIUM 9

ONION CRACKERS

1 cup all-purpose flour
¾ cup whole wheat flour
¼ teaspoon baking soda
⅛ teaspoon salt
2 tablespoons minced onion
½ cup plain nonfat yogurt
2 tablespoons vegetable oil
1 tablespoon honey
Vegetable cooking spray

Combine first 4 ingredients in a medium bowl; stir well. Stir in onion. Combine yogurt, oil, and honey; add to dry ingredients, stirring until mixture resembles coarse crumbs. Knead until dough is smooth.

Divide dough into 32 equal portions. Shape each portion into a ball, and place 3 inches apart on baking sheets coated with cooking spray. Flatten each to a 2-inch circle, and pierce circles with a fork. Bake at 350° for 10 to 12 minutes or until crisp and lightly browned. Yield: 32 crackers (35 calories each).

PROTEIN 1.0   FAT 1.0   CARBOHYDRATE 5.7   CHOLESTEROL 0
IRON 0.3   SODIUM 19   CALCIUM 10

WALKING STRATEGIES

To get the most from your walking expedition, the President's Council on Physical Fitness and Sports encourages you to follow these basic strategies:

• Hold head erect and back straight. Keep toes pointed straight ahead and let arms swing loosely at your side.
• Land on the heel of the foot and then roll forward; push off from the ball of the foot for the next step.
• Take long, easy strides but don't strain for distance. When walking up or down hills, lean forward slightly.
• Breathe deeply to get the most efficient workout for all the muscles.

COCKTAIL THINS

2 cups all-purpose flour
¼ cup cracked wheat
1½ teaspoons celery seeds
1 teaspoon baking powder
¼ teaspoon cracked pepper
2 tablespoons unsalted margarine, softened
⅔ cup plus 1 tablespoon spicy vegetable juice
    cocktail

Combine first 5 ingredients in a large bowl; cut in margarine with a pastry blender until mixture resembles coarse meal. Add vegetable juice cocktail, stirring just until dry ingredients are moistened. Shape into a ball.

Roll dough to ¹⁄₁₆-inch thickness between 2 sheets of heavy-duty plastic wrap. Remove top sheet of plastic wrap, and cut dough into 2-inch squares. Remove squares from bottom sheet of plastic wrap, and place on ungreased baking sheets. Bake at 325° for 15 to 18 minutes or until crisp and lightly browned. Remove from baking sheets, and let cool on wire racks. Yield: 6 dozen (17 calories each).

PROTEIN 0.4 FAT 0.4 CARBOHYDRATE 2.9 CHOLESTEROL 0
IRON 0.2 SODIUM 4 CALCIUM 4

CINNAMON-RAISIN BISCUITS

1¾ cups all-purpose flour
2 teaspoons baking powder
⅓ cup raisins
2 tablespoons sugar
1¼ teaspoons ground cinnamon
⅔ cup nonfat buttermilk
2 tablespoons vegetable oil
Vegetable cooking spray
½ cup sifted powdered sugar
2 tablespoons unsweetened apple juice

Combine first 5 ingredients in a large bowl; make a well in center of mixture. Combine buttermilk and oil; add to dry ingredients, stirring just until dry ingredients are moistened.

Turn dough out onto work surface, and knead lightly 3 to 5 times. Roll dough to ½-inch thickness; cut into rounds with a 1½-inch biscuit cutter. Place on a baking sheet coated with cooking spray. Bake at 400° for 8 to 10 minutes or until golden.

Combine powdered sugar and apple juice; stir well. Drizzle over warm biscuits. Yield: 2½ dozen (108 calories each).

PROTEIN 6.7 FAT 1.7 CARBOHYDRATE 17.1 CHOLESTEROL 0
IRON 0.4 SODIUM 190 CALCIUM 22

EAST INDIAN SPICE BISCUITS

2 cups all-purpose flour
2 teaspoons baking powder
½ teaspoon baking soda
¼ teaspoon salt
1 teaspoon ground cumin
1 teaspoon coriander seed
1 teaspoon ground turmeric
¼ to ½ teaspoon ground red pepper
Vegetable cooking spray
2 tablespoons minced onion
¾ teaspoon minced fresh ginger
2 cloves garlic, minced
1 (8-ounce) carton lemon low-fat yogurt
3 tablespoons skim milk

Combine first 8 ingredients in a medium bowl; stir well, and set aside.

Coat a small nonstick skillet with cooking spray; place over medium-high heat until hot. Add onion, ginger, and garlic; sauté until tender. Add to flour mixture, stirring well; make a well in center of mixture. Combine yogurt and milk; add to dry ingredients, stirring just until dry ingredients are moistened.

Drop dough by rounded tablespoonfuls, 2 inches apart, onto baking sheets coated with cooking spray. Bake at 450° for 10 minutes or until lightly browned. Yield: 2 dozen (47 calories each).

PROTEIN 1.6 FAT 0.3 CARBOHYDRATE 9.2 CHOLESTEROL 1
IRON 0.6 SODIUM 78 CALCIUM 40

A medley of flavor and color, Harvest Corn Muffins are tasty additions to any meal.

HARVEST CORN MUFFINS

1 cup all-purpose flour
1 cup cornmeal
1 tablespoon plus 1 teaspoon baking powder
¼ teaspoon salt
2 tablespoons brown sugar
½ teaspoon dried whole oregano
¼ teaspoon ground white pepper
1 cup skim milk
1 cup cooked mashed pumpkin
3 tablespoons diced pimiento
2 tablespoons vegetable oil
1 egg, lightly beaten
2 egg whites, lightly beaten
1 jalapeño pepper, seeded and minced
Vegetable cooking spray
½ cup (2 ounces) finely shredded reduced-fat
  Cheddar cheese

Combine first 4 ingredients in a large bowl; add brown sugar, oregano, and white pepper. Make a well in center of mixture.

Combine milk, mashed pumpkin, diced pimiento, vegetable oil, egg, egg whites, and jalapeño pepper; add to dry ingredients, stirring just until dry ingredients are moistened.

Spoon batter into muffin pans coated with vegetable cooking spray, filling two-thirds full. Sprinkle finely shredded Cheddar cheese evenly over corn muffins. Bake at 400° for 20 minutes or until muffins are lightly browned. Remove muffins from pans immediately. Yield: 1½ dozen (98 calories each).

PROTEIN 3.6 FAT 2.9 CARBOHYDRATE 14.3 CHOLESTEROL 13
IRON 1.0 SODIUM 141 CALCIUM 93

FRUITED YOGURT PANCAKES

1 cup all-purpose flour
1 teaspoon baking powder
½ teaspoon baking soda
¼ cup toasted wheat germ
1 tablespoon brown sugar
¼ teaspoon salt
1 (8-ounce) carton strawberry-banana
  low-fat yogurt
½ cup skim milk
2 tablespoons margarine, melted
1 egg, lightly beaten
1 cup cooked brown rice (cooked without
  salt or fat)
1 cup fresh blueberries
Vegetable cooking spray

Combine first 6 ingredients in a large bowl; make a well in center of mixture.

Combine yogurt, milk, margarine, and egg; add to dry ingredients, stirring just until dry ingredients are moistened. Fold in cooked rice and fresh blueberries.

For each pancake, spread ¼ cup batter onto a hot griddle or skillet coated with cooking spray. Turn pancakes when tops are covered with bubbles and edges look cooked. Yield: 14 (4-inch) pancakes (100 calories each).

PROTEIN 3.1 FAT 2.6 CARBOHYDRATE 16.1 CHOLESTEROL 15
IRON 0.7 SODIUM 131 CALCIUM 60

PUMPERNICKEL QUICK BREAD

1 cup rye flour
½ cup all-purpose flour
½ cup whole wheat flour
2 teaspoons baking powder
¼ teaspoon baking soda
1½ teaspoons caraway seeds
¾ cup skim milk
¼ cup vegetable oil
¼ cup molasses
2 eggs, lightly beaten
1 teaspoon cider vinegar
½ cup finely chopped onion
½ cup (2 ounces) finely shredded reduced-fat
  Cheddar cheese
Vegetable cooking spray

Combine first 6 ingredients in a large bowl; make a well in center of mixture. Combine milk, oil, molasses, eggs, and vinegar; add to dry ingredients, stirring just until dry ingredients are moistened. Stir in onion and cheese.

Spoon batter into an 8½- x 4½- x 3-inch loafpan coated with cooking spray. Bake at 350° for 50 to 60 minutes or until a wooden pick inserted in center comes out clean. Let cool in pan 10 minutes; remove from pan, and let cool on a wire rack. Yield: 16 servings (116 calories per ½-inch slice).

PROTEIN 3.7 FAT 5.0 CARBOHYDRATE 14.4 CHOLESTEROL 27
IRON 1.0 SODIUM 93 CALCIUM 95

USE IT OR LOSE IT

Stop exercising and your fitness level immediately begins to decline. This is sad but true, say fitness experts. One study at Washington University School of Medicine in St. Louis documented the effect. Researchers took a group of regular exercisers—runners, cyclists, and swimmers—all of whom had been working out consistently and vigorously for several years, and asked them to quit exercising cold-turkey. In just 12 weeks, the exercisers had lost more than half of their aerobic conditioning.

In another study, researchers coaxed a group of inactive people to bicycle regularly for eight weeks. The participants then quit the cycling routine, going back to old habits. In just eight weeks, it was as if these people had never cycled. All of the participants lost 100 percent of their aerobic gains. The fitness message to be gleaned is this: Never stop exercising completely. It's much easier to maintain fitness than to get into shape again after taking a long hiatus from exercising.

SWISS HERB LOAF

1¾ cups whole wheat flour
¾ cup all-purpose flour
1 tablespoon baking powder
1 teaspoon baking soda
¼ cup firmly packed brown sugar
½ teaspoon salt
1 tablespoon instant minced onion
¼ teaspoon dry mustard
1½ cups skim milk
¼ cup vegetable oil
1 egg, lightly beaten
2 egg whites, lightly beaten
1 teaspoon hot sauce
¾ cup (3 ounces) shredded reduced-fat
  Swiss cheese
1 tablespoon minced fresh parsley
1 tablespoon minced fresh chives
1½ teaspoons minced fresh thyme
Vegetable cooking spray

Combine whole wheat flour, all-purpose flour, baking powder, and baking soda in a large bowl; add brown sugar, salt, onion, and dry mustard. Make a well in center of mixture.

Combine milk, oil, egg, egg whites, and hot sauce; add mixture to dry ingredients, stirring just until dry ingredients are moistened. Stir in shredded Swiss cheese, minced parsley, minced chives, and minced thyme.

Spoon batter into an 8½- x 4½- x 3-inch loaf-pan coated with cooking spray. Bake at 375° for 50 to 55 minutes or until a wooden pick inserted in center comes out clean. Let cool in pan 10 minutes; remove loaf from pan, and let cool on a wire rack. Yield: 16 servings (140 calories per ½-inch slice).

PROTEIN 5.8 FAT 5.0 CARBOHYDRATE 18.7 CHOLESTEROL 16
IRON 1.0 SODIUM 216 CALCIUM 149

RASPBERRY PINWHEELS

2 cups all-purpose flour
1 tablespoon baking powder
¼ teaspoon salt
¼ cup plus 1 tablespoon margarine
½ cup skim milk
1 egg, lightly beaten
2 tablespoons all-purpose flour
⅓ cup no-sugar-added raspberry
  spread
Vegetable cooking spray
½ cup sifted powdered sugar
2 teaspoons water
½ teaspoon almond extract

Combine first 3 ingredients in a large bowl; stir well. Cut in margarine with a pastry blender until mixture resembles coarse meal; make a well in center of mixture. Combine milk and egg; add to dry ingredients, stirring just until dry ingredients are moistened.

Sprinkle 2 tablespoons flour evenly over work surface. Turn dough out onto floured surface, and knead 10 to 12 times. Cover and chill dough 15 minutes.

Place dough between 2 sheets of heavy-duty plastic wrap, and roll to 12- x 8-inch rectangle; remove top sheet of plastic wrap. Stir raspberry spread with a whisk until smooth; spread evenly over dough. Roll up dough, jellyroll fashion, starting with long side; pinch seam to seal (do not seal ends). Cut roll into ¾-inch slices. Place slices, cut side down, 2 inches apart on baking sheets coated with cooking spray. Bake at 375° for 12 to 15 minutes or until lightly browned.

Combine powdered sugar, water, and extract in a small bowl, stirring well. Drizzle over warm rolls. Yield: 16 rolls (116 calories each).

PROTEIN 2.3 FAT 4.1 CARBOHYDRATE 17.2 CHOLESTEROL 13
IRON 0.8 SODIUM 143 CALCIUM 50

COUNTRY WHITE BREAD

2⅔ cups plus 1 tablespoon all-purpose flour,
   divided
¼ teaspoon baking soda
½ teaspoon salt
1 package yeast
1 cup nonfat buttermilk
2 tablespoons honey
1 tablespoon unsalted margarine
2 tablespoons all-purpose flour, divided
Vegetable cooking spray

Combine 1⅓ cups flour, soda, salt, and yeast.

Combine buttermilk, honey, and margarine in a saucepan; cook over medium heat until margarine melts; stir occasionally. Cool to 120° to 130°.

Gradually add liquid mixture to flour mixture; beat at low speed of an electric mixer until well blended. Beat an additional 3 minutes at high speed. Stir in enough of the remaining 1⅓ cups plus 1 tablespoon flour to make a soft dough.

Sprinkle 1 tablespoon flour evenly over work surface. Turn dough out onto floured surface, and knead until smooth and elastic (about 8 to 10 minutes). Place dough in a large bowl coated with cooking spray, turning to coat top. Cover and let rise in a warm place (85°), free from drafts, 1 hour or until doubled in bulk.

Punch dough down. Sprinkle remaining 1 tablespoon flour over work surface. Roll dough to 10- x 6-inch rectangle. Roll up dough, jellyroll fashion, starting at short side, pressing firmly to eliminate air pockets. Pinch ends to seal. Place dough, seam side down, in an 8½- x 4½- x 3-inch loafpan coated with cooking spray.

Cover and let rise in a warm place, free from drafts, 35 minutes or until doubled in bulk. Bake at 375° for 25 minutes or until loaf sounds hollow when tapped. (Cover with aluminum foil the last 10 minutes of baking to prevent over-browning, if necessary.) Remove from pan; cool on a wire rack. Yield: 17 servings (91 calories per ½-inch slice).

PROTEIN 2.8 FAT 1.1 CARBOHYDRATE 18.6 CHOLESTEROL 0
IRON 1.0 SODIUM 113 CALCIUM 6

WHOLE WHEAT FRENCH BREAD

1 package dry yeast
1 tablespoon sugar, divided
1⅔ cups warm water (105° to 115°)
½ teaspoon salt
1½ cups whole wheat flour
2½ cups all-purpose flour
2 tablespoons all-purpose flour, divided
Vegetable cooking spray
1 tablespoon cornmeal
1 egg white, lightly beaten
1 tablespoon skim milk

Dissolve yeast and 1 teaspoon sugar in water in a large bowl; let stand 5 minutes. Add remaining 2 teaspoons sugar, salt, and whole wheat flour; beat at medium speed of an electric mixer until blended. Gradually stir in enough of the 2½ cups all-purpose flour to make a soft dough.

Sprinkle 1 tablespoon all-purpose flour evenly over work surface. Turn dough out onto floured surface, and knead until smooth and elastic (about 8 to 10 minutes). Place dough in a large bowl coated with cooking spray, turning to coat top. Cover and let rise in a warm place (85°), free from drafts, 1 hour or until doubled in bulk.

Spray 2 French bread loafpans with cooking spray; sprinkle each pan with cornmeal. Set aside.

Sprinkle remaining 1 tablespoon all-purpose flour evenly over work surface. Punch dough down; divide in half. Flatten each half into an oval on floured surface. Fold dough over lengthwise, and flatten with open hand. Fold again, and roll with palms of hands to a 15- x 2-inch rope; place ropes of dough in prepared pans.

Cover and let rise in a warm place, free from drafts, 30 minutes or until doubled in bulk. Combine egg white and milk, stirring well; brush loaves with egg mixture. Bake at 375° for 25 minutes or until loaves sound hollow when tapped. Remove from pans, and let cool completely on wire racks. Yield: 32 servings (57 calories per 1-inch slice).

PROTEIN 2.0 FAT 0.2 CARBOHYDRATE 12.0 CHOLESTEROL 0
IRON 0.7 SODIUM 39 CALCIUM 4

ITALIAN TOMATO BREAD

2 cups whole wheat flour
2 packages dry yeast
½ teaspoon salt
2 cups peeled, seeded, and chopped tomato
½ cup Burgundy or other dry red wine
2 tablespoons olive oil
2 tablespoons honey
¼ cup minced fresh rosemary
2½ cups all-purpose flour
1 tablespoon all-purpose flour
Vegetable cooking spray
2 tablespoons cornmeal
1 egg white, lightly beaten
1 tablespoon water
2 tablespoons grated Parmesan cheese

Combine first 3 ingredients in bowl; set aside. Position knife blade in food processor bowl. Add tomato; process until smooth.

Combine tomato puree, wine, oil, and honey in a saucepan; cook until very warm (120° to 130°). Add to flour mixture; beat at low speed of an electric mixer until blended. Beat an additional 3 minutes at medium speed. Stir in rosemary and enough of the 2½ cups flour to make a soft dough.

Sprinkle 1 tablespoon flour over work surface. Turn dough out onto floured surface; knead until smooth and elastic (about 8 to 10 minutes). Place in a bowl coated with cooking spray; turn to coat top. Cover; let rise in a warm place (85°), free from drafts, 45 minutes or until doubled in bulk.

Punch dough down; divide in half. Shape each portion into a round, slightly flat loaf. Coat a baking sheet with cooking spray; sprinkle with cornmeal. Place loaves on prepared baking sheet.

Cover and let rise in a warm place, free from drafts, 45 minutes or until doubled in bulk. Combine egg white and water; brush over loaves, and sprinkle with cheese. Bake at 325° for 40 to 45 minutes or until loaves sound hollow when tapped. Yield: 32 servings (79 calories per wedge).

PROTEIN 2.5 FAT 1.3 CARBOHYDRATE 14.8 CHOLESTEROL 0
IRON 0.9 SODIUM 46 CALCIUM 12

HARD SPICY PRETZELS

1 package dry yeast
1 cup warm flat light beer (105° to 115°)
1 cup warm skim milk (105° to 115°)
3 tablespoons unsalted margarine, melted
3 tablespoons molasses
1 cup medium rye flour
5¾ cups all-purpose flour, divided
¾ teaspoon baking powder
1 teaspoon salt
¼ cup spicy brown mustard
¼ cup all-purpose flour
Vegetable cooking spray
2 eggs, lightly beaten
2 tablespoons caraway seeds

Dissolve yeast in beer in a large bowl; let stand 5 minutes. Stir in milk, margarine, molasses, rye flour, and 2½ cups all-purpose flour; beat at low speed of an electric mixer until smooth. Cover and let rise in a warm place (85°), free from drafts, 40 minutes or until light and bubbly.

Add baking powder, salt, and mustard to beer mixture; stir well. Gradually stir in enough of the remaining 3¼ cups flour to make a soft dough.

Sprinkle ¼ cup flour over work surface. Turn dough out onto floured surface; knead until smooth and elastic (about 8 to 10 minutes). Divide dough into thirds. Working with 1 portion at a time, divide into 12 pieces; roll each into 14-inch rope. Twist each rope into a pretzel shape. Place pretzels, with loose ends turned under, on baking sheets coated with cooking spray.

Brush pretzels with beaten egg, and sprinkle lightly with caraway seeds. Bake at 400° for 12 to 14 minutes or until golden.

After all pretzels have been baked, turn oven off. Place baked pretzels onto 2 ungreased baking sheets, and place in warm oven for 2 hours or until completely dry (break one to test). Yield: 3 dozen (102 calories each).

PROTEIN 3.0 FAT 1.7 CARBOHYDRATE 18.6 CHOLESTEROL 12
IRON 1.2 SODIUM 103 CALCIUM 28

For special snacks that are also healthful, try (from right) Orange-Wheat Germ Twist (page 110) and Hard Spicy Pretzels.

ORANGE-WHEAT GERM TWIST

2 packages dry yeast
½ cup warm water (105° to 115°)
1 cup nonfat buttermilk
½ cup unsweetened orange juice
3 tablespoons unsalted margarine
¼ cup firmly packed brown sugar
2 eggs
2 cups whole wheat flour
½ teaspoon ground ginger
¾ cup toasted wheat germ, divided
2 tablespoons grated orange rind
½ teaspoon salt
3 cups all-purpose flour
3 tablespoons all-purpose flour
Vegetable cooking spray
1 egg white, lightly beaten
1 tablespoon water

Dissolve yeast in warm water in a large bowl; let stand 5 minutes. Combine buttermilk, orange juice, and margarine in a small saucepan; cook over medium heat until margarine melts, stirring constantly. Let cool to room temperature.

Add cooled buttermilk mixture, brown sugar, eggs, whole wheat flour, and ginger to yeast mixture; beat at medium speed of an electric mixer until well blended. Stir in ½ cup wheat germ, orange rind, salt, and enough of the 3 cups all-purpose flour to make a soft dough.

Sprinkle 3 tablespoons flour evenly over work surface. Turn dough out onto floured surface, and knead until smooth and elastic (about 8 to 10 minutes). Place dough in a large bowl coated with cooking spray, turning to coat top. Cover and let rise in a warm place (85°), free from drafts, 1½ hours or until doubled in bulk.

Punch dough down, and divide in half. Divide each half into 3 equal portions. Shape each portion into a 15-inch rope. Combine egg white and 1 tablespoon water; brush over ropes. Sprinkle ropes with remaining ¼ cup wheat germ.

Braid 3 ropes together on a baking sheet coated with cooking spray, pinching ends to seal; tuck ends under. Repeat with remaining ropes.

Cover and let rise in a warm place, free from drafts, 45 minutes or until doubled in bulk. Place in a cold oven, and bake at 350° for 25 minutes or until loaves sound hollow when tapped. Remove from baking sheet, and let cool on wire racks. Yield: 26 servings (128 calories per 1-inch slice).

PROTEIN 4.8   FAT 2.5   CARBOHYDRATE 22.1   CHOLESTEROL 15
IRON 1.5   SODIUM 64   CALCIUM 12

MOLASSES RYE ROLLS

1 package dry yeast
1¼ cups warm water (105° to 115°)
1 tablespoon dark molasses
1 cup rye flour
2 teaspoons anise seeds
2 teaspoons fennel seeds
2 teaspoons grated orange rind
1 teaspoon caraway seeds
½ teaspoon salt
2 teaspoons vegetable oil
3 cups all-purpose flour
2 tablespoons all-purpose flour
Vegetable cooking spray
1 egg white
1 tablespoon water
1 teaspoon caraway seeds

Dissolve yeast in warm water in a large bowl; add molasses, and let stand 5 minutes. Add rye flour and next 6 ingredients; beat at medium speed of an electric mixer until well blended. Gradually stir in enough of the 3 cups all-purpose flour to make a soft dough.

Sprinkle 2 tablespoons flour evenly over work surface. Turn dough out onto floured surface, and knead until smooth and elastic (about 8 to 10 minutes). Place dough in a large bowl coated with cooking spray, turning to coat top. Cover and let rise in a warm place (85°), free from drafts, 1 hour and 15 minutes or until doubled in bulk.

Punch dough down, and divide into 16 equal portions; shape each portion into a ball, and place

3 inches apart on a baking sheet coated with cooking spray.

Cover and let rise in a warm place, free from drafts, 45 minutes or until doubled in bulk. Combine egg white and 1 tablespoon water; brush over rolls. Sprinkle 1 teaspoon caraway seeds over rolls. Bake at 375° for 15 to 20 minutes or until golden. Remove from baking sheet, and let cool on wire racks. Yield: 16 rolls (116 calories each).

PROTEIN 3.3   FAT 1.1   CARBOHYDRATE 23.1   CHOLESTEROL 0
IRON 1.5   SODIUM 78   CALCIUM 17

PULL APART MAPLE-CHEDDAR ROLLS

2 cups whole wheat flour
¼ cup sugar
1 package dry yeast
1 teaspoon onion powder
½ teaspoon salt
1½ cups water
½ cup skim milk
¼ cup plus 1 tablespoon reduced-calorie maple
   syrup, divided
3 tablespoons margarine
3¾ cups all-purpose flour, divided
1 cup (4 ounces) shredded reduced-fat sharp
   Cheddar cheese
¼ cup minced fresh parsley
1 tablespoon all-purpose flour
Vegetable cooking spray
¼ cup water

Combine first 5 ingredients in a large bowl; stir well. Set aside.

Combine 1½ cups water, milk, 3 tablespoons maple syrup, and margarine in a saucepan; cook over medium heat until very warm (120° to 130°). Add water mixture to flour mixture; beat at medium speed of an electric mixer 2 minutes. Add ¾ cup all-purpose flour; beat 2 minutes at high speed. Stir in cheese, parsley, and enough of the remaining 3 cups flour to make a soft dough.

Sprinkle 1 tablespoon flour evenly over work surface. Turn dough out onto floured surface, and knead until smooth and elastic (about 8 to 10 minutes). Place dough in a large bowl coated with cooking spray, turning to coat top. Cover and let rise in a warm place (85°), free from drafts, 1 hour or until doubled in bulk.

Punch dough down, and divide into 32 equal portions; shape each portion into a ball. Place in two 9-inch square baking pans coated with cooking spray.

Combine remaining 2 tablespoons maple syrup and ¼ cup water; stir well. Brush syrup mixture over rolls. Cover and let rise in a warm place, free from drafts, 45 minutes or until doubled in bulk.

Bake at 350° for 15 minutes. Brush rolls with remaining maple syrup mixture. Bake an additional 2 to 5 minutes or until golden. Remove from pans, and let cool on wire racks. Yield: 32 rolls (105 calories each).

PROTEIN 3.7   FAT 2.1   CARBOHYDRATE 18.2   CHOLESTEROL 2
IRON 1.0   SODIUM 79   CALCIUM 39

EYES ON THE SIZE

Counting calories is meaningless unless you relate those numbers to portion size. When a calorie listing says a 2-inch square brownie carries 160 calories, don't assume that's the portion of brownie sold at your favorite bakery. Bakery brownies are usually double or triple that size and can yield 320 to 480 calories each.

For packaged food products, be aware that some manufacturers do list small portion sizes. It's a way to make a product seem lower in calories or lower in fat without adjusting the ingredients in the recipe. That's why those who are watching their weight need to have a better concept of amounts. Measuring cups, measuring spoons, and food scales are excellent tools for getting accurate ideas of portion size. Chefs and food professionals utilize food measuring equipment; it may pay to follow their example.

OVERNIGHT SOUR CREAM-CINNAMON ROLLS

2 packages dry yeast
¼ cup warm water (105° to 115°)
¼ cup sugar
¾ teaspoon salt
½ cup frozen egg substitute, thawed
⅓ cup reduced-calorie margarine, melted
1 teaspoon vanilla extract
1 (8-ounce) carton low-fat sour cream
4¼ cups all-purpose flour, divided
¼ cup flour, divided
2 tablespoons reduced-calorie margarine,
   melted
¼ cup sugar
1½ teaspoons ground cinnamon
Vegetable cooking spray
½ cup sifted powdered sugar
2 teaspoons skim milk
½ teaspoon clear vanilla extract

Dissolve yeast in warm water in a large bowl; let stand 5 minutes. Stir in sugar and next 5 ingredients. Add 2 cups flour; beat at medium speed of an electric mixer until smooth. Gradually stir in enough of the remaining 2¼ cups flour to make a soft dough. Cover and refrigerate 8 hours.

Sprinkle 1 tablespoon flour evenly over work surface. Punch dough down; turn dough out onto prepared surface, and knead 8 to 10 times, using remaining 3 tablespoons flour, if necessary, to keep dough from sticking. Roll dough to an 18- x 15-inch rectangle. Brush with 2 tablespoons melted margarine. Combine ¼ cup sugar and cinnamon; sprinkle over dough. Carefully roll up dough, jellyroll fashion, starting with long side; pinch seam to seal (do not seal ends). Cut roll into ¾-inch slices; place slices, cut side down, in two 9-inch square pans coated with cooking spray.

Cover and let rise in a warm place (85°), free from drafts, 1 hour. Bake at 350° for 20 to 25 minutes or until golden. Combine powdered sugar, milk, and ½ teaspoon vanilla, stirring well. Drizzle over hot rolls. Serve warm. Yield: 2 dozen (141 calories each).

PROTEIN 3.2 FAT 3.6 CARBOHYDRATE 24.0 CHOLESTEROL 4
IRON 1.3 SODIUM 119 CALCIUM 18

For the star of your meal, serve Braided Flounder with Tropical Relish (page 114). Pineapple, cantaloupe, mango, and lime combine to give the dish an island flavor.

Fish & Shellfish

OVEN-FRIED CATFISH FILLETS

⅓ cup corn flake crumbs
1½ tablespoons grated Parmesan cheese
1 tablespoon dried parsley flakes
4 (4-ounce) farm-raised catfish fillets
2 tablespoons reduced-calorie margarine,
  melted
Vegetable cooking spray

Combine corn flake crumbs, cheese, and parsley flakes in a small bowl; stir well. Brush fillets with melted margarine; dredge in crumb mixture.

Place fillets in an 11- x 7- x 2-inch baking dish coated with cooking spray. Bake, uncovered, at 400° for 20 minutes or until fish flakes easily when tested with a fork. Transfer to a serving platter, and serve immediately. Yield: 4 servings (223 calories per serving).

PROTEIN 23.0 FAT 9.7 CARBOHYDRATE 10.1 CHOLESTEROL 69
IRON 2.0 SODIUM 305 CALCIUM 95

BRAIDED FLOUNDER WITH TROPICAL RELISH

6 (4-ounce) flounder fillets
Vegetable cooking spray
3 tablespoons lemon juice
¾ pound fresh spinach
Tropical Relish
Lemon rind strips (optional)
Lime rind strips (optional)

Place fillets on a baking sheet coated with cooking spray. Cut each fillet lengthwise into 3 equal strips, leaving about 1 inch at one end of each fillet connected. Braid strips; tuck ends under. Brush fillets with lemon juice. Broil 5½ inches from heat 6 to 8 minutes or until fish flakes easily when tested with a fork.

Remove stems from spinach; wash leaves thoroughly. Arrange spinach in a vegetable steamer over boiling water. Cover and steam 1 to 2 minutes or just until spinach wilts.

Arrange spinach on individual plates. Place a fillet in center of each plate. Spoon Tropical Relish around fillets. If desired, garnish with rind strips. Yield: 6 servings (197 calories per serving).

Tropical Relish

1 cup diced fresh pineapple
1 cup diced cantaloupe
½ cup diced ripe mango
¼ cup chopped purple onion
1 (7-ounce) jar roasted red peppers in water,
  drained and chopped
2 tablespoons white wine vinegar
1 tablespoon minced fresh cilantro
1 tablespoon lime juice

Combine all ingredients in a medium bowl, and toss gently. Cover relish and chill at least 1 hour. Yield: 3 cups.

PROTEIN 28.3 FAT 2.4 CARBOHYDRATE 16.5 CHOLESTEROL 72
IRON 2.5 SODIUM 164 CALCIUM 93

GRILLED GROUPER

⅓ cup reduced-calorie mayonnaise
2 tablespoons Dijon mustard
2 teaspoons lemon juice
1 teaspoon low-sodium soy sauce
¼ teaspoon ground white pepper
¼ teaspoon minced garlic
2 (8-ounce) grouper fillets, halved
Vegetable cooking spray
1 tablespoon chopped fresh chives

Combine first 6 ingredients. Spread mixture on both sides of fillets. Cover and chill 2 hours. Coat grill rack with cooking spray; place on grill over medium-hot coals. Place fillets on rack; grill 8 minutes on each side or until fish flakes easily when tested with a fork. Sprinkle with chives. Yield: 4 servings (180 calories per serving).

PROTEIN 24.0 FAT 7.4 CARBOHYDRATE 2.2 CHOLESTEROL 51
IRON 1.1 SODIUM 453 CALCIUM 22

GROUPER BROCHETTES

2 (8-ounce) grouper fillets, cut into 1½-inch
    pieces
1 tablespoon olive oil
1 tablespoon lemon juice
1 tablespoon reduced-sodium soy sauce
2 teaspoons chopped fresh basil
2 teaspoons chopped fresh oregano
2 teaspoons chopped fresh thyme
1 teaspoon chopped fresh rosemary
6 large fresh mushrooms
1 medium zucchini, cut into ½-inch slices
1 medium onion, cut into 6 wedges
1 medium-size sweet red pepper, cut into
    1-inch pieces
1 medium-size green pepper, cut into 1-inch
    pieces
6 large cherry tomatoes

Place fillet pieces in a bowl. Combine oil and next 6 ingredients. Pour over fish; toss gently to coat. Cover and marinate in refrigerator 2 hours.

Arrange mushrooms, zucchini, onion, and peppers in a vegetable steamer over boiling water. Cover and steam 3 minutes.

Remove fish from marinade; discard marinade. Arrange fish, mushrooms, zucchini, onion, peppers, and tomatoes alternately on 6 (12-inch) skewers. Place kabobs on rack of a broiler pan coated with cooking spray. Bake at 400° for 10 minutes. Turn kabobs, and bake an additional 5 minutes or until fish flakes easily when tested with a fork. Yield: 6 servings (104 calories per serving).

PROTEIN 13.8   FAT 2.2   CARBOHYDRATE 7.8   CHOLESTEROL 23
IRON 1.8   SODIUM 82   CALCIUM 30

ORANGE ROUGHY WITH ARTICHOKES AND
RED PEPPER SAUCE

2 medium-size sweet red peppers
Vegetable cooking spray
1 teaspoon olive oil
½ cup peeled, chopped tomato
¼ cup minced green onions
1 tablespoon chopped fresh basil
1 clove garlic, minced
¼ cup canned low-sodium chicken broth,
    undiluted
¼ cup Chablis or other dry white wine
½ teaspoon sugar
⅛ teaspoon ground white pepper
⅛ teaspoon freshly ground pepper
1 (9-ounce) package frozen artichoke hearts,
    thawed
4 (4-ounce) orange roughy fillets
¼ teaspoon ground white pepper
¼ teaspoon pepper
1 tablespoon lemon juice

Cut peppers in half lengthwise; remove and discard seeds and membranes. Place peppers,

skin side up, on a baking sheet; flatten with palm of hand. Broil peppers 5½ inches from heat 15 to 20 minutes or until charred. Place in ice water; chill 5 minutes. Remove from water; peel peppers and discard skins. Coarsely chop peppers.

Coat a nonstick skillet with cooking spray; add oil. Place over medium-high heat until hot. Add red pepper, tomato, green onions, basil, and garlic; sauté 5 minutes. Add chicken broth and next 4 ingredients; stir well. Cook, uncovered, 7 minutes or just until thickened, stirring occasionally.

Coat an 11- x 7- x 2-inch baking dish with cooking spray; arrange artichoke hearts in dish. Place fillets over artichoke hearts; sprinkle with ¼ teaspoon ground white pepper, ¼ teaspoon pepper, and lemon juice. Spoon red pepper sauce over fillets. Bake, uncovered, at 400° for 20 minutes or until fish flakes easily when tested with a fork. Yield: 4 servings (204 calories per serving).

PROTEIN 19.2   FAT 9.8   CARBOHYDRATE 10.4   CHOLESTEROL 23
IRON 1.7   SODIUM 101   CALCIUM 276

Surprise your family with south-of-the-border flavor hidden inside Mexican Fish Packets.

MEXICAN FISH PACKETS

14 dried cornhusks
Vegetable cooking spray
¾ cup chopped onion
1½ teaspoons minced garlic
¾ cup peeled, seeded, and chopped tomato
3 tablespoons chopped green chiles
9 ripe olives, sliced
1½ tablespoons balsamic vinegar
¼ teaspoon chili powder
⅛ teaspoon ground cumin
6 (4-ounce) orange roughy fillets (¾ inch thick)

Cover dried cornhusks with hot water; let stand 1 hour or until cornhusks are softened. Drain well, and pat with paper towels to remove excess water.

Coat a nonstick skillet with cooking spray; place over medium-high heat until hot. Add onion and garlic; sauté until tender. Remove from heat; add chopped tomato and next 5 ingredients, stirring well to combine.

Tear 2 cornhusks into 24 (¼-inch) strips. Tie 2 strips together at ends, making 12 strips; set aside.

Overlap 2 cornhusks; place one fillet in center of cornhusks. Top with ¼ cup tomato mixture. Fold bottom and top of cornhusks over fillet; tie with a cornhusk strip. Fold right and left sides of cornhusk over fillet, forming a square; tie with a cornhusk strip. Repeat procedure.

Place fish packets in a 2-quart baking dish coated with cooking spray. Bake, uncovered, at 350° for 30 to 35 minutes or until fish flakes easily when tested with a fork. Yield: 6 servings (167 calories per serving).

PROTEIN 17.4 FAT 8.9 CARBOHYDRATE 3.9 CHOLESTEROL 23
IRON 0.8 SODIUM 123 CALCIUM 15

ORANGE BAKED SNAPPER

4 (4-ounce) red snapper fillets (about
　¾ inch thick)
Vegetable cooking spray
1¼ cups orange juice, divided
¼ teaspoon ground cloves, divided
2 teaspoons cornstarch
2 medium oranges, peeled, seeded, and
　sectioned (about 1 cup)

Arrange fillets in a 10- x 6- x 2-inch baking dish coated with cooking spray.

Combine ½ cup orange juice and ⅛ teaspoon cloves; stir well. Pour orange juice mixture over fillets; cover fillets and marinate in refrigerator at least 30 minutes.

Bake, uncovered, at 400° for 20 minutes or until fish flakes easily when tested with a fork, basting occasionally with orange juice mixture. Transfer fillets to a serving platter, and keep warm.

Combine remaining orange juice and cornstarch in a small nonaluminum saucepan, stirring well until blended. Bring to a boil; cook 1 minute or until mixture is thickened, stirring constantly with a wire whisk. Remove from heat; stir in remaining ⅛ teaspoon cloves and orange sections. Spoon sauce over fish. Serve immediately. Yield: 4 servings (174 calories per serving).

PROTEIN 24.2　FAT 1.8　CARBOHYDRATE 14.5　CHOLESTEROL 42
IRON 0.3　SODIUM 74　CALCIUM 61

COLORFUL SWORDFISH STIR-FRY

2 (8-ounce) swordfish steaks (1 inch thick)
2 tablespoons reduced-sodium soy
　sauce
2 tablespoons dry sherry
1 teaspoon minced garlic
1 teaspoon minced fresh ginger
½ cup canned low-sodium chicken broth,
　undiluted
¼ cup unsweetened pineapple juice
1 tablespoon cornstarch
3 tablespoons no-salt-added tomato
　paste
2 tablespoons vinegar
1 teaspoon sugar
Vegetable cooking spray
1 tablespoon peanut oil
1 small onion, thinly sliced
⅔ cup diagonally sliced carrot
¼ pound fresh snow pea pods, trimmed
1⅓ cups sliced fresh mushrooms
⅓ cup chopped green onions
1 cup fresh broccoli flowerets
3 cups cooked long-grain rice (cooked without
　salt or fat)

Cut swordfish steaks into 1-inch pieces, and place in a shallow dish. Combine soy sauce, sherry, garlic, and ginger; pour over steak pieces. Cover and marinate in refrigerator up to 4 hours.

Combine chicken broth and next 5 ingredients; stir well. Set aside.

Remove steak pieces from marinade, discarding marinade. Coat a wok or large nonstick skillet with cooking spray. Add oil; place over medium-high heat (375°) until hot. Add swordfish, and stir-fry 5 minutes. Remove from wok; keep warm.

Coat wok with cooking spray, and place over medium-high heat until hot. Add onion, and stir-fry 1 minute. Add carrot, and stir-fry 1 minute. Add snow peas, mushrooms, and green onions; stir-fry 2 minutes or until crisp-tender. Add broccoli, and stir-fry 1 minute. Return swordfish to wok. Stir in reserved broth mixture. Cook, stirring constantly, until mixture is thickened. Serve swordfish mixture over cooked rice. Yield: 6 servings (297 calories per serving).

PROTEIN 21.1　FAT 6.1　CARBOHYDRATE 38.2　CHOLESTEROL 32
IRON 2.8　SODIUM 170　CALCIUM 49

CRAB EN COCOTTE

1 pound fresh lump crabmeat, drained
½ cup chopped celery
½ cup chopped onion
½ cup chopped green pepper
¼ cup reduced-calorie mayonnaise
¼ cup frozen egg substitute, thawed
1 (2-ounce) jar diced pimiento, drained
1 tablespoon white wine Worcestershire sauce
1 tablespoon lemon juice
¼ teaspoon ground white pepper
⅛ teaspoon ground red pepper
2 drops hot sauce
Vegetable cooking spray
½ cup whole wheat breadcrumbs
1 tablespoon reduced-calorie margarine, melted

Combine first 12 ingredients in a medium bowl; stir well. Spoon mixture into a 1½-quart baking dish coated with cooking spray. Combine breadcrumbs and margarine; sprinkle over mixture. Bake, uncovered, at 350° for 30 minutes. Yield: 4 servings (206 calories per serving).

PROTEIN 24.9 FAT 7.6 CARBOHYDRATE 9.1 CHOLESTEROL 100
IRON 1.9 SODIUM 610 CALCIUM 137

CHEESE-STUFFED CALAMARI

1 tablespoon olive oil
¼ cup finely chopped green onions
1 teaspoon minced garlic
2½ cups peeled, chopped tomato
1½ cups chopped fresh mushrooms
¼ cup chopped green pepper
¼ cup chopped fresh basil, divided
½ teaspoon pepper, divided
¾ cup (3 ounces) finely shredded part-skim
  mozzarella cheese
¾ cup (3 ounces) finely shredded reduced-fat
  Monterey Jack cheese
2 tablespoons grated Parmesan cheese
16 medium-size cleaned, skinned calamari
  (squid) (about 2 pounds)

Heat oil in a large nonstick skillet over medium-high heat until hot. Add green onions and garlic; sauté 3 minutes or until tender. Add tomato, mushrooms, green pepper, 2 tablespoons basil, and ¼ teaspoon pepper. Reduce heat; cover and simmer 20 minutes.

Combine remaining 2 tablespoons basil, ¼ teaspoon pepper, and cheeses. Spoon cheese mixture evenly into each calamari. Place calamari in a 13- x 9- x 2-inch baking dish coated with cooking spray. Bake at 375° for 12 to 14 minutes or until done. Transfer calamari to a serving platter, and top with tomato sauce. Serve immediately. Yield: 8 servings (170 calories per serving).

PROTEIN 19.3 FAT 7.1 CARBOHYDRATE 7.0 CHOLESTEROL 196
IRON 1.2 SODIUM 182 CALCIUM 203

SHRIMP-STUFFED EGGPLANT

3 medium eggplants (about 2¼ pounds)
Vegetable cooking spray
1 cup chopped onion
¾ cup chopped green onions
½ cup chopped green pepper
½ cup chopped celery
1 tablespoon minced garlic
¾ pound medium-size fresh shrimp, cooked,
  peeled, and deveined
¾ cup no-salt-added tomato sauce
½ cup fine, dry breadcrumbs
3 tablespoons frozen egg substitute, thawed
1 teaspoon dried whole basil
1 teaspoon dried whole thyme
1 teaspoon dried whole oregano
¼ teaspoon ground white pepper
¼ teaspoon black pepper
¼ teaspoon ground red pepper
½ cup (2 ounces) shredded reduced-fat
  Monterey Jack cheese
3 tablespoons grated Parmesan cheese

Prick each eggplant several times with a fork. Place eggplant on a baking sheet, and bake at 350° for 20 minutes. Let cool. Cut each eggplant in half lengthwise; remove pulp, leaving a ¼-inch shell. Chop pulp; set shells and chopped pulp aside.

Coat a large nonstick skillet with cooking spray; place over medium-high heat until hot. Add onion, green onions, green pepper, celery, and garlic; sauté 5 minutes or until vegetables are tender. Remove from heat, and stir in chopped eggplant.

Coarsely chop shrimp; add shrimp and next 9 ingredients to vegetable mixture. Place eggplant shells in a 13- x 9- x 2-inch baking dish coated with cooking spray. Spoon mixture into shells; cover and bake at 350° for 25 minutes. Sprinkle with cheeses; bake, uncovered, 3 minutes or until thoroughly heated and cheese is melted. Transfer to individual serving plates. Yield: 6 servings (203 calories per serving).

PROTEIN 20.3 FAT 3.9 CARBOHYDRATE 23.3 CHOLESTEROL 119
IRON 4.0 SODIUM 327 CALCIUM 233

BAYOU DIRTY RICE

6 cups water
2 stalks celery with leaves
1 small onion, quartered
1 clove garlic, minced
1 pound unpeeled medium-size fresh shrimp
½ cup chopped onion
⅓ cup chopped green pepper
⅓ cup chopped celery
1 teaspoon minced garlic
½ pound fresh lump crabmeat,
    drained
2 cups cooked brown rice (cooked without
    salt or fat)
⅓ cup chopped green onions
½ cup no-salt-added tomato sauce
½ cup skim milk
½ teaspoon dried whole thyme
½ teaspoon dried whole basil
¼ teaspoon salt
¼ teaspoon ground white pepper
¼ teaspoon pepper
⅛ teaspoon ground red pepper

Combine first 4 ingredients in a Dutch oven. Bring to a boil; add shrimp, and cook 3 to 5 minutes or until done. Drain; reserve 1 cup liquid. Rinse shrimp thoroughly with cold water. Peel and devein shrimp.

Place reserved liquid in a 10-inch ovenproof skillet. Bring to a boil. Add onion, green pepper, celery, and garlic. Reduce heat, and simmer 15 minutes or until vegetables are tender. Stir in shrimp, crabmeat, and remaining ingredients. Cover and bake at 325° for 25 minutes. Yield: 6 servings (180 calories per serving).

PROTEIN 21.5 FAT 2.2 CARBOHYDRATE 17.6 CHOLESTEROL 107
IRON 2.4 SODIUM 613 CALCIUM 99

CHILDREN AND CHOLESTEROL

Monitoring blood cholesterol is not just for adults. New guidelines from the National Cholesterol Education Program set standards for children, too. Specifically, a healthy level of blood cholesterol for a child is anything lower than 170 milligrams per deciliter (mg/dl) as compared to the acceptable level of 200 milligrams for an adult.

For children, a level between 170 and 199 is considered borderline high, and a value of 200 or more is considered high. Many parents aren't aware of their child's cholesterol level. The panel of experts that put together the guidelines recommends selective screening for children. The children who really need screening, say the experts, are those with a family history of heart disease (mother, father, sibling, or grandparent) or have at least one parent with a blood cholesterol level of 240 milligrams or greater.

Regardless of risk, however, youngsters do need to start taking steps to prevent heart disease. High on the list of preventive strategies: an active lifestyle and a diet low in fat. Once children pass the age of two, it's safe to start trimming the fat. The same recommendation that holds true for adults—no more than 30 percent of the calories from fat—is perfect for pint-sized palates.

Serve Marinated Shrimp Kabobs on a bed of rice for a striking presentation.

MARINATED SHRIMP KABOBS

32 large fresh unpeeled shrimp (about 1½ pounds)
1 (15¼-ounce) can pineapple chunks in juice, undrained
½ cup commercial oil-free Italian dressing
1 (8-ounce) can no-salt-added tomato sauce
1½ tablespoons brown sugar
1 teaspoon prepared mustard
1 large green pepper, cut into 1-inch cubes
1 large sweet red pepper, cut into 1-inch cubes
12 pearl onions
Vegetable cooking spray
2 cups cooked long-grain rice (cooked without salt or fat)

Peel and devein shrimp, leaving tails intact. Set aside. Drain pineapple, reserving ¼ cup juice. Set pineapple aside.

Combine reserved juice, Italian dressing, tomato sauce, brown sugar, and mustard. Place shrimp in a shallow dish; add juice mixture, and toss gently. Cover and marinate in refrigerator at least 3 hours; stir occasionally.

Remove shrimp from marinade. Place marinade in a small saucepan; bring to a boil. Reduce heat, and simmer 5 minutes.

Alternate shrimp, pineapple chunks, peppers, and onions on 4 metal skewers. Coat grill rack with cooking spray; place on grill over medium-hot coals. Place kabobs on rack, and cook 3 to 4 minutes on each side or until done, basting frequently with reserved marinade. Serve over cooked rice. Yield: 4 servings (283 calories per serving).

PROTEIN 15.1 FAT 1.7 CARBOHYDRATE 50.9 CHOLESTEROL 85
IRON 3.5 SODIUM 389 CALCIUM 60

SCALLOPS IN TANGERINE SAUCE

1 cup clam juice
2 tablespoons chopped fresh parsley
1 tablespoon lemon juice
1 teaspoon dried whole thyme
1 teaspoon dried whole basil
¼ teaspoon pepper
1 pound fresh bay scallops
4 ounces spinach fettuccine, uncooked
⅔ cup fresh squeezed tangerine juice (about 3
  medium tangerines)
1 tablespoon lemon juice
1 tablespoon cornstarch
¼ cup water

Combine first 6 ingredients in a small saucepan; bring to a boil. Reduce heat, and simmer 10
minutes. Add scallops; cook 5 to 7 minutes or until
scallops are opaque. Drain scallops, reserving ½
cup liquid. Set scallops aside, and keep warm.

Cook fettuccine according to package directions,
omitting salt and fat; drain well, and keep warm.

Combine reserved ½ cup liquid, tangerine juice,
and 1 tablespoon lemon juice in a small nonaluminum saucepan; bring juice mixture to a boil
over medium heat.

Combine cornstarch and water; add to juice
mixture. Reduce heat, and cook until mixture is
thickened and bubbly, stirring constantly.

Transfer fettuccine to a serving platter; top with
scallops, and spoon tangerine sauce over scallops.
Yield: 4 servings (229 calories per serving).

PROTEIN 23.7 FAT 1.4 CARBOHYDRATE 31.2 CHOLESTEROL 37
IRON 2.2 SODIUM 251 CALCIUM 66

SWEET-AND-HOT SCALLOPS

Vegetable cooking spray
2 teaspoons peanut oil
½ cup diagonally sliced carrot
½ cup sliced onion
1 (8-ounce) can pineapple chunks in juice,
  undrained
6 ounces fresh snow pea pods, trimmed
1 (8-ounce) can water chestnuts, drained
1 pound sea scallops
¼ cup chopped green onions
½ cup canned low-sodium chicken broth,
  undiluted
1 tablespoon cornstarch
2 tablespoons rice wine vinegar
1 tablespoon hot bean paste
1 teaspoon low-sodium soy sauce
3 cups cooked long-grain rice (cooked without
  salt or fat)

Coat a wok or large nonstick skillet with cooking
spray; add oil. Place over medium-high heat
(375°) until hot. Add carrot, and stir-fry 1 minute.
Add onion, and stir-fry 1 minute.

Drain pineapple, reserving juice. Add pineapple,
snow peas, and water chestnuts to wok; stir-fry 1
minute. Add scallops and chopped green onions;
stir-fry 3 minutes. Combine broth and next 4
ingredients; add to scallop mixture. Cook until
mixture is thickened and thoroughly heated, stirring constantly. Serve over cooked rice. Yield: 6
servings (272 calories per serving).

PROTEIN 16.9 FAT 2.7 CARBOHYDRATE 43.7 CHOLESTEROL 25
IRON 2.3 SODIUM 178 CALCIUM 58

SEAFOOD SAFETY

Even though Americans eat more seafood
now than ever before, there is less foodborne
illness associated with eating seafood. The National
Academy of Sciences has come to this conclusion
about the safety of American seafood. The illnesses
tied to seafood are traced mostly to raw shellfish.

Also, pollutants can contaminate waters closer to
shore and may be picked up by fish and shellfish.
Deep-water ocean fish are less likely to be contami-
nated. Food safety experts agree that fish bought
from a reputable dealer, and then stored and cooked
properly, shouldn't be a cause for concern.

SEAFOOD LASAGNA

Vegetable cooking spray
1½ teaspoons olive oil
1½ cups finely chopped onion
¾ cup finely chopped green pepper
¼ cup plus 2 tablespoons chopped fresh parsley
1½ teaspoons minced garlic
3¾ cups peeled, chopped tomato (about 2¾ pounds)
¾ cup Chablis or other dry white wine
¼ cup plus 1½ teaspoons no-salt-added tomato paste
3 tablespoons chopped fresh basil
1½ tablespoons chopped fresh oregano
1 tablespoon chopped fresh thyme
1½ teaspoons chopped fresh marjoram
½ teaspoon freshly ground pepper
1½ pounds medium-size fresh shrimp, peeled and deveined
¾ pound bay scallops
2 tablespoons reduced-calorie margarine
2 tablespoons all-purpose flour
½ cup canned low-sodium chicken broth, undiluted
½ cup skim milk
¼ teaspoon salt
¼ teaspoon ground white pepper
¼ teaspoon freshly grated nutmeg
9 cooked lasagna noodles (cooked without salt or fat)
1 cup 1% low-fat cottage cheese
1 cup (4 ounces) shredded part-skim mozzarella cheese

Coat a large nonstick skillet with cooking spray; add oil. Place over medium-high heat until hot. Add onion, green pepper, parsley, and garlic; sauté until vegetables are tender. Add tomato and next 7 ingredients; cook over medium heat 20 minutes, stirring frequently. Add shrimp and scallops; cook an additional 10 to 12 minutes or until shrimp turn pink, stirring frequently.

Melt margarine in a medium saucepan; add flour, stirring until smooth. Cook 1 minute, stirring constantly. Gradually add broth and milk; cook over medium heat, stirring constantly, until mixture is thickened and bubbly. Stir in salt, white pepper, and nutmeg.

Coat a 13- x 9- x 2-inch baking dish with cooking spray. Place 3 lasagna noodles in bottom of dish. Top with half of tomato mixture. Place 3 lasagna noodles over tomato mixture. Top with white sauce. Place remaining 3 lasagna noodles over sauce. Top with cottage cheese and remaining half of tomato mixture. Sprinkle with mozzarella cheese. Bake, uncovered, at 375° for 30 to 40 minutes or until thoroughly heated. Let stand 10 minutes before serving. Yield: 12 servings (190 calories per serving).

PROTEIN 18.6   FAT 5.1   CARBOHYDRATE 18.6   CHOLESTEROL 65
IRON 3.6   SODIUM 296   CALCIUM 203

Serve Cheesy Chile Fettuccine (page 131) topped with diced tomato for your next pasta night, or spoon a topping over one of these fresh pastas for a delectable pasta dish: (clockwise from top left) Curried Pasta (page 129), Black Pepper Pasta (page 129), and Sweet Red Pepper Pasta (page 130).

Grains & Pastas

MINTED COUSCOUS

1¾ cups water
2 teaspoons minced fresh mint
1 teaspoon chicken-flavored bouillon
   granules
⅛ teaspoon salt
1 cup couscous, uncooked
¾ cup frozen English peas, thawed
Fresh mint sprigs (optional)

Combine first 4 ingredients in a medium saucepan; bring to a boil. Remove from heat. Add couscous and peas; cover and let stand 5 minutes or until couscous is tender and liquid is absorbed.

Fluff couscous with a fork, and transfer to a serving bowl. Garnish with fresh mint sprigs, if desired. Yield: 7 servings (102 calories per ½-cup serving).

PROTEIN 3.9   FAT 0.1   CARBOHYDRATE 20.5   CHOLESTEROL 0
IRON 0.7   SODIUM 177   CALCIUM 13

HARVEST COUSCOUS

2 cups water
¾ cup peeled, diced sweet potato
¼ cup diced dried figs
⅓ cup diced dried apricots
½ teaspoon pumpkin pie spice
¾ cup couscous, uncooked

Combine first 5 ingredients in a medium saucepan; bring to a boil. Cover, reduce heat, and simmer 15 minutes or until potato is tender. Remove from heat. Add couscous; cover and let stand 5 minutes or until couscous is tender and liquid is absorbed. Fluff couscous with a fork, and transfer to a serving bowl. Yield: 6 servings (124 calories per ½-cup serving).

PROTEIN 3.4   FAT 0.2   CARBOHYDRATE 27.7   CHOLESTEROL 0
IRON 1.0   SODIUM 8   CALCIUM 23

SUNNY ORANGE GRITS

2 cups water
1 cup unsweetened orange juice
½ teaspoon salt
½ teaspoon grated orange rind
1 cup quick-cooking grits, uncooked
1 tablespoon reduced-calorie margarine

Combine water, orange juice, salt, and orange rind in a medium saucepan; bring to a boil. Stir in grits. Cook over medium heat 3 minutes, stirring constantly. Remove from heat, and stir in margarine. Serve immediately. Yield: 6 servings (119 calories per ½-cup serving).

PROTEIN 2.5   FAT 1.4   CARBOHYDRATE 24.4   CHOLESTEROL 0
IRON 1.0   SODIUM 215   CALCIUM 5

LEMON RICE

1 cup basmati rice
2 cups water
Vegetable cooking spray
¼ cup chopped green onions
1 teaspoon minced jalapeño pepper
½ teaspoon grated lemon rind
3 tablespoons fresh lemon juice
¼ teaspoon ground white pepper
3 tablespoons minced fresh parsley

Rinse rice in 5 changes of cold water; drain. Bring 2 cups water to a boil in a small saucepan; add rice. Cover, reduce heat, and simmer 20 minutes. Remove from heat, and let rice stand 10 minutes.

Coat a large heavy skillet with cooking spray; place over medium-high heat until hot. Add onion and jalapeño pepper; sauté until tender. Add rice, and stir well. Add lemon rind, lemon juice, and white pepper; stir gently. Stir in parsley. Yield: 8 servings (91 calories per ½-cup serving).

PROTEIN 1.8   FAT 0.3   CARBOHYDRATE 20.0   CHOLESTEROL 0
IRON 1.2   SODIUM 2   CALCIUM 11

Reap the rewards of summer with Country-Style Brown Rice, a savory blend of brown rice, vegetables, and seasonings.

COUNTRY-STYLE BROWN RICE

Vegetable cooking spray
2 cups chopped collard greens
1 cup sliced leek
1 cup diced sweet red pepper
2 cloves garlic, minced
2½ cups water
1½ teaspoons vegetable-flavored bouillon
  granules
¼ teaspoon ground white pepper
¼ teaspoon hot sauce
1 cup long-grain brown rice, uncooked
½ cup minced fresh parsley
Sweet red pepper fan (optional)
Leek fan (optional)

Coat a large saucepan with cooking spray; place over medium-high heat until hot. Add collard greens and next 3 ingredients; sauté 5 minutes or until vegetables are tender. Add water, bouillon granules, white pepper, and hot sauce; stir well.

Bring mixture to a boil; stir in rice. Cover, reduce heat, and simmer 45 minutes or until rice is tender and liquid is absorbed. Stir in parsley; transfer to a serving bowl. If desired, garnish with a sweet red pepper fan and leek fan. Serve warm. Yield: 10 servings (89 calories per ½-cup serving).

PROTEIN 2.3   FAT 0.7   CARBOHYDRATE 18.6   CHOLESTEROL 0
IRON 0.9   SODIUM 247   CALCIUM 33

SPICY GREEN RICE

Vegetable cooking spray
2 teaspoons vegetable oil
½ cup chopped green onions
2 cloves garlic, minced
1 cup long-grain rice, uncooked
2 Anaheim chiles, seeded and finely chopped
1 jalapeño pepper, seeded and finely chopped
1¾ cups plus 2 tablespoons water
¼ teaspoon salt
½ cup chopped fresh parsley
¼ cup chopped fresh cilantro
1 tablespoon balsamic vinegar
¼ teaspoon cracked pepper

Coat a saucepan with cooking spray; add oil. Place over medium-high heat until hot. Add onions and garlic; sauté until tender. Add rice and chopped peppers; sauté 3 minutes. Stir in water and salt; bring to a boil. Cover, reduce heat, and simmer 15 minutes. Stir in parsley and remaining ingredients. Cover and cook an additional 5 minutes or until rice is tender and liquid is absorbed. Yield: 3½ cups (126 calories per ½-cup serving).

PROTEIN 2.7 FAT 1.6 CARBOHYDRATE 25.0 CHOLESTEROL 0
IRON 2.0 SODIUM 90 CALCIUM 25

ELEGANT RICE

1⅔ cups canned low-sodium chicken broth, undiluted
1 cup long-grain rice, uncooked
½ cup Chablis or other dry white wine
¼ teaspoon freshly ground pepper
Vegetable cooking spray
1 cup sliced fresh mushrooms
¼ cup finely chopped celery
¼ cup finely chopped green onions
1 (14-ounce) can artichoke hearts, drained and chopped
¾ cup peeled, seeded, and diced tomato
3 tablespoons minced fresh parsley
¼ teaspoon salt

Combine first 4 ingredients in a medium saucepan; bring to a boil. Cover, reduce heat, and simmer 20 minutes or until liquid is absorbed. Set aside, and keep warm.

Coat a large nonstick skillet with cooking spray; place over medium-high heat until hot. Add mushrooms, celery, and green onions; sauté until tender.

Add reserved rice, artichoke hearts, tomato, parsley, and salt; stir well. Cover and cook over medium heat 2 to 3 minutes or until thoroughly heated. Yield: 10 servings (89 calories per ½-cup serving).

PROTEIN 2.3 FAT 0.3 CARBOHYDRATE 19.0 CHOLESTEROL 0
IRON 1.5 SODIUM 81 CALCIUM 22

RICE CON QUESO

Vegetable cooking spray
½ cup chopped onion
½ cup chopped green pepper
1 cup water
1 (14½-ounce) can no-salt-added whole tomatoes, undrained and chopped
1 cup long-grain rice, uncooked
1 (4-ounce) can chopped green chiles, drained
2 tablespoons minced fresh cilantro
½ cup (2 ounces) shredded reduced-fat Monterey Jack cheese

Coat a small nonstick skillet with cooking spray; place over medium-high heat until hot. Add onion and green pepper; sauté until tender. Transfer mixture to a large saucepan.

Add water and tomatoes, stirring well; bring to a boil. Stir in rice and chiles; bring to a boil. Cover, reduce heat, and simmer 20 to 30 minutes or until rice is tender and liquid is absorbed. Stir in cilantro. Transfer rice mixture to a serving bowl, and sprinkle with cheese. Yield: 12 servings (82 calories per ½-cup serving).

PROTEIN 2.8 FAT 1.2 CARBOHYDRATE 15.0 CHOLESTEROL 3
IRON 0.9 SODIUM 40 CALCIUM 19

SAFFRON RICE

Vegetable cooking spray
2 teaspoons olive oil
½ cup chopped onion
2 cloves garlic, minced
1 cup plus 2 tablespoons long-grain rice,
   uncooked
1 (13¾-ounce) can no-salt-added chicken broth
⅓ cup Chablis or other dry white wine
½ teaspoon cracked pepper
¼ teaspoon salt
⅛ teaspoon ground saffron
¼ pound fresh asparagus spears

Coat a large skillet with cooking spray; add oil. Place over medium-high heat until hot. Add onion and garlic; sauté until tender. Add rice, and cook 1 minute, stirring constantly. Add chicken broth and next 4 ingredients; bring to a boil. Cover, reduce heat, and simmer 15 minutes or until rice is tender and liquid is absorbed. Remove from heat; let stand 5 minutes.

Snap off tough ends of asparagus. Remove scales with a knife or vegetable peeler, if desired. Cut asparagus into 1-inch pieces; arrange in a vegetable steamer over boiling water. Cover and steam 4 to 5 minutes or until crisp-tender.

Combine rice mixture and asparagus in a serving bowl, stirring well. Yield: 8 servings (127 calories per ½-cup serving).

PROTEIN 3.0 FAT 1.8 CARBOHYDRATE 24.0 CHOLESTEROL 0
IRON 1.4 SODIUM 30 CALCIUM 16

WILD RICE WITH MUSHROOMS

1 cup wild rice, uncooked
3½ cups water
½ cup Chablis or other dry white wine
¼ teaspoon salt
Vegetable cooking spray
2 cups sliced fresh oyster mushrooms
⅓ cup sliced green onions
2 tablespoons minced fresh parsley
1 teaspoon dried whole rosemary,
   crushed
½ teaspoon dried whole thyme
¼ teaspoon pepper

Rinse rice in 3 changes of hot water; drain. Combine 3½ cups water, wine, and salt in a saucepan; bring to a boil. Add rice; cover, reduce heat, and simmer 1 hour. Drain; set aside.

Coat a large nonstick skillet with cooking spray; place over medium-high heat until hot. Add mushrooms and green onions; sauté until tender. Stir in rice, parsley, and remaining ingredients. Yield: 8 servings (80 calories per ½-cup serving).

PROTEIN 3.5 FAT 0.4 CARBOHYDRATE 16.5 CHOLESTEROL 0
IRON 1.0 SODIUM 77 CALCIUM 14

 FRESH PASTA MADE EASY

When time is limited but you would like to serve fresh pasta, help is at hand. Several food manufacturers now produce made-from-scratch pasta flavored with herbs, garlic, or vegetables. While most commercial dried pasta is cholesterol-free and contains no added fat, the addition of eggs and oils in fresh pasta increases the fat and cholesterol content slightly.

Adding spinach, sweet red peppers, tomatoes, and herbs does little to change the nutrition profile of either fresh or dried pasta. Visual appeal and flavor are the main reasons companies add vegetables.

FRESH PASTA MADE EASY

Make a well in the center of dry ingredients; add beaten eggs. Stir until all flour is incorporated. Add seasonings such as roasted sweet red pepper, curry powder, ground black pepper, or fresh herbs, if desired.

To roll dough by hand, flatten dough with palm of hand. With rolling pin in center of dough, roll dough away from you, and then rotate dough a quarter-turn. Continue rolling until dough is as thin as possible.

Allow dough to dry slightly. Fold dough in thirds lengthwise. If dough sticks when folded over, it has not been sufficiently dried. Cut dough into ¼- to ½-inch slices according to desired width, using a sharp knife.

To use a pasta maker, divide dough into small portions, and flatten each portion into a disc shape. Pass each portion of dough through the smooth rollers of the pasta machine until it becomes a wide, thin sheet.

Adjust the control to the next smaller setting, and feed the entire sheet through the machine, guiding it gently with your hands. Continue narrowing the setting until the desired thickness is achieved.

Select the cutting attachment for the desired width of pasta (for spaghetti, linguine, or fettuccine). Pass each sheet of dough through the machine's cutting rollers, gently guiding cut pasta out of the cutting rollers.

BASIC EGG PASTA

2 eggs
1 teaspoon olive oil
½ teaspoon salt
1½ cups unbleached flour
1 tablespoon water
1 tablespoon unbleached flour
3 quarts boiling water

Position mixing blade in food processor bowl; add eggs, olive oil, and salt. Process 30 seconds or until blended. Add 1½ cups flour; process 30 seconds to 1 minute or until mixture forms pea-size balls. Slowly add 1 tablespoon water through food chute with processor running, blending just until mixture forms a ball.

Sprinkle 1 tablespoon flour evenly over work surface. Turn dough out onto floured surface. Knead dough until smooth and elastic (about 10 to 15 minutes). Wrap dough in plastic wrap, and let rest 10 minutes.

Divide dough in half. Working with 1 portion at a time, pass dough through smooth rollers of pasta machine on widest setting. Continue moving width gauge to narrower settings; pass dough through rollers once at each setting.

Roll dough to desired thinness (about $1/16$ inch). Pass each dough sheet through fettuccine cutting rollers of machine. Hang pasta on a wooden drying rack (dry no longer than 30 minutes).

Cook pasta in boiling water 2 minutes. Drain; serve immediately. Yield: 4½ cups (91 calories per ½-cup serving).

PROTEIN 3.5 FAT 1.8 CARBOHYDRATE 15.1 CHOLESTEROL 47
IRON 0.9 SODIUM 145 CALCIUM 6

BLACK PEPPER PASTA

2 eggs
1½ to 2 tablespoons coarsely
  ground pepper
1 teaspoon olive oil
½ teaspoon salt
1½ cups unbleached flour
2 tablespoons plus 2 teaspoons water

Position knife blade in food processor bowl; add first 4 ingredients. Process 30 seconds or until blended. Add flour, and process 30 seconds to 1 minute or until mixture forms pea-size balls. Slowly add water through food chute with processor running, blending until mixture forms a ball. Continue to process 2 minutes or until dough is smooth and elastic. Wrap dough in plastic wrap, and let stand 10 minutes. Follow procedure for Basic Egg Pasta. Yield: 4½ cups (90 calories per ½-cup serving).

PROTEIN 3.5 FAT 1.8 CARBOHYDRATE 15.2 CHOLESTEROL 44
IRON 1.2 SODIUM 146 CALCIUM 11

CILANTRO PASTA

1 (4-ounce) can chopped green chiles, drained
2 tablespoons fresh cilantro
1 egg
1 teaspoon olive oil
¼ teaspoon salt
2 cups unbleached flour

Position knife blade in food processor bowl; add chiles and cilantro. Process until smooth. Add egg, oil, and salt. Process 30 seconds to 1 minute; scrape sides of bowl once. Add flour; process until mixture forms a ball. Continue to process 2 minutes or until smooth and elastic. Wrap in plastic wrap, and let stand 10 minutes. Follow procedure for Basic Egg Pasta. Yield: 4½ cups (104 calories per ½-cup serving).

PROTEIN 3.4 FAT 1.3 CARBOHYDRATE 19.7 CHOLESTEROL 22
IRON 1.2 SODIUM 85 CALCIUM 4

CURRIED PASTA

2 eggs
1 tablespoon curry powder
1 teaspoon olive oil
½ teaspoon salt
½ teaspoon turmeric
⅛ teaspoon ground red pepper
1½ cups unbleached flour
2 tablespoons water

Position knife blade in food processor bowl; add first 6 ingredients. Process 30 seconds. Add flour; process 30 seconds or until pea-size balls form. Slowly add water through food chute with processor running; blend until mixture forms a ball. Continue to process 2 minutes or until smooth and elastic. Wrap in plastic wrap; let stand 10 minutes. Follow procedure for Basic Egg Pasta. Yield: 4½ cups (91 calories per ½-cup serving).

PROTEIN 3.5 FAT 1.9 CARBOHYDRATE 15.0 CHOLESTEROL 47
IRON 1.2 SODIUM 145 CALCIUM 10

SPICY SESAME PASTA

3 tablespoons sesame seeds, toasted
2 eggs
1 tablespoon sesame oil
½ teaspoon salt
½ teaspoon crushed red pepper
1½ cups unbleached flour
2 tablespoons water

Position knife blade in food processor bowl. Add sesame seeds; process 30 seconds or until minced. Add eggs, oil, salt, and red pepper; process 30 seconds or until blended. Add flour, and process 30 seconds to 1 minute or until mixture forms pea-size balls. Slowly add water through food chute with processor running, blending until mixture forms a ball. Continue to process 2 minutes or until dough is smooth and elastic. Wrap dough in plastic wrap; let stand 10 minutes. Follow procedure for Basic Egg Pasta. Yield: 5 cups (103 calories per ½-cup serving).

PROTEIN 3.6   FAT 3.9   CARBOHYDRATE 13.8   CHOLESTEROL 40
IRON 1.3   SODIUM 131   CALCIUM 33

SWEET RED PEPPER PASTA

1 large sweet red pepper (½ pound), seeded
  and cut into 1-inch cubes
Olive oil-flavored vegetable cooking spray
1 egg
1 teaspoon olive oil
½ teaspoon salt
1¾ cups unbleached flour

Place pepper cubes in an 11- x 7- x 2-inch baking dish coated with cooking spray. Cover and bake at 400° for 45 minutes or until peppers are soft, stirring every 15 minutes. Remove from oven; uncover and let cool.

Position knife blade in food processor bowl; add pepper cubes. Process until smooth, scraping

sides of processor bowl occasionally. Add egg, olive oil, and salt. Process 30 seconds or until mixture is blended. Add flour, and process 30 seconds to 1 minute or until mixture forms a ball. Continue to process 2 minutes or until dough is smooth and elastic. Wrap dough in plastic wrap, and let stand 10 minutes. Follow procedure for Basic Egg Pasta. Yield: 5 cups (87 calories per ½-cup serving).

PROTEIN 2.9   FAT 1.3   CARBOHYDRATE 16.1   CHOLESTEROL 20
IRON 1.1   SODIUM 125   CALCIUM 4

CORKSCREW PASTA TOSS

3 tablespoons sun-dried tomatoes (without salt
  or oil)
1¾ cups diced tomato
½ cup sliced green onions
2 teaspoons olive oil
1 tablespoon white wine vinegar
¼ teaspoon garlic powder
¼ teaspoon ground white pepper
6 ounces tri-colored corkscrew macaroni,
  uncooked
2 tablespoons minced fresh basil
1 cup (4 ounces) shredded part-skim
  mozzarella cheese

Place sun-dried tomatoes in a small bowl; cover with hot water. Let stand 15 minutes. Drain well; mince tomatoes.

Combine minced tomato, diced tomato, and next 5 ingredients in a large bowl. Cover and let stand at room temperature 2 hours.

Cook pasta according to package directions, omitting salt and fat; drain well.

Add hot pasta and basil to tomato mixture; toss well. Top with shredded cheese. Yield: 10 servings (115 calories per ½-cup serving).

PROTEIN 5.7   FAT 3.1   CARBOHYDRATE 16.3   CHOLESTEROL 7
IRON 1.2   SODIUM 102   CALCIUM 97

CREAMY GORGONZOLA PASTA

8 ounces radiatore pasta, uncooked
1 cup part-skim ricotta cheese
½ cup water
1 cup frozen English peas, thawed
¼ teaspoon ground red pepper
¼ cup chopped fresh parsley
2 ounces Gorgonzola cheese, crumbled
1 tablespoon chopped walnuts,
   toasted

Cook pasta according to package directions, omitting salt and fat. Drain and set aside.

Combine ricotta cheese and water in container of an electric blender; top with cover, and process until smooth. Transfer mixture to a small saucepan. Stir in peas and red pepper; cook until thoroughly heated, stirring constantly.

Place pasta in a serving bowl. Add ricotta mixture and parsley; toss gently. Sprinkle with Gorgonzola cheese and walnuts. Serve immediately. Yield: 11 servings (142 calories per ½-cup serving).

PROTEIN 7.2 FAT 3.9 CARBOHYDRATE 18.7 CHOLESTEROL 11
IRON 1.2 SODIUM 118 CALCIUM 96

HOT SESAME NOODLES

3½ tablespoons creamy peanut butter
3 tablespoons brewed tea
3 tablespoons rice vinegar
2 tablespoons low-sodium soy sauce
1 tablespoon minced fresh ginger
2 teaspoons chili oil
1 teaspoon honey
½ teaspoon sesame oil
8 ounces capellini (angel hair pasta),
   uncooked
2 tablespoons sesame seeds, toasted
3 tablespoons sliced green onions

Combine first 8 ingredients in container of an electric blender or food processor; top with cover, and process until smooth.

Cook pasta according to package directions, omitting salt and fat; drain. Place pasta in a serving bowl. Add peanut butter sauce and sesame seeds; toss well. Sprinkle with green onions. Serve immediately. Yield: 8 servings (177 calories per ½-cup serving).

PROTEIN 6.1 FAT 6.5 CARBOHYDRATE 24.0 CHOLESTEROL 0
IRON 1.6 SODIUM 135 CALCIUM 29

CHEESY CHILE FETTUCCINE

8 ounces fettuccine, uncooked
1 cup evaporated skimmed milk
1 tablespoon cornstarch
3 ounces Brie cheese, rind removed and
   softened
2 (4-ounce) cans chopped green chiles,
   drained
¾ cup peeled, seeded, and diced tomato
Fresh chervil sprigs (optional)

Cook fettuccine according to package directions, omitting salt and fat. Drain well, and set aside.

Combine milk and cornstarch in a medium saucepan; stir well using a wire whisk. Cook over medium heat, stirring frequently, until thickened. Cut cheese into small pieces, and add to milk mixture; cook over low heat until cheese melts, stirring constantly. Stir in chiles. Place pasta in a bowl. Pour sauce over pasta; toss gently. Sprinkle with tomato. Garnish with chervil sprigs, if desired. Yield: 8 servings (172 calories per ½-cup serving).

PROTEIN 9.1 FAT 3.5 CARBOHYDRATE 28.0 CHOLESTEROL 12
IRON 1.4 SODIUM 107 CALCIUM 126

CAPELLINI WITH ROASTED TOMATOES AND GOAT CHEESE

2 tablespoons olive oil
6 cloves garlic, halved
6 green onions, cut into 1-inch pieces
20 small cherry tomatoes
6 ounces capellini (angel hair pasta), uncooked
½ pound firm tofu, drained and diced
4 ounces goat cheese, crumbled
2 tablespoons pine nuts, toasted
1 teaspoon freshly ground pepper

Pour olive oil into a 13- x 9- x 2-inch baking dish. Add garlic, and toss to coat. Bake at 400° for 10 minutes. Add green onions, and toss to coat. Bake an additional 10 minutes. Add tomatoes, and stir well. Reduce heat to 375°, and bake 6 to 8 minutes or until vegetables are golden; remove from oven, and set aside.

Cook pasta according to package directions, omitting salt and fat; drain.

Place pasta in a large bowl. Add green onion mixture, diced tofu, goat cheese, toasted pine nuts, and pepper; toss gently to combine. Serve immediately. Yield: 6 servings (268 calories per 1-cup serving).

PROTEIN 11.4 FAT 13.4 CARBOHYDRATE 27.8 CHOLESTEROL 17
IRON 4.2 SODIUM 223 CALCIUM 158

A MAIN EVENT

For a recipe to be classified as a main dish in *Cooking Light*, it must contain at least 10 grams of protein per serving. If the analysis shows less than 10 grams, the recipe is considered a side dish accompaniment.

A filling one-dish meal, Colorful Ziti Medley boasts the flavors of fresh asparagus, toasted pine nuts, and Parmesan cheese.

COLORFUL ZITI MEDLEY

1 large sweet red pepper
1 large sweet yellow pepper
1 large green pepper
¾ pound fresh asparagus
Vegetable cooking spray
2 cloves garlic, minced
1 tablespoon lemon juice
¾ cup part-skim ricotta cheese
¾ cup plain nonfat yogurt
6 ounces ziti pasta, uncooked
¼ cup freshly grated Parmesan cheese
2 tablespoons pine nuts, toasted

Cut peppers in half lengthwise; remove and discard seeds and membrane. Place peppers, skin side up, on an ungreased baking sheet; flatten peppers with palm of hand. Broil 5½ inches from heat 15 to 20 minutes or until peppers blister and turn dark. Place peppers in ice water for 5 minutes. Peel and discard skins from peppers. Cut into julienne strips, and set aside.

Snap off tough ends of asparagus. Remove scales with a knife or vegetable peeler, if desired. Cut asparagus into 1-inch pieces. Cook asparagus in a small amount of boiling water 2 to 3 minutes or until crisp-tender. Drain well, and set aside.

Coat a large nonstick skillet with cooking spray; place over medium-high heat until hot. Add pepper strips and garlic; sauté 2 minutes. Add asparagus; sauté 1 minute. Stir in lemon juice. Remove from heat, and set aside.

Combine ricotta cheese and yogurt in container of an electric blender or food processor; top with cover, and process until smooth. Add ricotta mixture to pepper mixture.

Cook pasta according to package directions, omitting salt and fat. Drain. Add pasta to ricotta cheese mixture, and toss well to combine. Transfer to a large serving bowl; sprinkle with Parmesan cheese and pine nuts. Yield: 6 servings (236 calories per 1-cup serving).

PROTEIN 13.6 FAT 6.7 CARBOHYDRATE 32.0 CHOLESTEROL 14
IRON 2.7 SODIUM 158 CALCIUM 237

SAGE-CHICKEN AND PASTA

Olive oil-flavored vegetable cooking spray
3 (4-ounce) skinned, boned chicken breast
  halves, cut into strips
1 medium-size purple onion, thinly sliced
1 medium carrot, thinly sliced
1 clove garlic, minced
¼ cup water
2 tablespoons Chablis or other dry white wine
6 ounces spaghetti, uncooked
1 tablespoon reduced-calorie margarine
3 plum tomatoes, seeded and chopped
¼ cup sliced ripe olives
¼ cup chopped fresh parsley
1 tablespoon minced fresh sage
¼ cup freshly grated Parmesan cheese

Coat a large nonstick skillet with cooking spray;
place over medium-high heat until hot. Add chicken,
onion, carrot, and garlic; sauté 4 minutes or until
chicken is lightly browned. Add water and wine;
reduce heat to medium, and simmer, uncovered,
5 minutes. Remove from heat; set aside.

Cook pasta according to package directions,
omitting salt and fat. Drain well. Place pasta in a
large serving bowl; add margarine, and toss until
margarine melts. Add reserved chicken mixture,
tomato, olives, parsley, and sage; toss gently. Sprinkle with Parmesan cheese. Yield: 6 servings (220
calories per 1-cup serving).

PROTEIN 19.1 FAT 4.4 CARBOHYDRATE 25.4 CHOLESTEROL 36
IRON 2.1 SODIUM 191 CALCIUM 85

FETTUCCINE WITH SHRIMP AND SPINACH

½ cup part-skim ricotta cheese
½ cup nonfat plain yogurt
¼ cup nonfat buttermilk
¼ cup grated Parmesan cheese
½ teaspoon chicken-flavored bouillon
  granules
¼ teaspoon garlic powder
¼ teaspoon salt
¼ teaspoon crushed red pepper
1 pound medium-size fresh shrimp,
  peeled and deveined
10½ ounces fettuccine, uncooked
2 cups shredded fresh spinach

Combine first 8 ingredients in a medium bowl;
stir well. Set aside.

Bring 1 quart of water to a boil in a large saucepan; add shrimp, and cook 3 to 5 minutes. Drain
well; rinse with water, and drain again. Set
shrimp aside.

Cook fettuccine in a Dutch oven, according to
package directions, omitting salt and fat; drain.
Immediately return fettuccine to pan; add spinach,
and stir mixture well to combine. Cover and let
stand 1 to 2 minutes or until spinach wilts. Add
ricotta mixture and shrimp, stirring well to combine. Serve immediately. Yield: 8 servings (229
calories per 1-cup serving).

PROTEIN 18.5 FAT 4.1 CARBOHYDRATE 31.4 CHOLESTEROL 67
IRON 2.6 SODIUM 315 CALCIUM 185

---

*Bean and Vegetable Tortilla Stacks
(page 137) are ideal for a quick and
easy supper. Stuffed with garbanzo
beans, shredded carrot, and two types
of cheese, the entire family will enjoy
this filling entrée.*

Satisfy even the heartiest appetite with Wild Mushroom Lasagna Roll-Ups. Just add a fresh green salad and a beverage to complete the meal.

WILD MUSHROOM LASAGNA ROLL-UPS

1 cup water
1 cup Burgundy or other dry red wine
½ ounce dried porcini mushrooms
¾ pound fresh shiitake mushrooms, chopped
1 (14½-ounce) can no-salt-added whole
    tomatoes, drained and chopped
½ cup sliced green onions
1 tablespoon low-sodium soy sauce
1 teaspoon sugar
1 teaspoon dried whole marjoram
2 tablespoons no-salt-added tomato paste
Vegetable cooking spray
1 cup part-skim ricotta cheese
½ cup freshly grated Parmesan cheese
½ cup minced fresh parsley
8 whole wheat lasagna noodles, uncooked
Tomato Sauce
Fresh marjoram sprigs (optional)

Combine water and wine in saucepan; bring to a boil. Add dried mushrooms. Cover, reduce heat, and simmer 30 minutes. Drain mushrooms, reserving 1 cup liquid; chop mushrooms. Set aside.

Place reserved liquid in a saucepan. Stir in shiitake mushrooms and next 5 ingredients. Cook over medium heat 20 minutes or until liquid is absorbed, stirring occasionally. Stir in tomato paste and porcini mushrooms. Spoon into an 8-inch square dish coated with cooking spray.

Combine cheeses and parsley in a small bowl.

Cook noodles according to package directions, omitting salt and fat. Drain well. Spread cheese mixture evenly on one side of each lasagna noodle. Roll lasagna noodles up, jellyroll fashion, beginning at narrow end. Arrange rolls, seam side down, over mushroom mixture. Bake at 300° for 10 to 12 minutes or until thoroughly heated.

Spoon Tomato Sauce evenly over lasagna rolls. Garnish with fresh marjoram sprigs, if desired. Yield: 8 servings (332 calories per serving).

Tomato Sauce

½ (14½-ounce) can no-salt-added stewed tomatoes, undrained and chopped
½ tablespoon cornstarch
¼ teaspoon dried whole basil

Combine all ingredients in a small saucepan; stir well. Cook over medium heat, stirring constantly, until mixture thickens and comes to a boil. Yield: ¾ cup.

PROTEIN 13.8 FAT 6.1 CARBOHYDRATE 51.6 CHOLESTEROL 43
IRON 2.3 SODIUM 228 CALCIUM 212

BEAN AND VEGETABLE TORTILLA STACKS

1½ cups (6 ounces) shredded farmer cheese, divided
1 cup part-skim ricotta cheese
1 cup shredded carrot
½ cup chopped radish
¼ cup chopped ripe olives
1 (15-ounce) can garbanzo beans, drained
3 cloves garlic, halved
½ cup firmly packed parsley sprigs
3 green onions, cut into ½-inch pieces
1 tablespoon lemon juice
½ teaspoon ground cumin
12 (6-inch) corn tortillas
Green or sweet red pepper rings (optional)
Red Chile Sauce

Combine 1 cup farmer cheese and next 4 ingredients; stir well, and set aside.

Position knife blade in food processor bowl; add garbanzo beans and garlic. Process bean mixture 1 minute or until smooth. Add parsley sprigs, green onions, lemon juice, and cumin; process 10 seconds or until onion is minced, scraping sides of processor bowl occasionally.

Place 4 tortillas on an ungreased baking sheet. Spread each with one-eighth of bean mixture; top with one-eighth of cheese mixture. Repeat with remaining tortillas, bean mixture, and cheese mixture, ending with remaining 4 tortillas. Sprinkle remaining ½ cup farmer cheese evenly over stacks. Bake at 375° for 15 minutes or until thoroughly heated. Cut each in half. Garnish with pepper rings, if desired. Serve with Red Chile Sauce. Yield: 8 servings (248 calories per serving).

Red Chile Sauce

1 large dried pasilla chile pepper
1 medium onion, quartered
4 cloves garlic, halved
1 (28-ounce) can plum tomatoes, drained
½ teaspoon ground cumin
¼ teaspoon hot sauce

Wash chile; remove stem, seeds, and veins. Place chile in a bowl; add boiling water to cover. Let stand 15 minutes or until chile is soft; drain and coarsely chop.

Position knife blade in food processor bowl; add chile, onion, and garlic. Pulse 4 or 5 times or until finely chopped. Add tomato, cumin, and hot sauce; process 1 minute or until smooth. Yield: 2 cups.

PROTEIN 13.3 FAT 7.6 CARBOHYDRATE 35.0 CHOLESTEROL 10
IRON 3.9 SODIUM 320 CALCIUM 218

TRYING TORTILLAS

Tortillas are to Mexico what bread is to this country. These thin pancakes of corn or flour are often fried and made into chips, taco shells, or flat crisp tostados. But another way to enjoy them is to simply warm them briefly in the oven.

Most stores carry several varieties of tortillas—corn, blue corn, whole wheat, or white flour—in the refrigerator case. If well wrapped and refrigerated, flour tortillas will stay fresh for at least a week. For longer storage, flour tortillas freeze well; the corn varieties, however, do not resoften if frozen. Refrigerate corn tortillas and eat within 3 to 5 days.

BAKED BEANS WITH HOT TOMATO SAUCE

1 (16-ounce) package dried navy beans
1½ quarts water
1 (12-ounce) bottle dark beer
1⅓ cups chopped onion
6 cloves garlic, minced
1 tablespoon chicken-flavored bouillon granules
¼ cup firmly packed brown sugar
¼ cup reduced-calorie chili sauce
3 jalapeño peppers, seeded and minced
3 tablespoons vinegar
1½ tablespoons reduced-sodium
    Worcestershire sauce
½ teaspoon ground cinnamon
Vegetable cooking spray
Hot Tomato Sauce

Sort and wash beans; place in a Dutch oven. Cover with water to a depth of 2 inches above beans; let soak overnight. Drain and rinse beans. Combine beans, 1½ quarts water, beer, onion, garlic, and bouillon granules in pan. Bring to a boil; cover, reduce heat, and simmer 1½ hours. Drain bean mixture, reserving 1½ cups liquid.

Combine bean mixture, reserved cooking liquid, brown sugar, and next 5 ingredients; stir well. Pour mixture into a 2½-quart casserole coated with cooking spray. Bake, uncovered, at 350° for 1 hour and 15 minutes, or until beans are tender. Spoon 1 cup beans into each individual serving bowl, and top each with ⅓ cup Hot Tomato Sauce. Yield: 6 servings (271 calories per serving).

Hot Tomato Sauce

2 cups peeled, seeded, and diced tomato
4 green onions, minced
1 jalapeño pepper, seeded and minced
1 tablespoon minced fresh basil
1 tablespoon vinegar
2 teaspoons sugar
1 clove garlic, minced
¼ teaspoon salt
¼ teaspoon ground allspice
¼ teaspoon ground red pepper

Combine all ingredients in a small bowl; stir well. Cover and chill at least 24 hours. Serve with a slotted spoon. Yield: 2 cups.

PROTEIN 13.9   FAT 1.3   CARBOHYDRATE 53.8   CHOLESTEROL 0
IRON 4.0   SODIUM 417   CALCIUM 135

TEX-MEX PATTIES

2 (16-ounce) cans pinto beans, drained
    and mashed
1 cup chopped onion
1 cup yellow cornmeal, divided
2 poblano chiles, seeded and minced
2 cups (8 ounces) shredded 40% less-fat
    Cheddar cheese
2 egg whites, lightly beaten
½ teaspoon chili powder
¼ teaspoon hot sauce
Vegetable cooking spray
2 tablespoons plus 2 teaspoons melted
    reduced-calorie margarine, divided
Salad Salsa

Combine beans, onion, and ¾ cup cornmeal; stir well. Add chiles and next 4 ingredients, stirring well. Shape mixture into 8 (1-inch-thick) patties. Coat patties with remaining ¼ cup cornmeal. Place patties on a baking sheet coated with cooking spray; drizzle each patty with 1 teaspoon margarine. Bake at 425° for 10 minutes; turn patties, and bake an additional 10 minutes. Top each with ¼ cup Salad Salsa. Serve immediately. Yield: 8 servings (254 calories per serving).

Salad Salsa

1 cup seeded, diced tomato
1 clove garlic, minced
1 stalk celery, minced
2 tablespoons sliced green onion
⅓ cup diced avocado
½ cup minced fresh cilantro
⅓ cup frozen whole kernel corn, thawed
¼ cup unsweetened orange juice
1 tablespoon lime juice

Combine all ingredients in a small bowl, stirring well to combine. Cover and let stand at least 1 hour. Yield: 2 cups.

PROTEIN 11.5 FAT 8.3 CARBOHYDRATE 37.0 CHOLESTEROL 15
IRON 2.0 SODIUM 450 CALCIUM 233

CURRIED LENTILS AND RICE

1 tablespoon olive oil
10 shallots, minced
2 cloves garlic, minced
8 cups canned low-sodium chicken broth,
    undiluted
1 pound dried lentils
½ cup sliced green onions
1 tablespoon plus 2 teaspoons chili
    powder
1 tablespoon ground coriander
2 teaspoons ground turmeric
⅓ cup lime juice
¼ teaspoon salt
5 cups cooked long-grain rice (cooked
    without salt or fat)

Heat olive oil in a Dutch oven over medium-high heat until hot. Add shallots and garlic; sauté until shallots are tender.

Add chicken broth and next 5 ingredients, stirring well. Bring to a boil; cover, reduce heat, and simmer 25 minutes or until lentils are tender. Stir in lime juice and salt.

Place ½ cup cooked rice in each individual serving bowl, and spoon 1 cup lentil mixture over each serving. Yield: 10 servings (326 calories per serving).

PROTEIN 16.7 FAT 2.4 CARBOHYDRATE 58.9 CHOLESTEROL 0
IRON 6.0 SODIUM 87 CALCIUM 61

SPICY VEGETABLE RAGOÛT

1 (1-pound) eggplant, cut into ¾-inch cubes
3 tablespoons olive oil, divided
3 cloves garlic, sliced
3 cups chopped onion
1 tablespoon dried whole thyme
2¼ cups diced zucchini
1⅔ cups diced sweet red pepper
2 jalapeño peppers, seeded and minced
1 (28-ounce) can plum tomatoes, undrained
    and coarsely chopped
5 large fresh plum tomatoes, diced
½ cup Burgundy or other dry red wine
1 tablespoon dried whole oregano
1 teaspoon fennel seeds, crushed
¼ teaspoon salt
1 (19-ounce) can cannellini beans, drained
2 tablespoons lemon juice
⅓ cup chopped fresh cilantro
5½ cups cooked linguine (cooked without
    salt or fat)
1 cup plus 1½ teaspoons freshly grated
    Parmesan cheese

Combine eggplant, 2 tablespoons olive oil, garlic, onion, and thyme in a bowl; toss gently. Place mixture into a 13- x 9- x 2-inch baking dish. Cover and bake at 350° for 20 minutes; uncover and stir well. Bake, uncovered, an additional 15 to 20 minutes or until eggplant is tender.

Heat remaining 1 tablespoon oil in a Dutch oven; add zucchini, sweet red pepper, and jalapeño pepper. Sauté 5 to 7 minutes or until vegetables are tender. Add chopped tomato and next 5 ingredients; bring to a boil. Reduce heat, and simmer, uncovered, 15 minutes. Stir in eggplant mixture, beans, and lemon juice; simmer 2 minutes. Remove from heat, and stir in cilantro.

Place ½ cup cooked linguine on each individual serving plate; spoon 1 cup vegetable mixture over each serving. Top each with 1½ tablespoons cheese. Yield: 11 servings (257 calories per serving).

PROTEIN 11.1 FAT 7.6 CARBOHYDRATE 37.6 CHOLESTEROL 7
IRON 3.7 SODIUM 427 CALCIUM 204

CUBAN BLACK BEANS AND RICE

1 pound dried black beans
Vegetable cooking spray
½ cup chopped onion
½ cup chopped green pepper
2 cloves garlic, minced
5 cups water
1 (6-ounce) can no-salt-added tomato
  paste
1 tablespoon vinegar
½ teaspoon sugar
½ teaspoon salt
½ teaspoon ground cumin
½ teaspoon hot sauce
4½ cups cooked long-grain rice (cooked
  without salt or fat)
½ cup plus 1 tablespoon (2¼ ounces) finely
  shredded 40% less-fat Cheddar cheese
½ cup plus 1 tablespoon peeled, seeded,
  and chopped tomato
½ cup plus 1 tablespoon chopped
  green onions

Sort and wash beans; place in a large Dutch oven. Cover with water to a depth of 3 inches above beans; let soak 8 hours. Drain well.

Coat a small nonstick skillet with cooking spray; place over medium-high heat until hot. Add onion, green pepper, and garlic; sauté until tender.

Combine beans, sautéed onion mixture, 5 cups water, and next 6 ingredients in pan; bring to a boil. Cover, reduce heat, and simmer 1½ hours or until beans are tender, stirring occasionally.

Place ½ cup rice in each individual serving bowl. Spoon 1 cup beans over rice, and top each serving with 1 tablespoon each of cheese, tomato, and green onions. Yield: 9 servings (340 calories per serving).

PROTEIN 15.8 FAT 2.2 CARBOHYDRATE 66.2 CHOLESTEROL 4
IRON 4.3 SODIUM 186 CALCIUM 136

SOUTHWESTERN GRAIN BURRITOS

2 cups water
1 cup whole grain wheat
¼ cup plus 2 tablespoons canned low-sodium
  chicken broth, undiluted
¼ cup lime juice
1 (4-ounce) can chopped green chiles, drained
1 tablespoon olive oil
10 sprigs fresh cilantro
½ teaspoon ground cumin
3 cups cooked brown rice (cooked without salt
  or fat)
1 (15-ounce) can black beans, rinsed and
  drained
1 (8¾-ounce) can no-salt-added whole kernel
  corn, drained
½ cup finely chopped sweet red pepper
½ cup thinly sliced green onions
8 (6-inch) corn tortillas
2 cups shredded leaf lettuce
2 cups seeded, chopped tomato

Combine water and whole grain wheat in a medium saucepan. Bring to a boil; cover, reduce heat, and simmer 1 hour, stirring occasionally. Drain well, and set aside.

Combine broth and next 5 ingredients in container of an electric blender; top with cover, and process until smooth. Combine broth mixture, cooked wheat, rice, beans, corn, sweet red pepper, and green onions; stir well. Set aside.

Place tortillas on baking sheets. Bake at 350° for 15 to 20 minutes or until crisp. Transfer to individual serving plates. Spoon ¼ cup lettuce onto each tortilla. Top each with 1 cup rice mixture and ¼ cup chopped tomato. Serve immediately. Yield: 8 servings (320 calories per serving).

PROTEIN 11.1 FAT 4.7 CARBOHYDRATE 61.7 CHOLESTEROL 0
IRON 4.2 SODIUM 180 CALCIUM 85

As colorful as it is nutritious, Vegetarian Couscous Casserole is a tasty meatless entrée.

VEGETARIAN COUSCOUS CASSEROLE

1½ cups water
¼ teaspoon salt
1 cup couscous, uncooked
1 (15-ounce) can black beans, drained
1 (8¾-ounce) can no-salt-added whole kernel
  corn, drained
1 (8-ounce) can sliced water chestnuts, drained
1 (7-ounce) jar roasted red peppers in water,
  drained and cut into strips
⅓ cup minced green onions
2 tablespoons minced pickled jalapeño pepper
1 cup part-skim ricotta cheese
2 tablespoons balsamic vinegar
2 teaspoons sesame oil
1 teaspoon ground cumin
Vegetable cooking spray
6 cups fresh spinach leaves

Combine water and salt in a saucepan; bring to a boil. Remove from heat. Add couscous; stir well. Cover and let stand 5 minutes or until couscous is tender and liquid is absorbed. Add black beans and next 5 ingredients; stir gently.

Combine ricotta cheese, vinegar, oil, and cumin; stir into couscous mixture. Spoon mixture into an 11- x 7- x 2-inch baking dish coated with cooking spray. Bake, uncovered, at 350° for 25 minutes or until thoroughly heated.

Cut spinach leaves into thin strips. Place 1 cup spinach on each serving plate; spoon couscous mixture evenly over spinach. Yield: 6 servings (299 calories per serving).

PROTEIN 15.3   FAT 5.8   CARBOHYDRATE 47.4   CHOLESTEROL 13
IRON 3.6   SODIUM 206   CALCIUM 185

VEGETABLE POLENTA SQUARES

6 cups water
½ teaspoon salt
2 cups instant polenta, uncooked
Vegetable cooking spray
1 teaspoon olive oil
2 cups diced eggplant
2 cups chopped fresh shiitake mushrooms
1 cup diced zucchini
¾ cup chopped onion
2 cloves garlic, minced
2 (14½-ounce) cans no-salt-added whole
    tomatoes, drained
2 tablespoons minced fresh thyme
2 cups (8 ounces) shredded part-skim
    mozzarella cheese, divided

Combine water and salt in a saucepan; bring to a boil. Add polenta in a slow, steady stream, stirring constantly. Reduce heat; cook, uncovered, over low heat 20 minutes or until mixture pulls away from sides of pan.

Pour mixture into a 15- x 10- x 1-inch jellyroll pan coated with cooking spray; spread mixture evenly, working quickly. Let cool.

Coat a large nonstick skillet with cooking spray; add oil. Place over medium-high heat until hot. Add eggplant, mushrooms, zucchini, onion, and garlic; sauté until tender.

Position knife blade in food processor bowl, and add whole tomatoes. Process until smooth. Add pureed tomato to vegetable mixture. Stir in minced fresh thyme.

Cut polenta into 16 pieces. Place 8 pieces in a 13- x 9- x 2-inch baking pan coated with cooking spray. Spoon one-half of vegetable mixture over polenta. Sprinkle with 1 cup mozzarella cheese. Top with remaining polenta, vegetable mixture, and cheese. Bake, uncovered, at 450° for 20 minutes or until thoroughly heated. Let polenta stand 10 minutes before serving. Yield: 8 servings (244 calories per serving).

PROTEIN 11.8 FAT 6.0 CARBOHYDRATE 36.3 CHOLESTEROL 16
IRON 2.5 SODIUM 291 CALCIUM 230

CURRIED WILD RICE AND ROASTED POTATOES

1 (6¾-ounce) package wild rice
2 teaspoons curry powder, divided
2 tablespoons reduced-calorie margarine,
    melted
Vegetable cooking spray
4 (8-ounce) baking potatoes, peeled and
    cut into 1-inch pieces
1¾ cups coarsely chopped onion
5 cloves garlic, minced
¼ teaspoon salt
Lentil Dal
Carrot Sauce
½ cup minced fresh parsley
2 medium tomatoes, cut into wedges

Wash rice in 3 changes of hot water; drain. Cook according to package directions, omitting salt and fat. Stir ½ teaspoon curry powder into rice.

Place margarine in 15- x 10- x 1-inch jellyroll pan coated with cooking spray. Add potato, onion, and garlic; stir well. Combine remaining 1½ teaspoons curry powder and salt; sprinkle over potato mixture. Bake, uncovered, at 450° for 40 to 50 minutes or until potatoes are tender and golden brown, stirring occasionally. Add wild rice, stirring well. Reduce heat to 350°, and bake 10 minutes or until thoroughly heated. Spoon mixture evenly into individual serving bowls. Top each serving with 4½ tablespoons Lentil Dal and 3 tablespoons Carrot Sauce; sprinkle with minced parsley. Serve with tomato wedges. Yield: 8 servings (285 calories per serving).

Lentil Dal

1 cup water
¾ cup canned low-sodium chicken broth,
    undiluted
½ cup dried lentils
1 jalapeño pepper, seeded and minced
1½ teaspoons ground ginger
½ teaspoon ground cumin
½ teaspoon ground turmeric
¼ teaspoon salt

Combine all ingredients in a small saucepan; bring to a boil. Reduce heat; cover, and simmer 20 minutes or until lentils are very tender. Position knife blade in food processor bowl; add lentil mixture. Process 30 seconds or until smooth. Return to saucepan; cook over medium-low heat until thoroughly heated. Yield: 2¼ cups.

Carrot Sauce

1½ cups sliced carrot
½ cup plus 2 tablespoons canned low-sodium
   chicken broth, undiluted
1 teaspoon ground cumin
⅔ cup part-skim ricotta cheese

Combine carrot, broth, and cumin in saucepan; bring to a boil. Reduce heat; cover and simmer 20 minutes or until carrot is very tender.

Place ricotta cheese in container of an electric blender; top with cover, and process mixture until smooth, scraping sides of container as necessary. Add carrot mixture, and process until smooth. Yield: 1½ cups.

PROTEIN 12.4 FAT 4.3 CARBOHYDRATE 51.3 CHOLESTEROL 6
IRON 3.4 SODIUM 222 CALCIUM 102

CILANTRO-STUFFED BAKED POTATOES

8 (8-ounce) baking potatoes
½ cup sliced green onions
1 cup diced tomato
Cilantro Cheese Sauce
1 cup (4 ounces) shredded reduced-fat
   Monterey Jack cheese

Wash potatoes; bake at 400° for 45 minutes to 1 hour or until done. Let potatoes cool to touch. Cut potatoes in half lengthwise, and fluff with a fork. Top each potato half with 1½ teaspoons green onions, 1 tablespoon tomato, 1½ tablespoons Cilantro Cheese Sauce, and 1 tablespoon shredded cheese. Serve immediately. Yield 8 servings (346 calories per serving).

Cilantro Cheese Sauce

2 (8-ounce) cartons fromage blanc
1 cup chopped fresh cilantro
½ cup firmly packed chopped fresh parsley
¼ cup grated Parmesan cheese
1 clove garlic, halved
¼ teaspoon salt

Position knife blade in food processor bowl; add all ingredients, and process until smooth. Yield: 1¾ cups.

PROTEIN 16.6 FAT 3.7 CARBOHYDRATE 62.9 CHOLESTEROL 12
IRON 3.8 SODIUM 304 CALCIUM 244

NUTTY RICE AND CHEESE CASSEROLE

1 (8-ounce) carton plain nonfat yogurt
1 tablespoon all-purpose flour
1½ cups 1% low-fat cottage cheese
1 egg white
½ teaspoon hot sauce
4 cups cooked brown rice (cooked without salt
   or fat)
½ cup sliced green onions
½ cup grated Parmesan cheese, divided
¼ cup slivered almonds, toasted and chopped
3 tablespoons minced fresh parsley
Vegetable cooking spray

Combine yogurt and flour in a medium bowl; stir until smooth. Add cottage cheese, egg white, and hot sauce, stirring well. Stir in brown rice, green onions, ¼ cup Parmesan cheese, almonds, and parsley; spoon mixture into a 2-quart casserole coated with cooking spray.

Sprinkle casserole with remaining ¼ cup Parmesan cheese. Bake, uncovered, at 350° for 25 minutes or until thoroughly heated. Yield: 6 servings (274 calories per serving).

PROTEIN 17.1 FAT 6.4 CARBOHYDRATE 36.9 CHOLESTEROL 8
IRON 1.2 SODIUM 404 CALCIUM 238

SPINACH SOUFFLÉ ROLL

Vegetable cooking spray
3 tablespoons reduced-calorie margarine
3 tablespoons all-purpose flour
1 cup skim milk
½ cup (2 ounces) shredded 40% less-fat
    Cheddar cheese
⅛ teaspoon salt
3 eggs, separated
3 egg whites
¾ teaspoon cream of tartar
2 tablespoons grated Parmesan cheese
Spinach Filling
Peppery Fennel Sauce

Coat a 15- x 10- x 1-inch jellyroll pan with cooking spray. Line with wax paper. Coat wax paper with cooking spray; set aside.

Melt margarine in a heavy saucepan; add flour, stirring until smooth. Cook 1 minute, stirring constantly. Gradually add milk; cook over medium heat, stirring constantly, until mixture is thickened and bubbly. Remove from heat, and stir in Cheddar cheese and salt.

Beat egg yolks until thick and lemon colored. Gradually stir about one-fourth of hot mixture into yolks. Add to remaining hot mixture, stirring well.

Beat 6 egg whites (at room temperature) in a large bowl at high speed of an electric mixer until foamy. Add cream of tartar; beat until stiff peaks form. Fold one-third of egg whites into cheese mixture; carefully fold in remaining egg whites.

Pour mixture into prepared pan, spreading evenly. Bake at 350° for 15 to 20 minutes or until puffed and lightly browned. Loosen edges of soufflé with a metal spatula; let cool 15 minutes in pan on a wire rack. Turn soufflé out onto a double layer of wax paper sprinkled with Parmesan cheese. Carefully peel off wax paper. Spread Spinach Filling evenly over soufflé. Starting at short side and using wax paper for support, roll soufflé, jellyroll fashion. Cut roll into 8 slices. Spoon ¼ cup Peppery Fennel Sauce onto each serving plate, and top with slices of soufflé. Serve immediately. Yield: 8 servings (175 calories per serving).

Spinach Filling

2 (10-ounce) packages frozen chopped spinach
Vegetable cooking spray
¼ cup finely chopped green onions
½ cup (2 ounces) shredded 40% less-fat
    Cheddar cheese
⅓ cup low-fat sour cream
3 tablespoons grated Parmesan cheese
⅛ teaspoon garlic powder

Cook spinach according to package directions, omitting salt; drain and press dry between layers of paper towels.

Coat a nonstick skillet with cooking spray; place over medium-high heat until hot. Add green onions, and sauté 2 minutes or until tender. Stir in spinach, Cheddar cheese and remaining ingredients. Yield: 2 cups.

Peppery Fennel Sauce

1 pound sweet red peppers (about 3 medium),
    seeded
½ pound fennel bulb (about 1 small)
¼ cup canned low-sodium chicken broth,
    undiluted
1 to 2 teaspoons sherry vinegar
½ teaspoon ground red pepper
⅛ teaspoon salt

Cut sweet red peppers into 1-inch pieces; place in a 2½-quart casserole. Trim off tough outer stalks from fennel bulb; cut bulb in half lengthwise, and remove core. Cut fennel into 1-inch pieces; place in casserole. Add chicken broth; cover and bake at 350° for 25 to 30 minutes or until vegetables are tender. Remove from oven, and let cool 10 minutes.

Position knife blade in food processor bowl; add sweet red pepper mixture. Process until smooth, scraping sides of processor bowl twice. Add vinegar, ground red pepper, and salt; process until blended. Yield: 2 cups.

PROTEIN 12.0 FAT 9.5 CARBOHYDRATE 13.7 CHOLESTEROL 9
IRON 3.0 SODIUM 389 CALCIUM 299

A stunning main course, Goat Cheese and Red Pepper Soufflé will add flair to your menu.

GOAT CHEESE AND RED PEPPER SOUFFLÉ

Vegetable cooking spray
2 large sweet red peppers
6 ounces Montrachet goat cheese, crumbled
3 tablespoons reduced-calorie margarine
3 tablespoons all-purpose flour
1 cup skim milk
2 eggs, separated
3 tablespoons chopped fresh chives
5 egg whites
1 teaspoon cream of tartar

Cut a piece of aluminum foil long enough to fit around a 1½-quart soufflé dish, allowing a 1-inch overlap; fold lengthwise into thirds. Coat one side of foil and bottom of dish with cooking spray; wrap foil around outside of dish, coated side against dish, allowing it to extend 3 inches above rim. Secure with string.

Place peppers on a baking sheet. Broil 5½ inches from heat, turning with tongs as peppers blister and turn dark on all sides. Place peppers in a paper bag; seal and let stand 10 minutes to loosen skins. Peel; discard skins and seeds.

Position knife blade in food processor bowl; add roasted pepper and cheese. Process 1 minute or until pureed but not smooth. Set aside.

Melt margarine in a heavy saucepan over low heat. Add flour; stir until smooth. Cook 1 minute, stirring constantly. Gradually add milk, stirring constantly. Cook over medium heat, stirring constantly, until mixture is thickened and bubbly. Beat egg yolks until thick and lemon colored. Gradually stir about one-fourth of hot mixture into egg yolks; add to remaining hot mixture, stirring constantly. Stir in cheese mixture and chives.

Beat 7 egg whites (at room temperature) and cream of tartar at high speed of an electric mixer until stiff peaks form. Fold one-third of egg whites into cheese mixture; fold in remaining egg whites. Spoon into prepared dish. Bake on lower rack of oven at 375° for 30 minutes. Reduce temperature to 350°; bake 20 minutes or until set. Serve immediately. Yield: 6 servings (177 calories per serving).

PROTEIN 10.9 FAT 11.6 CARBOHYDRATE 7.9 CHOLESTEROL 93
IRON 1.0 SODIUM 474 CALCIUM 204

SUMMER VEGETABLE DINNER

1 small eggplant, cut into ½-inch cubes
2 tablespoons lemon juice
2 teaspoons olive oil
½ pound small fresh mushrooms, halved
2 medium-size yellow squash, cut into
    ½-inch-thick slices
2 small zucchini, cut into ½-inch-thick slices
1 medium-size sweet red pepper, seeded
    and cut into 1-inch cubes
3 tablespoons minced fresh basil
¾ teaspoon freshly ground pepper
¼ teaspoon salt
2 medium tomatoes, cut into wedges
8 ounces firm tofu, drained and cut into
    ½-inch cubes
1½ cups (6 ounces) shredded reduced-fat
    Monterey Jack cheese
5½ cups cooked brown rice (cooked without
    salt or fat)

Combine eggplant and lemon juice; toss well.
Heat oil in a Dutch oven over medium heat until
hot. Add eggplant, mushrooms, and next 6 ingredients; sauté 3 to 4 minutes or until vegetables
are crisp-tender. Cover and cook 3 minutes. Add
tomato, tofu, and cheese, stirring gently; cook,
uncovered, 2 minutes or until thoroughly heated.
Place brown rice on a serving platter. Spoon vegetable mixture over rice, and serve immediately.
Yield: 11 servings (211 calories per serving).

PROTEIN 10.8 FAT 6.0 CARBOHYDRATE 30.8 CHOLESTEROL 10
IRON 3.0 SODIUM 165 CALCIUM 205

BEAN AND TOFU JAMBALAYA

Vegetable cooking spray
½ cup chopped onion
½ cup chopped green pepper
1 clove garlic, minced
2 (14½-ounce) cans no-salt-added whole
    tomatoes, undrained and chopped
1 (15-ounce) can pinto beans, drained
1 (15.8-ounce) can Great Northern beans,
    drained
¼ cup low-sodium Worcestershire sauce
1 tablespoon vinegar
1 teaspoon chili powder
½ teaspoon salt
½ teaspoon dried whole thyme
½ teaspoon rubbed sage
½ teaspoon ground red pepper
½ teaspoon freshly ground pepper
¼ teaspoon garlic powder
⅔ cup long-grain rice, uncooked
6 ounces firm tofu, drained and cut into
    ½-inch cubes

Coat a large saucepan with cooking spray; place
over medium-high heat until hot. Add onion, green
pepper, and garlic; sauté until tender. Add tomato
and next 11 ingredients; stir well. Bring mixture to a boil; stir in rice. Cover, reduce heat, and
simmer 20 minutes. Add tofu, stirring gently; cover and cook an additional 5 minutes or until rice is
tender. Yield: 6 servings (235 calories per serving).

PROTEIN 10.3 FAT 2.4 CARBOHYDRATE 44.2 CHOLESTEROL 0
IRON 4.5 SODIUM 414 CALCIUM 110

*No one can resist Chestnut-Sage Stuffed
Pork Tenderloin (page 161), a savory
blend of chestnuts, sage, and seasonings.*

SWEET-AND-SOUR MEATBALLS WITH YELLOW RICE

1 pound ground chuck
⅓ cup fine, dry breadcrumbs
2 egg whites, lightly beaten
3 tablespoons minced fresh parsley
2 tablespoons minced onion
¼ teaspoon salt
¼ teaspoon garlic powder
¼ teaspoon pepper
Vegetable cooking spray
½ cup chopped onion
1 (14½-ounce) can no-salt-added whole
    tomatoes, drained and chopped
1 cup no-salt-added tomato sauce
½ cup jellied cranberry sauce
1 tablespoon lemon juice
⅛ teaspoon ground red pepper
3 cups cooked yellow rice (cooked without salt
    or fat)

Combine first 8 ingredients in a medium bowl; stir well. Shape mixture into 24 (1-inch) meatballs; place on a rack in a roasting pan coated with cooking spray. Bake at 350° for 25 minutes. Drain and pat dry with paper towels.

Coat a large nonstick skillet with cooking spray; place over medium-high heat until hot. Add onion; sauté until tender. Stir in tomato, tomato sauce, cranberry sauce, lemon juice, and red pepper; stir well. Bring to a boil; cover, reduce heat, and simmer 5 minutes. Stir in meatballs; cover and simmer an additional 10 minutes. Serve over cooked rice. Yield: 6 servings (349 calories per serving).

PROTEIN 19.5   FAT 10.3   CARBOHYDRATE 43.0   CHOLESTEROL 48
IRON 2.9   SODIUM 224   CALCIUM 48

DESKERCISE

Workout at the workplace? Create your own fitness center right at your desk by exercising while you are seated.

• Abdominal Strengtheners. Lift your left knee toward your right elbow as far as you can comfortably. Repeat knee lift 10 times, and change to opposite side.

• Alternate Leg Extensions. Extend your right leg forward, straighten it, and then lower it. Change to your left leg. Alternate in "can-can" style. Repeat 10 to 15 times for each leg.

• Knee Hugs. Pull your right knee to your chest. Hold 10 seconds and repeat with left knee. Repeat exercise 3 times.

• Torso Twist. Keeping legs planted on the floor, twist torso to the right, and look over your right shoulder. Repeat to the left side. Repeat 3 times.

• Sidebends. Keeping your back straight, bend your torso to the left and hold 5 seconds. Repeat on the right side. Repeat 3 times.

• Toe Touches. Reach forward and touch your toes. Hold 10 seconds and repeat 3 times.

HEARTY BEEF POT PIE

1¼ pounds lean round steak
Vegetable cooking spray
2 cups thinly sliced carrot
1 cup chopped onion
2 cloves garlic, minced
2 tablespoons all-purpose flour
1 teaspoon dried whole oregano
½ teaspoon dried whole thyme
¼ teaspoon salt
¼ teaspoon ground red pepper
1 (12-ounce) can light beer
Pastry

Trim fat from steak; cut steak into 1-inch pieces. Coat a large nonstick skillet with cooking spray; place over medium-high heat until hot. Add steak;

Filled with vegetables and beef, Hearty Beef Pot Pie is a tasty, no-fuss dish.

cook, turning occasionally, until browned on all sides. Set aside.

Wipe drippings from skillet with a paper towel; coat skillet with cooking spray. Add carrot, and sauté for 8 minutes, stirring frequently. Add onion and garlic; sauté until onion is tender. Combine flour and next 4 ingredients; stir well. Stir in flour mixture; cook 1 minute, stirring constantly. Add beer and reserved beef; stir well. Spoon beef mixture into a 9-inch deep-dish pieplate.

Roll pastry to an 11½-inch circle between 2 sheets of heavy-duty plastic wrap. Place in freezer 10 minutes or until plastic wrap can be removed easily. Remove bottom sheet of plastic wrap; fit pastry over beef mixture in pieplate. Remove top sheet of plastic wrap. Cut v-shaped slits in top crust for steam to escape. Fold edges under and flute; seal to edges of pieplate.

Bake at 425° for 30 minutes or until pastry is golden. Transfer to a wire rack. Let stand 10 minutes before serving. Yield: 8 servings (257 calories per serving).

Pastry

⅓ cup reduced-calorie margarine
1¼ cups all-purpose flour
⅛ teaspoon salt
3 to 4 tablespoons ice water
1 tablespoon all-purpose flour

Drop margarine by ½ teaspoonfuls onto wax paper; freeze 15 minutes or until hard.

Combine 1¼ cups flour and salt; add frozen margarine, and cut in with a pastry blender until mixture resembles coarse meal. Sprinkle ice water, 1 tablespoon at a time, evenly over surface. Stir with a fork until dough forms a ball.

Sprinkle 1 tablespoon flour evenly over work surface. Turn dough out onto floured surface, and knead 4 or 5 times. Flatten dough into a disk; wrap in heavy-duty plastic wrap, and chill 20 minutes. Yield: 1 (9-inch) top crust.

PROTEIN 18.3 FAT 9.7 CARBOHYDRATE 21.6 CHOLESTEROL 45
IRON 2.8 SODIUM 234 CALCIUM 27

SESAME-LEMON MARINATED STEAK

1 (1-pound) lean flank steak
½ cup lemon juice
1 tablespoon water
1 tablespoon dark sesame oil
1 teaspoon hot sauce
½ teaspoon garlic powder
Vegetable cooking spray
1 tablespoon sesame seeds, toasted
Lemon rind curls (optional)

Trim fat from steak. Place steak in a large shallow dish. Combine lemon juice and next 4 ingredients; pour over steak. Turn steaks to coat. Cover and marinate in refrigerator 8 hours; turn occasionally.

Remove steak from marinade, reserving marinade. Transfer marinade to a small saucepan; bring to a boil. Reduce heat, and simmer marinade 2 minutes.

Coat a grill rack with cooking spray; place on grill over medium-hot coals. Sprinkle sesame seeds over steak. Place steak on rack, and cook 3 minutes on each side or to desired degree of doneness, basting frequently with marinade.

Slice steak diagonally across grain into ¼-inch slices. Garnish with lemon rind curls, if desired. Yield: 4 servings (267 calories per serving).

PROTEIN 23.0 FAT 17.9 CARBOHYDRATE 3.1 CHOLESTEROL 61
IRON 2.4 SODIUM 83 CALCIUM 11

PEPPERY PINEAPPLE SWISS STEAK

1½ pounds lean round steak
¾ teaspoon black pepper
½ teaspoon chili powder
Vegetable cooking spray
½ teaspoon vegetable oil
1 (20-ounce) can pineapple chunks in juice,
    undrained
⅓ cup reduced-calorie chili sauce
¼ cup water
¼ teaspoon ground red pepper
⅛ teaspoon ground white pepper
½ cup sliced green onions
½ medium carrot, cut into julienne strips
¼ cup minced celery

Trim fat from steak; cut steak into 2-inch pieces. Place steak between 2 sheets of heavy-duty plastic wrap, and flatten to ¼-inch thickness, using a meat mallet or rolling pin. Sprinkle steak with black pepper and chili powder.

Coat a large nonstick skillet with cooking spray; add oil. Place over medium-high heat until hot. Add steak, and cook 1 minute on each side or until browned. Remove steak from skillet. Drain and pat dry with paper towels. Wipe drippings from skillet with a paper towel.

Drain pineapple, reserving liquid; set aside. Combine pineapple juice, chili sauce, and next 3 ingredients, stirring well; set aside.

Coat skillet with cooking spray; place over medium-high heat until hot. Add green onions, carrot, and celery; sauté until crisp-tender. Return steak to skillet. Add juice mixture; stir well. Cover, reduce heat, and simmer 1½ hours or until steak is tender. Stir in pineapple chunks, and simmer an additional 5 minutes or until thoroughly heated. Yield: 6 servings (294 calories per serving).

PROTEIN 22.6 FAT 13.8 CARBOHYDRATE 18.7 CHOLESTEROL 61
IRON 2.8 SODIUM 95 CALCIUM 27

MARINATED STEAK AND ONIONS

2 pounds lean round steak
2 large sweet onions
1 cup water
¼ cup low-sodium Worcestershire sauce
1 teaspoon beef-flavored bouillon
   granules
1 bay leaf
½ teaspoon crushed red pepper
¼ teaspoon ground nutmeg
⅛ teaspoon ground allspice
Vegetable cooking spray
Fresh parsley sprigs (optional)

Trim fat from steak. Cut onions into ¼-inch slices, and separate into rings.

Combine water and next 6 ingredients in a large zip-top heavy-duty plastic bag; add steak and onions. Seal and marinate in refrigerator at least 8 hours, turning occasionally.

Remove steak from bag, reserving onion and marinade. Place steak on rack of a broiler pan coated with vegetable cooking spray. Broil 5½ inches from heat 7 to 8 minutes on each side or to desired degree of doneness. Set steak aside, and keep warm.

Coat a large nonstick skillet with cooking spray, and place over medium-high heat until hot. Add onion, and sauté until crisp-tender. Add reserved marinade; cover, reduce heat, and simmer onion mixture 5 minutes or until onion is tender. Remove and discard bay leaf.

Transfer steak to a serving platter, and spoon onion mixture over steak. Garnish with fresh parsley sprigs, if desired. Yield: 8 servings (211 calories per serving).

PROTEIN 30.0   FAT 6.1   CARBOHYDRATE 7.5   CHOLESTEROL 77
IRON 2.9   SODIUM 205   CALCIUM 21

MUSHROOM-STUFFED BEEF TENDERLOIN

Vegetable cooking spray
1 (8-ounce) package presliced fresh
   mushrooms
4 ounces fresh shiitake mushrooms, coarsely
   chopped
½ cup chopped fresh parsley
3 tablespoons minced green onion
2 cloves garlic, minced
¼ cup freshly grated Parmesan cheese
¼ cup frozen egg substitute, thawed
2 tablespoons bourbon
½ teaspoon salt
1 (4½-pound) beef tenderloin

Coat a large nonstick skillet with cooking spray; place over medium-high heat until hot. Add mushrooms, parsley, onion, and garlic; sauté until tender. Remove from heat; stir in cheese, egg substitute, bourbon, and salt. Set aside.

Trim fat from tenderloin. Slice tenderloin lengthwise to, but not through, the center, leaving one long side connected. Spoon mushroom mixture into opening of tenderloin. Fold top side over mushroom mixture, and tie securely with heavy string at 2-inch intervals. Place tenderloin, seam side down, on a rack in a roasting pan coated with cooking spray. Insert meat thermometer into thickest part of tenderloin, if desired.

Heat oven to 500°; place tenderloin in oven. Reduce heat to 350°, and bake for 50 to 55 minutes or until meat thermometer registers 140° (rare) or 160° (medium). Remove from oven, and let stand 10 minutes. Slice diagonally across grain into ¼-inch-thick slices, and arrange on a serving platter. Yield: 18 servings (183 calories per serving).

PROTEIN 24.8   FAT 7.9   CARBOHYDRATE 1.6   CHOLESTEROL 71
IRON 3.4   SODIUM 158   CALCIUM 30

Veal Shanks À La Végétal, accompanied by julienned vegetables, will add a fresh flair to your meal.

VEAL SHANKS À LA VÉGÉTAL

6 (5-ounce) veal shanks
Vegetable cooking spray
½ cup Chablis or other dry white wine
½ cup chopped onion
½ cup thinly sliced celery
½ cup diced zucchini
½ cup shredded carrot
1 clove garlic, sliced
2 cups canned no-salt-added chicken broth,
 undiluted
2 tablespoons no-salt-added tomato paste
¼ teaspoon salt
¼ teaspoon pepper
12 small new potatoes (about 1 pound)
1 medium carrot, cut into julienne strips
1 small zucchini, cut into julienne strips

Trim fat from veal. Coat a Dutch oven with cooking spray; place over medium-high heat until hot. Add veal; cook 3 minutes on each side or until browned. Drain and pat dry with paper towels. Wipe drippings from pan with a paper towel.

Coat pan with cooking spray. Add wine and next 5 ingredients; bring to a boil, and cook 4 minutes over medium-high heat. Return shanks to pan. Stir in broth, tomato paste, salt, and pepper. Bring to a boil; cover, reduce heat, and simmer 1 hour or until veal is tender. Transfer veal to a platter; keep warm. Reserve vegetable mixture.

Wash potatoes. Cook in boiling water to cover 15 minutes or until tender; drain and cool slightly. Cut potatoes in quarters; set aside.

Arrange carrot and zucchini strips in a vegetable steamer over boiling water. Cover and steam 3 to 4 minutes or until crisp-tender.

Position knife blade in food processor bowl; add reserved vegetable mixture, and process until smooth. Divide pureed vegetable mixture among 6 serving plates, and top with shanks. Arrange potatoes, carrot, and zucchini around veal. Yield: 6 servings (257 calories per serving).

PROTEIN 24.5 FAT 8.0 CARBOHYDRATE 21.0 CHOLESTEROL 93
IRON 2.5 SODIUM 251 CALCIUM 58

VEAL-VEGETABLE LOAF

1 (10-ounce) package frozen chopped spinach,
 thawed
1 pound ground veal
1 cup soft breadcrumbs
¾ cup chopped onion
½ cup finely shredded carrot
4 egg whites
2 cloves garlic, minced
2 tablespoons minced fresh parsley
¼ teaspoon salt
¼ teaspoon ground red pepper
2 tablespoons white wine Worcestershire sauce
2 tablespoons no-salt-added vegetable juice
 cocktail
Vegetable cooking spray
¼ cup plus 2 tablespoons reduced-calorie chili
 sauce
2 tablespoons no-salt-added vegetable juice
 cocktail
¼ teaspoon dry mustard
Carrot curls (optional)

Drain spinach; press between paper towels to remove excess moisture. Combine spinach, veal, and next 10 ingredients in a large bowl; stir well. Spoon mixture into an 8½- x 4½- x 3-inch loafpan coated with cooking spray. Place loafpan in a 13- x 9- x 2-inch baking pan; add hot water to pan to a depth of 1 inch. Bake at 350° for 55 minutes. Remove loafpan from water bath; invert veal loaf onto a wire rack to drain fat. Pat loaf dry with paper towels.

Combine chili sauce, 2 tablespoons vegetable juice cocktail, and dry mustard in a small saucepan; cook over medium heat until thoroughly heated.

Slice veal loaf into 6 slices; place 1 slice on each of 6 individual serving plates. Spoon chili sauce mixture evenly over slices. Garnish with carrot curls, if desired. Yield: 6 servings (198 calories per serving).

PROTEIN 20.6 FAT 13.5 CARBOHYDRATE 15.9 CHOLESTEROL 62
IRON 2.2 SODIUM 384 CALCIUM 97

MUSHROOM-STUFFED VEAL CHOPS

Vegetable cooking spray
1 (8-ounce) package presliced fresh
  mushrooms
½ cup water
½ cup Chablis or other dry white wine
3 tablespoons minced fresh thyme, divided
½ teaspoon beef-flavored bouillon granules
6 (6-ounce) loin veal chops (¾ inch thick)
½ teaspoon freshly ground pepper
1 cup water
Fresh thyme sprigs (optional)

Coat a large nonstick skillet with cooking spray; place over medium-high heat until hot. Add mushrooms; sauté until tender. Add ½ cup water, wine, 2 tablespoons thyme, and bouillon. Bring to a boil; cook over medium-high heat 12 minutes or until liquid is reduced to 2 tablespoons.

Trim fat from veal chops. Cut each chop crosswise to, but not through, the center, leaving side connected along bone.

Stuff mushroom mixture evenly into pockets of chops, and secure openings with wooden picks. Sprinkle remaining 1 tablespoon minced thyme and pepper evenly over chops.

Place chops on a rack in a roasting pan coated with cooking spray. Coat surface of chops with cooking spray. Pour 1 cup water in roasting pan. Bake, uncovered, at 325° for 40 minutes or until veal is tender. Let stand 10 minutes. Transfer chops to a large serving platter; garnish with fresh thyme sprigs, if desired. Yield: 6 servings (184 calories per serving).

PROTEIN 20.2   FAT 10.2   CARBOHYDRATE 2.2   CHOLESTEROL 80
IRON 1.3   SODIUM 153   CALCIUM 19

VEAL MARSALA

1 pound veal cutlets (¼ inch thick)
¼ cup all-purpose flour, divided
¼ teaspoon salt
¼ teaspoon pepper
Vegetable cooking spray
1 tablespoon olive oil, divided
1½ cups sliced fresh mushrooms
¾ cup Marsala
¼ cup water
¼ teaspoon beef-flavored bouillon granules
Fresh parsley sprigs (optional)

Trim fat from cutlets. Place cutlets between 2 sheets of heavy-duty plastic wrap, and flatten to ⅛-inch thickness, using a meat mallet or rolling pin. Combine 3 tablespoons flour, salt, and pepper; stir well. Dredge cutlets in flour mixture.

Coat a large nonstick skillet with cooking spray; add 2 teaspoons oil. Place over medium heat until

hot. Add cutlets; cook 4 minutes on each side or until browned. Remove cutlets from skillet. Drain and pat dry with paper towels. Set aside. Wipe drippings from skillet with a paper towel.

Add remaining 1 teaspoon oil to skillet, and place over medium heat until hot. Add sliced mushrooms, and sauté until tender. Sprinkle remaining 1 tablespoon flour over mushrooms, stirring until well blended. Add Marsala, water, and bouillon granules. Cook, stirring constantly, 2 minutes or until mushroom mixture is thickened. Add cutlets; cover and simmer 5 minutes or until cutlets are tender. Transfer cutlets to a large serving platter; spoon mushroom mixture over cutlets. Garnish with fresh parsley sprigs, if desired. Yield: 4 servings (236 calories per serving).

PROTEIN 28.5   FAT 9.3   CARBOHYDRATE 7.7   CHOLESTEROL 100
IRON 1.8   SODIUM 283   CALCIUM 26

VEAL CUTLETS WITH CRANBERRY-APPLE CHUTNEY

Butter-flavored vegetable cooking spray
2 medium-size cooking apples, peeled, cored and thinly sliced
2 tablespoons unsweetened apple juice
1½ tablespoons brown sugar
1 tablespoon water
½ teaspoon grated orange rind
¾ cup jellied whole-berry cranberry sauce
¼ teaspoon salt
⅛ teaspoon pepper
1½ pounds veal cutlets (¼ inch thick)
2 tablespoons chopped pecans, toasted

Coat a large nonstick skillet with cooking spray; place over medium-high heat until hot. Add apple and next 4 ingredients; cook 5 to 6 minutes or until apple is tender. Stir in cranberry sauce; cook an additional 2 to 3 minutes or until sauce melts, stirring constantly. Let cool 5 minutes.

Position knife blade in food processor bowl; add ¾ cup apple mixture, and process until smooth. Stir in salt and pepper; set aside.

Trim fat from cutlets; cut cutlets into 2-inch pieces. Coat a large nonstick skillet with cooking spray; place over medium heat until hot. Add cutlets; cook 4 minutes on each side or until browned. Remove cutlets from skillet. Drain and pat dry with paper towels. Wipe drippings from skillet with a paper towel.

Return cutlets to skillet; add pureed apple mixture, and cook until thoroughly heated. Transfer to a serving platter, and sprinkle with pecans. Serve with remaining apple-cranberry mixture. Yield: 6 servings (299 calories per serving).

PROTEIN 27.7 FAT 9.7 CARBOHYDRATE 24.7 CHOLESTEROL 100
IRON 1.4 SODIUM 190 CALCIUM 3

MUSHROOM-VEAL ROULADES

6 (4-ounce) veal cutlets (¼ inch thick)
2½ cups chopped fresh mushrooms
½ cup chopped onion
2 tablespoons chopped fresh parsley
1 teaspoon no-salt-added herb salad seasoning
¼ teaspoon coarsely ground pepper
2 teaspoons low-sodium soy sauce
1 cup hot water
1 teaspoon beef-flavored bouillon granules
Vegetable cooking spray
3 tablespoons all-purpose flour
¼ cup dry sherry
¼ teaspoon salt
⅛ teaspoon pepper
½ cup low-fat sour cream
3 cups cooked medium egg noodles (cooked without salt or fat)
1 tablespoon chopped fresh parsley

Trim fat from cutlets. Place cutlets between 2 sheets of heavy-duty plastic wrap; flatten to ⅛-inch thickness, using a meat mallet or rolling pin.

Combine mushrooms and next 4 ingredients. Spoon ¼ cup mixture onto center of each cutlet. Reserve remaining mixture. Roll up cutlets, jelly-roll fashion, starting at short side. Secure with wooden picks. Place rolls in a 9-inch square baking dish; brush with soy sauce.

Combine water and bouillon granules; pour around rolls. Cover and bake at 350° for 30 minutes or until veal is tender. Remove from dish, using a slotted spoon. Reserve bouillon mixture.

Coat a skillet with cooking spray; place over medium heat until hot. Add mushroom mixture; sauté until tender. Stir in flour. Add bouillon mixture. Cook over medium heat; stir constantly, until thickened and bubbly. Stir in sherry, salt, and pepper. Remove from heat; let stand 1 minute. Stir in sour cream. Add veal to mushroom sauce. Serve over noodles; sprinkle with 1 tablespoon parsley. Yield: 6 servings (294 calories per serving).

PROTEIN 28.6 FAT 7.3 CARBOHYDRATE 27.0 CHOLESTEROL 128
IRON 3.0 SODIUM 410 CALCIUM 58

VEAL MEDAILLONS IN CREAM SAUCE

1 (8-ounce) carton plain nonfat yogurt
1 pound veal cutlets (¼ inch thick)
2 tablespoons all-purpose flour
¼ teaspoon pepper
Vegetable cooking spray
1 teaspoon olive oil
½ small onion
1 cup sliced fresh mushrooms
¾ cup water
3 tablespoons brandy
½ teaspoon beef-flavored bouillon granules
½ teaspoon dried whole basil
¼ teaspoon dried whole rosemary
¼ teaspoon pepper
3 cups cooked medium egg noodles (cooked
    without salt or fat)

Line a colander or sieve with a double layer of cheesecloth that has been rinsed out and squeezed dry; allow cheesecloth to overlap sides of colander. Stir yogurt until smooth; pour into colander, and fold edges of cheesecloth over to cover yogurt. Place colander in a small bowl; refrigerate 12 to 24 hours. Remove yogurt from colander, and discard liquid in bowl.

Trim fat from cutlets. Cut cutlets into 2-inch pieces. Combine flour and ¼ teaspoon pepper; stir well. Dredge cutlets in flour mixture.

Coat a large nonstick skillet with cooking spray; add oil. Place over medium-high heat until hot. Add cutlets; cook 2 to 3 minutes on each side or until browned. Remove cutlets from skillet. Drain and pat dry with paper towels. Wipe drippings from skillet with a paper towel.

Cut onion into ¼-inch slices, and separate into rings. Coat skillet with cooking spray; place over medium-high heat until hot. Add onion and mushrooms; sauté until tender. Return cutlets to skillet.

Combine water and next 5 ingredients, stirring well. Pour over cutlets. Bring to a boil; cover, reduce heat, and simmer 5 minutes. Remove from heat. Transfer cutlets to a serving platter, using a slotted spoon, and keep warm. Let mushroom mixture stand 3 minutes. Stir in drained yogurt. Return cutlets to skillet, and cook over low heat 1 minute. Serve cutlets in cream sauce over cooked egg noodles. Yield: 6 servings (278 calories per serving).

PROTEIN 24.8   FAT 6.0   CARBOHYDRATE 29.8   CHOLESTEROL 94
IRON 2.4   SODIUM 161   CALCIUM 106

ROSEMARY ROASTED LAMB WITH CRUSTY NEW POTATOES

1 (3½-pound) lean boneless leg of lamb
6 cloves garlic, minced
2 tablespoons chopped fresh rosemary
½ teaspoon salt
Vegetable cooking spray
2¾ pounds round red potatoes
1 teaspoon freshly ground pepper
1 cup water
Fresh rosemary sprigs (optional)

Trim fat from leg of lamb. Starting from center, slice horizontally through thickest part of lamb almost to, but not through, outer edge. Flip cut piece over to enlarge leg of lamb. Combine garlic, chopped rosemary, and salt; stir well. Rub half of garlic mixture over cut surface. Roll leg of lamb, and tie securely with string. Rub remaining garlic mixture over entire surface of lamb. Place on a rack in a roasting pan coated with cooking spray. Insert meat thermometer into thickest part of roast, if desired.

Arrange potatoes around roast; sprinkle potatoes with pepper. Pour water into roasting pan. Bake, uncovered, at 350° for 2 hours or until meat thermometer registers 140° (rare) to 160° (medium). Transfer lamb to a serving platter, and remove string; arrange potatoes around lamb. Garnish with fresh rosemary sprigs, if desired. Yield: 14 servings (232 calories per serving).

PROTEIN 26.1   FAT 6.8   CARBOHYDRATE 15.4   CHOLESTEROL 76
IRON 3.1   SODIUM 148   CALCIUM 24

Apricots, currants, pecans, and brandy add robust flavor to Lamb with Fruit and Nut Sauce.

LAMB WITH FRUIT AND NUT SAUCE

8 dried apricots, cut into strips
½ cup canned no-salt-added beef broth,
   undiluted
¼ cup currants
¼ cup brandy
4 (4-ounce) slices leg of lamb
2 tablespoons all-purpose flour
Vegetable cooking spray
2 teaspoons vegetable oil
1 tablespoon chopped pecans, toasted
Flowering kale (optional)

Combine first 4 ingredients in a small bowl; stir well. Cover and refrigerate at least 8 hours.

Place lamb between 2 sheets of heavy-duty plastic wrap, and flatten to ½-inch thickness, using a meat mallet or rolling pin. Dredge in flour.

Coat a nonstick skillet with cooking spray; add oil. Place over medium-high heat until hot. Add lamb; cook 5 minutes on each side or until lightly browned. Add apricot mixture and pecans; cover, reduce heat, and simmer 15 minutes or until lamb is tender. Transfer lamb to a platter lined with kale, if desired; spoon apricot mixture over lamb. Yield: 4 servings (281 calories per serving).

PROTEIN 24.8   FAT 9.1   CARBOHYDRATE 25.4   CHOLESTEROL 73
IRON 3.3   SODIUM 77   CALCIUM 23

GRECIAN LAMB WITH HERBED YOGURT SAUCE

6 (6-ounce) lean lamb loin chops (1 inch thick)
¼ cup plus 2 tablespoons lemon juice
1½ tablespoons water
1 tablespoon olive oil
1½ teaspoons dried whole rosemary
3 cloves garlic, minced
Vegetable cooking spray
Herbed Yogurt Sauce
Cucumber curls (optional)

Trim fat from chops. Place chops in a zip-top heavy-duty plastic bag. Combine lemon juice and next 4 ingredients; stir well. Pour lemon juice mixture over chops; seal bag, and shake until chops are well coated. Marinate in refrigerator 8 hours, turning bag occasionally.

Remove chops from marinade. Place marinade in a small saucepan. Bring to a boil over medium heat; reduce heat, and simmer 2 minutes.

Coat grill rack with vegetable cooking spray; place on grill over medium-hot coals. Place chops on rack, and cook 7 to 9 minutes on each side or to desired degree of doneness, basting chops occasionally with marinade. Transfer chops to individual serving plates. Serve with Herbed Yogurt Sauce. Garnish chops with cucumber curls, if desired. Yield: 6 servings (236 calories per serving).

Herbed Yogurt Sauce

1 (8-ounce) carton plain nonfat yogurt
½ cup peeled, seeded, and chopped cucumber
1 tablespoon sliced green onions
½ teaspoon dried whole oregano
½ teaspoon coarsely ground pepper
⅛ teaspoon dried whole rosemary, crumbled

Combine all ingredients in a small bowl; stir gently. Cover and chill yogurt sauce at least 3 hours. Yield: 1⅓ cups.

PROTEIN 28.0 FAT 10.8 CARBOHYDRATE 5.6 CHOLESTEROL 82
IRON 2.0 SODIUM 102 CALCIUM 105

INDIVIDUAL MUSHROOM-HAM SOUFFLÉS

Vegetable cooking spray
1 tablespoon reduced-calorie margarine
2 cups sliced fresh mushrooms
¼ cup minced green onions
¼ cup plus 2 tablespoons all-purpose flour
1½ cups skim milk
½ cup (2 ounces) shredded reduced-fat sharp Cheddar cheese
⅛ to ¼ teaspoon ground red pepper
1 cup chopped lean cooked ham
1 cup cooked long-grain rice (cooked without salt and fat)
½ cup frozen egg substitute, thawed
3 egg whites
1 teaspoon sugar
1 tablespoon grated Parmesan cheese

Coat a large saucepan with cooking spray; add margarine. Place over medium heat until hot. Add mushrooms and green onions; sauté until tender. Sprinkle flour over mushroom mixture; cook 1 minute, stirring constantly. Gradually stir in milk. Cook over medium heat, stirring constantly, until thickened and bubbly. Remove from heat; add Cheddar cheese and red pepper, stirring until cheese melts. Stir in ham, rice, and egg substitute; cool to room temperature.

Beat egg whites (at room temperature) at high speed of an electric mixer until foamy. Add sugar, and beat until stiff peaks form (2 to 4 minutes). Gently fold egg white mixture into ham mixture. Spoon 1 cup mixture into each of 6 individual 1½-cup soufflé dishes. Sprinkle each with ½ teaspoon Parmesan cheese. Bake at 350° for 30 minutes or until puffed and golden. Serve immediately. Yield: 6 servings (204 calories per serving).

PROTEIN 17.1 FAT 5.3 CARBOHYDRATE 21.5 CHOLESTEROL 22
IRON 2.1 SODIUM 524 CALCIUM 187

EASY SKILLET BARBECUE DINNER

6 (4-ounce) lean boneless center-cut loin
   pork chops
Vegetable cooking spray
½ small onion
½ small green pepper, seeded and cut
   into strips
⅔ cup commercial reduced-calorie
   barbecue sauce
½ cup orange juice
2 tablespoons dark brown sugar
1 tablespoon cider vinegar

Trim fat from chops. Place chops between 2 sheets of heavy-duty plastic wrap, and flatten to ¼-inch thickness, using a meat mallet or rolling pin. Coat a large nonstick skillet with cooking spray; place over medium-high heat until hot.

Add chops, and cook 3 minutes on each side or until browned. Remove chops from skillet. Drain and pat dry with paper towels. Wipe drippings from skillet with a paper towel.

Cut onion into ¼-inch slices, and separate into rings. Coat skillet with vegetable cooking spray; place over medium-high heat until hot. Add onion and green pepper; sauté until tender. Return chops to skillet.

Combine barbecue sauce and remaining ingredients, stirring well; pour over chops. Bring to a boil; cover, reduce heat, and simmer 10 minutes or until pork chops are tender. Yield: 6 servings (284 calories per serving).

PROTEIN 27.3   FAT 12.7   CARBOHYDRATE 12.7   CHOLESTEROL 86
IRON 1.4   SODIUM 227   CALCIUM 14

PORK BURGERS DIJON

2 egg whites
1 (1-ounce) slice white bread, cubed
1 pound lean ground pork
2 cups finely shredded cabbage
¼ cup grated onion
½ teaspoon sugar
½ teaspoon pepper
¼ teaspoon ground coriander
⅛ teaspoon ground nutmeg
Vegetable cooking spray
1 (8-ounce) package presliced fresh mushrooms
1 cup water
1 tablespoon Dijon mustard
1 teaspoon beef-flavored bouillon granules
2 tablespoons water
1 tablespoon plus 1 teaspoon cornstarch

Combine egg whites and bread cubes in a large bowl; let stand 5 minutes. Add pork and next 6 ingredients; stir well. Shape mixture into 6 patties.

Coat a large nonstick skillet with cooking spray; place over medium heat until hot. Add pork patties, and cook 7 minutes on each side. Drain and pat dry with paper towels. Wipe drippings from skillet with a paper towel.

Coat skillet with cooking spray, and place over medium-high heat until hot. Add mushrooms, and sauté until tender. Stir in 1 cup water, mustard, and bouillon granules, stirring well. Return pork patties to skillet. Cover, reduce heat, and simmer 10 minutes. Transfer patties to a large serving platter.

Combine 2 tablespoons water and cornstarch; stir well. Add to mushroom mixture, and cook just until thickened, stirring constantly. Spoon over patties, and serve immediately. Yield: 6 servings (198 calories per serving).

PROTEIN 18.6   FAT 9.5   CARBOHYDRATE 8.8   CHOLESTEROL 54
IRON 1.3   SODIUM 319   CALCIUM 25

PORK PAELLA

2 (10½-ounce) cans no-salt-added chicken
   broth, undiluted
¼ teaspoon saffron threads
¾ pound lean ground pork
2 cloves garlic, minced
¾ teaspoon dried Italian seasoning
¼ teaspoon fennel seeds, crushed
Vegetable cooking spray
¾ pound lean boneless pork loin, cut into
   1-inch pieces
¾ cup chopped green onions
2 cloves garlic, minced
1 cup long-grain rice, uncooked
1 bay leaf
½ teaspoon dried whole oregano
¼ teaspoon salt
¾ cup frozen English peas, thawed
2 tablespoons chopped fresh parsley
1 (2-ounce) jar sliced pimientos, drained

Combine chicken broth and saffron; let stand
15 minutes.

Combine ground pork, 2 cloves garlic, Italian
seasoning, and fennel seeds in a large bowl; stir
well. Shape mixture into 1-inch balls. Coat a large
nonstick skillet with cooking spray; place over
medium-high heat until hot. Add meatballs, and
cook until browned, stirring occasionally. Remove meatballs from skillet. Drain and pat dry
with paper towels. Wipe drippings from skillet
with a paper towel.

Coat skillet with cooking spray, and place over
medium-high heat until hot. Add pork pieces,
green onions, and 2 cloves garlic; cook until pork
is browned on all sides. Drain and pat dry with
paper towels. Wipe drippings from skillet with a
paper towel.

Return meatballs and pork mixture to skillet;
add broth mixture, rice, and next 3 ingredients.
Bring to a boil; cover, reduce heat, and simmer
25 minutes. Stir in peas, parsley, and pimiento.
Cook, uncovered, an additional 10 minutes or until rice is tender and liquid is absorbed. Remove
and discard bay leaf. Yield: 6 servings (359 calories per serving).

PROTEIN 27.7 FAT 13.1 CARBOHYDRATE 29.4 CHOLESTEROL 77
IRON 3.2 SODIUM 239 CALCIUM 42

PORK CHOPS WITH MAPLE-PECAN SAUCE

4 (4-ounce) lean boneless center-cut loin
   pork chops
2 teaspoons Dijon mustard
2 tablespoons all-purpose flour
½ teaspoon ground ginger
Vegetable cooking spray
2 teaspoons vegetable oil
2 tablespoons reduced-calorie maple syrup
1 tablespoon chopped toasted pecans
Celery leaves (optional)

Trim fat from chops. Place chops between 2
sheets of heavy-duty plastic wrap, and flatten
to ¼-inch thickness, using a meat mallet or rolling
pin. Spread mustard on both sides of chops.

Combine flour and ginger; stir well. Dredge pork
chops in flour mixture.

Coat a large nonstick skillet with cooking spray;
add oil. Place over medium heat until hot. Add
chops, and cook 3 minutes on each side or until
chops are browned. Combine maple syrup and
pecans; add to pork chops, stirring to coat. Cover
and simmer 4 minutes or until chops are tender,
turning once.

Transfer chops to a large serving platter, and
garnish with celery leaves, if desired. Yield: 4
servings (234 calories per serving).

PROTEIN 25.5 FAT 11.9 CARBOHYDRATE 4.4 CHOLESTEROL 71
IRON 1.1 SODIUM 151 CALCIUM 7

CHESTNUT-SAGE STUFFED PORK TENDERLOIN

2 (½-pound) pork tenderloins
½ cup soft whole wheat breadcrumbs
⅓ cup coarsely chopped chestnuts
2 cloves garlic, minced
½ teaspoon rubbed sage
1 tablespoon frozen orange juice concentrate,
    thawed
½ teaspoon coarsely ground pepper
¼ teaspoon salt
¼ teaspoon poultry seasoning
¼ teaspoon rubbed sage
Vegetable cooking spray
Fresh sage sprigs (optional)
Orange sections (optional)

Trim fat from pork. Cut pork lengthwise to within ½ inch of outer edge of each tenderloin, leaving 1 long side connected; flip cut piece over to enlarge pork. Place pork between 2 sheets of heavy-duty plastic wrap, and flatten to ¼ inch thickness, using a meat mallet or rolling pin.

Combine breadcrumbs, chestnuts, garlic, and ½ teaspoon sage; stir well. Divide mixture evenly and sprinkle in center of each tenderloin to within ½ inch of sides. Roll up tenderloins, jellyroll fashion, starting at narrow end. Secure at 2-inch intervals with string. Combine orange juice concentrate and next 4 ingredients in a small bowl; rub mixture over entire surface of tenderloins.

Place tenderloins on a rack in a roasting pan coated with cooking spray. Bake, uncovered, at 400° for 45 minutes. Let stand 10 minutes; slice into 12 slices, and arrange on a serving platter. If desired, garnish with fresh sage and orange sections. Yield: 4 servings (201 calories per serving).

PROTEIN 25.4 FAT 4.8 CARBOHYDRATE 13.2 CHOLESTEROL 77
IRON 1.8 SODIUM 250 CALCIUM 29

For an easy entrée with lots of flavor, serve Pork Chops with Maple-Pecan Sauce.

APPLE-GLAZED PORK LOIN ROAST

1 (6-ounce) can frozen apple juice concentrate, thawed
⅓ cup sherry
⅓ cup red currant jelly
1 teaspoon pepper
¼ teaspoon ground red pepper
1 (3½-pound) lean boneless double pork loin roast, tied
1 tablespoon rubbed sage
1 teaspoon coarsely ground pepper
Vegetable cooking spray
Fresh sage sprigs (optional)

Combine first 5 ingredients in a small saucepan; cook over low heat until jelly melts, stirring occasionally. Remove from heat, and let cool.

Untie roast, and trim fat. Retie roast. Place roast in a large zip-top heavy-duty plastic bag. Pour apple juice mixture over roast. Seal bag securely. Place bag in a large bowl; marinate roast in refrigerator 8 hours, turning occasionally.

Remove roast from marinade. Place marinade in a small saucepan; bring to a boil. Reduce heat, and simmer 5 minutes.

Combine sage and coarsely ground pepper; rub mixture over surface of roast. Place roast on a rack in a roasting pan coated with cooking spray. Insert meat thermometer into thickest part of roast, if desired. Place roast in a 450° oven. Reduce heat to 350°, and bake 1 hour and 45 minutes or until meat thermometer registers 165°, basting frequently with marinade.

Let roast stand 10 minutes. Remove string; slice roast diagonally across grain into ¼-inch slices, and arrange on a large serving platter. Serve with remaining marinade. Yield: 14 servings (220 calories per serving).

PROTEIN 21.3 FAT 9.8 CARBOHYDRATE 10.5 CHOLESTEROL 68
IRON 1.2 SODIUM 56 CALCIUM 13

CHEESE-AND-BASIL-STUFFED PORK TENDERLOIN

3 ounces Montrachet goat cheese
¼ cup chopped fresh basil
¼ teaspoon salt, divided
⅛ teaspoon pepper
1 (1-pound) pork tenderloin
8 thin slices plum tomato
2 tablespoons commercial oil-free Italian dressing
¼ cup fine, dry breadcrumbs
Vegetable cooking spray
1 teaspoon vegetable oil
Plum tomato slices (optional)
Fresh basil sprigs (optional)

Combine cheese, basil, ⅛ teaspoon salt, and pepper, stirring well; set aside.

Trim fat from tenderloin; slice tenderloin into fourths. Cut each portion crosswise to, but not through, the center, leaving 1 side connected.

Place 2 slices tomato on one side of each butterflied tenderloin; spoon cheese mixture evenly over tomato. Fold tenderloin over tomato and cheese mixture; secure with wooden picks. Brush both sides with Italian dressing, and sprinkle with remaining ⅛ teaspoon salt. Dredge in breadcrumbs, and set aside.

Coat a large nonstick skillet with cooking spray; add oil. Place over medium-high heat until hot. Add stuffed tenderloins. Cover and cook 10 minutes on each side or until done. Transfer to a serving platter. If desired, garnish with plum tomato slices and fresh basil sprigs. Yield: 4 servings (230 calories per serving).

PROTEIN 28.0 FAT 9.0 CARBOHYDRATE 7.8 CHOLESTEROL 93
IRON 2.1 SODIUM 556 CALCIUM 127

*Serve Vegetable-Stuffed Turkey Breast
(page 174) to family and friends.
Everyone will enjoy the pleasing
combination of flavors.*

Poultry

CHICKEN EMPANADAS

1 cup finely chopped cooked chicken breast
   (skinned before cooking and cooked without
   salt)
1 (4-ounce) can chopped green chiles, drained
½ cup 1% low-fat cottage cheese
¼ cup (1 ounce) shredded reduced-fat Monterey
   Jack cheese
¾ cup all-purpose flour
¼ cup plus 2 teaspoons cornmeal, divided
¼ teaspoon ground red pepper
3 tablespoons reduced-calorie margarine
¼ cup cold water
1 tablespoon all-purpose flour
Vegetable cooking spray
2 teaspoons skim milk

Combine first 4 ingredients in a medium bowl; stir well. Set aside.

Combine ¾ cup flour, ¼ cup cornmeal, and red pepper in a large bowl; cut in margarine with a pastry blender until mixture resembles coarse meal. Sprinkle cold water, 1 tablespoon at a time, evenly over surface of mixture; stir with a fork until dry ingredients are moistened. Shape into a ball; cover and chill 10 minutes.

Sprinkle 1 tablespoon flour evenly over work surface. Divide dough into fourths; roll each portion to a 5-inch circle on floured surface. Place circles on a baking sheet coated with cooking spray. Spoon ½ cup chicken mixture on one-half of each pastry circle. To seal, fold circles in half, making sure edges are even. Press edges of filled pastry firmly together with a fork. Brush tops with milk, and sprinkle with remaining 2 teaspoons cornmeal. Bake, uncovered, at 400° for 20 minutes or until lightly browned. Let stand 10 minutes. Yield: 4 servings (280 calories per serving).

PROTEIN 22.0 FAT 9.3 CARBOHYDRATE 26.3 CHOLESTEROL 42
IRON 1.9 SODIUM 297 CALCIUM 88

CURRIED CHICKEN AND VEGETABLE PIE

1 cup corn flake crumbs
3 tablespoons reduced-calorie margarine, melted
1 tablespoon water
½ cup chopped fresh broccoli
¼ cup shredded carrot
¼ cup chopped onion
¼ cup chopped sweet red pepper
1 cup diced cooked chicken breast (skinned before
   cooking and cooked without salt)
1 cup (4 ounces) shredded part-skim
   mozzarella cheese
¾ cup skim milk
¾ cup frozen egg substitute, thawed
½ teaspoon curry powder
¼ teaspoon ground coriander
¼ teaspoon salt
¼ teaspoon ground white pepper

Combine corn flake crumbs, margarine, and water; stir well. Press mixture into bottom and up sides of a 9-inch pieplate. Set aside.

Arrange broccoli, carrot, onion, and red pepper in a vegetable steamer over boiling water. Cover and steam 5 to 7 minutes or until crisp-tender; drain well.

Layer vegetables and chicken in crust; sprinkle with cheese. Combine milk and egg substitute; beat well. Stir in curry powder and remaining ingredients. Pour over chicken and vegetables. Bake at 350° for 30 to 35 minutes or until set. Let stand 10 minutes before serving. Yield: 6 servings (224 calories per serving).

PROTEIN 18.9 FAT 8.1 CARBOHYDRATE 18.6 CHOLESTEROL 36
IRON 2.2 SODIUM 490 CALCIUM 182

CHICKEN STIR-FRY CALCUTTA

1 (10½-ounce) can low-sodium chicken broth
2 tablespoons cornstarch
1 tablespoon grated fresh ginger
2 teaspoons low-sodium soy sauce
½ teaspoon coriander seed
½ teaspoon ground cumin
¼ teaspoon salt
¼ teaspoon ground cardamom
¼ teaspoon pepper
¾ pound fresh snow pea pods
Vegetable cooking spray
2 teaspoons vegetable oil, divided
4 (4-ounce) skinned, boned chicken breast halves,
    cut into thin strips
1 medium-size sweet red pepper, cut into
    thin strips
5 green onions, cut diagonally into 1-inch pieces
1 cup sliced celery
3 cups cooked long-grain rice (cooked without salt
    or fat)
2 tablespoons chopped unsalted peanuts

Combine first 9 ingredients in a small bowl; stir well. Set aside.

Wash snow peas; trim ends, and remove strings. Set aside.

Coat a wok or large nonstick skillet with cooking spray; add 1 teaspoon oil. Place over medium-high heat (375°) until hot. Add chicken, and stir-fry 3 minutes or until lightly browned. Remove chicken from wok. Drain and pat dry with paper towels. Wipe drippings from wok with a paper towel.

Add remaining 1 teaspoon oil to wok; place over medium-high heat until hot. Add snow peas, sweet red pepper, green onions, and celery; stir-fry 3 to 4 minutes or until vegetables are crisp-tender. Add reserved chicken broth mixture; stir well.

Return chicken to wok. Cook, stirring constantly, until mixture is thickened and thoroughly heated. Serve over rice; sprinkle with chopped peanuts. Yield: 6 servings (290 calories per serving).

PROTEIN 23.0 FAT 6.5 CARBOHYDRATE 33.4 CHOLESTEROL 47
IRON 3.2 SODIUM 209 CALCIUM 64

CHICKEN AND VEGETABLE COUSCOUS

3 (4-ounce) skinned, boned chicken breast halves
4¼ cups water, divided
½ teaspoon curry powder
Olive oil-flavored vegetable cooking spray
1 teaspoon olive oil
2 cups peeled, cubed eggplant
1½ cups cubed zucchini
1 cup chopped onion
1 cup chopped sweet red pepper
1 clove garlic, minced
1 (14½-ounce) can no-salt-added whole
    tomatoes, undrained and chopped
1 teaspoon chopped fresh mint
½ teaspoon ground cumin
½ teaspoon ground coriander
¼ teaspoon salt
¼ teaspoon pepper
1 cup plus 2 tablespoons couscous, uncooked
1 tablespoon pine nuts, toasted

Combine chicken, 2 cups water, and curry powder in a saucepan. Bring to a boil; cover, reduce heat, and simmer 15 minutes or until chicken is tender. Remove chicken from broth, and cut into 1-inch pieces; set aside. Skim and discard fat from broth; reserve broth for another use.

Coat a saucepan with cooking spray; add oil. Place over medium-high heat until hot. Add eggplant, zucchini, onion, red pepper, and garlic; sauté until tender. Stir in tomato and next 5 ingredients. Cover and cook over medium heat 10 minutes. Stir in chicken; cook until thoroughly heated.

Bring remaining 2¼ cups water to a boil in a medium saucepan. Remove from heat. Add couscous; cover and let stand 5 minutes or until couscous is tender and liquid is absorbed. Transfer to a serving platter. Spoon chicken mixture over couscous, and sprinkle with pine nuts. Yield: 6 servings (246 calories per serving).

PROTEIN 19.3 FAT 3.8 CARBOHYDRATE 34.1 CHOLESTEROL 35
IRON 2.3 SODIUM 141 CALCIUM 68

SOUTHWESTERN CHICKEN ROULADES

½ cup frozen whole kernel corn, thawed
¼ cup (1 ounce) shredded reduced-fat
   Monterey Jack cheese
2 tablespoons grated onion
2 tablespoons finely chopped sweet red pepper
2 tablespoons chopped fresh cilantro
1 teaspoon minced fresh jalapeño pepper
4 (4-ounce) skinned, boned chicken breast halves
¼ teaspoon pepper
⅛ teaspoon salt
⅛ teaspoon garlic powder
Vegetable cooking spray
2 teaspoons vegetable oil
½ cup seeded, chopped tomato
2 tablespoons reduced-calorie catsup
2 tablespoons lime juice
2 tablespoons tequila
⅛ teaspoon ground cumin
⅛ teaspoon ground cinnamon

Combine first 6 ingredients in a small bowl; stir well. Set aside.

Place chicken between 2 sheets of heavy-duty plastic wrap, and flatten to ¼-inch thickness, using a meat mallet or rolling pin. Divide corn mixture evenly among chicken breast halves, spooning mixture into center of each half. Roll up chicken breast halves, lengthwise, tucking ends under. Secure with wooden picks. Combine pepper, salt, and garlic powder; sprinkle over chicken rolls.

Coat a large nonstick skillet with cooking spray; add oil. Place over medium-high heat until hot. Add chicken rolls; cook until browned on all sides.

Combine tomato, catsup, lime juice, tequila, cumin, and cinnamon; stir well. Spoon over chicken. Cover, reduce heat, and simmer 30 to 35 minutes or until chicken is tender. Transfer chicken to a serving platter; remove wooden picks. Spoon sauce over chicken. Yield: 4 servings (204 calories per serving).

PROTEIN 29.0 FAT 5.3 CARBOHYDRATE 9.3 CHOLESTEROL 70
IRON 1.2 SODIUM 201 CALCIUM 77

GRILLED CHICKEN BURGUNDY

4 (4-ounce) skinned, boned chicken breast halves
⅓ cup Burgundy or other dry red wine
2 tablespoons low-sodium soy sauce
1 tablespoon brown sugar
1 tablespoon grated fresh ginger
1 tablespoon sesame oil
½ teaspoon dry mustard
1 clove garlic, crushed
Vegetable cooking spray

Place chicken in a dish. Combine Burgundy and next 6 ingredients; pour over chicken. Cover and marinate in refrigerator 4 hours; turn twice.

Remove chicken from marinade; place marinade in a small saucepan. Bring to a boil; reduce heat, and simmer 5 minutes.

Coat grill rack with cooking spray; place on grill over medium-hot coals. Place chicken on rack, and cook 10 to 12 minutes or until chicken is tender, turning and basting frequently with marinade. Yield: 4 servings (184 calories per serving).

PROTEIN 25.8 FAT 6.6 CARBOHYDRATE 3.0 CHOLESTEROL 70
IRON 1.0 SODIUM 259 CALCIUM 18

GRILLED CHICKEN PIQUANT

4 (4-ounce) skinned, boned chicken breast halves
3 tablespoons lime juice
3 tablespoons lemon juice
1 tablespoon low-sodium soy sauce
1 tablespoon honey
2 teaspoons vegetable oil
¼ teaspoon ground ginger
¼ teaspoon ground cardamom
⅛ teaspoon ground coriander
1 cup shredded red cabbage
1 cup shredded Boston lettuce
1 cup shredded Bibb lettuce
1 cup shredded red leaf lettuce
1 small purple onion, thinly sliced
½ cup shredded carrot
Vegetable cooking spray

Flavorful chicken is served over wilted greens in Grilled Chicken Piquant. The greens are wilted with a warm citrus-spice dressing.

Place chicken in a shallow dish. Combine lime juice and next 7 ingredients in a small bowl, stirring well; pour over chicken. Cover and marinate in refrigerator 4 hours, turning occasionally.

Combine red cabbage, shredded lettuces, onion, and carrot; toss well. Cover and chill.

Drain chicken, reserving marinade. Coat grill rack with cooking spray, and place on grill over medium-hot coals. Place chicken on rack, and cook 5 to 6 minutes on each side or until chicken is tender. Set aside, and keep warm.

Place reserved marinade in a small saucepan. Bring to a boil; reduce heat, and simmer 5 minutes. Spoon hot marinade over lettuce mixture, and toss gently.

Place lettuce mixture evenly on individual serving plates. Top lettuce mixture with grilled chicken breasts. Serve immediately. Yield: 4 servings (204 calories per serving).

PROTEIN 26.8 FAT 5.6 CARBOHYDRATE 10.9 CHOLESTEROL 70
IRON 1.3 SODIUM 168 CALCIUM 34

JALAPEÑO CHICKEN-PEPPER KABOBS

⅓ cup unsweetened pineapple juice
3 tablespoons jalapeño jelly
1 tablespoon lemon juice
2 teaspoons olive oil
¼ teaspoon garlic powder
¼ teaspoon salt
¼ teaspoon crushed red pepper
6 (4-ounce) skinned, boned chicken
  breast halves
1 medium-size green pepper, seeded
1 medium-size sweet red pepper,
  seeded
1 medium-size sweet yellow pepper,
  seeded
Vegetable cooking spray

Combine first 7 ingredients in a small sauce-pan. Bring to a boil; reduce heat, and simmer until jelly melts, stirring occasionally.

Cut chicken into 1-inch cubes; set aside. Cut peppers into 1-inch pieces. Thread chicken and peppers alternately on 6 (12-inch) skewers.

Coat grill rack with cooking spray; place on grill over medium-hot coals. Place kabobs on rack, and cook 12 to 14 minutes or until chicken is done, turning and basting frequently with pine-apple juice mixture. Yield: 6 servings (201 cal-ories per serving).

PROTEIN 26.3   FAT 4.8   CARBOHYDRATE 12.2   CHOLESTEROL 70
IRON 1.8   SODIUM 163   CALCIUM 22

GRILLED JAMAICAN CHICKEN

4 (6-ounce) skinned chicken breast halves
3 tablespoons lime juice
3 tablespoons lemon juice
3 tablespoons sweet vermouth
2 tablespoons Dijon mustard
1 jalapeño pepper, seeded and finely
  chopped
1 clove garlic, minced
¼ teaspoon ground coriander
¼ teaspoon ground cumin
¼ teaspoon dried whole thyme
¼ teaspoon dried whole oregano
¼ teaspoon salt
Vegetable cooking spray
Lime twists (optional)

Place chicken in a dish. Combine lime juice and next 10 ingredients; pour over chicken. Cover and marinate in refrigerator 8 hours; turn twice.

Remove chicken from marinade. Place mari-nade in a small saucepan. Bring to a boil; reduce heat, and simmer 5 minutes. Set aside.

Coat grill rack with cooking spray; place on grill over medium-hot coals. Place chicken on rack, and cook 20 to 25 minutes or until chicken is tender, turning and basting frequently with re-served marinade. Garnish with lime twists, if de-sired. Yield: 4 servings (158 calories per serving).

PROTEIN 25.9   FAT 3.7   CARBOHYDRATE 3.6   CHOLESTEROL 70
IRON 1.1   SODIUM 432   CALCIUM 23

SPICE STORAGE TIPS

Cinnamon, cloves, and other dried spices can lose their flavors if stored improperly or for too long. Exposure to air, heat, and light can contribute to this deterioration. A few rules of thumb: Store spices away from heat, hot stoves, or heat-generating kitchen appliances. Direct sunlight should also be avoided. For this reason, spices stored in tins have a slight advantage over those in clear bottles.

In hot, humid summer months, consider placing delicate spices such as paprika in the refrigerator. The same is true for poppy seeds and sesame seeds. Keeping these seeds in the refrigerator prevents the oils they contain from turning rancid.

Taco-Tico Chicken features a spicy flavor blend of chili powder, cumin, and red pepper.

TACO-TICO CHICKEN

½ teaspoon chili powder
¼ teaspoon ground cumin
⅛ teaspoon garlic powder
⅛ teaspoon ground red pepper
6 (6-ounce) skinned chicken breast halves
Vegetable cooking spray
1 teaspoon vegetable oil
1 (14½-ounce) can no-salt-added whole
    tomatoes, undrained and chopped
½ cup sliced green onions
¼ cup sliced ripe olives
1 tablespoon golden tequila
1 teaspoon seeded, chopped jalapeño pepper
2 teaspoons cornstarch
2 tablespoons water
¼ cup plus 2 tablespoons low-fat sour cream
¼ cup (1 ounce) shredded 40% less-fat
    Cheddar cheese
2 tablespoons chopped fresh cilantro

Combine first 4 ingredients; sprinkle over both sides of chicken. Coat a large nonstick skillet with cooking spray; add oil. Place over medium-high heat until hot. Add chicken; cook 2 minutes on each side or until browned. Remove chicken from skillet. Drain and pat dry with paper towels. Wipe drippings from skillet with a paper towel.

Return chicken to skillet. Add tomato and next 4 ingredients. Bring to a boil; cover, reduce heat, and simmer 20 minutes or until tender. Transfer chicken to a serving platter, using a slotted spoon. Combine cornstarch and water; stir well. Add to tomato mixture; bring to a boil. Cook 1 minute or until slightly thickened; stir constantly. Spoon over chicken; top with sour cream, cheese, and cilantro. Yield: 6 servings (200 calories per serving).

PROTEIN 27.6 FAT 6.2 CARBOHYDRATE 7.8 CHOLESTEROL 77
IRON 1.6 SODIUM 145 CALCIUM 91

APPLE-KISSED CHICKEN

½ cup unsweetened apple juice
3 tablespoons apple butter
1 teaspoon grated lemon rind
1 tablespoon lemon juice
6 (6-ounce) skinned chicken breast
   halves
½ teaspoon poultry seasoning
Vegetable cooking spray
1 small onion, thinly sliced
1 small cooking apple, cored and
   cut into 12 wedges
1 tablespoon plus 1 teaspoon
   cornstarch
1 tablespoon plus 1 teaspoon water
2 tablespoons chopped walnuts,
   toasted
Apple wedges (optional)
Fresh sage sprigs (optional)

Combine first 4 ingredients in a small bowl; stir well. Set aside.

Sprinkle chicken with poultry seasoning. Coat a large nonstick skillet with cooking spray; place over medium-high heat until hot. Add chicken, and cook 5 minutes on each side or until browned. Remove chicken; drain on paper towels. Wipe drippings from skillet with a paper towel. Return chicken to skillet. Pour apple juice mixture over chicken, and top with onion slices. Cover, reduce heat, and simmer 10 minutes. Add 12 apple wedges. Cover and simmer 12 minutes or until chicken is tender.

Transfer chicken and apple wedges to a serving platter, using a slotted spoon. Dissolve cornstarch in water in a small bowl. Add to apple juice mixture in skillet, stirring constantly. Cook over medium heat, stirring constantly, until mixture is thickened. Spoon sauce over chicken, and sprinkle with walnuts. If desired, garnish with apple wedges and fresh sage sprigs. Yield: 6 servings (229 calories per serving).

PROTEIN 29.8 FAT 5.6 CARBOHYDRATE 13.9 CHOLESTEROL 78
IRON 1.3 SODIUM 70 CALCIUM 26

CHICKEN PAPRIKA

1 (3-pound) broiler-fryer, cut up and skinned
Vegetable cooking spray
1 teaspoon vegetable oil
1 medium onion, thinly sliced
1 cup sliced fresh mushrooms
1 clove garlic, minced
1 tablespoon paprika
¼ cup hot water
½ teaspoon chicken-flavored bouillon granules
¼ teaspoon ground white pepper
1 (8-ounce) carton plain nonfat yogurt
1 tablespoon all-purpose flour

Trim excess fat from chicken. Rinse chicken under cold, running water, and pat dry.

Coat a large nonstick skillet with cooking spray; add oil. Place over medium-high heat until hot. Add chicken, and cook until lightly browned on all sides. Remove chicken; drain and pat dry with paper towels. Wipe drippings from skillet with a paper towel.

Return chicken to skillet. Arrange onion, mushrooms, and garlic over chicken. Sprinkle with paprika. Combine water, bouillon granules, and pepper, stirring well; pour over chicken. Bring to a boil; cover, reduce heat, and simmer 30 minutes or until chicken is tender. Transfer chicken to a serving platter, using a slotted spoon.

Combine yogurt and flour, stirring until smooth. Stir yogurt mixture into onion mixture. Cook over low heat 3 minutes or until thickened. Spoon sauce over chicken. Yield: 6 servings (205 calories per serving).

PROTEIN 26.6 FAT 7.3 CARBOHYDRATE 7.1 CHOLESTEROL 73
IRON 1.6 SODIUM 164 CALCIUM 96

BOURBON BARBECUED CHICKEN

⅓ cup unsweetened orange juice
2 tablespoons bourbon
2 tablespoons reduced-calorie catsup
2 tablespoons molasses
2 teaspoons red wine vinegar
2 teaspoons olive oil
1 teaspoon low-sodium Worcestershire sauce
¼ teaspoon salt
¼ teaspoon garlic powder
⅛ teaspoon ground cloves
⅛ teaspoon ground red pepper
1 (3-pound) broiler-fryer, skinned
Vegetable cooking spray

Combine first 7 ingredients in a small saucepan. Add salt, garlic powder, cloves, and red pepper, stirring well. Cook over medium-low heat 10 minutes, stirring occasionally. Cool slightly.

Trim excess fat from chicken; remove giblets and neck from chicken, and reserve for other uses. Rinse chicken under cold, running water, and pat dry. Place chicken, breast side up, on a rack in a roasting pan coated with cooking spray.

Truss chicken. Insert meat thermometer in meaty part of thigh, making sure it does not touch bone. Brush chicken with orange juice mixture. Bake, uncovered, at 375° for 1½ hours or until meat thermometer registers 185°, basting frequently with orange juice mixture. Yield: 6 servings (206 calories per serving).

PROTEIN 23.7 FAT 7.7 CARBOHYDRATE 9.0 CHOLESTEROL 73
IRON 1.3 SODIUM 174 CALCIUM 26

LEMON-SAGE GRILLED CORNISH HENS

4 (1-pound) Cornish hens, skinned
3 tablespoons chopped fresh sage
2 teaspoons grated lemon rind
½ teaspoon poultry seasoning
¼ teaspoon salt-free lemon-pepper seasoning
½ cup lemon juice
3 tablespoons vodka
1 tablespoon honey
2 teaspoons vegetable oil
1 teaspoon white wine Worcestershire sauce
Vegetable cooking spray

Remove giblets from hens; reserve for another use. Rinse hens under cold, running water, and pat dry. Split each hen in half lengthwise, using an electric knife. Place hens in 2 (11- x 7- x 2-inch) baking dishes.

Combine sage and next 8 ingredients; pour over hens. Cover and marinate in refrigerator 8 hours.

Remove hens from marinade, reserving marinade. Place hens, cut side down, in a baking dish. Bake, uncovered, at 400° for 15 minutes.

Place marinade in a saucepan. Bring marinade to a boil; reduce heat, and simmer 5 minutes.

Coat a grill rack with cooking spray; place on grill over medium-hot coals. Place hens on rack, and cook 10 to 15 minutes or until done, turning and basting frequently with marinade. Yield: 8 servings (204 calories per serving).

PROTEIN 25.8 FAT 7.9 CARBOHYDRATE 6.6 CHOLESTEROL 79
IRON 1.2 SODIUM 83 CALCIUM 21

FINICKY PINT-SIZED PALATES

Nutritionists have a word of advice for parents worried about their child's food jags, erratic eating, and aversion to vegetables: Relax—finicky appetites are the norm during early years. Studies continue to reinforce that the successful feeding of children requires only that parents provide an assortment of nutritious foods. Children innately know what to pick and choose. A study reported in *The New England Journal of Medicine* showed that children, when given the choice, ate the amount of food their bodies needed.

Sometimes a child will pack it all into one meal and then eat lightly at the next. But it ends up being about the same by the end of the day.

Spoon cooked apples and pears over Cornish Hens with Autumn Fruit for a warming weeknight dinner.

CORNISH HENS WITH AUTUMN FRUIT

½ teaspoon ground coriander
¼ teaspoon salt
¼ teaspoon ground cardamom
¼ teaspoon pepper
3 (1-pound) Cornish hens, skinned
Vegetable cooking spray
2 teaspoons vegetable oil
1 medium onion, thinly sliced
2 cloves garlic, minced
2 cups cubed cooking apple
1⅓ cups cubed pear
2 teaspoons lemon juice
3 tablespoons unsweetened apple juice
3 tablespoons applejack or other apple-flavored
    brandy
1 teaspoon dried whole rosemary
Fresh rosemary sprigs (optional)

Combine first 4 ingredients. Remove giblets from hens; reserve for another use. Rinse hens; pat dry. Split each hen in half lengthwise, using an electric knife. Sprinkle hens with coriander mixture.

Coat a large nonstick skillet with cooking spray; add oil. Place over medium-high heat until hot. Add hens; cook until hens are lightly browned on both sides, turning occasionally. Remove hens from skillet; drain and pat dry with paper towels. Wipe drippings from skillet with a paper towel.

Coat skillet with cooking spray; place skillet over medium-high heat until hot. Add onion and garlic; sauté until crisp-tender.

Combine apple, pear, and lemon juice; toss to coat. Add hens, apple mixture, apple juice, applejack, and 1 teaspoon rosemary to skillet. Cover, reduce heat, and simmer 20 to 30 minutes or until hens are done and fruit is tender. Transfer hens and fruit mixture to a serving platter, using a slotted spoon. Garnish with fresh rosemary sprigs, if desired. Yield: 6 servings (192 calories per serving).

PROTEIN 20.3 FAT 4.9 CARBOHYDRATE 16.9 CHOLESTEROL 64
IRON 1.2 SODIUM 170 CALCIUM 28

GET A PHYSICAL

Fitness experts urge both men and women who are inactive or out of shape, particularly if they are past the age of 40, to undergo a complete medical checkup before starting an exercise program.

Some medical problems automatically make aerobic exercise off limits: severe obesity (50 pounds above ideal body weight), certain types of heart disease, uncontrolled diabetes, high blood pressure that medications can't control, and acute infectious diseases. People with these conditions may be allowed to exercise but only under medical supervision. Other indications that you may not be a good candidate for strenuous aerobics include shortness of breath during mild activity, chest pain, irregular heartbeats, and chronic back pain. If in doubt about whether or not you are physically able to exercise, check with your physician.

TARRAGON TURKEY CUTLETS

½ cup soft whole wheat breadcrumbs
2 tablespoons chopped fresh parsley
1 teaspoon dried whole tarragon
1 teaspoon grated lemon rind
¼ teaspoon salt
¼ teaspoon salt-free lemon-pepper seasoning
⅛ teaspoon garlic powder
2 tablespoons lemon juice
1 teaspoon olive oil
1 pound turkey breast cutlets
Olive oil-flavored vegetable cooking spray
Lemon wedges (optional)
Fresh tarragon sprigs (optional)

Combine first 7 ingredients, stirring well. Combine lemon juice and olive oil; dip cutlets in lemon juice mixture, and dredge in crumb mixture. Cover and refrigerate 1 hour.

Coat a large nonstick skillet with cooking spray; place over medium-high heat until hot. Add cutlets, and cook 3 to 4 minutes on each side or until browned. Transfer cutlets to a serving platter. If desired, garnish with lemon wedges and fresh tarragon sprigs. Yield: 4 servings (176 calories per serving).

PROTEIN 28.1   FAT 3.4   CARBOHYDRATE 7.1   CHOLESTEROL 68
IRON 1.8   SODIUM 285   CALCIUM 33

TURKEY BREASTS WITH PINEAPPLE-CRANBERRY SALSA

¾ cup finely chopped fresh pineapple
½ cup finely chopped fresh cranberries
¼ cup thinly sliced green onions
¼ cup finely chopped dried dates
1 tablespoon honey
1 teaspoon lemon juice
1 teaspoon grated fresh ginger
¼ teaspoon ground red pepper
½ teaspoon ground coriander
¼ teaspoon salt
¼ teaspoon ground white pepper
⅛ teaspoon ground ginger
1½ pounds boneless fresh turkey breast slices
Vegetable cooking spray
2 teaspoons vegetable oil
½ cup unsweetened orange juice
1 tablespoon lemon juice

Combine first 8 ingredients in a small bowl; stir well. Cover and chill salsa 1 hour.

Combine coriander, salt, white pepper, and ground ginger; sprinkle over both sides of each turkey slice.

Coat a large nonstick skillet with cooking spray; add oil. Place over medium heat until hot. Add turkey; cook until lightly browned on both sides. Add orange juice and 1 tablespoon lemon juice. Cover, reduce heat, and simmer 10 minutes or until turkey is done. Transfer turkey to individual serving plates. Spoon ¼ cup salsa over each serving. Yield: 6 servings (212 calories per serving).

PROTEIN 27.3   FAT 3.6   CARBOHYDRATE 17.5   CHOLESTEROL 68
IRON 1.7   SODIUM 171   CALCIUM 27

VEGETABLE-STUFFED TURKEY BREAST

1 (3-pound) boneless turkey breast, skinned
Vegetable cooking spray
1 teaspoon reduced-calorie margarine
½ cup finely chopped onion
½ cup chopped fresh mushrooms
½ cup shredded carrot
1 cup soft whole wheat breadcrumbs
¼ cup chopped fresh parsley
½ teaspoon dried whole thyme
½ teaspoon grated lemon rind
¼ teaspoon pepper
¼ cup canned low-sodium chicken broth,
  undiluted
1 egg, lightly beaten
2 teaspoons lemon juice
2 tablespoons reduced-calorie margarine, melted
1 tablespoon white wine Worcestershire sauce
Baby carrots, cut lengthwise (optional)
Lemon slices (optional)

Trim fat from turkey; remove tendons. Place turkey breast, boned side up, on heavy-duty plastic wrap. From center, slice horizontally through thickest part of each side of breast almost to outer edge; flip each cut piece over to enlarge breast. Place heavy-duty plastic wrap over turkey, and flatten to ½-inch thickness using a meat mallet or rolling pin.

Coat a large nonstick skillet with cooking spray; add 1 teaspoon margarine. Place over medium-high heat until hot. Add onion, mushrooms, and shredded carrot; sauté until crisp-tender. Stir in breadcrumbs and next 7 ingredients; stir well.

Spoon mushroom mixture in center of turkey breast, leaving a 2-inch border at sides; roll up, jellyroll fashion, starting with short side. Tie turkey breast securely at 2-inch intervals with string. Place, seam side down, on a rack in a roasting pan coated with cooking spray. Insert meat thermometer. Bake, uncovered, at 325° for 45 minutes.

Combine 2 tablespoons margarine and Worcestershire sauce; brush over turkey. Bake, uncovered, an additional 1½ hours or until meat thermometer registers 185°, brushing with remaining margarine mixture after 1 hour. Transfer to a large serving platter; remove string. Let stand 10 minutes before slicing. If desired, garnish with baby carrots and lemon slices. Yield: 12 servings (129 calories per serving).

PROTEIN 21.8   FAT 2.6   CARBOHYDRATE 3.9   CHOLESTEROL 74
IRON 1.4   SODIUM 98   CALCIUM 20

Show off Tropical Shrimp Salad (page 185) by arranging shrimp, mango, kiwifruit, and pineapple on lettuce-lined plates and drizzling with the honey-citrus dressing.

Salads & Salad Dressings

SUMMER FRUIT SALAD IN LEMONADE GLAZE

1 (11-ounce) can mandarin oranges in water,
  undrained
¼ teaspoon unflavored gelatin
¼ cup frozen lemonade concentrate, thawed
1 teaspoon poppy seeds
2 cups fresh cherries, pitted and halved
2 cups sliced fresh peaches
1½ cups sliced fresh plums

Drain oranges, reserving ¼ cup liquid. Combine reserved liquid and gelatin in a small non-aluminum saucepan; let stand 1 minute. Add lemonade concentrate; stir well. Bring to a boil, and cook 2 minutes or until gelatin dissolves, stirring constantly. Remove from heat, and stir in poppy seeds. Cover and chill 3 hours or until mixture is thickened.

Combine oranges, cherries, peaches, and plums; toss gently. Pour lemonade mixture over fruit mixture, and toss gently. Yield: 6 servings (85 calories per 1-cup serving).

PROTEIN 1.3 FAT 0.9 CARBOHYDRATE 19.7 CHOLESTEROL 0
IRON 0.4 SODIUM 3 CALCIUM 18

FRESH PEACH SALAD WITH CREAMY GINGER DRESSING

4 cups sliced fresh peaches
2 tablespoons sugar
2 tablespoons rum
2 tablespoons lime juice
½ cup vanilla low-fat yogurt
2 teaspoons minced crystallized ginger
2 cups fresh raspberries
16 spinach leaves

Combine first 4 ingredients in a medium bowl; stir gently. Cover and chill 2 hours. Drain peaches, reserving 2 tablespoons marinade. Combine 1 cup peaches, reserved marinade, yogurt, and ginger in container of an electric blender or food processor; top with cover, and process until smooth.

Arrange remaining 3 cups peaches and raspberries on a spinach-lined serving platter. Drizzle yogurt mixture evenly over sliced peaches and raspberries. Serve immediately. Yield: 8 servings (82 calories per serving).

PROTEIN 1.8 FAT 0.5 CARBOHYDRATE 16.7 CHOLESTEROL 1
IRON 0.7 SODIUM 21 CALCIUM 50

FRESH PINEAPPLE SLAW

2 cups chopped fresh pineapple
1 cup shredded carrot
1 medium-size green pepper, cut into
  julienne strips
3 tablespoons white wine vinegar
3 tablespoons unsweetened pineapple
  juice
1 tablespoon honey
1 teaspoon vegetable oil
2 ounces blue cheese, crumbled

Combine pineapple, carrot, and green pepper in a medium bowl; toss gently.

Combine vinegar and next 3 ingredients; stir well with a wire whisk. Pour over pineapple mixture; toss gently. Cover and chill 1 hour. Top with blue cheese just before serving. Yield: 7 servings (90 calories per ½-cup serving).

PROTEIN 2.2 FAT 3.4 CARBOHYDRATE 13.9 CHOLESTEROL 6
IRON 0.5 SODIUM 119 CALCIUM 53

Chives and shredded cheese add exciting flavor to sautéed pears in Peppered Pears with Jarlsberg Cheese.

PEPPERED PEARS WITH JARLSBERG CHEESE

3 medium-size ripe pears
Vegetable cooking spray
1 teaspoon reduced-calorie margarine
6 Boston lettuce leaves
2 tablespoons lemon juice
½ teaspoon sugar
½ teaspoon Dijon mustard
1 tablespoon chopped fresh chives
¼ cup (1 ounce) shredded reduced-fat Jarlsberg
   cheese
Dash of freshly ground pepper
Fresh chives (optional)

Peel and core pears; cut in half lengthwise, and set aside.

Coat a large nonstick skillet with cooking spray; add margarine. Place over medium heat; cook until margarine melts. Add pears; sauté 10 to 15 minutes or until pears are tender, turning frequently. Transfer hot pears to lettuce-lined salad plates; set aside.

Add lemon juice, sugar, and mustard to skillet; cook over medium heat until bubbly. Drizzle lemon juice mixture over pears. Sprinkle with chopped chives, cheese, and freshly ground pepper. Garnish with fresh chives, if desired. Yield: 6 servings (70 calories per serving).

PROTEIN 1.7 FAT 1.5 CARBOHYDRATE 13.6 CHOLESTEROL 2
IRON 0.2 SODIUM 39 CALCIUM 10

FRUITED BROCCOLI SALAD

3 cups fresh broccoli flowerets
⅓ cup golden raisins
¼ cup sweet onion slices, separated into rings
¼ cup reduced-calorie mayonnaise
¼ cup fromage blanc
2 tablespoons minced water chestnuts
1 tablespoon white wine vinegar
1 tablespoon unsweetened orange juice
2 teaspoons sugar
¼ teaspoon grated orange rind
Orange rind strips (optional)

Combine broccoli, raisins, and onion slices in a medium bowl; toss gently.

Combine mayonnaise and next 6 ingredients in a small bowl; stir well. Add mayonnaise mixture to broccoli mixture, and toss gently to coat vegetables. Cover and chill thoroughly. Garnish with orange rind strips before serving, if desired. Yield: 8 servings (57 calories per ½-cup serving).

PROTEIN 1.9 FAT 2.1 CARBOHYDRATE 8.5 CHOLESTEROL 2
IRON 0.3 SODIUM 71 CALCIUM 26

HARVARD BEET SALAD

1 (15¼-ounce) can sliced beets, drained
⅓ cup sugar
⅓ cup cider vinegar
2 teaspoons cornstarch
¼ teaspoon salt
1 tablespoon low-sugar orange marmalade
2 medium-size oranges, peeled and sectioned
Green leaf lettuce (optional)

Place beets in an 8-inch square baking dish.

Combine sugar, vinegar, cornstarch, and salt in a small saucepan. Bring to a boil over medium heat. Stir in marmalade; let cool slightly. Pour over beets; cover and marinate in refrigerator 8 hours, stirring occasionally.

Drain beets, reserving 2 tablespoons marinade. Combine reserved marinade and orange sections; toss gently. Stir in beets. Arrange salad on individual lettuce-lined salad plates, if desired. Serve immediately. Yield: 4 servings (111 calories per serving).

PROTEIN 0.9 FAT 0.1 CARBOHYDRATE 28.6 CHOLESTEROL 0
IRON 0.4 SODIUM 177 CALCIUM 24

MINTED CUCUMBER AND SWEET ONION SALAD

½ cup plain nonfat yogurt
2 cups peeled, seeded, and sliced cucumber
¾ cup chopped sweet onion
¼ cup diced sweet red pepper
¼ cup diced sweet yellow pepper
3 tablespoons minced fresh parsley
2 tablespoons chopped fresh mint
1 tablespoon lemon juice
1 teaspoon white wine vinegar
½ teaspoon sugar
⅛ teaspoon ground red pepper
Dash of garlic powder
Fresh mint sprigs (optional)

Spoon yogurt onto several layers of paper towels; spread to ½-inch thickness. Cover with additional paper towels; let stand 5 minutes. Scrape yogurt into a bowl, using a rubber spatula; cover and refrigerate.

Combine cucumber and next 5 ingredients in a medium bowl; stir well. Combine drained yogurt, lemon juice, vinegar, sugar, ground red pepper, and garlic powder in a small bowl, stirring well; pour over cucumber mixture, and stir gently.

Cover and chill 2 hours. Garnish with fresh mint sprigs, if desired. Yield: 6 servings (28 calories per ½-cup serving).

PROTEIN 1.7 FAT 0.2 CARBOHYDRATE 5.4 CHOLESTEROL 0
IRON 0.4 SODIUM 18 CALCIUM 51

Summer Corn and Basil Salad, with a variety of flavorful and colorful ingredients, offers cool refreshment for summer dining.

SUMMER CORN AND BASIL SALAD

1 (10-ounce) package, frozen whole kernel corn,
 thawed
½ cup chopped sweet red pepper
¼ cup thinly sliced green onions
8 cherry tomatoes, quartered
12 fresh basil leaves, thinly sliced
Spicy Tomato Dressing
½ pound fresh snow pea pods

Combine first 5 ingredients in a medium bowl, tossing gently. Stir in Spicy Tomato Dressing; cover and chill 3 hours.

Blanch snow peas in boiling water 30 seconds or until crisp-tender; drain. Rinse under cold water until cool; drain. Arrange snow peas on a platter. Spoon corn mixture over snow peas. Yield: 6 servings (86 calories per ½-cup serving).

Spicy Tomato Dressing

½ cup no-salt-added tomato sauce
2 tablespoons golden raisins
2 tablespoons white wine vinegar
1 tablespoon sliced green onions
3 fresh basil leaves
¼ teaspoon salt
Dash of ground red pepper

Combine tomato sauce, raisins, white wine vinegar, green onions, basil leaves, salt, and pepper in container of an electric blender; top with cover, and process tomato sauce mixture until smooth. Yield: ½ cup.

PROTEIN 3.2 FAT 0.6 CARBOHYDRATE 19.2 CHOLESTEROL 0
IRON 1.6 SODIUM 109 CALCIUM 41

MINTED PEAS IN LETTUCE CUPS

2 cups frozen English peas, thawed
½ cup sliced parsnips
1 tablespoon vegetable oil
2 tablespoons white wine vinegar
1 tablespoon frozen orange juice concentrate,
    thawed
2 tablespoons chopped fresh mint
1 tablespoon chopped fresh parsley
½ teaspoon sugar
8 Boston lettuce leaves
Fresh mint leaves (optional)

Blanch peas and parsnips in boiling water 2 to 4 minutes or until crisp-tender; drain. Rinse under cold water; drain. Place in a medium bowl.

Combine oil and next 5 ingredients; stir well with a wire whisk. Pour over peas and parsnips; let stand until cool, stirring often.

Spoon pea mixture onto lettuce leaves, using a slotted spoon. Drizzle 1 teaspoon orange juice mixture over each serving. Garnish with fresh mint leaves, if desired. Yield: 4 servings (110 calories per ½-cup serving).

PROTEIN 4.0 FAT 2.4 CARBOHYDRATE 14.8 CHOLESTEROL 0
IRON 1.3 SODIUM 83 CALCIUM 28

MARINATED TOMATO AND JICAMA

2 large ripe tomatoes
½ medium jicama, peeled and cut into julienne
    strips (about 1 cup)
¼ cup white wine vinegar
2 tablespoons unsweetened apple juice
1 tablespoon olive oil
1 teaspoon white wine Worcestershire sauce
2 tablespoons chopped fresh chives
1 tablespoon chopped fresh basil
¼ teaspoon freshly ground pepper
Dash of garlic powder
Red leaf lettuce (optional)
Fresh chives (optional)

Cut tomatoes into ½-inch slices; arrange on one side of an 11-x 7-x 2-inch baking dish. Arrange jicama on other side of dish. Combine vinegar and next 7 ingredients. Pour vinegar mixture over tomato and jicama. Cover and marinate in refrigerator 8 hours, turning occasionally.

Drain vegetables, reserving ¼ cup plus 2 tablespoons marinade. Arrange tomato on a lettuce-lined platter, if desired. Arrange jicama strips over tomatoes. Garnish with fresh chives, if desired. Drizzle reserved marinade over salad. Serve immediately. Yield: 6 servings (46 calories per serving).

PROTEIN 0.8 FAT 2.5 CARBOHYDRATE 5.4 CHOLESTEROL 0
IRON 0.5 SODIUM 16 CALCIUM 9

ICY HOT BEANS AND POTATO SALAD

1 pound small new potatoes
½ pound fresh green beans
¼ cup lemon juice
2 tablespoons water
1 tablespoon vegetable oil
¼ cup thinly sliced green onions
½ teaspoon ground cumin
½ teaspoon ground red pepper
¼ teaspoon mustard seeds, crushed
⅛ teaspoon ground coriander

Wash potatoes. Cook in boiling water to cover 15 minutes or until tender; drain and cool slightly. Cut into quarters; place in a bowl. Set aside.

Wash beans; trim ends, and remove strings. Cut into 2-inch pieces. Arrange in a vegetable steamer over boiling water. Cover and steam 5 minutes or until crisp-tender. Add to potato.

Combine lemon juice, water, and oil in a small saucepan; bring to a boil. Stir in green onions and remaining ingredients; pour over vegetable mixture, and toss gently. Cover and chill. Yield: 8 servings (70 calories per ½-cup serving).

PROTEIN 1.9 FAT 1.9 CARBOHYDRATE 12.5 CHOLESTEROL 0
IRON 1.2 SODIUM 6 CALCIUM 22

BLACK BEAN SLAW

2½ cups finely shredded cabbage
1 (15-ounce) can black beans, rinsed and drained
½ cup shredded carrot
½ cup chopped purple onion
¼ cup chopped fresh cilantro
½ cup plain nonfat yogurt
½ cup no-salt-added salsa
2 tablespoons reduced-calorie mayonnaise
2 teaspoons white wine vinegar
2 teaspoons lime juice
Fresh cilantro sprigs (optional)

Combine cabbage, beans, carrot, onion, and chopped cilantro in a large bowl; toss well. Combine yogurt and next 4 ingredients in a small bowl, stirring well. Pour over cabbage mixture, and toss gently. Cover and chill at least 2 hours. Garnish with fresh cilantro sprigs, if desired. Yield: 8 servings (58 calories per ½-cup serving).

PROTEIN 3.1 FAT 1.2 CARBOHYDRATE 9.3 CHOLESTEROL 2
IRON 0.9 SODIUM 132 CALCIUM 55

GARBANZO BEAN SALAD

1 (15-ounce) can garbanzo beans, drained
¾ cup chopped purple onion
¾ cup peeled, seeded, and chopped tomato
¾ cup diced sweet red pepper
½ cup chopped ripe olives
3 tablespoons minced fresh parsley
2 tablespoons lemon juice
2 tablespoons red wine vinegar
2 tablespoons canned low-sodium chicken broth, undiluted
2 teaspoons olive oil
1 clove garlic, minced
¼ teaspoon salt
¼ teaspoon freshly ground pepper

Combine beans, onion, tomato, sweet red pepper, and olives in a medium bowl; stir well. Combine parsley and remaining ingredients in a

small bowl; beat well with a wire whisk. Pour parsley mixture over vegetable mixture, and stir gently. Cover and chill 1 hour. Yield: 9 servings (68 calories per ½-cup serving).

PROTEIN 2.0 FAT 2.3 CARBOHYDRATE 10.5 CHOLESTEROL 0
IRON 1.0 SODIUM 223 CALCIUM 24

MIXED GREENS AND ORANGE SALAD

1 small purple onion
4 cups torn Bibb lettuce
4 cups torn curly leaf lettuce
2 large oranges, peeled and sectioned
Cranberry Dressing
¼ teaspoon freshly ground pepper

Cut onion into ¼-inch slices, and separate into rings. Set aside.
Combine Bibb and leaf lettuce in a large bowl. Place 1 cup salad greens on each of 8 individual salad plates. Arrange onion and orange sections on greens; spoon 2 tablespoons Cranberry Dressing over each salad. Sprinkle pepper evenly over each salad. Yield: 8 servings (83 calories per serving).

Cranberry Dressing

1¼ cups frozen cranberries, thawed
⅓ cup sugar
3 tablespoons orange juice
1 tablespoon white wine vinegar
1 tablespoon vegetable oil
¼ teaspoon grated orange rind

Combine cranberries, sugar, and orange juice in a medium saucepan; cook over medium-low heat 8 minutes or until cranberries pop and mixture thickens, stirring frequently. Remove from heat. Add vinegar, oil, and orange rind, stirring well. Cover and chill thoroughly. Yield: 1 cup.

PROTEIN 1.4 FAT 1.9 CARBOHYDRATE 16.3 CHOLESTEROL 0
IRON 0.7 SODIUM 5 CALCIUM 34

SPICY SESAME-NOODLE SALAD

1 medium carrot, scraped and cut into 1½-inch
  julienne strips
1 green onion
3 tablespoons low-sodium soy sauce
1 tablespoon sesame oil
1 tablespoon water
¾ teaspoon garlic powder
¾ teaspoon crushed red pepper
½ teaspoon pepper
8 ounces linguine, uncooked

Cook carrot strips in boiling water 1 minute;
drain. Rinse under cold water; drain well, and set
aside. Cut green onion in half lengthwise; cut into
1-inch pieces. Set aside.

Combine soy sauce and next 5 ingredients in a
small bowl, stirring well.

Break linguine in half, and cook according to
package directions, omitting salt and fat; drain.
Combine linguine, soy sauce mixture, and vegetables in a large bowl; toss gently. Cover and chill
thoroughly. Yield: 9 servings (113 calories per ½-
cup serving).

PROTEIN 3.6 FAT 1.9 CARBOHYDRATE 19.9 CHOLESTEROL 0
IRON 1.2 SODIUM 203 CALCIUM 7

CREAMY PASTA SALAD

4½ ounces rotini pasta, uncooked
16 cherry tomatoes, quartered
2 tablespoons sliced ripe olives
2 teaspoons sugar
½ teaspoon salt
¼ teaspoon pepper
⅛ teaspoon garlic powder
½ cup fromage blanc
¼ cup reduced-calorie mayonnaise
1 tablespoon prepared mustard
2 teaspoons white wine vinegar

Cook pasta according to package directions,
omitting salt and fat. Drain; rinse pasta under cold

water, and drain. Combine pasta, tomatoes, and
olives in a large bowl.

Combine sugar and next 7 ingredients in a
small bowl; stir well. Add pasta mixture; toss to
combine. Yield: 5 servings (173 calories per 1-cup
serving).

PROTEIN 6.9 FAT 4.6 CARBOHYDRATE 26.7 CHOLESTEROL 4
IRON 1.5 SODIUM 334 CALCIUM 42

TOSS AND SERVE WILD RICE SALAD

1 cup canned no-salt-added chicken broth,
  undiluted
1 cup quick-cooking wild rice, uncooked
2 cups frozen broccoli flowerets
6 fresh asparagus spears, cut into 1-inch pieces
½ cup seeded, chopped tomato
¼ cup shredded carrot
Fresh Basil Vinaigrette
Fresh basil sprigs (optional)

Combine chicken broth and rice in a medium
saucepan; bring to a boil over medium heat. Reduce heat, and simmer, uncovered, 5 minutes.
Drain; set aside.

Arrange broccoli and asparagus in a vegetable
steamer over boiling water. Cover and steam 7 to
9 minutes or just until tender; let cool.

Combine cooked rice, steamed vegetables, tomato, and carrot in a large bowl; toss gently. Shake
Fresh Basil Vinaigrette vigorously, and pour over
salad; toss gently. Garnish with basil sprigs, if
desired. Yield: 4 servings (121 calories per 1-cup
serving).

Fresh Basil Vinaigrette

1 tablespoon minced fresh basil
2 tablespoons crumbled feta cheese
2 tablespoons white wine vinegar
2 tablespoons olive oil
2 teaspoons lemon juice
¼ teaspoon salt
⅛ teaspoon pepper

Combine all ingredients in a jar; cover tightly, and shake vigorously. Chill. Yield: 1/3 cup.

PROTEIN 5.1   FAT 3.7   CARBOHYDRATE 16.8   CHOLESTEROL 3
IRON 0.5   SODIUM 242   CALCIUM 43

MOROCCAN PORK SALAD

1/2 pound fresh snow pea pods
1/4 cup boiling water
3/4 pound lean boneless pork loin
1/4 cup low-sodium soy sauce
2 tablespoons honey
1 tablespoon minced fresh ginger
1/4 teaspoon garlic powder
1 1/3 cups canned no-salt-added chicken broth,
    undiluted
1 tablespoon rice vinegar
3/4 teaspoon honey
1/8 teaspoon dry mustard
Dash of ground ginger
3/4 cup uncooked couscous
Vegetable cooking spray

Wash snow peas; trim ends, and remove strings. Cook snow peas in boiling water until crisp-tender. Drain well, and set aside.

Trim fat from pork. Cut pork lengthwise to within 1/2-inch of outer edge, leaving 1 long side connected; flip cut piece over to enlarge pork loin.

Combine soy sauce, honey, ginger, and garlic powder in a large zip-top heavy-duty plastic bag; add pork. Seal and marinate in refrigerator at least 2 hours.

Combine broth and next 4 ingredients in a medium saucepan; bring to a boil. Remove from heat. Add couscous; cover and let stand 5 minutes or until couscous is tender and liquid is absorbed. Fluff couscous with a fork; transfer to a bowl. Cover and chill at least 1 hour.

Remove pork from marinade. Place marinade in a saucepan; bring to a boil, reduce heat, and simmer 2 minutes. Insert meat thermometer into thickest part of pork, if desired. Coat grill rack with cooking spray; place on grill over medium-hot coals. Place pork on rack; cook 15 minutes or until meat thermometer registers 165°, turning once and basting with reserved marinade. Let stand 10 minutes. Slice diagonally into 1/4-inch slices.

Add snow peas to couscous mixture; toss gently. Spoon mixture onto a large serving platter; top with pork slices. Yield: 6 servings (230 calories per serving).

PROTEIN 16.2   FAT 6.2   CARBOHYDRATE 25.5   CHOLESTEROL 39
IRON 1.6   SODIUM 321   CALCIUM 25

SMOKED TURKEY SALAD WITH BROWN AND WILD RICE

1/2 cup wild rice, uncooked
2 1/2 cups water
1/2 cup brown rice, uncooked
12 ounces smoked turkey breast, cut into
    3/4-inch cubes
14 cherry tomatoes, quartered
1/2 medium-size green pepper, cut into julienne
    strips
1/4 cup chopped green onions
2 tablespoons minced fresh parsley
3 tablespoons balsamic vinegar
1 tablespoon vegetable oil
1 teaspoon minced fresh ginger
1 clove garlic, crushed
2 tablespoons sliced almonds, toasted

Rinse and drain wild rice. Place water in a medium saucepan; bring to a boil. Stir in wild rice and brown rice; cover, reduce heat, and simmer 50 minutes or until rice is tender.

Combine cooked rice, turkey, and next 4 ingredients in a large bowl. Combine vinegar, oil, ginger, and garlic in a small jar; cover tightly, and shake vigorously. Pour over turkey mixture. Toss well. Spoon mixture onto a large serving platter. Sprinkle with toasted almonds. Yield: 7 servings (204 calories per 1-cup serving).

PROTEIN 15.3   FAT 6.7   CARBOHYDRATE 21.6   CHOLESTEROL 27
IRON 2.2   SODIUM 341   CALCIUM 22

Crabmeat and shrimp, accented with chili sauce and horseradish, blend flavors in Spicy Seafood Aspics.

SPICY SEAFOOD ASPICS

1½ cups no-salt-added vegetable juice cocktail,
    divided
½ cup reduced-calorie chili sauce
¼ cup no-salt-added tomato paste
3 tablespoons lemon juice
2 tablespoons grated onion
2 teaspoons sugar
1½ teaspoons prepared horseradish
1 teaspoon low-sodium Worcestershire sauce
¾ teaspoon hot sauce
2 envelopes unflavored gelatin
1 pound cooked shrimp, peeled, deveined, and
    coarsely chopped
8 ounces fresh lump crabmeat, drained and flaked
Vegetable cooking spray
Curly endive (optional)
Cucumber slices (optional)
Lemon wedges (optional)

Combine 1¼ cups vegetable juice cocktail and next 8 ingredients in a saucepan; bring to a boil. Reduce heat, and simmer, uncovered, 5 minutes.

Sprinkle gelatin over remaining ¼ cup vegetable juice cocktail; let stand 1 minute. Add gelatin mixture to hot juice mixture. Cook mixture over medium heat 5 minutes or until gelatin dissolves, stirring constantly. Remove from heat; chill until mixture reaches the consistency of unbeaten egg white. Fold in shrimp and crabmeat.

Coat 8 (4-ounce) molds with cooking spray. Spoon mixture into molds. Cover and chill until firm. Unmold aspics onto serving platter. If desired, garnish with endive, cucumber, and lemon. Yield: 8 servings (102 calories per serving).

PROTEIN 15.2 FAT 1.0 CARBOHYDRATE 7.6 CHOLESTEROL 93
IRON 1.8 SODIUM 201 CALCIUM 51

TROPICAL SHRIMP SALAD

1 pound medium-size fresh shrimp
3 cups water
1 medium banana, peeled and cut into ½-inch
    slices
1 tablespoon lemon juice
½ small fresh pineapple, peeled, cored, and sliced
1 small ripe mango, peeled, seeded, and sliced
1 kiwifruit, peeled and cut into 8 pieces
4 green leaf lettuce leaves
¼ cup unsweetened orange juice
3 tablespoons reduced-calorie mayonnaise
1 tablespoon honey
Dash of ground ginger

Peel and devein shrimp, leaving tails intact. Bring water to a boil; add shrimp, and cook 3 to 5 minutes. Drain well; rinse with cold water.

Brush banana slices with lemon juice. Arrange shrimp, banana slices, pineapple, mango, and kiwifruit on individual lettuce-lined plates.

Combine orange juice and next 3 ingredients in container of an electric blender; top with cover, and process 5 seconds. Drizzle evenly over salads. Yield: 4 servings (217 calories per serving).

PROTEIN 14.6 FAT 4.4 CARBOHYDRATE 31.9 CHOLESTEROL 128
IRON 2.6 SODIUM 229 CALCIUM 43

SMOKED TROUT WITH MELON

1 pound smoked trout fillets, skinned and flaked
4¼ cups cubed honeydew melon
3 cups cubed cantaloupe
¼ teaspoon freshly ground pepper
Curly leaf lettuce leaves (optional)

Combine first 4 ingredients in a large bowl; toss gently. Serve on lettuce-lined salad plates, if desired. Yield: 8 servings (142 calories per 1-cup serving).

PROTEIN 15.1 FAT 2.6 CARBOHYDRATE 15.7 CHOLESTEROL 39
IRON 1.5 SODIUM 35 CALCIUM 60

CREAMY HERB DRESSING

⅓ cup part-skim ricotta cheese
¼ cup skim milk
2 tablespoons chopped onion
2 tablespoons grated Parmesan cheese
¼ cup nonfat sour cream
¼ cup plain nonfat yogurt
2 teaspoons minced fresh basil
1 teaspoon minced fresh thyme
1 teaspoon minced fresh oregano
1 teaspoon minced fresh parsley
⅛ teaspoon ground white pepper

Combine ricotta cheese and milk in container of an electric blender or food processor; top with cover, and process until smooth. Add onion and Parmesan cheese; top with cover, and process until smooth. Add sour cream and remaining ingredients, stirring well. Serve with salad greens. Yield: 1¼ cups (13 calories per tablespoon).

PROTEIN 1.0 FAT 0.5 CARBOHYDRATE 1.0 CHOLESTEROL 2
IRON 0.1 SODIUM 20 CALCIUM 30

HOUSE DRESSING

⅔ cup no-salt-added vegetable juice cocktail
3 tablespoons nonfat buttermilk
2 tablespoons reduced-calorie mayonnaise
1½ teaspoons salt-free lemon-pepper seasoning

Combine all ingredients in a small bowl, stirring well with a wire whisk. Cover and chill at least 4 hours. Serve with salad greens or steamed fresh vegetables. Yield: 1 cup (9 calories per tablespoon).

PROTEIN 0.3 FAT 0.5 CARBOHYDRATE 0.8 CHOLESTEROL 1
IRON 0.1 SODIUM 19 CALCIUM 2

Toss a fresh salad anytime with delicious make-ahead dressings such as (clockwise from top left) Salad Dressing Dijon, Chutney Vinaigrette, Gazpacho Salad Dressing (page 188), and Citrus Salad Dressing.

CITRUS SALAD DRESSING

2 medium oranges
1 lime
3 tablespoons white wine vinegar
3 tablespoons sugar
½ cup plus 1 tablespoon water, divided
2 teaspoons cornstarch

Remove rind from 1 orange, using a sharp knife. Slice rind into thin strips. Place in a nonaluminum saucepan; add water to cover. Bring to a boil; drain rind, and discard liquid. Repeat procedure twice; set aside. Juice oranges and lime. Add vinegar and enough water to equal ¾ cup; set aside.

Combine reserved rind strips and sugar in a small saucepan. Stir in ½ cup water. Bring to a boil; reduce heat, and simmer 15 minutes, stirring frequently. Stir in reserved juice mixture.

Combine remaining 1 tablespoon water and cornstarch. Add to juice mixture. Bring to a boil, stirring constantly. Reduce heat; simmer 1 minute, stirring constantly. Remove from heat. Cover and chill thoroughly. Serve with salad greens. Yield: 1¼ cups (12 calories per tablespoon).

PROTEIN 0.1   FAT 0.0   CARBOHYDRATE 3.5   CHOLESTEROL 0
IRON 0.0   SODIUM 0   CALCIUM 4

SALAD DRESSING DIJON

½ cup white wine vinegar
¼ cup plus 1 tablespoon water
2 tablespoons olive oil
1 tablespoon Dijon mustard
1 clove garlic, minced
1 teaspoon sugar
⅛ teaspoon freshly ground pepper

Combine all ingredients in a small jar; cover tightly, and shake vigorously to blend. Cover and refrigerate at least 8 hours. Serve with salad greens. Yield: ¾ cup (24 calories per tablespoon).

PROTEIN 0.0 FAT 2.3 CARBOHYDRATE 0.5 CHOLESTEROL 0
IRON 0.0 SODIUM 38 CALCIUM 1

RAISIN-NUT DRESSING

¼ cup plus 2 tablespoons unsweetened
    apple juice, divided
1½ teaspoons cornstarch
3 tablespoons cider vinegar
1 tablespoon plus 1 teaspoon honey
2 teaspoons Dijon mustard
½ vanilla bean, split lengthwise
⅓ cup golden raisins
1 tablespoon chopped almonds, toasted

Combine 2 tablespoons apple juice and cornstarch in a small saucepan; stir well. Gradually add remaining ¼ cup apple juice; cook over medium heat until thickened and bubbly. Remove from heat; stir in vinegar, honey, and mustard.
Scrape seeds from vanilla bean; stir into apple juice mixture. Stir in raisins and almonds; chill thoroughly. Serve with fresh fruit salad or salad greens. Yield: ¾ cup (25 calories per tablespoon).

PROTEIN 0.2 FAT 0.4 CARBOHYDRATE 5.4 CHOLESTEROL 0
IRON 0.1 SODIUM 26 CALCIUM 4

WARM CITRUS-SHALLOT VINAIGRETTE

Vegetable cooking spray
1 tablespoon olive oil
½ cup minced shallot
¾ cup frozen orange juice concentrate, thawed
    and undiluted
¼ cup water
1 tablespoon plus 1 teaspoon balsamic vinegar
½ teaspoon grated orange rind

Coat a small saucepan with cooking spray; add olive oil. Place over medium-high heat until hot. Add shallot, and sauté until tender. Add orange juice concentrate and remaining ingredients. Cook over low heat until thoroughly heated. Serve warm with salad greens. Yield: 1¼ cups (25 calories per tablespoon).

PROTEIN 0.3 FAT 0.7 CARBOHYDRATE 4.6 CHOLESTEROL 0
IRON 0.1 SODIUM 1 CALCIUM 5

CHUTNEY VINAIGRETTE

¼ cup white wine vinegar
3 tablespoons mango chutney
2 tablespoons coarse grind Dijon mustard
2 teaspoons sugar
1 clove garlic, minced
1½ tablespoons vegetable oil
1½ tablespoons water
⅛ teaspoon freshly ground pepper

Combine first 5 ingredients in container of an electric blender; top with cover, and blend at high speed 30 seconds. Combine oil and water. With blender running, gradually add oil mixture in a slow, steady stream. Blend 15 seconds. Stir in pepper. Cover and chill thoroughly. Stir well before serving. Serve with salad greens. Yield: ¾ cup (32 calories per tablespoon).

PROTEIN 0.1 FAT 1.9 CARBOHYDRATE 3.6 CHOLESTEROL 0
IRON 0.1 SODIUM 83 CALCIUM 2

AVOCADO DRESSING

½ cup nonfat buttermilk
1 small avocado, peeled and
   cut into chunks
¼ cup plain nonfat yogurt
¼ small onion, cut into chunks
1 slice pickled jalapeño pepper
¼ teaspoon chili powder
⅛ teaspoon salt
Dash of garlic powder

Combine first 5 ingredients in container of an electric blender or food processor; top with cover, and process until smooth. Stir in chili powder, salt, and garlic powder. Cover and chill thoroughly. Serve with salad greens or Mexican salad. Yield: 1 cup (11 calories per tablespoon).

PROTEIN 0.6   FAT 0.5   CARBOHYDRATE 1.1   CHOLESTEROL 0
IRON 0.0   SODIUM 31   CALCIUM 8

GAZPACHO SALAD DRESSING

½ cup reduced-calorie chili sauce
⅓ cup no-salt-added vegetable juice cocktail
2 tablespoons red wine vinegar
1 tablespoon vegetable oil
1 tablespoon lime juice
1 teaspoon sugar
¼ teaspoon salt
⅛ teaspoon hot sauce
¼ cup peeled, seeded, and chopped cucumber
¼ cup seeded, chopped tomato

Combine first 8 ingredients in a small bowl; stir well with a wire whisk until blended. Stir in cucumber and tomato. Cover and chill thoroughly. Serve with salad greens or Mexican salad. Yield: 1½ cups (11 calories per tablespoon).

PROTEIN 0.1   FAT 0.6   CARBOHYDRATE 1.3   CHOLESTEROL 0
IRON 0.0   SODIUM 30   CALCIUM 1

 FORGOTTEN FLEXIBILITY
Genetics dictates flexibility to some degree, but with a little effort anyone can improve what nature provides. The best tool for increasing flexibility is static stretching, which means stretching a muscle beyond its normal length (such as doing toe touches), and then holding the completed stretch for 10 to 60 seconds. Optimally, static stretches should be done daily; at minimum, three times per week. The goal is to gradually increase the length of the muscle stretched.

Fitness experts feel that static stretches performed with the help of a partner or done using antagonistic muscles may be even more likely to improve flexibility. Contracting an antagonistic muscle allows for a longer stretch. Working with a partner can do the same. For example, if you're doing sitting toe touches, a partner can push gently on your back to help lengthen the stretch.

Ballistic (bouncing) stretches are not recommended, although many people stretch in this manner. There is a greater chance of muscle injury or soreness when ballistic stretches are performed on muscles that have not gone through a warm-up phase.

The benefits of proper stretching include reduced chances of muscle injury or soreness, less back pain, improved posture, and improved productivity. That's quite a long list of pluses for an activity that takes only minutes out of your schedule.

All-American foods combine with a flavorful marinade in tasty Grilled Chicken Sandwiches (page 193).

Sandwiches & Snacks

WARM ASPARAGUS SANDWICHES

1 cup 1% low-fat cottage cheese
1 tablespoon plus 2 teaspoons freshly grated
  Parmesan cheese, divided
1 teaspoon chopped green onions
2 teaspoons lemon juice
16 fresh asparagus spears (about 10 ounces)
8 (1-ounce) slices white bread
8 (1-ounce) slices whole wheat bread
Vegetable cooking spray
1 tablespoon plus 1 teaspoon reduced-calorie
  margarine, melted

Position knife blade in food processor bowl; add cottage cheese, 2 teaspoons Parmesan cheese, green onions, and lemon juice. Process until smooth; set aside.

Snap off tough ends of asparagus. Remove scales from stalks with a knife or vegetable peeler, if desired. Arrange asparagus in a vegetable steamer over boiling water. Cover and steam 4 to 5 minutes or until crisp-tender.

Remove crust from bread slices. Roll each slice to ⅛-inch thickness with a rolling pin. Spread 1 tablespoon cottage cheese mixture over each slice. Place an asparagus spear on each slice, and roll up. Place seam side down on a baking sheet coated with cooking spray. Brush with melted margarine, and sprinkle with remaining 1 tablespoon Parmesan cheese. Bake at 400° for 10 minutes or until golden. Yield: 16 servings (78 calories per serving).

PROTEIN 4.6 FAT 1.9 CARBOHYDRATE 11.3 CHOLESTEROL 2
IRON 0.6 SODIUM 201 CALCIUM 47

AVOCADO DELUXE SANDWICH

2 tablespoons reduced-calorie mayonnaise
8 (¾-ounce) slices reduced-calorie oatmeal bread
4 (1-ounce) slices low-fat process American cheese
8 tomato slices (¼ inch thick)
8 thin slices avocado, peeled
1 cup alfalfa sprouts

Spread mayonnaise evenly over each slice of bread. Top each of 4 bread slices with 1 cheese slice, 2 tomato slices, 2 avocado slices, and ¼ cup alfalfa sprouts. Top with remaining bread slices. Serve immediately. Yield: 4 servings (147 calories per serving).

PROTEIN 4.7 FAT 6.3 CARBOHYDRATE 13.2 CHOLESTEROL 6
IRON 0.3 SODIUM 261 CALCIUM 55

OPEN-FACED ROASTED RED PEPPER SANDWICH

2 medium-size sweet red peppers
1 tablespoon olive oil
2 teaspoons rice wine vinegar
½ teaspoon dry mustard
½ teaspoon coarsely ground pepper
¼ teaspoon sugar
¼ teaspoon salt
¼ cup julienne-cut green onions
¼ cup julienne-cut zucchini
1 tablespoon julienne-cut fresh basil
8 (½-inch) slices French bread, toasted
½ cup (2 ounces) shredded Gruyére cheese

Cut peppers in half lengthwise; remove and discard seeds and membrane. Place peppers, skin side up, on a baking sheet; flatten with palm of hand. Broil 5½ inches from heat 12 minutes or until charred. Place peppers in ice water; chill 5 minutes. Remove from water; peel and discard skins. Cut into julienne strips; set aside.

Combine oil and next 5 ingredients in a zip-top heavy-duty plastic bag. Add red pepper, green onions, and zucchini. Seal and marinate in refrigerator 3 hours. Add fresh basil; toss well.

Arrange bread slices on an ungreased baking sheet; top with pepper mixture. Sprinkle cheese over pepper mixture. Broil 5½ inches from heat 2 minutes or until cheese melts. Serve immediately. Yield: 4 servings (202 calories per serving).

PROTEIN 7.9 FAT 9.3 CARBOHYDRATE 22.0 CHOLESTEROL 17
IRON 1.5 SODIUM 388 CALCIUM 168

SPINACH SALAD SANDWICH

¼ cup reduced-calorie mayonnaise
1½ tablespoons reduced-calorie catsup
8 (¾-ounce) slices reduced-calorie rye bread
4 (⅔-ounce) slices low-fat process Swiss
   cheese
2 hard-cooked eggs, thinly sliced
2 cups torn fresh spinach leaves
1 cup sliced fresh mushrooms

Combine mayonnaise and catsup in a small bowl; stir well. Evenly divide mixture among bread slices. Top each of 4 bread slices with a cheese slice. Arrange even amounts of egg, spinach, and mushrooms over cheese slices. Top with remaining 4 bread slices. Cut sandwiches in half. Yield: 4 servings (178 calories per serving).

PROTEIN 9.6 FAT 8.7 CARBOHYDRATE 23.9 CHOLESTEROL 105
IRON 1.4 SODIUM 422 CALCIUM 74

HERBED TOMATO SANDWICH

1 (3-ounce) package Neufchâtel cheese,
   softened
1 tablespoon chopped fresh parsley
1 teaspoon fresh lemon juice
¼ teaspoon minced garlic
⅛ teaspoon dried whole thyme
8 (¾-ounce) slices reduced-calorie whole
   wheat bread
8 tomato slices (¼ inch thick)
4 large Boston lettuce leaves
1 cup alfalfa sprouts

Combine first 5 ingredients in a bowl; stir well. Spread cheese mixture evenly over bread slices. Place 2 tomato slices, 1 lettuce leaf, and ¼ cup alfalfa sprouts on each of 4 bread slices; top with remaining 4 bread slices. Cut sandwiches in half. Yield: 4 servings (141 calories per serving).

PROTEIN 6.7 FAT 7.0 CARBOHYDRATE 15.8 CHOLESTEROL 16
IRON 1.8 SODIUM 283 CALCIUM 61

VEGETABLE CHEESE BURRITO

4 cups peeled, seeded, and chopped tomato
1½ cups cubed avocado
1 cup chopped green onions
¼ cup fresh lime juice
1 tablespoon chopped fresh cilantro
2 teaspoons minced fresh jalapeño pepper
8 (6-inch) flour tortillas
Vegetable cooking spray
2 cups (8 ounces) shredded reduced-fat Monterey
   Jack cheese
½ cup nonfat sour cream
Chopped tomatoes (optional)
Fresh cilantro sprigs (optional)

Combine first 6 ingredients in a medium bowl; stir well, and set aside.

Place tortillas on a baking sheet coated with cooking spray. Top each tortilla evenly with ¼ cup cheese. Bake at 400° for 1½ minutes or just until cheese melts.

Divide tomato mixture evenly among tortillas. Roll up tortillas, and place seam side down on a serving platter. Top each with 1 tablespoon sour cream. Sprinkle with tomatoes, if desired. Garnish with cilantro sprigs, if desired. Yield: 8 servings (274 calories per serving).

PROTEIN 13.3 FAT 12.3 CARBOHYDRATE 31.4 CHOLESTEROL 19
IRON 1.7 SODIUM 204 CALCIUM 270

 **LOW IMPACT YIELDS
HIGH ACHIEVEMENT**
Movements done during low-impact aerobics are more likely to be side-to-side rather than the up-and-down motions used during high-impact aerobics. To help achieve the same cardiovascular benefits, the upper body is moved around almost continuously. It's this upper-body action that has put low-impact movements in the same cardiovascular category as high-impact. Another bonus with low-impact is that it can be modified to suit any intensity.

GRILLED FLANK STEAK SANDWICH

1 (1½-pound) lean flank steak
½ cup Chablis or other dry white wine
2 tablespoons balsamic vinegar
2 teaspoons coarsely ground pepper
2 teaspoons minced garlic
1 teaspoon dried whole oregano
Vegetable cooking spray
2 teaspoons olive oil
1 cup thinly sliced green pepper
1 cup thinly sliced sweet red pepper
½ cup thinly sliced onion
½ teaspoon minced garlic
¼ teaspoon sugar
¼ teaspoon salt
8 reduced-calorie whole wheat sandwich buns,
    toasted

Trim fat from steak. Place steak in a large shallow dish. Combine wine and next 4 ingredients; pour over steak. Cover and marinate in refrigerator 8 hours, turning occasionally.

Coat a large nonstick skillet with cooking spray; add oil. Place over medium-high heat until hot. Add peppers, onion, and ½ teaspoon garlic; sauté 4 minutes. Sprinkle with sugar and salt; sauté an additional 2 minutes or until crisp-tender. Remove from heat, and keep warm.

Remove steak from marinade. Place marinade in a small saucepan; bring to a boil. Reduce heat, and simmer 5 minutes.

Coat grill rack with cooking spray; place on grill over medium-hot coals. Place steak on rack, and cook 6 to 7 minutes on each side or to desired degree of doneness, basting frequently with marinade. Slice steak diagonally across grain into ¼-inch-thick slices. Place bottom halves of buns on a serving platter. Divide steak evenly among bottom halves. Spoon pepper mixture evenly over steak. Top with remaining halves of buns. Yield: 8 servings (272 calories per serving).

PROTEIN 19.7 FAT 12.5 CARBOHYDRATE 19.0 CHOLESTEROL 47
IRON 2.5 SODIUM 352 CALCIUM 17

MOCK GYROS

½ cup chopped cucumber
½ cup nonfat sour cream
¼ cup plain nonfat yogurt
1 teaspoon olive oil
1 pound lean ground lamb
1 teaspoon dried whole oregano
½ teaspoon dried whole thyme
¼ teaspoon salt
1 tablespoon lemon juice
2 (6-inch) pita bread rounds, cut in half crosswise
1 cup thinly sliced onion
1½ cups shredded lettuce

Combine first 3 ingredients in a small bowl; stir well. Cover and chill 30 minutes.

Heat oil in a large nonstick skillet over medium heat until hot. Add lamb, oregano, thyme, and salt; cook until browned, stirring to crumble. Drain and pat dry with paper towels. Transfer mixture to a bowl. Add lemon juice, and stir well.

Spoon lamb mixture evenly into pita halves. Top evenly with onion and lettuce. Serve with sour cream mixture. Yield: 4 servings (334 calories per serving).

PROTEIN 30.9 FAT 10.3 CARBOHYDRATE 25.3 CHOLESTEROL 81
IRON 3.4 SODIUM 252 CALCIUM 97

BASIL CHICKEN SALAD SANDWICH

6 (4-ounce) skinned, boned chicken breast halves
½ cup chopped celery
⅓ cup chopped green onions
2 tablespoons pine nuts, toasted
⅓ cup plain nonfat yogurt
3 tablespoons reduced-calorie mayonnaise
1 tablespoon lemon juice
1 tablespoon chopped fresh basil
½ teaspoon salt
3 (6-inch) pita bread rounds, cut in half
    crosswise
¾ cup alfalfa sprouts

Place chicken in a medium saucepan; add water to cover. Bring to a boil; cover, reduce heat, and simmer 30 minutes or until chicken is tender. Drain chicken, and cut into ¾-inch pieces.

Combine chicken, celery, and next 7 ingredients, stirring well. Divide mixture evenly among 6 pita halves. Top each pita half with 2 tablespoons alfalfa sprouts. Yield: 6 servings (278 calories per serving).

PROTEIN 29.4 FAT 7.3 CARBOHYDRATE 20.9 CHOLESTEROL 73
IRON 2.6 SODIUM 332 CALCIUM 89

GRILLED CHICKEN SANDWICH

¼ cup fresh lime juice
2 tablespoons minced shallots
2 tablespoons Chablis or other dry white wine
1 teaspoon dried whole thyme
2 teaspoons vegetable oil
½ teaspoon sugar
½ teaspoon dried whole marjoram
¼ teaspoon coarsely ground pepper
6 (4-ounce) skinned, boned chicken breast
  halves
Vegetable cooking spray
3 tablespoons reduced-calorie mayonnaise
1 teaspoon spicy brown mustard
6 reduced-calorie whole wheat hamburger buns
6 green leaf lettuce leaves
1 small purple onion
6 tomato slices (¼ inch thick)

Combine first 8 ingredients in a zip-top heavy-duty plastic bag. Add chicken, turning to coat. Seal and marinate in refrigerator at least 1 hour.

Remove chicken from marinade; place marinade in a small saucepan. Bring to a boil; reduce heat, and simmer 5 minutes.

Coat grill rack with cooking spray; place rack on grill over medium-hot coals. Place chicken on rack, and cook 5 to 6 minutes on each side or until done, basting frequently with marinade. Set aside, and keep warm.

Combine mayonnaise and mustard; spread mixture evenly over bottom halves of buns. Top each with a green lettuce leaf. Place grilled chicken breasts on lettuce.

Cut onion into 6 slices, and separate into rings. Divide onion evenly among grilled chicken breasts, and top each with a tomato slice. Top with remaining bun halves. Yield: 6 servings (290 calories per serving).

PROTEIN 29.0 FAT 7.9 CARBOHYDRATE 24.3 CHOLESTEROL 73
IRON 2.2 SODIUM 356 CALCIUM 45

SHRIMP-VEGETABLE PITA POCKETS

1 cup fresh snow pea pods
¾ pound medium-size fresh shrimp, cooked,
  peeled, and deveined
3 cups shredded fresh spinach
1½ cups sliced fresh mushrooms
1 cup bean sprouts
2 tablespoons red wine vinegar
1 tablespoon olive oil
1 teaspoon minced fresh garlic
½ teaspoon dry mustard
¼ teaspoon salt
⅛ teaspoon ground white pepper
3 (6-inch) pita bread rounds, cut in half
  crosswise

Wash snow peas; trim ends, remove strings and cut in half. Cut shrimp into ¾-inch pieces. Combine snow peas, cooked shrimp, shredded spinach, sliced mushrooms, and bean sprouts in a large bowl; toss well.

Combine vinegar and next 5 ingredients in a small bowl; stir well using a wire whisk. Pour over shrimp mixture, and toss well. Spoon 1 cup mixture into each pita half. Serve immediately. Yield: 6 servings (168 calories per serving).

PROTEIN 9.7 FAT 3.6 CARBOHYDRATE 22.6 CHOLESTEROL 55
IRON 3.3 SODIUM 180 CALCIUM 75

Take a break from ordinary sandwiches by serving open-faced Shrimp Remoulade Sandwiches.

SHRIMP REMOULADE SANDWICHES

1½ cups coarsely chopped cooked shrimp
⅓ cup chopped celery
3 tablespoons reduced-calorie mayonnaise
1 teaspoon chopped green onions
1 teaspoon capers
½ teaspoon tarragon vinegar
¼ teaspoon salt
¼ teaspoon prepared horseradish
4 (¾-ounce) slices reduced-calorie oatmeal bread,
    toasted
1½ cups shredded romaine lettuce
4 lemon twists (optional)

Combine shrimp, celery, mayonnaise, and green onions in a small bowl, stirring well.

Add capers and next 3 ingredients, stirring well to combine.

Place bread slices on a serving platter. Divide lettuce evenly among bread slices. Spoon shrimp mixture evenly over lettuce. Garnish with lemon twists, if desired. Yield: 4 servings (148 calories per serving).

PROTEIN 17.4 FAT 4.9 CARBOHYDRATE 12.1 CHOLESTEROL 142
IRON 2.4 SODIUM 560 CALCIUM 42

CRAB SALAD ON ENGLISH MUFFIN

½ cup light process cream cheese product
2 tablespoons reduced-calorie mayonnaise
1 tablespoon lemon juice
1 teaspoon prepared horseradish
1 teaspoon Dijon mustard
2 tablespoons chopped celery
1 tablespoon chopped green onions
1 tablespoon toasted sesame seeds
8 ounces fresh lump crabmeat, drained
3 English muffins, split and toasted
1 tablespoon chopped fresh parsley
⅛ teaspoon paprika
6 lemon wedges (optional)

Combine first 5 ingredients in a small bowl; stir well. Add celery, green onions, and sesame seeds; stir well. Stir in crabmeat. Spoon crab mixture evenly over English muffin halves. Broil 5½ inches from heat 3 to 4 minutes or until lightly browned. Top each sandwich with parsley and paprika. Garnish with lemon wedges, if desired. Yield: 6 servings (185 calories per serving).

PROTEIN 11.8 FAT 6.4 CARBOHYDRATE 19.8 CHOLESTEROL 31
IRON 1.5 SODIUM 719 CALCIUM 115

OPEN-FACED TUNA MELT

1 (6½-ounce) can no-salt-added white tuna in
   spring water, drained
¼ cup chopped celery
1 tablespoon minced sweet pickle
3 tablespoons reduced-calorie mayonnaise
2 English muffins, split and toasted
4 tomato slices (¼ inch thick)
4 (1-ounce) slices low-fat process American cheese

Combine tuna, celery, pickle, and mayonnaise; stir well. Place muffin halves on an ungreased baking sheet. Spoon tuna mixture evenly onto each half. Top each with 1 tomato slice and 1 cheese slice. Broil 5½ inches from heat 2 to 3 minutes or until cheese melts. Yield: 4 servings (208 calories per serving).

PROTEIN 19.7 FAT 5.7 CARBOHYDRATE 19.0 CHOLESTEROL 19
IRON 1.3 SODIUM 650 CALCIUM 237

FLAVORED YOGURT CHEESE

2 cups plain nonfat yogurt
1 teaspoon salt-free lemon-pepper seasoning
½ teaspoon dried whole thyme
¼ teaspoon salt
¼ teaspoon garlic powder

Line a colander or sieve with a double layer of cheesecloth that has been rinsed out and squeezed dry; allow cheesecloth to extend over outside edge of colander. Stir yogurt until smooth; pour into colander, and fold edges of cheesecloth over to cover yogurt. Place colander in a large bowl to drain; refrigerate 8 hours. Remove yogurt from colander, and discard liquid. Remove yogurt from cheesecloth.
Combine yogurt, lemon-pepper seasoning, thyme, salt, and garlic powder; stir well. Cover and chill. Serve with unsalted crackers or raw fresh vegetables. Yield: 1 cup (16 calories per tablespoon).

PROTEIN 1.7 FAT 0.1 CARBOHYDRATE 2.3 CHOLESTEROL 1
IRON 0.1 SODIUM 58 CALCIUM 58

 NONFAT YOGURTS FOR CHEESE

For dips, cheesecakes, and other rich and creamy recipes, be sure to make "yogurt cheese" with the right type of nonfat yogurt. Select a yogurt that does not have gelatin added. This thickener binds the liquid to the solids, preventing the whey from weeping out. Typically, it's the less expensive yogurts that rely on gelatin to improve thickness and to solidify texture. A close look at the ingredient panel will let you know which is the best yogurt for your yogurt cheese.

HOT BEAN DIP WITH CORN CHIPS

6 (6-inch) corn tortillas
Butter-flavored vegetable cooking spray
¼ teaspoon salt
¼ teaspoon garlic powder
1 (16-ounce) can pinto beans, drained
3 tablespoons water
1 tablespoon finely chopped onion
2 teaspoons minced jalapeño pepper
½ teaspoon ground cumin
½ teaspoon white wine vinegar

Coat tortillas with cooking spray; sprinkle with salt and garlic powder. Cut each tortilla into 8 wedges, and place on an ungreased baking sheet. Bake at 350° for 6 minutes. Turn chips, and bake an additional 2 to 3 minutes or until golden and crisp. Let cool; store in an airtight container.

Combine pinto beans and remaining ingredients in a small saucepan. Mash beans slightly. Cook over low heat, 8 to 10 minutes or until thoroughly heated. Serve bean mixture warm with tortilla wedges. Yield: 6 servings (88 calories per 8 chips and ¼ cup dip).

PROTEIN 3.6 FAT 1.2 CARBOHYDRATE 16 CHOLESTEROL 0
IRON 1.6 SODIUM 296 CALCIUM 44

FRESH SALSA WITH PITA CHIPS

1¼ cups chopped tomato
2½ tablespoons chopped green onions
2 tablespoons cold water
1½ teaspoons chopped fresh cilantro
1½ teaspoons fresh lime juice
½ teaspoon minced jalapeño pepper
¼ teaspoon salt
3 (8-inch) pita bread rounds

Combine first 7 ingredients in a medium bowl; stir well. Cover and chill salsa at least 1 hour.

Separate each pita bread into 2 rounds; cut each round into 4 wedges, and place on an ungreased baking sheet. Bake at 400° for 7 minutes or until lightly browned. Yield: 6 servings (100 calories per 4 chips and ¼ cup salsa).

PROTEIN 2.2 FAT 0.8 CARBOHYDRATE 19.5 CHOLESTEROL 0
IRON 1.3 SODIUM 102 CALCIUM 35

HONEY-SESAME SNACK

1 (8-inch) flour tortilla, quartered
1½ teaspoons honey
1½ teaspoons sesame seeds, toasted

Place tortilla wedges on an ungreased baking sheet; bake at 400° for 3 minutes. Brush each with honey; sprinkle with sesame seeds. Bake an additional 2 minutes or until golden. Yield: 4 servings (54 calories per serving).

PROTEIN 1.2 FAT 1.5 CARBOHYDRATE 10.1 CHOLESTEROL 0
IRON 0.4 SODIUM 1 CALCIUM 11

TOASTED HERB STICKS

2 tablespoons reduced-calorie margarine,
   softened
1 teaspoon minced shallot
¼ teaspoon dried whole basil
¼ teaspoon dried whole dillweed
¼ teaspoon dried whole marjoram
6 (½-ounce) slices reduced-calorie whole wheat
   bread

Combine first 5 ingredients in a small bowl; stir well. Spread herb mixture evenly on bread slices.

Cut each bread slice into 4 narrow strips. (Do not remove crusts.) Place strips on an ungreased baking sheet. Bake at 350° for 10 minutes; turn strips over, and bake 4 to 5 minutes or until lightly browned. Remove from baking sheet; let cool on a wire rack. Store in an airtight container. Yield: 2 dozen (14 calories each).

PROTEIN 0.4 FAT 0.7 CARBOHYDRATE 1.7 CHOLESTEROL 0
IRON 0.1 SODIUM 27 CALCIUM 4

Top a flour tortilla with tomato sauce and cheese for Quick After-School Pizzas, a snack that everyone will enjoy.

QUICK AFTER-SCHOOL PIZZAS

1 (8-inch) flour tortilla
Vegetable cooking spray
2½ tablespoons no-salt-added
   tomato sauce
2 teaspoons minced onion
¼ teaspoon dried whole oregano
¼ cup (1 ounce) shredded part-skim
   mozzarella cheese
2 teaspoons grated Parmesan
   cheese

Place tortilla on a baking sheet coated with cooking spray. Bake at 400° for 3 minutes. Turn tortilla; spread tomato sauce evenly over tortilla, leaving a ½-inch border around edge. Sprinkle with onion, oregano, and cheeses. Bake an additional 5 minutes or until golden. Cut into 4 wedges. Yield: 4 servings (66 calories per serving).

PROTEIN 3.1 FAT 2.3 CARBOHYDRATE 9.1 CHOLESTEROL 5
IRON 0.3 SODIUM 51 CALCIUM 69

PINEAPPLE-NEUFCHÂTEL SNACK

1½ tablespoons Neufchâtel cheese, softened
1 teaspoon brown sugar
Dash of cinnamon
2 tablespoons crushed pineapple in juice, drained
1 (¾-ounce) slice reduced-calorie whole wheat
　bread, toasted
Dash of cinnamon

　Combine first 3 ingredients in a small bowl; stir well. Stir in pineapple. Spread mixture on toast. Sprinkle with cinnamon. Cut toast to form 2 triangles. Yield: 2 servings (72 calories each).

PROTEIN 2.4　FAT 3.8　CARBOHYDRATE 8.0　CHOLESTEROL 11
IRON 0.5　SODIUM 106　CALCIUM 25

RASPBERRY-BANANA FROSTY

1 cup frozen unsweetened raspberries
½ cup peeled, sliced banana
½ cup crushed ice
¼ cup skim milk
1 tablespoon sugar

　Combine all ingredients in container of an electric blender; top with cover, and process until smooth. Serve immediately. Yield: 3 servings (70 calories per ½-cup serving).

PROTEIN 1.4　FAT 0.4　CARBOHYDRATE 16.7　CHOLESTEROL 0
IRON 0.3　SODIUM 11　CALCIUM 36

PEACH FRAPPÉ

1¼ cups frozen unsweetened sliced peaches
½ cup plain nonfat yogurt
½ cup unsweetened orange juice
2 teaspoons sugar

　Combine all ingredients in container of an electric blender; top with cover, and process until smooth. Serve immediately. Yield: 4 servings (57 calories per ½-cup serving).

PROTEIN 2.2　FAT 0.1　CARBOHYDRATE 12.6　CHOLESTEROL 1
IRON 0.1　SODIUM 22　CALCIUM 62

COCONUT-ALMOND POPS

1 (8-ounce) carton vanilla low-fat yogurt
½ cup skim milk
1 tablespoon unsweetened coconut, toasted
½ teaspoon almond extract
4 (3-ounce) paper cups
4 wooden sticks

　Combine first 4 ingredients in a small bowl; stir well. Pour into paper cups. Cover tops of cups with aluminum foil, and insert a stick through foil into center of each cup. Freeze until firm. To serve, remove foil, and peel paper cup away from pop. Yield: 4 servings (67 calories per serving).

PROTEIN 3.9　FAT 1.4　CARBOHYDRATE 9.6　CHOLESTEROL 3
IRON 0.1　SODIUM 54　CALCIUM 135

Mango, apple, ginger, and allspice blend together in flavorful Mango Chutney (page 206). It is delicious served with roast beef, grilled pork, or broiled poultry.

Sauces

(From top): Red Plum Sauce and Peach and Apricot Sauce can be served over angel food cake, ice milk, or fresh fruit.

Sauces

(From top): Red Plum Sauce and Peach and Apricot Sauce can be served over angel food cake, ice milk, or fresh fruit.

CHUNKY BRANDIED APPLE SAUCE

1½ cups peeled, chopped apple
1 cup unsweetened apple juice
2 tablespoons applejack or other
    apple-flavored brandy
1 teaspoon sugar
1 teaspoon lemon juice
1 tablespoon cornstarch
2 tablespoons water
½ teaspoon apple pie spice

Combine first 5 ingredients in a saucepan; bring to a boil. Reduce heat, and simmer, uncovered, 8 minutes or until apple is tender.

Combine cornstarch and water, stirring until smooth; add to apple mixture. Add apple pie spice, and stir well. Bring to a boil, stirring constantly; cook 1 minute or until mixture is thickened. Serve warm over ice milk or angel food cake. Yield: 1¾ cups (11 calories per tablespoon).

PROTEIN 0.0   FAT 0.0   CARBOHYDRATE 2.8   CHOLESTEROL 0
IRON 0.0   SODIUM 0   CALCIUM 1

PEACH AND APRICOT SAUCE

1 (16-ounce) can sliced peaches in light syrup,
    drained
1 (16-ounce) can apricots in light syrup, drained
2 tablespoons cornstarch
½ cup water
1 tablespoon lemon juice
2 tablespoons bourbon
¼ teaspoon ground cinnamon
⅛ teaspoon ground nutmeg

Combine peaches and apricots in container of an electric blender or food processor; top with cover, and process until smooth.

Combine cornstarch, water, and lemon juice in a medium saucepan; stir until smooth. Add pureed fruit; stir well. Cook over medium heat until thickened and bubbly, stirring often. Remove from heat; stir in bourbon, cinnamon, and nutmeg. Serve warm or chilled over ice milk or angel food cake. Yield: 3¾ cups (8 calories per tablespoon).

PROTEIN 0.1   FAT 0.0   CARBOHYDRATE 2.0   CHOLESTEROL 0
IRON 0.0   SODIUM 0   CALCIUM 1

RED PLUM SAUCE

¾ pound red plums, pitted and quartered
2 tablespoons port wine
2 tablespoons frozen orange juice concentrate,
    thawed
1 tablespoon honey
1 teaspoon lemon juice

Combine all ingredients in a saucepan. Bring to a boil; cover, reduce heat, and simmer 15 minutes or until plums are tender. Place mixture in container of an electric blender or food processor; top with cover, and process until smooth. Cover and chill. Serve over ice milk or angel food cake. Yield: 1 cup (19 calories per tablespoon).

PROTEIN 0.2   FAT 0.1   CARBOHYDRATE 4.6   CHOLESTEROL 0
IRON 0.0   SODIUM 0   CALCIUM 2

DOUBLE BERRY DESSERT SAUCE

2 cups sliced fresh strawberries
2 cups cranberry juice cocktail
¼ cup rum
2 tablespoons cornstarch
1 teaspoon coconut extract

Combine first 4 ingredients in container of an electric blender or food processor; top with cover, and process until smooth. Transfer to a saucepan; cook over medium heat until thickened, stirring constantly. Remove from heat. Stir in extract. Yield: 3¼ cups (12 calories per tablespoon).

PROTEIN 0.0   FAT 0.0   CARBOHYDRATE 2.1   CHOLESTEROL 0
IRON 0.0   SODIUM 0   CALCIUM 1

PRALINE SAUCE

¼ cup firmly packed dark brown sugar
1 tablespoon cornstarch
1 cup skim milk
1 teaspoon reduced-calorie margarine
1 teaspoon vanilla extract
3 tablespoons chopped pecans, toasted

Combine first 3 ingredients in a saucepan. Cook over medium heat; stir constantly until mixture thickens and comes to a boil. Cook an additional 2 minutes; stir constantly. Add margarine, vanilla, and pecans; stir until margarine melts. Serve warm. Yield: 1½ cups (23 calories per tablespoon).

PROTEIN 0.4   FAT 0.9   CARBOHYDRATE 3.3   CHOLESTEROL 0
IRON 0.1   SODIUM 8   CALCIUM 15

TOMATO-CLAM PASTA SAUCE

Olive oil-flavored vegetable cooking spray
1 teaspoon olive oil
½ cup chopped purple onion
½ cup chopped sweet red pepper
2 cloves garlic, minced
1 (14½-ounce) can no-salt-added whole
　 tomatoes, undrained and chopped
1 (8-ounce) can no-salt-added tomato sauce
2 tablespoons chopped fresh parsley
1 teaspoon dried whole marjoram
½ teaspoon dried whole basil
½ teaspoon ground white pepper
¼ teaspoon salt
1 (6½-ounce) can minced clams, drained

Coat a saucepan with cooking spray; add oil. Place over medium-high heat until hot. Add onion, red pepper, and garlic; sauté until tender. Stir in tomato and next 6 ingredients. Bring to a boil; cover, reduce heat, and simmer 30 minutes. Add clams; cook until thoroughly heated. Serve over pasta. Yield: 3 cups (8 calories per tablespoon).

PROTEIN 0.5   FAT 0.1   CARBOHYDRATE 1.1   CHOLESTEROL 1
IRON 0.5   SODIUM 16   CALCIUM 6

SPANISH SAUCE

Olive oil-flavored vegetable cooking spray
1 teaspoon olive oil
½ cup plus 2 tablespoons chopped green
　 pepper
½ cup chopped onion
1 clove garlic, minced
1 (14½-ounce) can no-salt-added whole
　 tomatoes, undrained and chopped
2 tablespoons Burgundy or other red wine
¼ teaspoon cracked pepper
⅛ teaspoon ground saffron
2 tablespoons capers
2 tablespoons sliced ripe olives

Coat a large saucepan with cooking spray; add olive oil. Place saucepan over medium-high heat until hot.

Add green pepper, onion, and garlic; sauté until tender. Stir in tomato, wine, pepper, and saffron. Bring to a boil; cover, reduce heat, and simmer 15 minutes. Stir in capers and olives; cook until thoroughly heated. Serve sauce warm over cooked pasta or chicken. Yield: 2¼ cups (5 calories per tablespoon).

PROTEIN 0.2   FAT 0.2   CARBOHYDRATE 0.8   CHOLESTEROL 0
IRON 0.1   SODIUM 41   CALCIUM 5

SPICY MARINADE

½ cup lemon juice
¼ cup dry sherry
2 tablespoons low-sodium
　 soy sauce
1 tablespoon olive oil
2 cloves garlic, minced
2 teaspoons grated lemon rind
1 teaspoon ground cumin
1 teaspoon chili powder
½ teaspoon ground turmeric
½ teaspoon ground ginger
¼ teaspoon crushed red pepper

Combine all ingredients in a jar. Cover tightly, and shake vigorously.

Use to marinate beef before cooking. Remove beef from marinade, and bring marinade to a boil in a saucepan. Simmer 5 minutes. Remove from heat, and use for basting beef while cooking. Yield: 1 cup (13 calories per tablespoon).

PROTEIN 0.1 FAT 0.9 CARBOHYDRATE 1.3 CHOLESTEROL 0
IRON 0.2 SODIUM 51 CALCIUM 5

CARIBBEAN SPICE MIX

¼ cup ground turmeric
2 tablespoons ground coriander
1 tablespoon ground cumin
1 tablespoon ground cinnamon
2¼ teaspoons ground ginger
2¼ teaspoons garlic powder
1 teaspoon pepper
½ teaspoon ground cloves

Combine all ingredients in a small bowl; stir well. Store in an airtight container. Use when recipe calls for curry powder. Yield: ½ cup plus 2 tablespoons (19 calories per tablespoon).

PROTEIN 0.6 FAT 0.5 CARBOHYDRATE 3.7 CHOLESTEROL 0
IRON 2.1 SODIUM 4 CALCIUM 26

GARLIC-HERB VINEGAR

½ cup chopped fresh basil
½ cup chopped fresh oregano
¼ cup chopped fresh parsley
4 cloves garlic, cut in half
3¾ cups white wine vinegar
    (5% acidity)
Additional sprigs of fresh oregano and
    basil (optional)

Place first 4 ingredients in a wide-mouth quart glass jar. Pour vinegar into a medium saucepan;

bring to a boil. Pour hot vinegar over herbs; cover. Let mixture stand at room temperature at least 1 week.

Strain vinegar into decorative jars, discarding herbs. If desired, add sprigs of fresh oregano and basil to jars. Carefully seal jars with a cork or other airtight lid. Yield: 3½ cups (3 calories per tablespoon).

PROTEIN 0.1 FAT 0.0 CARBOHYDRATE 0.3 CHOLESTEROL 0
IRON 0.1 SODIUM 2 CALCIUM 5

CRANBERRY-CORN RELISH

Vegetable cooking spray
1 teaspoon vegetable oil
1 cup finely chopped onion
1 cup finely chopped green
    pepper
1 cup finely chopped sweet red
    pepper
2 cups fresh cranberries
1 (10-ounce) package frozen whole
    kernel corn, thawed
½ cup sugar
½ cup red wine vinegar
½ teaspoon crushed red pepper
¼ teaspoon ground ginger
¼ teaspoon ground turmeric

Coat a large saucepan with cooking spray; add oil. Place over medium-high heat until hot. Add chopped onion and peppers; sauté until vegetables are tender.

Stir in cranberries; cook 3 minutes, stirring occasionally. Stir in corn and remaining ingredients. Reduce heat to medium, and cook 20 minutes, stirring occasionally. Transfer mixture to a medium bowl. Cover and refrigerate 4 hours. Serve with poultry or pork. Yield: 3½ cups (17 calories per tablespoon).

PROTEIN 0.3 FAT 0.2 CARBOHYDRATE 3.8 CHOLESTEROL 0
IRON 0.1 SODIUM 1 CALCIUM 2

Cilantro, cumin, and red pepper add southwestern flavor to Tomatillo Salsa.

TOMATILLO SALSA

1 cup husked, diced tomatillos
¼ cup diced sweet red pepper
¼ cup diced sweet yellow pepper
¼ cup diced onion
2 tablespoons white wine vinegar
1 tablespoon sugar
1 tablespoon unsweetened orange juice
1 tablespoon lime juice
1 tablespoon lemon juice
2 teaspoons chopped fresh cilantro
½ teaspoon ground cumin
¼ teaspoon ground red pepper

Combine diced tomatillos, sweet red pepper, sweet yellow pepper, and onion in a large glass bowl, stirring well. Add vinegar, sugar, orange juice, lime juice, and lemon juice, stirring well to combine. Stir in cilantro, cumin, and ground red pepper; stir well to combine. Cover and refrigerate at least 2 hours. Serve salsa with unsalted tortilla chips, beef, pork, or chicken. Yield: 1¾ cups (5 calories per tablespoon).

PROTEIN 0.1   FAT 0.0   CARBOHYDRATE 1.2   CHOLESTEROL 0
IRON 0.1   SODIUM 1   CALCIUM 1

BLACK BEAN SALSA

1 (15-ounce) can black beans, rinsed and drained
1 cup seeded, chopped tomato
½ cup frozen whole kernel corn, thawed
½ cup chopped onion
¼ cup chopped fresh cilantro
1 serrano pepper, seeded and chopped
1 clove garlic, minced
1 tablespoon balsamic vinegar
¼ teaspoon salt
⅛ teaspoon pepper

Combine all ingredients in a medium bowl; toss well. Let stand 1 hour. Serve with unsalted chips. Yield: 3½ cups (7 calories per tablespoon).

PROTEIN 0.4   FAT 0.0   CARBOHYDRATE 1.3   CHOLESTEROL 0
IRON 0.1   SODIUM 26   CALCIUM 2

AUTUMN FRUIT SALSA

1 cup diced fresh apple
1 cup diced fresh pear
1 cup diced fresh plums
½ cup thinly sliced green onions
1 tablespoon lemon juice
3 tablespoons unsweetened apple juice
1 tablespoon cider vinegar
½ teaspoon ground ginger
¼ teaspoon ground coriander
¼ teaspoon ground allspice
Dash of crushed red pepper

Combine apple, pear, plums, green onions, and lemon juice; toss well. Add apple juice and remaining ingredients; toss gently. Let stand at room temperature 1 hour. Serve with pork or chicken. Yield: 3 cups (6 calories per tablespoon).

PROTEIN 0.1   FAT 0.0   CARBOHYDRATE 1.4   CHOLESTEROL 0
IRON 0.0   SODIUM 0   CALCIUM 1

 COVETING CILANTRO
Although it's been a staple seasoning in the Mediterranean and the Orient for thousands of years, cilantro (coriander) is receiving renewed interest by American cooks. Part of the reason is the popularity of ethnic food, particularly Mexican cuisine. Cilantro makes a distinct, strong contribution to many Mexican dishes.

Most supermarkets stock this fresh green herb; it may be labeled as Chinese parsley and is found along with fresh dillweed, basil, and regular parsley in the produce section. The ripple-edged flat leaf and fragrant aroma should make cilantro easy to identify. Cilantro doesn't hold up well under excessive periods of high heat, so add it toward the end of the cooking period to get the best flavor.

PLUM-PINEAPPLE BUTTER

1½ pounds plums, pitted and quartered
1 (8-ounce) can crushed pineapple in juice, undrained
2 tablespoons honey
2 teaspoons lemon juice
½ teaspoon ground cardamom
¼ teaspoon ground ginger

Combine all ingredients in a large saucepan. Bring to a boil over medium heat; reduce heat, and simmer 10 minutes or until plums are tender.

Position knife blade in food processor bowl; add fruit mixture. Process until smooth. Return mixture to saucepan. Cook over medium heat 15 to 20 minutes or until thickened, stirring frequently. Serve warm or chilled with toast or muffins. Yield: 2½ cups (16 calories per tablespoon).

PROTEIN 0.2   FAT 0.1   CARBOHYDRATE 4.0   CHOLESTEROL 0
IRON 0.0   SODIUM 0   CALCIUM 2

MANGO CHUTNEY

2¾ cups diced ripe mango
½ cup diced Red Delicious apple
½ cup diced Granny Smith apple
¾ cup plus 2 tablespoons finely chopped onion
¼ cup golden raisins
2 tablespoons brown sugar
1 teaspoon grated orange rind
1 teaspoon ground ginger
¼ teaspoon ground allspice
2 cloves garlic, minced
1 cup unsweetened apple juice

Combine all ingredients in a large saucepan; stir well. Bring mixture to a boil; reduce heat, and simmer 30 to 35 minutes or until thickened, stirring occasionally. Serve with beef, pork, or poultry. Yield: 3 cups (17 calories per tablespoon).

PROTEIN 0.1 FAT 0.1 CARBOHYDRATE 4.3 CHOLESTEROL 0
IRON 0.1 SODIUM 1 CALCIUM 3

PEACH CHUTNEY

4 cups finely chopped frozen unsweetened peaches
½ cup chopped onion
¼ cup firmly packed brown sugar
3 tablespoons currants
1 tablespoon mustard seeds
1 teaspoon ground ginger
½ teaspoon ground allspice
¼ teaspoon crushed red pepper
⅛ teaspoon garlic powder
½ cup unsweetened orange juice
¼ cup vinegar

Combine all ingredients in a saucepan. Bring to a boil over medium heat; reduce heat, and simmer, uncovered, 35 minutes or until thickened, stirring frequently. Serve with chicken or pork. Yield: 3½ cups (13 calories per tablespoon).

PROTEIN 0.2 FAT 0.1 CARBOHYDRATE 3.2 CHOLESTEROL 0
IRON 0.1 SODIUM 1 CALCIUM 4

 STUFFERS, SKIPPERS, AND STARVERS

One weight-control expert sees three eating patterns that cause weight gain. Overweight people, he says, are either stuffers, skippers, or starvers.

Stuffers basically eat all of the time, nibbling on food at every opportunity. This constant eating keeps their metabolism running high, a factor that can be advantageous for weight loss. If you are a stuffer, simply cutting back to the number of calories your body burns at rest will help start the weight-loss cycle.

Skippers get in the habit of skipping breakfast and sometimes lunch, and then going out of control at night. Consuming a lot of calories at night continues the cycle because the skipper wakes up not hungry. To get back on track, skippers need to follow a regular meal schedule, getting at least 20 to 25 percent of their calories at breakfast. Within a few weeks, they'll start losing weight and become adjusted to eating more regularly. Nighttime food jags will become unnecessary.

Starvers usually restrict their calorie intake for long periods, which causes their bodies to react abnormally to refeeding. Sometimes they actually gain weight, swelling with fluid, when they are put on a regular weight-loss regimen. The answer to this dilemma is to find the amount of food that will bring the metabolic rate back to normal without causing any gain of body fat.

Although none of these eating habits can be solved overnight, with time and effort they can be changed to a healthy course leading to better weight control.

Prepare Colorful Vegetable Medley (page 214) fresh from the garden. Julienne strips of carrot, sweet red pepper, yellow squash, and zucchini retain their fresh-picked flavor.

Side Dishes

ASPARAGUS TIMBALES

2 cups finely chopped fresh asparagus
1½ cups skim milk
1 cup frozen egg substitute, thawed
½ teaspoon dry mustard
¼ teaspoon white wine Worcestershire sauce
Dash of hot sauce
3 tablespoons grated Parmesan cheese
Vegetable cooking spray
Steamed fresh asparagus tips (optional)
Pimiento strips (optional)

Arrange chopped asparagus in a vegetable steamer over boiling water. Cover and steam 8 minutes or until tender. Set aside.

Combine milk and next 4 ingredients; beat with a wire whisk until smooth. Stir in asparagus and cheese. Spoon into 6 (6-ounce) timbale molds or custard cups coated with cooking spray.

Place molds in a 9-inch square baking dish; add hot water to baking dish to a depth of 1 inch. Bake at 350° for 40 minutes or until set. Remove from water; cool 5 minutes before unmolding.

Loosen edges of timbales with a spatula; invert onto serving plates. If desired, garnish with asparagus tips and pimiento strips. Yield: 6 servings (65 calories per serving).

PROTEIN 8.5   FAT 1.2   CARBOHYDRATE 5.4   CHOLESTEROL 3
IRON 1.1   SODIUM 142   CALCIUM 133

RASPBERRY-SPIKED BEETS

1 pound medium-size fresh beets
2 tablespoons raspberry schnapps
1 tablespoon honey
2 teaspoons vegetable oil
½ teaspoon grated orange rind
Vegetable cooking spray
2 tablespoons no-sugar-added raspberry
   spread

Leave root and 1-inch of stem on beets; scrub with a vegetable brush. Place beets in a medium saucepan; add water to cover. Bring to a boil; cover, reduce heat, and simmer 35 to 40 minutes or until beets are tender. Drain; pour cold water over beets, and drain. Trim off stems and roots; rub off skins. Slice beets into ¼-inch slices.

Combine schnapps, honey, oil, and orange rind; stir well. Pour over beets; cover and chill 1 hour.

Coat a nonstick skillet with cooking spray; place over medium heat until hot. Add beet mixture; cover and cook 4 to 5 minutes or until thoroughly heated, stirring occasionally. Stir in raspberry spread, and cook an additional 3 minutes. Yield: 8 servings (55 calories per ½-cup serving).

PROTEIN 0.6   FAT 1.3   CARBOHYDRATE 11.1   CHOLESTEROL 0
IRON 0.4   SODIUM 31   CALCIUM 7

BROCCOLI WITH CREAMY ORANGE SAUCE

1½ pounds fresh broccoli
2 tablespoons reduced-calorie margarine
2 tablespoons all-purpose flour
½ teaspoon grated orange rind
½ cup unsweetened orange juice
¼ teaspoon salt
½ cup plain nonfat yogurt

Trim off large leaves of broccoli, and remove tough ends of lower stalks. Wash broccoli thoroughly, and cut into spears. Arrange in a vegetable steamer over boiling water. Cover and steam 5 minutes or until crisp-tender. Drain; transfer to a serving platter, and keep warm.

Melt margarine in a small heavy saucepan over medium heat. Add flour; cook 1 minute, stirring constantly with a wire whisk. Gradually add orange rind, orange juice, and salt. Cook until thickened and bubbly, stirring constantly. Remove from heat, and stir in yogurt. Pour sauce over broccoli, and serve immediately. Yield: 6 servings (73 calories per serving).

PROTEIN 4.1   FAT 2.8   CARBOHYDRATE 10.1   CHOLESTEROL 0
IRON 0.9   SODIUM 173   CALCIUM 83

Your family will enjoy San Antonio Beans because it's delicious; you will like it because it's so easy to prepare.

SAN ANTONIO BEANS

Vegetable cooking spray
½ cup chopped green pepper
¼ cup chopped onion
1 (16-ounce) can pinto beans, drained
1 (15-ounce) can red kidney beans, drained
¾ cup no-salt-added tomato sauce
2 to 3 tablespoons no-salt-added salsa
1 tablespoon prepared mustard
1 teaspoon liquid smoke

Coat a saucepan with cooking spray; place over medium-high heat until hot. Add green pepper and onion; sauté until tender. Add pinto beans and remaining ingredients. Cover, reduce heat, and simmer 10 minutes or until thoroughly heated. Yield: 7 servings (108 calories per ½-cup serving).

PROTEIN 6.0   FAT 0.8   CARBOHYDRATE 19.8   CHOLESTEROL 0
IRON 1.9   SODIUM 184   CALCIUM 31

CONFETTI CABBAGE CASSEROLE

4 cups coarsely shredded cabbage
3 tablespoons chopped green pepper
3 tablespoons chopped sweet red pepper
2 tablespoons all-purpose flour
1 teaspoon sugar
¼ teaspoon salt
⅛ teaspoon ground red pepper
1 (12-ounce) can evaporated skimmed milk
¾ cup frozen egg substitute, thawed
1 teaspoon spicy brown mustard
Vegetable cooking spray

Combine first 7 ingredients in a bowl; stir well. Combine milk, egg substitute, and mustard, stirring well. Add to cabbage mixture; stir well.

Spoon mixture into a 1½-quart casserole coated with cooking spray. Place in a 13- x 9- x 2-inch baking pan; add hot water to pan to a depth of 1 inch. Bake at 350° for 1 hour or until a knife inserted in center comes out clean. Serve immediately. Yield: 6 servings (83 calories per serving).

PROTEIN 8.1   FAT 0.4   CARBOHYDRATE 11.9   CHOLESTEROL 2
IRON 1.1   SODIUM 226   CALCIUM 195

MINTED CARROTS

1½ pounds carrots, scraped and thinly sliced
¼ cup water
2 teaspoons sugar
¼ teaspoon salt
1 tablespoon chopped fresh mint

Combine carrot, water, sugar, and salt in a medium saucepan, stirring well. Bring mixture to a boil; cover, reduce heat, and simmer 12 minutes or until carrot is tender. Drain well. Gently stir in chopped fresh mint. Transfer mixture to a large serving dish, and serve warm. Yield: 7 servings (40 calories per ½-cup serving).

PROTEIN 0.8   FAT 0.1   CARBOHYDRATE 9.6   CHOLESTEROL 0
IRON 0.4   SODIUM 113   CALCIUM 24

CELERY ORIENTAL

Vegetable cooking spray
1 teaspoon sesame oil
3¼ cups diagonally sliced celery
1 cup sliced fresh mushrooms
½ cup sliced water chestnuts
2 tablespoons sliced almonds
2 teaspoons tamari sauce

Coat a nonstick skillet with vegetable cooking spray; add sesame oil. Place over medium-high heat until hot. Add sliced celery, and sauté until crisp-tender. Add sliced mushrooms, water chestnuts, and almonds; sauté 2 to 3 minutes or until mushrooms are tender. Add tamari sauce, stirring until mixture is well combined. Transfer celery mixture to a large serving bowl, and serve warm. Yield: 8 servings (36 calories per ½-cup serving).

PROTEIN 1.1   FAT 1.7   CARBOHYDRATE 4.6   CHOLESTEROL 0
IRON 0.4   SODIUM 123   CALCIUM 23

TINY CORNCAKES

¼ cup plus 2 tablespoons all-purpose
    flour
¼ cup plus 2 tablespoons cornmeal
2 tablespoons whole wheat flour
1 teaspoon baking powder
¼ teaspoon salt
½ teaspoon sugar
1 (8¾-ounce) can no-salt-added
    cream-style corn
¼ cup plus 2 tablespoons skim milk
2 tablespoons frozen egg substitute,
    thawed
Vegetable cooking spray
No-salt-added picante sauce (optional)

Combine first 6 ingredients in a large bowl, stirring well; make a well in center of mixture. Combine corn, milk, and egg substitute in a bowl, stirring well; add to dry ingredients, stirring just until dry ingredients are moistened.

For each corncake, pour 2 tablespoons batter onto a hot griddle or skillet coated with cooking spray. Turn corncakes when tops are covered with bubbles and edges look cooked. Serve with picante sauce, if desired. Yield: 15 (3-inch) corncakes (43 calories each).

PROTEIN 1.4   FAT 0.3   CARBOHYDRATE 9.1   CHOLESTEROL 0
IRON 0.4   SODIUM 66   CALCIUM 23

TANGY BLACK-EYED PEAS

1½ cups water
1 (10-ounce) package frozen black-eyed
 peas
1 cup chopped onion
2 cloves garlic, crushed
3 tablespoons red wine vinegar
1 tablespoon low-sodium Worcestershire
 sauce
¼ teaspoon pepper

Combine water, peas, onion, and garlic in a medium saucepan; cook according to package directions, omitting salt and fat. Drain. Add vinegar, Worcestershire, and pepper; stir well. Transfer to a serving dish, and serve warm. Yield: 4 servings (116 calories per ½-cup serving).

PROTEIN 6.8 FAT 0.5 CARBOHYDRATE 21.5 CHOLESTEROL 0
IRON 1.8 SODIUM 20 CALCIUM 30

CURRIED SNOW PEAS

½ pound fresh snow pea pods
2 small oranges
¼ teaspoon curry powder
Vegetable cooking spray
¼ teaspoon sesame seeds

Wash snow peas; trim ends, and remove strings. Set aside.

Peel and section oranges over a bowl, reserving juice. Set orange sections aside. Combine reserved juice and curry powder; stir well.

Coat a large nonstick skillet with cooking spray; place over medium-high heat until hot. Add snow peas, and sauté 2 minutes. Add curry mixture and sesame seeds, stirring well. Add orange sections, and stir gently. Cook over medium heat until thoroughly heated, stirring gently. Yield: 4 servings (41 calories per ½-cup serving).

PROTEIN 1.7 FAT 0.4 CARBOHYDRATE 8.0 CHOLESTEROL 0
IRON 1.1 SODIUM 2 CALCIUM 38

SAUTÉED PEPPERS AND ONION

1 large onion
1 large green pepper
1 large sweet red pepper
1 large sweet yellow pepper
Vegetable cooking spray
2 teaspoons olive oil
¼ teaspoon dried whole thyme
⅛ teaspoon salt
⅛ teaspoon pepper

Cut onion into ¼-inch slices, and separate into rings. Slice peppers into ¼-inch rings; remove and discard membranes and seeds.

Coat a large nonstick skillet with cooking spray; add oil. Place over medium-high heat until hot. Add onion and pepper slices; sauté 6 to 8 minutes or until crisp-tender. Sprinkle with thyme, salt, and pepper. Yield: 8 servings (37 calories per ½-cup serving).

PROTEIN 0.8 FAT 1.5 CARBOHYDRATE 5.9 CHOLESTEROL 0
IRON 0.7 SODIUM 41 CALCIUM 11

GLAZED PEARL ONIONS

40 pearl onions
1½ tablespoons reduced-calorie maple
 syrup
1 tablespoon plus 2 teaspoons
 reduced-sodium soy sauce
2 teaspoons white wine vinegar
¼ teaspoon ground ginger

Place onions in a medium saucepan, and cover with water. Bring onions to a boil; reduce heat, and simmer 8 to 10 minutes or just until onions are tender. Drain.

Combine syrup and remaining ingredients; stir well. Pour over onions, and toss well. Yield: 4 servings (32 calories per ½-cup serving).

PROTEIN 1.0 FAT 0.0 CARBOHYDRATE 7.7 CHOLESTEROL 0
IRON 0.4 SODIUM 258 CALCIUM 26

SPINACH-STUFFED BAKED POTATOES

2 small baking potatoes
½ (10-ounce) package frozen chopped spinach,
  thawed and drained
¼ cup grated Parmesan cheese, divided
2 tablespoons nonfat sour cream
2 tablespoons diced pimiento
1 tablespoon reduced-calorie margarine,
  softened
1 tablespoon chopped green onions
1 clove garlic, crushed
Dash of ground red pepper

Scrub potatoes; prick several times with a fork. Bake at 400° for 45 minutes or until potatoes are soft. Cool slightly.

Cut potatoes in half lengthwise, and carefully scoop out potato pulp, leaving ¼-inch-thick shells. Set shells aside. Place pulp in a small bowl; mash until smooth. Add spinach, 3 tablespoons cheese, and next 6 ingredients; stir well. Fill potato shells with spinach mixture, and sprinkle with remaining 1 tablespoon cheese. Place potatoes in an ungreased 13- x 9- x 2-inch baking dish. Bake at 350° for 30 minutes or until thoroughly heated. Yield: 4 servings (124 calories per serving).

PROTEIN 6.1   FAT 4.1   CARBOHYDRATE 16.6   CHOLESTEROL 6
IRON 1.7   SODIUM 186   CALCIUM 132

STEAMED SWISS CHARD

3 pounds Swiss chard
Vegetable cooking spray
1 cup thinly sliced onion
2 tablespoons hot pepper sauce
2 teaspoons olive oil
½ teaspoon dried whole oregano
¼ teaspoon pepper

Remove and discard stalks and tough stems from Swiss chard; wash leaves, and tear into bite-size pieces. Set aside.

Coat a Dutch oven with cooking spray; place over medium heat until hot. Add onion; sauté 4 minutes. Add Swiss chard; cover and cook over medium heat 6 minutes or until tender, stirring occasionally. Remove from heat; stir in hot pepper sauce and remaining ingredients. Yield: 5 servings (54 calories per ½-cup serving).

PROTEIN 2.4   FAT 2.3   CARBOHYDRATE 7.7   CHOLESTEROL 0
IRON 2.2   SODIUM 284   CALCIUM 69

MEXICAN-STYLE SPAGHETTI SQUASH

1 (4-pound) spaghetti squash
Vegetable cooking spray
1 teaspoon olive oil
1 cup chopped onion
2 cloves garlic, minced
1 (14½-ounce) can Mexican-flavored stewed
  tomatoes, undrained and chopped
1 (4-ounce) can chopped green chiles,
  undrained
¼ teaspoon dried whole oregano
¼ teaspoon pepper
½ cup low-fat sour cream
¼ cup (1 ounce) shredded reduced-fat
  Monterey Jack cheese
¼ cup (1 ounce) shredded 40% less-fat
  Cheddar cheese

Wash squash; cut in half lengthwise. Remove and discard seeds. Place squash, cut sides down, in a Dutch oven; add water to pan to a depth of 2 inches. Bring water to a boil; cover, reduce heat, and simmer 20 to 25 minutes or until squash is tender. Drain squash; let cool. Using a fork, remove spaghetti-like strands from squash; discard shells. Place strands in a bowl; set aside.

Coat a large skillet with cooking spray; add oil. Place over medium-high heat until hot. Add onion and garlic; sauté until tender. Add tomato, chiles, oregano, and pepper; cook over medium-high heat 5 minutes, stirring frequently. Pour tomato mixture over squash; stir well. Stir in sour cream.

Transfer mixture to a 2-quart casserole coated with cooking spray. Bake at 375° for 15 minutes. Top with cheeses; bake an additional 5 minutes or until cheese melts. Yield: 8 servings (103 calories per ½-cup serving).

PROTEIN 3.7   FAT 4.1   CARBOHYDRATE 14.2   CHOLESTEROL 10
IRON 0.8   SODIUM 199   CALCIUM 114

 NUTRITIONAL NO-NO'S

Many people have at least one bad eating habit that is difficult to break. And it can be hard to realize how these attitudes and behaviors hurt the chances of eating healthy. If any of the following nutritional negatives sound like you, shape up.

• Eating without a schedule. Weight-control experts say that people need to eat with some regularity to establish eating patterns and to keep appetite under control. Skipping meals can lead to binge eating.

• Letting fat take a prime spot in the diet. It's not something most people do consciously, but high-fat foods are so widely available that it's easy to lose track of what you're eating. Start reading labels and totaling your fat intake.

• Cleaning your plate. Eating everything on your plate is fine if you're hungry. But don't eat food just because it is sitting in front of you or because you don't want to have any leftovers. All those extra bites can add up to extra pounds.

• Viewing foods as good or bad. Despite all the press about "bad" or unhealthy foods, nutritionists say it's not foods that are really good or bad but diets. By practicing moderation, there's really no particular food that you should not eat.

• Neglecting grains, fruits, and vegetables. Along with eating too much fat, this is probably the other big mistake many Americans make. Whole grains and fibrous fruits and vegetables are filling foods with concentrated sources of vitamins, minerals, and complex carbohydrates. And they're low in fat.

SUMMER SQUASH RING

1 pound yellow squash, cut into ½-inch slices
1 (8-ounce) carton frozen egg substitute, thawed
¼ cup grated onion
¼ cup (1 ounce) shredded 40% less-fat Cheddar cheese
¼ cup evaporated skimmed milk
2 tablespoons all-purpose flour
¼ teaspoon salt
⅛ teaspoon pepper
Vegetable cooking spray
1 (10-ounce) package frozen English peas
¼ teaspoon dried whole dillweed

Cook squash in a small amount of boiling water until tender; drain well. Mash squash with a potato masher.

Combine squash, egg substitute, and next 6 ingredients in a large bowl; stir well. Spoon mixture into a 4-cup ring mold coated with cooking spray. Cover tightly with aluminum foil. Place in a shallow baking pan; add hot water to pan to a depth of 1 inch. Bake at 350° for 45 minutes or until a knife inserted in ring comes out clean. Remove from oven, and let cool on a wire rack 15 minutes.

Cook peas according to package directions, omitting salt; drain. Stir in dillweed.

Invert squash ring onto a serving platter; spoon peas into center of ring. Yield: 8 servings (79 calories per serving).

PROTEIN 6.8   FAT 0.8   CARBOHYDRATE 11.7   CHOLESTEROL 2.3
IRON 1.5   SODIUM 176   CALCIUM 79

COLORFUL VEGETABLE MEDLEY

2 cups water
1 teaspoon chicken-flavored bouillon granules
¾ teaspoon dried Italian seasoning
1 clove garlic, minced
2 medium zucchini, cut into julienne strips
2 medium-size yellow squash, cut into julienne strips
2 medium carrots, scraped and cut into julienne strips
1 medium-size sweet red pepper, cut into julienne strips
1 tablespoon minced fresh parsley

Combine first 4 ingredients in a large skillet. Bring to a boil; add zucchini, squash, carrot, and sweet red pepper. Cover, reduce heat, and simmer 6 to 8 minutes or until vegetables are tender. Drain well. Transfer mixture to a serving dish, and sprinkle with parsley. Yield: 7 servings (26 calories per ½-cup serving).

PROTEIN 1.2 FAT 0.4 CARBOHYDRATE 5.4 CHOLESTEROL 0
IRON 0.9 SODIUM 125 CALCIUM 23

CRANBERRY-APPLE-ORANGE BAKE

¾ cup cranberry juice cocktail
½ cup fresh cranberries
2 tablespoons brown sugar
2 teaspoons lemon juice
¼ teaspoon ground cardamom
¼ teaspoon ground cinnamon
4 medium cooking apples, cored and sliced into rings
3 oranges, peeled and cut into ¼-inch slices

Combine first 6 ingredients in a medium saucepan. Bring to a boil; cook until cranberry skins pop and mixture is thickened, stirring frequently. Remove from heat; set aside.
Arrange apple and orange slices in a 2½-quart casserole; pour cranberry mixture over fruit. Bake,

covered, at 350° for 40 minutes or until apple is tender. Serve warm, using a slotted spoon. Yield: 8 servings (83 calories per ½-cup serving).

PROTEIN 0.6 FAT 0.3 CARBOHYDRATE 21.2 CHOLESTEROL 0
IRON 0.3 SODIUM 2 CALCIUM 27

BROILED GRAPEFRUIT SUPREME

2 large pink grapefruit
2 tablespoons low-sugar orange marmalade
2 teaspoons cream sherry
1 tablespoon brown sugar

Cut grapefruit in half crosswise; remove seeds, and loosen sections. Place grapefruit, cut side up, on rack of a broiler pan. Combine marmalade and sherry. Drizzle over grapefruit; sprinkle with brown sugar. Broil 5½ inches from heat 6 minutes or until thoroughly heated and sugar melts. Yield: 4 servings (70 calories per serving).

PROTEIN 1.2 FAT 0.2 CARBOHYDRATE 17.7 CHOLESTEROL 0
IRON 0.2 SODIUM 2 CALCIUM 28

FLAMING PEACHES

2 (16-ounce) cans peach halves in juice, drained
¼ teaspoon ground nutmeg
12 sugar cubes
1 tablespoon lemon extract

Arrange peaches, cut side up, on rack of a broiler pan; sprinkle with nutmeg. Broil 5½ inches from heat for 4 minutes or until thoroughly heated.
Transfer peaches to a serving platter. Place 1 sugar cube in center of each peach half. Spoon ¼ teaspoon extract over each sugar cube; ignite with a long match. Serve immediately. Yield: 6 servings (58 calories per serving).

PROTEIN 0.4 FAT 0.1 CARBOHYDRATE 10.1 CHOLESTEROL 0
IRON 0.3 SODIUM 3 CALCIUM 2

Nectarines, peaches, kiwifruit, carambola, and tropical fruits cherimoya and mamey create an unusual presentation in Fruit en Papillote.

FRUIT EN PAPILLOTE

2 medium-size fresh nectarines, cut into 8
   wedges each
2 medium-size fresh peaches, peeled and cut
   into 8 wedges each
1 kiwifruit, peeled and sliced
2 carambola (starfruit), sliced
1 cherimoya, peeled and sliced
1 mamey fruit, peeled and cut into 16 wedges
Vegetable cooking spray
2 tablespoons brown sugar
1 tablespoon reduced-calorie margarine,
   melted
1 tablespoon lime juice
½ teaspoon vanilla extract

Combine first 6 ingredients in a large bowl, and toss gently.

Cut 8 (12-inch) squares of parchment paper; fold in half diagonally, forming a triangle. Place paper triangles on large baking sheets, and open out flat. Coat open side of parchment paper with cooking spray.

Evenly divide fruit mixture on half of each square near the crease. Combine brown sugar, margarine, lime juice, and vanilla, stirring well; drizzle evenly over fruit. Fold edges over to seal securely.

Starting at one pointed end of triangle, carefully pleat and crimp edges of parchment paper to make an airtight seal. Bake at 400° for 10 minutes or until packets are puffed and lightly browned.

Place packets on individual serving plates; cut an opening in the top of each packet, and fold paper back. Serve immediately. Yield: 8 servings (78 calories per serving).

PROTEIN 1.1 FAT 1.6 CARBOHYDRATE 17.4 CHOLESTEROL 0
IRON 0.3 SODIUM 21 CALCIUM 8

HONEYED PEARS

2 medium-size ripe pears
2 tablespoons pear nectar
2 tablespoons honey
2 teaspoons vinegar
⅛ teaspoon ground cinnamon
Dash of salt
Ground cinnamon (optional)

Core pears; cut crosswise into ½-inch slices, and set aside.

Combine nectar and next 4 ingredients in a large nonstick skillet; bring to a boil. Add pears; reduce heat, and simmer 10 minutes or until pears are tender, turning once. Garnish with additional cinnamon, if desired. Serve warm. Yield: 4 servings (97 calories per ½-cup serving).

PROTEIN 0.4 FAT 0.4 CARBOHYDRATE 25.4 CHOLESTEROL 0
IRON 0.3 SODIUM 37 CALCIUM 13

TANGY PINEAPPLE PUFF

1 (8-ounce) can crushed pineapple in juice, undrained
½ cup frozen egg substitute, thawed
¼ cup skim milk
¼ cup no-sugar-added peach spread
2 tablespoons sugar
2 teaspoons prepared mustard
2 (1¼-ounce) slices French bread, cut into ½-inch cubes
Vegetable cooking spray

Drain pineapple, reserving juice. Add enough water to juice to equal ¾ cup. Set pineapple aside.

Combine juice, egg substitute, and next 4 ingredients. Stir in pineapple and bread cubes. Pour into a 1½-quart casserole coated with cooking spray. Bake at 350° for 1 hour. Serve immediately. Yield: 6 servings (69 calories per serving).

PROTEIN 3.1 FAT 0.4 CARBOHYDRATE 13.5 CHOLESTEROL 0
IRON 0.6 SODIUM 92 CALCIUM 28

TIPSY MINCEMEAT PLUMS

Vegetable cooking spray
1 tablespoon reduced-calorie margarine
1¼ pounds small ripe plums, pitted and quartered
⅓ cup unsweetened grape juice
1 tablespoon brown sugar
1 tablespoon lemon juice
¼ teaspoon ground cinnamon
¼ cup condensed mincemeat
2 tablespoons brandy

Coat a large nonstick skillet with cooking spray; add margarine. Place over medium heat until margarine melts. Add plums and next 4 ingredients; stir well. Cover, reduce heat, and simmer 10 to 12 minutes or until plums are tender and lightly glazed. Stir in mincemeat and brandy; cook until thoroughly heated. Yield: 5 servings (122 calories per ½-cup serving).

PROTEIN 0.9 FAT 2.6 CARBOHYDRATE 25.6 CHOLESTEROL 0
IRON 0.2 SODIUM 79 CALCIUM 9

With beef, green chiles, and tomatoes, Mexican Meatball Stew (page 226) will warm you all over. This stew teams nicely with a crisp green salad.

Soups & Stews

CHERRIES-AND-CREAM SOUP

2½ cups cherry juice, divided
3 tablespoons cornstarch
½ cup muscatel or other sweet white wine
1 tablespoon fresh lemon juice
⅓ cup nonfat sour cream
1 (16-ounce) package frozen sweet cherries, thawed

Combine ¼ cup cherry juice and cornstarch in a small bowl; stir well. Combine 1¼ cups cherry juice, wine, and lemon juice in a nonaluminum saucepan; cook over medium heat until warm. Stir in cornstarch mixture, and cook until thickened and bubbly, stirring constantly. Transfer mixture to a bowl.

Combine remaining 1 cup cherry juice and sour cream in container of an electric blender; top with cover, and process until smooth. Add to juice mixture in bowl, and stir well. Skim foam from top of juice mixture.

Chop cherries, reserving juice. Stir cherries and reserved juice into thickened juice mixture; stir well. Cover cherry mixture and chill at least 4 hours. Stir before serving. Yield: 5 cups (83 calories per ½-cup serving).

PROTEIN 1.5   FAT 0.5   CARBOHYDRATE 19.3   CHOLESTEROL 0
IRON 0.2   SODIUM 6.9   CALCIUM 8

PEAR BRIE SOUP

1 (4-ounce) round Brie cheese
2 cups peeled, chopped fresh pear
1 (10½-ounce) can low-sodium chicken broth, undiluted
1 teaspoon grated fresh ginger
¼ teaspoon ground nutmeg
2 tablespoons reduced-calorie margarine
2 tablespoons all-purpose flour
⅔ cup evaporated skimmed milk
½ cup Sauternes or other sweet white wine
½ cup unpeeled, shredded pear
1 tablespoon lime juice

Remove rind from Brie; cut cheese into small pieces. Set aside.

Combine chopped pear, broth, ginger, and nutmeg in a saucepan. Bring to a boil over medium heat. Cover, reduce heat, and simmer 20 minutes or until pear is tender. Transfer to container of an electric blender or food processor; top with cover, and process until smooth. Set aside.

Melt margarine in a heavy saucepan over low heat; add flour, stirring until smooth. Cook 1 minute, stirring constantly. Gradually add milk and wine; cook over medium heat until mixture is thickened and bubbly, stirring constantly. Stir in cheese; cook until cheese melts and mixture is smooth. Add pureed pear mixture, stirring well. Ladle soup into individual bowls. Toss shredded pear with lime juice, and sprinkle over soup. Yield: 3½ cups (117 calories per ½-cup serving).

PROTEIN 4.9   FAT 5.7   CARBOHYDRATE 12.0   CHOLESTEROL 13
IRON 0.4   SODIUM 138   CALCIUM 100

CARROTS FOR THE HEART

Preliminary data from a Harvard Medical School study reports that beta carotene, a vitamin A-like compound, may protect against heart disease. When a group of physicians with beginning signs of coronary heart disease consumed 50 milligrams of beta carotene (about the amount in 2 cups of cooked carrots) every other day, their risk of heart attack, stroke, and cardiovascular disease was actually cut in half.

Since this is the first such finding relating beta carotene to a lowered heart disease risk, researchers hesitate to make any firm recommendations. But remember, too, that several studies have found that beta carotene appears to offer protection against certain types of cancer.

What's more, the body converts beta carotene into vitamin A. Eating any food rich in beta carotene —carrots, melons, sweet potatoes, and leafy greens such as kale—is a super way to net healthy amounts of this fat-soluble vitamin.

CURRIED CARROT SOUP

Vegetable cooking spray
1 cup chopped onion
1 teaspoon minced fresh ginger
1 teaspoon curry powder
3 cups scraped, diced carrot
2 (10½-ounce) cans low-sodium chicken broth, undiluted
1 cup unsweetened orange juice
Shredded carrot (optional)

Coat a Dutch oven with cooking spray; place over medium-high heat until hot. Add onion and ginger; sauté until tender. Add curry powder; sauté 1 minute. Stir in diced carrot, broth, and orange juice; cover and cook over medium heat 40 minutes or until carrot is tender. Remove from heat.

Pour carrot mixture into container of an electric blender or food processor; top with cover, and process until smooth. Ladle soup into individual bowls. Garnish with shredded carrot, if desired. Yield: 4½ cups (67 calories per ¾-cup serving).

PROTEIN 1.5 FAT 0.3 CARBOHYDRATE 14.3 CHOLESTEROL 0
IRON 0.5 SODIUM 27 CALCIUM 28

CHILLED ZUCCHINI BISQUE

3 cups canned low-sodium chicken broth, undiluted
2 cups diced zucchini
1 cup diced onion
1 cup peeled, diced potato
2 cloves garlic, minced
1 cup plain nonfat yogurt
1 cup peeled, seeded, and diced tomato
½ cup sliced green onions
2 tablespoons minced fresh parsley
2 tablespoons white wine vinegar
¼ teaspoon salt
¼ teaspoon dry mustard
⅛ teaspoon ground white pepper
3 drops hot sauce

Combine broth, zucchini, onion, potato, and garlic in a large saucepan. Bring to a boil over high heat; cover, reduce heat, and simmer 15 minutes or until potato is tender.

Transfer mixture in batches to container of an electric blender or food processor; top with cover, and process until smooth. Pour into a bowl; let cool. Stir in yogurt and next 8 ingredients. Cover and chill. Yield: 1½ quarts (72 calories per 1-cup serving).

PROTEIN 4.1 FAT 0.3 CARBOHYDRATE 12.6 CHOLESTEROL 1
IRON 0.8 SODIUM 140 CALCIUM 102

HARVEST CABBAGE SOUP

Vegetable cooking spray
3 cups shredded cabbage
2½ cups peeled, chopped Rome apple
1 cup diced carrot
½ cup diced green pepper
1 clove garlic, minced
4 cups water
2 cups unsweetened apple juice
2 teaspoons beef-flavored bouillon granules
2 cups cooked egg noodles (cooked without salt or fat)
1½ cups diced cooked lean pork loin
½ teaspoon caraway seeds
½ cup (2 ounces) shredded reduced-fat Swiss cheese
3 tablespoons minced fresh parsley

Coat a Dutch oven with cooking spray; place over medium-high heat until hot. Add cabbage and next 4 ingredients; sauté 5 minutes or until cabbage begins to wilt. Stir in water, apple juice, and bouillon granules. Bring to a boil. Add noodles, pork, and caraway seeds. Reduce heat; simmer 10 minutes or until thoroughly heated. Ladle soup into bowls; sprinkle with cheese and parsley. Yield: 9 cups (186 calories per 1-cup serving).

PROTEIN 12.0 FAT 4.7 CARBOHYDRATE 24.3 CHOLESTEROL 39
IRON 1.4 SODIUM 251 CALCIUM 101

HUNGARIAN VEGETABLE SOUP

1½ pounds lean boneless round steak (½ inch thick)
Vegetable cooking spray
1 teaspoon vegetable oil
3 cups chopped onion
3 cloves garlic, minced
5 cups water
2 cups no-salt-added tomato juice
1 (14½-ounce) can no-salt-added whole tomatoes, undrained and chopped
3 tablespoons Hungarian paprika
1 tablespoon beef-flavored bouillon granules
1½ teaspoons dried whole marjoram
¾ teaspoon cracked pepper
1 small dried red chile, seeded and minced
2 cups peeled, cubed potato
1 cup diced carrot

Trim fat from steak, and cut steak into 1-inch pieces. Set aside.

Coat a large Dutch oven with cooking spray; add oil. Place over medium-high heat until hot. Add onion and garlic; sauté until tender. Reduce heat to medium. Add steak; cook until browned, stirring frequently. Drain well, and pat dry with paper towels. Wipe steak drippings from pan with a paper towel.

Return meat to pan; add water and next 7 ingredients. Bring to a boil; cover, reduce heat, and simmer 1 hour. Add potato and carrot. Cover and simmer 45 minutes or until meat and vegetables are tender. Yield: 3½ quarts (130 calories per 1-cup serving).

PROTEIN 12.5 FAT 3.9 CARBOHYDRATE 11.9 CHOLESTEROL 31
IRON 1.9 SODIUM 243 CALCIUM 26

TARRAGON-CHICKEN NOODLE SOUP

1 (4-pound) broiler-fryer, skinned
10 cups water
1 large onion, quartered
2 carrots, scraped and cut into ½-inch pieces
1 cup diced celery with leaves
5 sprigs fresh parsley
1 teaspoon poultry seasoning
½ teaspoon salt
½ teaspoon ground turmeric
8 whole black peppercorns, crushed
4 whole cloves
1 cup diced carrot
½ cup thinly sliced celery
1 tablespoon minced fresh tarragon
¼ teaspoon cracked pepper
2 ounces fine egg noodles, uncooked

Remove giblets and neck from chicken; reserve for other uses. Rinse chicken under cold, running water, and pat dry. Place chicken and next 10 ingredients in a large Dutch oven. Bring to a boil; cover, reduce heat, and simmer 3 hours or until chicken is tender.

Remove chicken from broth, reserving broth. Let chicken cool to touch. Bone and shred chicken into bite-size pieces; set aside. Strain broth through a double layer of cheesecloth, discarding vegetables and spices. Skim off fat.

Combine broth, diced carrot, sliced celery, tarragon, and pepper in pan. Bring to a boil; cover, reduce heat, and simmer 5 minutes. Stir in noodles; simmer, uncovered, 5 minutes. Add chicken, and cook until thoroughly heated. Ladle soup into individual bowls. Yield: 9 cups (171 calories per 1-cup serving).

PROTEIN 22.5 FAT 3.4 CARBOHYDRATE 11.8 CHOLESTEROL 74
IRON 1.7 SODIUM 240 CALCIUM 43

Thai Chicken Soup has a wonderful flavor and is simple to prepare. Served with breadsticks, crackers, or warm bread, it's a good choice to serve for lunch or dinner.

THAI CHICKEN SOUP

4 (6-ounce) skinned chicken breast halves
2 quarts water
3 stalks lemon grass, cut into 2-inch pieces
2 small dried red chiles, seeded and minced
2 teaspoons chicken-flavored bouillon granules
8 ounces fresh or frozen baby corn, thawed
1 cup thinly sliced celery
3 tablespoons fresh lime juice
3 tablespoons minced fresh cilantro
3 tablespoons minced green onions
1 small dried red chile, seeded and sliced

Combine first 5 ingredients in a large Dutch oven. Bring to a boil; cover, reduce heat, and simmer 30 minutes or until chicken is tender. Strain broth through a double layer of cheese cloth, reserving broth and chicken. Bone chicken, and cut into ½-inch pieces. Set chicken aside.

Combine chicken broth, corn, and sliced celery in pan; bring to a boil. Add reserved chicken and lime juice; cook over medium heat until soup is thoroughly heated. Ladle soup into individual bowls. Top soup evenly with minced cilantro, minced green onions, and sliced chile. Yield: 2 quarts (102 calories per 1-cup serving).

PROTEIN 17.1   FAT 1.9   CARBOHYDRATE 3.2   CHOLESTEROL 44
IRON 0.7   SODIUM 286   CALCIUM 17

CHICKEN MINESTRONE

Vegetable cooking spray
3 (4-ounce) skinned, boned chicken breast
   halves, cut in ½-inch cubes
1 teaspoon olive oil
1 cup chopped onion
2 cloves garlic, minced
Fresh Herb Stock
2 (8-ounce) cans no-salt-added tomato sauce
1 cup diced zucchini
½ cup chopped celery
½ cup diced carrot
¼ cup minced fresh parsley
1 tablespoon minced fresh basil
¼ teaspoon dried whole thyme
¼ teaspoon cracked pepper
2 cups peeled, seeded, and diced tomato
½ cup orzo, uncooked

Coat a Dutch oven with cooking spray; place over medium-high heat until hot. Add chicken; sauté 3 minutes or until lightly browned. Remove chicken from pan; pat dry with paper towels. Wipe drippings from pan with a paper towel.

Add oil, onion, and garlic to pan; sauté until tender. Stir in chicken, Fresh Herb Stock, and next 8 ingredients. Bring to a boil; cover, reduce heat, and simmer 15 minutes. Add tomato and orzo.

Return to a boil; cover and cook 50 to 60 minutes or until orzo is tender and soup is thickened. Ladle soup into individual bowls. Yield: 9 cups (145 calories per 1-cup serving).

Fresh Herb Stock

4 cups water
1 cup no-salt-added tomato juice
1 medium potato, peeled and chopped
¼ cup minced fresh parsley
¼ cup minced fresh basil
¼ cup chopped onion
2 tablespoons minced fresh thyme
2 tablespoons minced fresh oregano
2 tablespoons minced fresh chives
¼ teaspoon salt
5 white peppercorns, crushed
1 clove garlic, minced

Combine all ingredients in a large saucepan. Bring to a boil; cover, reduce heat, and simmer 30 minutes. Remove from heat, and let cool to room temperature. Strain broth through a double layer of cheesecloth. Yield: 4 cups.

PROTEIN 11.9 FAT 2.0 CARBOHYDRATE 20.4 CHOLESTEROL 23
IRON 1.5 SODIUM 115 CALCIUM 32

LINGUINE-CLAM SOUP

Vegetable cooking spray
½ cup diced sweet yellow pepper
2 cloves garlic, minced
4 cups water
2 tablespoons minced fresh basil
2 teaspoons chicken-flavored bouillon granules
2 ounces linguine, uncooked and broken into
   2-inch pieces
2 cups peeled, seeded, and diced tomato
2 (6½-ounce) cans minced clams, undrained
¼ cup minced fresh parsley
¼ teaspoon cracked pepper
2 tablespoons plus 1 teaspoon grated
   Parmesan cheese

Coat a Dutch oven with cooking spray; place over medium-high heat until hot. Add yellow pepper and garlic; sauté 2 minutes. Add water, basil, and bouillon granules. Bring to a boil.

Add linguine; return to a boil, and cook 11 minutes or until linguine is tender. Add tomato, clams, parsley, and cracked pepper. Cook until thoroughly heated. Ladle soup into individual bowls, and sprinkle each serving with 1 teaspoon Parmesan cheese. Yield: 7 cups (82 calories per 1-cup serving).

PROTEIN 6.6 FAT 1.3 CARBOHYDRATE 11.1 CHOLESTEROL 18
IRON 3.0 SODIUM 338 CALCIUM 63

SPICY CRAB SOUP

Vegetable cooking spray
1 cup chopped onion
¾ cup chopped celery
2 cups no-salt-added vegetable juice cocktail
1 (10½-ounce) can low-sodium chicken broth, undiluted
2 (14½-ounce) cans no-salt-added whole tomatoes, undrained and chopped
1½ cups peeled, diced potato
1 tablespoon Old Bay seasoning
1 pound fresh lump crabmeat, drained
¼ cup chopped fresh parsley

Coat a Dutch oven with cooking spray; place over medium-high heat until hot. Add onion and celery; sauté until tender. Stir in vegetable juice cocktail and next 4 ingredients. Bring to a boil; cover, reduce heat, and simmer 40 to 50 minutes or until potato is tender. Add crabmeat and parsley; stir well. Cook over low heat 2 minutes or until thoroughly heated. Yield: 2½ quarts (97 calories per 1-cup serving).

PROTEIN 10.2 FAT 0.8 CARBOHYDRATE 12.1 CHOLESTEROL 23
IRON 1.4 SODIUM 516 CALCIUM 69

CARIBBEAN FISH SOUP

¾ pound swordfish steaks, cut into 1-inch cubes
¼ cup lime juice
1 tablespoon minced fresh ginger
1 jalapeño pepper, seeded and finely diced
2 cloves garlic, minced
Vegetable cooking spray
½ cup sliced green onions
½ cup diced sweet red pepper
2 cups no-salt-added vegetable broth
½ (8-ounce) bottle clam juice
2 cups peeled, seeded, and diced tomato
1 cup diced papaya
¼ cup minced fresh parsley
¼ teaspoon cracked pepper

Place swordfish in a large glass bowl. Combine lime juice, ginger, jalapeño pepper, and garlic. Pour over swordfish; stir gently. Cover and marinate in refrigerator 1 hour.

Coat a large saucepan with cooking spray; place over medium-high heat until hot. Add green onions and sweet red pepper; sauté 5 minutes or until tender. Stir in broth and clam juice; simmer, uncovered, 15 minutes. Stir in fish with marinade, tomato, and papaya. Reduce heat to low, and simmer 15 minutes or until fish flakes easily when tested with a fork. Stir in parsley and pepper. Yield: 1½ quarts (96 calories per 1-cup serving).

PROTEIN 10.4 FAT 2.6 CARBOHYDRATE 8.6 CHOLESTEROL 18
IRON 1.1 SODIUM 92 CALCIUM 26

HEARTY BAKED SPLIT PEA SOUP

1 pound lean boneless lamb
4 cups water
1½ cups dried split peas
1 cup diced onion
⅔ cup chopped carrot
1 teaspoon dried whole thyme
1 teaspoon minced garlic
¼ teaspoon salt
¼ teaspoon ground white pepper
1 (14½-ounce) can no-salt-added whole tomatoes, undrained and chopped

Trim fat from lamb; cut lamb into 1-inch cubes. Combine lamb, water, and next 7 ingredients in a 3-quart casserole. Cover and bake at 325° for 1 hour and 35 minutes. Stir in tomato. Cover and bake an additional 10 minutes or until peas are tender. Ladle soup into individual bowls. Yield: 9 cups (209 calories per 1-cup serving).

PROTEIN 20.0 FAT 2.8 CARBOHYDRATE 26.9 CHOLESTEROL 32
IRON 3.0 SODIUM 112 CALCIUM 49

Cheesy Potato Chowder, filled with colorful fresh vegetables and topped with cheese, looks good and is good for you.

CHEESY POTATO CHOWDER

Vegetable cooking spray
½ cup sliced green onions
½ cup chopped sweet red pepper
1 jalapeño pepper, seeded and diced
3 tablespoons cornstarch
4 cups water, divided
3¾ cups peeled, diced potato
2 teaspoons chicken-flavored bouillon granules
¼ teaspoon salt
⅛ teaspoon ground white pepper
1½ cups frozen whole kernel corn
1 cup (4 ounces) shredded 40% less-fat
   Cheddar cheese, divided
2 tablespoons minced fresh parsley

Coat a Dutch oven with cooking spray; place over medium-high heat until hot. Add sliced green onions, red pepper, and jalapeño pepper; sauté until tender.

Combine cornstarch and ¼ cup water; stir until smooth. Stir in remaining 3¾ cups water. Add cornstarch mixture to pan. Stir in potato, bouillon granules, salt, and white pepper. Bring to a boil; reduce heat and simmer, uncovered, 10 minutes, stirring constantly. Add corn, and cook an additional 15 minutes, stirring occasionally. Add ¾ cup plus 2 tablespoons cheese; stir until cheese melts. Ladle chowder into individual bowls, and sprinkle with remaining 2 tablespoons cheese and parsley. Yield: 7 cups (167 calories per 1-cup serving).

PROTEIN 6.2 FAT 3.1 CARBOHYDRATE 31.8 CHOLESTEROL 9
IRON 1.3 SODIUM 412 CALCIUM 125

FISH AND OKRA STEW

Vegetable cooking spray
1 cup diced onion
⅔ cup diced carrot
½ cup diced green pepper
½ cup diced celery
3 (6-ounce) cans spicy hot vegetable juice
    cocktail
½ cup water
2 medium-size sweet potatoes, peeled and
    diced
6 cups sliced fresh okra
1 cup peeled, diced tomato
1 pound red snapper fillets, cut into 1-inch
    pieces

Coat a Dutch oven with cooking spray; place over medium-high heat until hot. Add onion and next 3 ingredients; sauté until tender. Add vegetable juice cocktail, water, sweet potato, okra, and tomato. Bring to a boil; cover, reduce heat, and simmer 35 minutes or until potato is tender.

Add fish; stir gently. Cover and cook 10 minutes or until fish flakes easily when tested with a fork. Yield: 9 cups (149 calories per 1-cup serving).

PROTEIN 12.9   FAT 1.1   CARBOHYDRATE 21.6   CHOLESTEROL 19
IRON 1.3   SODIUM 268   CALCIUM 74

EASY BRUNSWICK STEW

4 (6-ounce) skinned chicken breast halves
4 cups water
1 cup chopped onion
¾ cup diced green pepper
2 teaspoons chicken-flavored bouillon granules
1 teaspoon pepper
1 (14½-ounce) can no-salt-added whole
    tomatoes, undrained and chopped
1½ cups frozen whole kernel corn
1 cup frozen baby lima beans
2 tablespoons vinegar
¼ teaspoon ground red pepper
2 tablespoons all-purpose flour
2 tablespoons water

Trim excess fat from chicken. Combine chicken and next 5 ingredients in a large Dutch oven. Bring to a boil; cover, reduce heat, and simmer 25 minutes or until chicken is tender. Remove chicken from broth; skim fat from broth, and set broth aside. Bone chicken, and cut into bite-size pieces.

Combine chicken, reserved broth, tomato, corn, lima beans, vinegar, and red pepper in pan. Bring to a boil; cover, reduce heat, and simmer 15 minutes. Combine flour and 2 tablespoons water, stirring until smooth. Add to stew, and stir well. Cook over medium heat until thickened and bubbly, stirring constantly. Yield: 9 cups (144 calories per 1-cup serving).

PROTEIN 17.1   FAT 2.2   CARBOHYDRATE 14.6   CHOLESTEROL 39
IRON 1.6   SODIUM 249   CALCIUM 34

HOPPIN' JOHN STEW

1 cup dried black-eyed peas
7 cups water
2 teaspoons chicken-flavored bouillon granules
½ teaspoon crushed red pepper
½ teaspoon liquid smoke
2 cloves garlic, minced
1 cup chopped onion
¾ cup long-grain rice, uncooked
4 cups coarsely chopped Swiss chard
2 cups peeled, seeded, and diced tomato
1 cup diced lean smoked turkey ham

Sort and wash peas; place in a Dutch oven. Add water; bring to a boil. Cover and cook 2 minutes; remove from heat, and let stand 1 hour.

Stir in bouillon and next 3 ingredients. Bring to a boil; cover, reduce heat, and simmer 1 hour or until peas are tender. Stir in onion and rice. Cover and simmer 25 minutes or until rice is tender. Transfer 1 cup mixture to a bowl; mash with a fork. Return to pan. Add chard, tomato, and ham. Cover and cook until thoroughly heated. Yield: 2½ quarts (111 calories per 1-cup serving).

PROTEIN 6.5   FAT 1.3   CARBOHYDRATE 18.8   CHOLESTEROL 0
IRON 1.7   SODIUM 409   CALCIUM 30

MEXICAN MEATBALL STEW

1 pound ground chuck
¼ cup soft breadcrumbs
1 egg, lightly beaten
1 (4-ounce) can chopped green chiles, drained
    and divided
½ teaspoon ground cumin
¼ teaspoon pepper
Vegetable cooking spray
⅓ cup all-purpose flour
2¼ cups water
1 cup frozen whole kernel corn
1 (14½-ounce) can no-salt-added whole
    tomatoes, undrained and chopped
1 (15-ounce) can kidney beans, drained
1 tablespoon chili powder
1 teaspoon beef-flavored bouillon granules
1 teaspoon dried whole oregano

Combine ground chuck, breadcrumbs, egg, 3 tablespoons chiles, cumin, and pepper in a medium bowl; stir well. Shape mixture into meatballs, using about 2 teaspoons mixture for each meatball. Arrange meatballs on rack of a broiler pan coated with cooking spray. Broil 5½ inches from heat 5 minutes; turn meatballs, and broil an additional 4 minutes or until browned. Drain and pat dry with paper towels.

Combine flour and water in a Dutch oven; stir well. Cook over medium heat until thickened and bubbly. Add meatballs, remaining chiles, corn, and remaining ingredients. Bring to a boil; cover, reduce heat, and simmer 30 minutes. Yield: 7 cups (255 calories per 1-cup serving).

PROTEIN 19.3   FAT 9.5   CARBOHYDRATE 24.0   CHOLESTEROL 71
IRON 3.6   SODIUM 204   CALCIUM 51

LENTIL-LAMB STEW

1 pound lean boneless leg of lamb
Vegetable cooking spray
7 cups water
2 cups dried lentils
1½ cups chopped tomato
1 cup diced onion
¾ cup diced carrot
¼ cup brown rice, uncooked
2 tablespoons fresh lemon juice
1 teaspoon dried whole oregano
½ teaspoon garlic powder
¼ teaspoon salt
1 cup shredded fresh spinach
10 thin lemon slices (optional)

Trim fat from lamb; cut lamb into 1-inch pieces.

Coat a Dutch oven with cooking spray; place over medium-high heat until hot. Add lamb, and cook 10 minutes or until lamb is browned on all sides, stirring occasionally. Drain and pat dry with paper towels. Wipe drippings from pan with a paper towel.

Return lamb to pan; add water and next 9 ingredients. Bring to a boil; cover, reduce heat, and simmer 1 hour or until lentils and lamb are tender. Stir in spinach; cook 1 minute. Ladle stew into individual bowls, and garnish with lemon slices, if desired. Yield: 2½ quarts (228 calories per 1-cup serving).

PROTEIN 21.3   FAT 3.4   CARBOHYDRATE 29.1   CHOLESTEROL 30
IRON 4.6   SODIUM 95   CALCIUM 36

For your next party, serve Raspberry Coeur à la Crème (page 233). This dessert looks pretty surrounded by fresh raspberries and accompanied with a raspberry sauce.

Desserts

AMBROSIA COMPOTE

1 (15¼-ounce) can pineapple chunks in juice,
    undrained
¼ cup sugar
¼ cup unsweetened apple juice
1 tablespoon lime juice
¼ teaspoon coconut extract
2 large oranges, peeled and sectioned (about
    1½ cups)
1 large banana, peeled and sliced
    (about 1 cup)
1 quart raspberry sherbet
1 (10-ounce) bottle club soda, chilled

Drain pineapple, reserving ¼ cup juice. Combine reserved pineapple juice, sugar, and next 3 ingredients; stir until sugar dissolves. Set aside.

Combine pineapple, orange, and banana in a medium bowl; pour juice mixture over fruit. Cover and chill at least 4 hours. To serve, spoon fruit mixture evenly into individual dessert bowls, using a slotted spoon. Top each with ½ cup sherbet and 3 tablespoons club soda. Serve immediately. Yield: 8 servings (187 calories per serving).

PROTEIN 1.5   FAT 1.0   CARBOHYDRATE 44.9   CHOLESTEROL 0
IRON 0.3   SODIUM 75   CALCIUM 59

MAPLE STREUSEL APPLES

¼ cup plain nonfat yogurt
2 teaspoons brown sugar
4 medium cooking apples
¼ cup plus 2 tablespoons reduced-calorie
    maple syrup
¼ cup unsweetened apple juice
¼ cup water
2 tablespoons quick-cooking oats,
    uncooked
1 tablespoon brown sugar
2 teaspoons all-purpose flour
½ teaspoon ground cinnamon
1 tablespoon unsalted margarine,
    softened

Combine yogurt and 2 teaspoons brown sugar, stirring well; cover and refrigerate.

Core apples to within ½ inch from bottom; peel top third of each apple. Combine syrup and juice; stir well. Spoon evenly into cavity of each apple. Place apples in a 10- x 6- x 2-inch baking dish. Pour water into dish. Cover and bake at 400° for 25 to 35 minutes or until apples are tender.

Combine oats, 1 tablespoon brown sugar, flour, and cinnamon; stir well. Cut in margarine with a pastry blender until mixture resembles coarse meal. Uncover apples, and sprinkle with oat mixture. Broil 5½ inches from heat 3 minutes or until lightly browned. Spoon 1 tablespoon yogurt mixture over each apple. Serve immediately. Yield: 4 servings (195 calories per serving).

PROTEIN 2.1   FAT 3.9   CARBOHYDRATE 41.5   CHOLESTEROL 0
IRON 0.9   SODIUM 18   CALCIUM 52

FRUIT AND CRÈME BRÛLÉE

2 cups fresh pineapple chunks
2 cups fresh strawberries, halved
2 medium kiwifruit, peeled and cut into ¼-inch
    slices
¼ cup low-fat sour cream
2 ounces Neufchâtel cheese, softened
⅓ cup firmly packed brown sugar

Combine pineapple, strawberries, and kiwifruit in a large bowl; stir gently. Spoon fruit mixture evenly into 6 (6-ounce) ovenproof ramekins or custard cups.

Combine sour cream and Neufchâtel cheese, stirring well. Spoon sour cream mixture evenly over fruit mixture.

Place ramekins on a baking sheet. Sprinkle each evenly with brown sugar. Broil 5½ inches from heat 2 minutes or until sugar melts. Serve immediately. Yield: 6 servings (136 calories per serving).

PROTEIN 2.0   FAT 3.9   CARBOHYDRATE 24.8   CHOLESTEROL 11
IRON 0.9   SODIUM 46   CALCIUM 43

TROPICAL FRUIT CRISP

½ cup all-purpose flour
⅓ cup quick-cooking oats, uncooked
3 tablespoons brown sugar
2 tablespoons chopped pistachios,
  toasted
½ teaspoon ground cardamom
3 tablespoons reduced-calorie margarine
2 cups cubed fresh pineapple
1 medium mango, peeled, seeded, and cubed
1 medium papaya, peeled, seeded, and cubed
2 tablespoons sugar
2 teaspoons quick-cooking tapioca, uncooked
¼ teaspoon ground nutmeg

Combine first 5 ingredients in a small bowl; cut in margarine with a pastry blender until mixture resembles coarse meal. Set aside.

Combine pineapple, mango, and papaya in an 8-inch square baking dish. Sprinkle sugar, tapioca, and nutmeg evenly over fruit; toss well. Sprinkle flour mixture evenly over fruit mixture. Bake at 350° for 25 minutes or until crust is golden and fruit is bubbly. Yield: 8 servings (159 calories per serving).

PROTEIN 2.6 FAT 4.5 CARBOHYDRATE 29.1 CHOLESTEROL 0
IRON 1.1 SODIUM 44 CALCIUM 21

CARAMEL-PEACH TRIFLE

2 (8-ounce) cartons vanilla low-fat yogurt
1½ cups skim milk
¼ cup plus 2 tablespoons sugar, divided
2 tablespoons cornstarch
1 teaspoon vanilla extract
¼ cup cream sherry
10 ladyfingers, split
⅔ cup low-sugar peach spread, melted
3 cups sliced fresh peaches
Cracked Sugar

Spoon yogurt onto several layers of heavy-duty paper towels; spread to ½-inch thickness. Cover with additional paper towels; let stand 5 minutes. Scrape yogurt from paper towels, using a rubber spatula; set aside.

Combine milk, ¼ cup sugar, and cornstarch in a medium saucepan; stir well. Cook over medium heat until mixture thickens, stirring constantly. Remove from heat; stir in vanilla. Let cool to room temperature. Cover and chill thoroughly. Stir in reserved yogurt.

Place remaining 2 tablespoons sugar in a small heavy saucepan. Cook over medium-low heat until sugar melts, stirring constantly. Continue to cook, without stirring, until golden. Reduce heat to low; add sherry in a slow stream, stirring constantly with a wire whisk. Cook over medium heat 3 minutes or until sugar dissolves, stirring constantly with a wire whisk. Remove from heat.

Arrange half of ladyfingers in bottom of a 1-quart trifle dish. Brush half of sugar syrup over ladyfingers; let stand 5 minutes. Brush with half of melted peach spread. Arrange half of peaches over ladyfingers, and spread half of yogurt mixture over peaches. Repeat layering procedure with remaining ladyfingers, sugar syrup, peach spread, peaches, and yogurt mixture. Cover and refrigerate 1 hour or just until set. Top with Cracked Sugar just before serving. Yield: 10 servings (171 calories per serving).

Cracked Sugar

Vegetable cooking spray
¼ cup sugar
1½ teaspoons water

Line a large baking sheet with aluminum foil; coat foil with cooking spray. Set aside.

Combine sugar and water in a small heavy saucepan. Cook over medium heat until sugar dissolves and mixture caramelizes and turns golden. Pour mixture onto prepared baking sheet. Tilt baking sheet to spread mixture to ¼-inch thickness. Cool completely; break mixture into bite-size pieces. Yield: 10 pieces.

PROTEIN 4.5 FAT 1.1 CARBOHYDRATE 36.6 CHOLESTEROL 3
IRON 1.2 SODIUM 143 CALCIUM 127

A drizzle of chocolate and a sauce made from cranberry juice make Cranberry Poached Pears perfect for dessert.

CRANBERRY POACHED PEARS

3 large firm pears (about 1½ pounds)
1 tablespoon unflavored gelatin
½ cup cold water
1½ cups cranberry-raspberry juice cocktail
½ cup unsweetened orange juice
1 (1-ounce) square unsweetened chocolate
1 tablespoon margarine

Peel and core pears, leaving stem end intact. Slice each pear in half lengthwise, leaving stem intact on one side.

Sprinkle gelatin over water in a Dutch oven; let stand 1 minute. Add juices; bring to a boil. Place pears in juice mixture. Cover, reduce heat, and simmer 15 minutes or until pears are tender. Transfer pears to a bowl, using a slotted spoon; cover and chill thoroughly. Chill juice mixture 2½ hours or until mixture is the consistency of unbeaten egg white.

Place pear halves, cut side down, on a flat cutting surface. Cut lengthwise slits in pears to within ½-inch of stem end, forming a fan. Spoon ¼ cup juice mixture onto each dessert plate. Arrange fanned pear halves over juice mixture. Chill 45 minutes or until juice mixture is partially set.

Combine chocolate and margarine in a small saucepan; cook over low heat until chocolate melts, stirring constantly. Drizzle chocolate mixture over pear halves. Yield: 6 servings (134 calories per serving).

PROTEIN 2.2   FAT 13.7   CARBOHYDRATE 14.4   CHOLESTEROL 0
IRON 3.8   SODIUM 24   CALCIUM 14

SPICED PEAR KISSES

1½ cups finely chopped firm ripe pear
2 teaspoons lemon juice
¼ cup firmly packed brown sugar
2 tablespoons all-purpose flour
¼ teaspoon ground cinnamon
¼ teaspoon ground nutmeg
4 sheets commercial frozen phyllo pastry, thawed
Vegetable cooking spray

Combine pear and lemon juice in a large bowl; toss well.

Combine brown sugar, flour, cinnamon, and nutmeg in a small bowl. Add to pear mixture, and toss to coat pear.

Cut each phyllo sheet in half lengthwise, and then into fourths crosswise to form 32 (6-x 4-inch) rectangles.

To assemble, lay 1 phyllo rectangle on a sheet of wax paper. Coat with cooking spray. Stack 3 more phyllo rectangles on top of first, coating each with cooking spray. Spoon one-eighth of pear mixture in center of pastry. Bring up corners of rectangle and pinch together to form a "kiss." Repeat procedure with remaining phyllo, cooking spray, and pear mixture. Place pastries on a baking sheet coated with cooking spray. Bake at 375° for 15 to 20 minutes or until golden. Serve warm. Yield: 8 servings (86 calories per serving).

PROTEIN 1.3   FAT 1.2   CARBOHYDRATE 18.2   CHOLESTEROL 0
IRON 0.7   SODIUM 3   CALCIUM 10

FRUIT AND CAKE KABOBS

2 tablespoons honey
1 tablespoon brown sugar
1 teaspoon lemon juice
1 teaspoon water
¼ teaspoon ground cinnamon
2 firm ripe nectarines, each cut into
    6 wedges
2 firm ripe plums, each cut into 6 wedges
12 (1-inch-thick) banana slices (about
    2 medium)
2 (1-ounce) slices angel food cake, each
    cut into 6 pieces
Vegetable cooking spray

Combine first 5 ingredients in a small bowl; stir well, and set aside.

Thread nectarine wedges, plum wedges, banana slices, and cake cubes alternately on 6 (8-inch) skewers. Brush kabobs with honey mixture, reserving any remaining honey mixture.

Coat grill rack with cooking spray, and place on grill over medium-hot coals. Place kabobs on rack; grill 5 minutes or until fruit is thoroughly heated and cake is lightly browned, turning once. Remove kabobs from grill, and drizzle remaining honey mixture over kabobs. Yield: 6 servings (133 calories per serving).

PROTEIN 1.6   FAT 0.8   CARBOHYDRATE 32.8   CHOLESTEROL 0
IRON 0.4   SODIUM 15   CALCIUM 18

MELON MOUSSE

3½ cups cubed cantaloupe
⅓ cup unsweetened apple juice
2 envelopes unflavored gelatin
¼ cup cold water
1 (8-ounce) container low-fat sour cream
2 tablespoons sugar
Vegetable cooking spray
Fresh mint sprigs (optional)
Melon wedges (optional)

Combine cantaloupe and apple juice in container of an electric blender or food processor; top with cover, and process until smooth.

Sprinkle gelatin over water in a small saucepan; let stand 1 minute. Cook over low heat until gelatin dissolves, stirring constantly. Remove from heat. Stir in cantaloupe mixture, sour cream, and sugar. Pour mixture into a 4-cup mold coated with cooking spray. Cover and chill 4 hours or until firm. Unmold onto a serving platter. If desired, garnish with fresh mint sprigs and melon wedges. Yield: 8 servings (87 calories per ½-cup serving).

PROTEIN 3.0   FAT 3.7   CARBOHYDRATE 11.4   CHOLESTEROL 11
IRON 0.2   SODIUM 20   CALCIUM 38

Raspberry Cream Bombe is a showy dessert that is surprisingly easy to prepare.

RASPBERRY CREAM BOMBE

1 (32-ounce) carton vanilla low-fat yogurt
1 (8-ounce) carton raspberry low-fat yogurt
Vegetable cooking spray
½ (10½-ounce) loaf commercial angel
  food cake
2 tablespoons cream sherry, divided
1 (10-ounce) package frozen raspberries in
  light syrup, thawed
¼ cup sugar
1½ teaspoons unflavored gelatin
¼ cup cold water
½ ounce semisweet chocolate, grated
Fresh raspberries (optional)
Fresh mint (optional)

Line a colander or sieve with a double layer of cheesecloth that has been rinsed out and squeezed dry; allow cheesecloth to extend over edge of colander.

Combine yogurts; stir until smooth. Pour into colander, and fold edges of cheesecloth over to cover yogurt. Place colander in a large bowl; refrigerate 12 hours. Remove yogurt from colander, and discard liquid. Cover and chill.

Coat a 1½-quart bowl with cooking spray; line with heavy-duty plastic wrap. Set aside.

Cut half of angel food cake into ½-inch-thick slices and half into ¼-inch-thick slices. Cut all cake slices in half diagonally to form triangles. Arrange ½-inch-thick triangles in bowl, with narrow ends pointing to center. (Crust sides of triangles should fit together so the center resembles a sunburst design.) Continue lining bowl with both ½-inch and ¼-inch triangles until inner surface of bowl is covered. Fill any gaps with small pieces of cake. Set remaining cake slices aside. Sprinkle 1 tablespoon sherry over cake-lined bowl. Set aside.

Press thawed raspberries through a sieve; discard seeds. Place strained raspberries in a saucepan. Bring to a boil; reduce heat, and simmer 20 minutes or until mixture reduces to ½ cup, stirring frequently. Add sugar, and cook until sugar dissolves, stirring constantly. Remove from heat.

Sprinkle gelatin over water in a small saucepan; let stand 1 minute. Cook mixture over low heat, stirring until gelatin dissolves. Add raspberry mixture, stirring until well blended.

Add gelatin mixture to chilled yogurt; stir well. Spoon yogurt mixture into cake-lined bowl. Arrange remaining cake triangles over yogurt mixture, filling gaps with trimmed portions of cake. Sprinkle remaining 1 tablespoon sherry over cake. Trim cake from sides of bowl to make a smooth top. Cover with heavy-duty plastic wrap, and chill at least 4 hours.

Remove plastic wrap, and invert bowl onto a serving platter. Remove bowl and plastic liner. Sift grated chocolate over bombe. If desired, garnish with fresh raspberries and mint. Yield: 10 servings (195 calories per serving).

PROTEIN 6.8 FAT 2.0 CARBOHYDRATE 37.8 CHOLESTEROL 5
IRON 0.3 SODIUM 95 CALCIUM 205

RASPBERRY COEUR À LA CRÈME

1 (10-ounce) package frozen raspberries in
　light syrup, thawed
1 cup skim milk
1 envelope unflavored gelatin
½ (8-ounce) package Neufchâtel cheese,
　softened
¼ cup sugar
1 (8-ounce) carton raspberry low-fat
　yogurt
Vegetable cooking spray
2 teaspoons cornstarch
Fresh raspberries (optional)

Drain raspberries, reserving syrup. Set aside.

Combine milk and 2 tablespoons reserved raspberry syrup in a small saucepan. Sprinkle gelatin over milk mixture; let stand 1 minute. Cook over low heat until gelatin dissolves, stirring constantly. Remove from heat, and let cool.

Position knife blade in food processor bowl. Add cheese, sugar, yogurt, and gelatin mixture; process until smooth. Pour mixture into a 4-cup heart-shaped mold coated with cooking spray. Cover and chill until firm.

Combine remaining raspberry syrup and cornstarch in a small nonaluminum saucepan; stir with a wire whisk until well blended. Bring to a boil; cook over medium heat until thickened, stirring constantly. Gently stir in reserved raspberries; cover and chill. Unmold gelatin mixture onto a large serving platter. Garnish with fresh raspberries, if desired. Serve with raspberry sauce. Yield: 6 servings (190 calories per serving).

PROTEIN 6.1 FAT 5.1 CARBOHYDRATE 31.0 CHOLESTEROL 17
IRON 0.4 SODIUM 119 CALCIUM 124

 TOP PARTICIPATION SPORTS

According to the National Sporting Goods Association, the sport of the moment is swimming. At last count, 71 million Americans, seven years of age and older, have chosen to swim to keep fit. Exercise walking ranks a close second, with 67 million followers, followed by bicycle riding with 57 million enthusiasts. Rounding out the top five sporting activities are fishing and camping.

Popularity polls aside, fitness experts say that fun and camaraderie should be major reasons for taking up a sport. But health benefits—both physical and mental—must also be factors. Fishing and camping are fine for relaxing and being with nature, but they do not provide cardiovascular benefits. If they have been your sole exercise program, start including aerobic workouts in your schedule. No matter what you choose to keep active, make sure your heart gets a good workout at least part of the time.

STRAWBERRY MOUSSE PARFAITS

1 envelope unflavored gelatin
¼ cup water
¼ cup plus 1 tablespoon sugar, divided
½ (8-ounce) package Neufchâtel cheese, softened
⅓ cup instant nonfat dry milk powder
1 cup unsweetened orange juice
⅓ cup water
2¾ cups fresh strawberries, hulled and divided
1 teaspoon grated orange rind

Sprinkle gelatin over ¼ cup water in a small saucepan; let stand 1 minute. Add 3 tablespoons sugar, and cook over medium heat until gelatin and sugar dissolve, stirring constantly. Remove gelatin mixture from heat, and let cool.

Combine Neufchâtel cheese and next 3 ingredients in container of an electric blender; top with cover, and process until smooth. With blender on high, gradually add gelatin mixture in a slow steady stream. Process 15 to 20 seconds or until smooth. Add 2 cups strawberries, and process 1 to 2 minutes or until berries are coarsely chopped. Pour mixture evenly into 6 (6-ounce) parfait glasses. Cover and chill 1 hour or until set.

Combine remaining ¾ cup strawberries, 2 tablespoons sugar, and orange rind in container of an electric blender; top with cover, and process until smooth. Top each parfait with 1 tablespoon strawberry sauce. Serve immediately. Yield: 6 servings (159 calories per ½-cup serving).

PROTEIN 6.0 FAT 4.8 CARBOHYDRATE 24.2 CHOLESTEROL 16
IRON 0.4 SODIUM 113 CALCIUM 112

ENGLISH SUMMER PUDDING

1½ pints fresh raspberries
3 tablespoons sugar
2 tablespoons Sauternes or other sweet
    white wine
12 (½-inch-thick) slices white bread
1 (8-ounce) carton vanilla low-fat yogurt

Combine first 3 ingredients in a nonaluminum saucepan. Bring to a boil; cook over medium heat, until sugar dissolves, stirring occasionally. Reduce heat, and simmer 5 minutes. Cool slightly; cover and chill thoroughly.

Cut rounds from bread slices, using a 3-inch cookie cutter. Discard crusts. Place half of rounds in bottom of 6 (6-ounce) ramekins or custard cups. Reserve ¼ cup raspberry mixture. Spoon remaining raspberry mixture evenly over bread rounds; top with remaining bread rounds.

Cover each custard cup with plastic wrap, pulling wrap tightly over bread to pack down. Refrigerate at least 8 hours.

Combine yogurt and ¼ cup reserved raspberry mixture; stir gently. Spoon 3 tablespoons yogurt sauce onto each of 6 serving plates. Unmold puddings onto sauce. Serve immediately. Yield: 6 servings (122 calories per serving).

PROTEIN 3.6 FAT 1.2 CARBOHYDRATE 25.1 CHOLESTEROL 2
IRON 0.7 SODIUM 127 CALCIUM 87

CHOCOLATE PUDDING PARFAIT

3 tablespoons unsweetened cocoa
2½ teaspoons cornstarch
1 cup skim milk
1 egg
3 tablespoons sugar
½ teaspoon rum extract
2 cups vanilla ice milk

Combine cocoa and cornstarch in a small saucepan; gradually stir in milk. Cook over medium heat until mixture comes to a boil, stirring constantly. Cook 1 minute, stirring constantly. Remove mixture from heat.

Combine egg and sugar in a small bowl; beat at medium speed of an electric mixer until blended. Gradually stir one-fourth of hot milk mixture into egg mixture; add to remaining hot mixture, stirring constantly with a wire whisk. Cook over low heat until thickened, stirring constantly. Remove from heat; stir in extract. Cool completely.

Spoon 1½ tablespoons sauce into each of 4 parfait glasses; top each with ¼ cup ice milk. Spoon 2 tablespoons sauce over each; top each with ¼ cup ice milk. Drizzle remaining sauce over ice milk. Cover and freeze at least 1 hour. Serve frozen. Yield: 4 servings (194 calories per serving).

PROTEIN 7.4 FAT 4.7 CARBOHYDRATE 30.4 CHOLESTEROL 64
IRON 1.0 SODIUM 102 CALCIUM 176

CHOCOLATE-FILLED PASTRY SHELLS

1 (10-ounce) package frozen strawberries in
  light syrup, thawed
2 tablespoons brandy
2 cups chocolate ice milk
Pastry Shells

Place strawberries in container of an electric blender; top with cover, and process until smooth. Transfer strawberries to a saucepan. Bring to a boil; reduce heat, and cook until mixture reduces to ⅔ cup. Add brandy; stir well. Cook an additional 1 to 2 minutes or until thoroughly heated. Remove from heat; cool completely.

To serve, spoon ⅓ cup ice milk into each pastry shell; spoon sauce over ice milk. Serve immediately. Yield: 6 servings (182 calories per serving).

Pastry Shells

1 cup sifted cake flour
1 tablespoon sugar
½ teaspoon baking powder
2½ tablespoons margarine
¼ cup cold water
½ teaspoon vanilla extract

Combine first 3 ingredients in a bowl; cut in margarine with a pastry blender until mixture resembles coarse meal. Sprinkle cold water, 1 tablespoon at a time, over surface; add vanilla. Stir

with a fork until dry ingredients are moistened. Shape into a ball. Divide into 6 equal portions.

Place dough between 2 sheets of heavy-duty plastic wrap, and gently press each portion to ½-inch thickness. Chill 30 minutes. Remove top sheet of plastic wrap; press each portion of dough firmly on back of a 5-inch baking shell.

Place shells on a baking sheet, and bake at 400° for 9 minutes or until lightly browned. Remove from oven; cool slightly. Remove pastry from shells; cool on wire racks. Yield: 6 pastry shells.

PROTEIN 2.5 FAT 5.7 CARBOHYDRATE 28.3 CHOLESTEROL 0
IRON 1.2 SODIUM 83 CALCIUM 20

REFRESHING CITRUS SORBET

3½ cups water
½ cup sugar
1 (6-ounce) can frozen orange juice concentrate,
  undiluted
1 tablespoon grated lime rind
1 tablespoon grated lemon rind
1 tablespoon fresh lime juice
1 tablespoon fresh lemon juice

Combine water and sugar in a medium saucepan; stir well. Bring to a boil; reduce heat, and simmer, stirring until sugar dissolves. Let cool to room temperature.

Combine sugar mixture, orange juice concentrate, and next 4 ingredients in container of an electric blender; top with cover, and process until smooth.

Pour mixture into freezer can of a 2-quart hand-turned or electric freezer. Freeze according to manufacturer's instructions. Let ripen 1 hour, if desired. Scoop sorbet into individual dessert bowls. Serve immediately. Yield: 4 cups (83 calories per ½-cup serving).

PROTEIN 0.5 FAT 0.1 CARBOHYDRATE 21.1 CHOLESTEROL 0
IRON 0.1 SODIUM 1 CALCIUM 9

Savor the flavor of fresh raspberries by turning them into Raspberry-Mint Sorbet, a frosty, sweet-tasting treat.

RASPBERRY-MINT SORBET

2 cups Burgundy or other dry red wine
1 cup water
½ cup sugar
⅓ cup minced fresh mint
1⅓ cups fresh raspberries
2 tablespoons unsweetened orange juice
1½ tablespoons lemon juice

Combine first 4 ingredients in a nonaluminum saucepan. Bring to a boil; cook over medium heat until sugar dissolves, stirring constantly. Boil 3 minutes without stirring. Remove from heat, and let cool completely.

Line a colander or sieve with a double layer of cheesecloth that has been rinsed out and squeezed dry. Allow cheesecloth to extend over edge of colander. Place colander in a large bowl to drain. Pour mixture into colander; discard mint.

Place raspberries in container of an electric blender; top with cover, and process until smooth. Strain puree, discarding seeds. Add puree, orange juice, and lemon juice to wine mixture; stir well.

Pour into freezer can of a 2-quart hand-turned or electric freezer. Freeze according to manufacturer's instructions. Let ripen 1 hour, if desired. Scoop sorbet into individual dessert bowls. Serve immediately. Yield: 3½ cups (72 calories per ½-cup serving).

PROTEIN 0.4   FAT 0.1   CARBOHYDRATE 18.5   CHOLESTEROL 0
IRON 0.4   SODIUM 5   CALCIUM 11

TROPICAL RUM SHAKE

1 (8-ounce) can crushed pineapple in juice, drained
1 cup evaporated skimmed milk, chilled
¼ cup sifted powdered sugar
¼ cup rum
½ teaspoon vanilla extract
½ cup crushed ice

Line a baking sheet with plastic wrap. Spread pineapple in a thin layer on baking sheet; freeze 15 minutes or until pineapple is firm.

Combine frozen pineapple and next 4 ingredients in container of an electric blender; top with cover, and process until smooth. Add crushed ice, and process until smooth. Pour into tall frosted glasses, and serve immediately. Yield: 4 cups (150 calories per 1-cup serving).

PROTEIN 5.0   FAT 0.2   CARBOHYDRATE 22.1   CHOLESTEROL 3
IRON 0.3   SODIUM 74   CALCIUM 192

AMARETTO CHEESECAKE ICE MILK

2 (8-ounce) cartons plain nonfat yogurt
⅔ cup instant nonfat dry milk powder
½ (8-ounce) package Neufchâtel cheese, softened
⅓ cup sugar
1 envelope unflavored gelatin
1 cup cold water
¼ cup amaretto
1 teaspoon vanilla extract

Combine first 4 ingredients in container of an electric blender; top with cover, and process until smooth.

Sprinkle gelatin over water in a saucepan; let stand 1 minute. Cook over low heat; stir until gelatin dissolves. Add amaretto; cook 5 minutes, stirring occasionally. Remove from heat. Add gelatin mixture and vanilla to container of electric blender; top with cover, and process until smooth.

Pour mixture into freezer can of a 2-quart hand-turned or electric freezer. Freeze according to manufacturer's instructions. Let ripen 2 hours (mixture will be soft). Yield: 5 cups (127 calories per ½-cup serving).

PROTEIN 7.4   FAT 3.8   CARBOHYDRATE 15.9   CHOLESTEROL 11
IRON 0.1   SODIUM 129   CALCIUM 199

PEANUT BUTTER ICE MILK SANDWICHES

3 tablespoons no-sugar-added peanut butter
2 cups vanilla ice milk, softened
12 (2-inch-diameter) gingersnaps

Gently swirl peanut butter into ice milk. Spread ⅓ cup ice milk mixture onto each of 6 gingersnaps. Top with remaining 6 gingersnaps. Place on a baking sheet; freeze until firm. Wrap sandwiches in heavy-duty plastic wrap, and store in freezer. Yield: 6 servings (165 calories per serving).

PROTEIN 4.8   FAT 8.1   CARBOHYDRATE 19.4   CHOLESTEROL 11
IRON 0.8   SODIUM 53   CALCIUM 83

FROZEN MARGARITA SQUARES

2 cups frozen unsweetened whole strawberries, halved
¼ cup lime juice
2 tablespoons tequila
2 tablespoons Triple Sec or other orange-flavored liqueur
6 cups vanilla ice milk, softened
Vegetable cooking spray
20 unsalted pretzel sticks, crushed

Combine first 4 ingredients; fold into ice milk. Spread into an 8-inch square baking pan coated with cooking spray; sprinkle with pretzels. Cover and freeze until firm. Cut into squares. Yield: 9 servings (153 calories per serving).

PROTEIN 3.6   FAT 3.9   CARBOHYDRATE 23.8   CHOLESTEROL 12
IRON 0.4   SODIUM 71   CALCIUM 123

EASY FRUIT TART

1¼ cups all-purpose flour
¼ cup sugar
1 teaspoon grated lemon rind
⅓ cup margarine
½ cup regular oats, uncooked
1 egg, lightly beaten
2 (8-ounce) cans apricot halves in juice,
    undrained
1 (20-ounce) can sliced pineapple in juice,
    undrained
1 (16-ounce) can sliced peaches in light
    syrup, undrained
1 envelope unflavored gelatin
2 tablespoons sugar
1 pint fresh strawberries,
    hulled

Combine flour, ¼ cup sugar, and lemon rind, stirring well; cut in margarine until mixture resembles coarse meal. Stir in oats. Add egg, and stir just until combined. Shape flour mixture into a ball; cover and chill at least 1 hour.

Roll dough between 2 sheets of heavy-duty plastic wrap to a 12-inch circle. Place in freezer 10 minutes or until plastic wrap can be removed easily. Remove top sheet of plastic wrap. Invert and fit pastry into a 9-inch springform pan, pressing crust about 1½ inches up sides of pan. Remove remaining plastic wrap. Prick bottom of pastry with a fork. Chill 15 minutes. Bake at 375° for 20 to 25 minutes or until lightly browned. Remove from oven, and cool completely.

Drain canned fruits, reserving ¾ cup liquid. Sprinkle gelatin over reserved liquid in a small saucepan; let stand 1 minute. Add 2 tablespoons sugar; cook over low heat until gelatin and sugar dissolve, stirring constantly. Cool slightly.

Arrange canned fruits and strawberries in crust; pour gelatin mixture over fruit. Chill until firm. Yield: 12 servings (191 calories per serving).

PROTEIN 3.4   FAT 5.9   CARBOHYDRATE 32.4   CHOLESTEROL 18
IRON 1.2   SODIUM 70   CALCIUM 18

CARROT CUSTARD TART

⅔ cup sugar
3 tablespoons margarine, softened
3 tablespoons all-purpose flour
2 eggs
1¼ cups evaporated skimmed milk
1¼ cups grated carrot
½ teaspoon ground cinnamon
2 egg whites
Vegetable cooking spray

Combine sugar and margarine in a medium bowl. Beat at medium speed of an electric mixer until light and fluffy. Stir in flour. Add eggs, 1 at a time, beating well after each addition. Add milk, carrot, and cinnamon; stir well.

Beat egg whites (at room temperature) in a small bowl at high speed of an electric mixer until soft peaks form. Gently fold egg white into carrot mixture. Spoon mixture into an 8-inch round cakepan coated with cooking spray. Bake at 425° for 15 minutes; reduce heat to 350°, and bake an additional 20 minutes or until knife inserted in center comes out clean. Yield: 8 servings (174 calories per serving).

PROTEIN 5.9   FAT 5.8   CARBOHYDRATE 25.0   CHOLESTEROL 55
IRON 0.6   SODIUM 131   CALCIUM 131

GINGERED PUMPKIN PIE

1 cup cooked, mashed pumpkin
¾ cup evaporated skimmed milk
½ cup unsweetened applesauce
¼ cup sugar
¼ cup reduced-calorie maple syrup
2 egg whites
1 egg
2 teaspoons cornstarch
1½ teaspoons pumpkin pie spice
Vegetable cooking spray
8 (2-inch-diameter) gingersnaps
2 tablespoons gingersnap crumbs

Combine first 9 ingredients in a large bowl; beat at medium speed of an electric mixer until well blended.

Coat a 9-inch pieplate with cooking spray. Cut gingersnaps in half, using a bread knife. Line side of pieplate with cookie halves, cut side down. Spoon pumpkin mixture into prepared pieplate. Sprinkle with gingersnap crumbs. Bake at 400° for 15 minutes. Reduce heat to 350°; bake an additional 20 minutes or until knife inserted in center comes out clean. Yield: 8 servings (119 calories per serving).

PROTEIN 4.4   FAT 2.3   CARBOHYDRATE 21.0   CHOLESTEROL 31
IRON 1.1   SODIUM 65   CALCIUM 99

 ## BEFORE VERSUS AFTER

Is it better to run before you eat or eat before you run? That depends on your size, according to researchers from Mount Sinai Hospital in New York City. If you're overweight, scheduling workouts before you sit down to a meal is probably better. For those with thin and trim bodies, exercising after meals may be best. It's all tied in with the body's response to food.

Researchers noticed that when feeding a group of thin men (less than 15 percent body fat) and a group of overweight men (greater than 25 percent body fat) exactly the same amount of food, their bodies reacted differently. The fatter bodies burned less energy in response to food than the thin ones did. Researchers suggest that body cells in overweight people are less sensitive to insulin, a hormone that's involved in regulating the amount of energy that the cells receive.

Interestingly, when each group took turns either fasting or eating before exercise, differences were again noted. Exercising before eating worked to speed up metabolisms of the overweight men and made their cells more receptive to insulin. For the thin men, the opposite was true. Eating first stepped up the metabolic rate.

DAIQUIRI SOUFFLÉ

Vegetable cooking spray
¼ cup plus 1 teaspoon sugar, divided
¾ cup skim milk
3 egg, separated
3 tablespoons all-purpose flour
3 tablespoons rum
1 tablespoon framboise or other raspberry-flavored liqueur
1 teaspoon grated lime rind
1 egg white
⅛ teaspoon cream of tartar

Coat a 1½-quart soufflé dish with cooking spray; sprinkle with 1 teaspoon sugar. Set aside.

Bring milk to a boil in a saucepan; remove from heat. Beat egg yolks and 3 tablespoons sugar at medium speed of an electric mixer 4 minutes or until thick and lemon colored. Add flour; stir well, using a wire whisk. Gradually stir about one-fourth of hot milk into egg mixture; add to remaining hot milk, stirring constantly with a wire whisk.

Cook over medium-low heat 2 minutes or until thick, stirring constantly. Remove from heat; pour into a large bowl. Add rum, liqueur, and lime rind; mix well, using a wire whisk. Cover with plastic wrap, and let cool to room temperature.

Beat 4 egg whites (at room temperature) and cream of tartar at high speed of electric mixer until soft peaks form. Add remaining 1 tablespoon sugar, beating until stiff peaks form. Gently fold egg white mixture into egg yolk mixture. Spoon into prepared dish.

Place dish in a 9-inch square baking pan; pour hot water into pan to a depth of 1 inch. Bake at 350° for 30 to 45 minutes or until golden. Serve immediately. Yield: 6 servings (101 calories per serving).

PROTEIN 5.2   FAT 2.8   CARBOHYDRATE 13.7   CHOLESTEROL 109
IRON 0.5   SODIUM 60   CALCIUM 52

SPICY APPLESAUCE CUPCAKES

1½ cups all-purpose flour
1½ teaspoons baking powder
1 teaspoon ground cinnamon
½ teaspoon ground nutmeg
¼ teaspoon ground cloves
2 tablespoons creamy peanut butter
2 tablespoons margarine, softened
¼ cup firmly packed brown sugar
1 egg
¾ cup unsweetened applesauce
¼ cup skim milk
¼ cup chopped unsalted dry-roasted
    peanuts
½ teaspoon vanilla extract
Vegetable cooking spray
¼ cup sifted powdered sugar
1 tablespoon creamy peanut butter,
    melted
1 to 2 teaspoons unsweetened apple
    juice

Combine first 5 ingredients in a small bowl; stir well. Set aside.

Cream 2 tablespoons peanut butter and margarine in a medium bowl; gradually add brown sugar, beating well at medium speed of an electric mixer. Add egg and applesauce; beat well. Add flour mixture to creamed mixture alternately with milk, beginning and ending with flour mixture. Mix well after each addition. Stir in peanuts and vanilla.

Spoon cupcake batter into muffin pans coated with cooking spray, filling each cup two-thirds full. Bake at 350° for 25 to 30 minutes or until a wooden pick inserted in centers comes out clean. Remove cupcakes from pans, and cool completely on wire racks.

Combine powdered sugar, melted peanut butter, and apple juice, stirring well. Drizzle powdered sugar mixture over cupcakes. Yield: 1 dozen (156 calories each).

PROTEIN 4.2 FAT 6.3 CARBOHYDRATE 21.5 CHOLESTEROL 18
IRON 1.1   SODIUM 90   CALCIUM 46

LEMON-FILLED CAKE

Vegetable cooking spray
¼ cup margarine, softened
½ cup sugar
2 cups sifted cake flour
2 teaspoons baking powder
⅛ teaspoon salt
¾ cup skim milk
¼ teaspoon lemon extract
1 tablespoon grated lemon rind, divided
4 egg whites
⅓ cup sugar
1 tablespoon plus 1 teaspoon cornstarch
1 egg yolk, beaten
⅓ cup lemon juice
⅓ cup water
Fluffy Frosting
Lemon curls (optional)
Fresh mint sprigs (optional)

Coat two 8-inch round cakepans with cooking spray; line with wax paper. Set aside.

Cream margarine; gradually add ½ cup sugar, beating well at medium speed of an electric mixer. Combine flour, baking powder, and salt; add to creamed mixture alternately with milk, beginning and ending with flour mixture. Mix just until blended after each addition. Add extract and 1 teaspoon lemon rind, stirring well.

Beat egg whites (at room temperature) at high speed of an electric mixer until stiff peaks form; fold into batter. Spoon batter evenly into prepared pans. Bake at 375° for 20 to 25 minutes or until a wooden pick inserted in center comes out clean. Cool in pans 10 minutes; remove from pans, and cool completely on wire racks.

Combine ⅓ cup sugar and next 4 ingredients in a small saucepan. Cook over medium heat until mixture comes to a boil, stirring constantly; boil 1 minute. Stir in remaining 2 teaspoons lemon rind, and let cool.

Spread lemon filling between layers; frost top and sides of cake with Fluffy Frosting. If desired, garnish with lemon curls and fresh mint sprigs. Yield: 12 servings (198 calories per serving).

Serve Lemon-Filled Cake for a delicious ending to a summer dinner. Lemon curls and fresh mint are the perfect garnish.

Fluffy Frosting

1 teaspoon unflavored gelatin
1 tablespoon cold water
⅓ cup light-colored corn syrup
½ teaspoon lemon extract
1 egg white
¼ teaspoon cream of tartar

Sprinkle gelatin over water in a small saucepan; let stand 1 minute. Add corn syrup; cook over medium heat until mixture comes to a boil and gelatin dissolves, stirring constantly. Remove from heat; stir in lemon extract.

Beat egg white (at room temperature) and cream of tartar in a small bowl at high speed of an electric mixer until foamy. Slowly add corn syrup mixture, and continue beating until stiff peaks form and frosting is of spreading consistency. Yield: 1⅓ cups.

PROTEIN 3.8 FAT 4.5 CARBOHYDRATE 35.6 CHOLESTEROL 18
IRON 1.6 SODIUM 162 CALCIUM 62

RUM-GLAZED APPLE CAKE

2 cups peeled, cored, and chopped cooking apple
⅔ cup sugar
1 cup all-purpose flour
1 teaspoon ground cinnamon
½ teaspoon baking powder
½ teaspoon baking soda
⅛ teaspoon salt
¼ cup vegetable oil
¼ cup frozen egg substitute, thawed
¼ cup strong cold coffee
1 teaspoon vanilla extract
Vegetable cooking spray
¼ cup sifted powdered sugar
1 teaspoon rum
1 teaspoon hot water

Combine apple and ⅔ cup sugar in a medium bowl; stir well. Combine flour and next 4 ingredients; add to apple mixture, stirring well. Combine oil, egg substitute, coffee, and vanilla; stir well. Add to apple mixture, and stir just until well blended.

Spoon batter into an 8-inch square baking pan coated with cooking spray. Bake at 350° for 25 to 30 minutes or until a wooden pick inserted in center comes out clean. Combine powdered sugar, rum, and water; stir well. Drizzle over warm cake. Yield: 9 servings (192 calories per serving).

PROTEIN 2.0   FAT 6.3   CARBOHYDRATE 32.0   CHOLESTEROL 0
IRON 0.9   SODIUM 107   CALCIUM 29

PINEAPPLE-OAT CAKE

¾ cup unsweetened pineapple juice
⅔ cup quick-cooking oats, uncooked
¾ cup all-purpose flour
¼ cup whole wheat flour
½ cup sugar
1 teaspoon baking soda
¼ teaspoon orange extract
¼ cup vegetable oil
1 egg, lightly beaten
Vegetable cooking spray
½ (8-ounce) package Neufchâtel cheese, softened
1 (8-ounce) can crushed pineapple in juice, drained

Bring pineapple juice to a boil in a nonaluminum saucepan. Remove from heat; stir in oats. Let stand 20 minutes. Combine all-purpose flour and next 6 ingredients in a large bowl; stir well. Add oat mixture; mix well. Spoon batter into an 8-inch square baking pan coated with cooking spray. Bake at 350° for 25 minutes or until a wooden pick inserted in center comes out clean. Let cool on a wire rack.

Beat cheese at high speed of an electric mixer until light and fluffy. Add pineapple, and beat well. Spread over cooled cake, and cut into squares. Yield: 12 servings (192 calories per serving).

PROTEIN 4.0   FAT 8.1   CARBOHYDRATE 26.5   CHOLESTEROL 25
IRON 1.0   SODIUM 112   CALCIUM 35

WHERE'S THE FAT?

Extra pounds create a definite health risk. But even more important, say health experts, is where the extra weight is stored. People who put on pounds around the middle section of the body—waist and upper torso—are at higher risk for diabetes, heart disease, high blood pressure, and stroke. If, on the other hand, your extra pounds settle below the waist—hips and thighs—health risk is minimal. Women naturally tend to deposit weight in lower body areas as preparation for child bearing.

But if you're not sure about your body's contour by looking in the mirror, calculate your waist-to-hip ratio. Take a tape measure and measure your waist and your hips in inches. Then divide the waist measurement by the hip measurement. Men with a measurement above 1.0 are at greater health risk; women are at risk if that number exceeds 0.8.

HURRY UP CHOCOLATE CAKE

1½ cups all-purpose flour
½ cup plus 3 tablespoons sugar
¼ cup unsweetened cocoa
1 teaspoon baking soda
½ teaspoon salt
½ cup skim milk
⅓ cup water
3 tablespoons vegetable oil
1 teaspoon vanilla extract
3 tablespoons semisweet chocolate
   mini-morsels
Vegetable cooking spray
1 teaspoon powdered sugar

Combine first 5 ingredients; make a well in center of mixture. Combine milk, water, oil, and vanilla; add to dry ingredients, stirring just until dry ingredients are moistened. Fold in chocolate. Spoon into an 8-inch square baking pan coated with cooking spray. Bake at 350° for 20 minutes or until a wooden pick inserted in center comes out clean. Sift powdered sugar over cooled cake; cut into squares. Yield: 12 servings (158 calories per serving).

PROTEIN 2.5 FAT 5.1 CARBOHYDRATE 26.2 CHOLESTEROL 0
IRON 1.1 SODIUM 173 CALCIUM 34

CRANBERRY-TOPPED CHOCOLATE SQUARES

¾ cup plus 2 tablespoons all-purpose flour
1 teaspoon baking powder
¼ teaspoon baking soda
1⅓ cups sugar, divided
¼ cup plus 2 tablespoons unsweetened cocoa
⅔ cup water
¼ cup margarine, softened
1 teaspoon vanilla extract
½ teaspoon rum extract
3 egg whites
Vegetable cooking spray
1 (12-ounce) package fresh cranberries
½ teaspoon ground cinnamon
3 tablespoons rum
2 (8-ounce) cartons vanilla low-fat yogurt
1 cup vanilla ice milk, softened
1 (1-ounce) package pre-melted unsweetened
   chocolate
Fresh mint sprigs (optional)

Combine flour, baking powder, soda, ⅔ cup sugar, and cocoa in a large bowl. Add water, margarine, and extracts. Beat at low speed of an electric mixer 1 minute. Beat at high speed 2 to 3 minutes or until mixture is smooth.

Beat egg whites (at room temperature) at high speed of electric mixer until stiff peaks form. Fold ½ cup beaten egg whites into chocolate batter. Fold in remaining egg whites. Spoon batter into a 15- x 10- x 1-inch jellyroll pan coated with cooking spray. Bake at 375° for 10 to 12 minutes or until a wooden pick inserted in center comes out clean. Cool brownie completely.

Place cranberries in a 15- x 10- x 1-inch jellyroll pan. Combine remaining ⅔ cup sugar and cinnamon; sprinkle evenly over cranberries. Stir well. Sprinkle with rum; stir well. Bake at 350° for 10 minutes, stirring occasionally. Cool completely.

Spoon yogurt onto several layers of heavy-duty paper towels; spread to ½-inch thickness. Cover with additional paper towels; let stand 5 minutes. Scrape yogurt into a bowl, using a rubber spatula; add ice milk, and stir well.

Cut brownie into 16 pieces. Spoon 2 tablespoons yogurt mixture onto each individual dessert plate. Place a brownie in sauce on each plate. Spoon melted chocolate over yogurt mixture in small circles around each brownie. Pull a wooden pick or the tip of a knife continuously through chocolate circles surrounding each brownie. Spoon cranberries evenly over brownies. Garnish with fresh mint sprigs, if desired. Yield: 16 servings (190 calories per serving).

PROTEIN 4.0 FAT 5.0 CARBOHYDRATE 32.8 CHOLESTEROL 3
IRON 0.8 SODIUM 102 CALCIUM 82

SPICED CHOCOLATE CAKE ROLL

⅔ cup water
1½ teaspoons instant coffee granules
4 eggs, separated
1 cup sugar
1¼ cups sifted cake flour
¼ cup unsweetened cocoa
1 teaspoon ground cinnamon
¼ teaspoon salt
1 teaspoon vanilla extract
1 teaspoon cream of tartar
2 tablespoons powdered sugar
3 cups vanilla ice milk, softened
1 teaspoon apple pie spice

Line the bottom of a 15- x 10- x 1-inch jellyroll pan with parchment paper. Set aside.

Combine water and coffee granules in a large bowl. Add egg yolks, and beat 5 minutes at high speed of an electric mixer. Gradually add 1 cup sugar, and beat 4 minutes.

Sift flour, cocoa, cinnamon, and salt over egg yolk mixture; beat at low speed of electric mixer until blended. Stir in vanilla.

Beat egg whites (at room temperature) at high speed of electric mixer just until foamy. Add cream of tartar, and beat until stiff peaks form. Fold into egg yolk mixture. Pour batter into prepared pan. Bake at 350° for 20 to 25 minutes or until top springs back when touched. When cake is done, immediately loosen from sides of pan. Invert cake onto a linen towel that has been dusted with powdered sugar; gently peel off parchment paper. Roll up cake and towel together lengthwise; place seam side down on a wire rack. Let cake cool completely.

Unroll cake. Combine ice milk and pie spice, stirring well; spread evenly over cake. Carefully reroll cake, without towel. Place seam side down on a baking sheet, and freeze until firm. To serve, remove from freezer, and let stand at room temperature 5 minutes. Cut into 1-inch slices. Serve immediately. Yield: 16 servings (140 calories per serving).

PROTEIN 3.6 FAT 2.6 CARBOHYDRATE 25.8 CHOLESTEROL 57
IRON 1.1 SODIUM 86 CALCIUM 45

MOCHA ANGEL FOOD CAKE

¾ cup sifted cake flour
3 tablespoons unsweetened cocoa
1 tablespoon instant espresso powder
¼ teaspoon baking soda
1 cup sugar, divided
11 egg whites
1½ teaspoons cream of tartar
¼ teaspoon salt
1½ teaspoons vanilla extract
1 tablespoon powdered sugar

Sift flour, cocoa, espresso powder, baking soda, and ½ cup sugar together 3 times; set aside.

Beat egg whites (at room temperature) in an extra-large bowl at high speed of an electric mixer until foamy. Add cream of tartar, salt, and vanilla; beat until soft peaks form. Gradually add remaining ½ cup sugar, 2 tablespoons at a time, beating until stiff peaks form. Sift flour mixture over egg white mixture, ¼ cup at a time, folding in carefully after each addition.

Spoon batter into an ungreased 10-inch tube pan; spread evenly with a spatula. Break large air pockets by cutting through batter with a knife. Bake at 350° for 35 to 40 minutes or until cake springs back when lightly touched. Remove cake from oven; invert pan, and cool completely. Loosen cake from sides of pan, using a narrow metal spatula; remove from pan. Sift powdered sugar over cooled cake. Yield: 12 servings (112 calories per serving).

PROTEIN 4.1 FAT 0.2 CARBOHYDRATE 23.1 CHOLESTEROL 0
IRON 0.7 SODIUM 142 CALCIUM 9

LEMON POPPY SEED POUNDCAKE

Vegetable cooking spray
1 teaspoon all-purpose flour
½ cup margarine, softened
¼ cup sugar
¾ cup water
¾ cup frozen egg substitute, thawed
¼ cup frozen lemonade concentrate, thawed
1 tablespoon grated lemon rind
2½ cups all-purpose flour
2 tablespoons poppy seeds
1 teaspoon baking soda
1 teaspoon baking powder
Lemon Syrup

Coat bottom and sides of a 9- x 5- x 3-inch loafpan with cooking spray; dust with 1 teaspoon flour, and set aside.

Cream margarine; add sugar, beating well. Combine water, egg substitute, lemonade concentrate, and lemon rind; stir well. Combine 2½ cups flour and next 3 ingredients; add to creamed mixture alternately with lemonade mixture, beginning and ending with dry ingredients.

Pour batter into prepared pan. Bake at 350° for 50 minutes or until a wooden pick inserted in center comes out clean. Remove cake from oven; prick top of cake at 2-inch intervals with a fork. Pour Lemon Syrup over cake. Cool in pan 10 minutes; remove from pan. Let cool on a wire rack. Yield: 18 servings (142 calories per ½-inch slice).

Lemon Syrup

⅓ cup sifted powdered sugar
¼ cup plus 1½ teaspoons lemon juice

Combine powdered sugar and lemon juice in a small saucepan; cook over medium heat until sugar dissolves, stirring constantly. Yield: ¼ cup plus 1 tablespoon.

PROTEIN 2.9   FAT 5.7   CARBOHYDRATE 20.1   CHOLESTEROL 0
IRON 1.1   SODIUM 138   CALCIUM 43

CRUMB-TOPPED GINGERBREAD

¼ cup firmly packed brown sugar
¼ cup reduced-calorie margarine, softened
¼ cup molasses
1 egg
1¼ cups all-purpose flour
½ teaspoon baking soda
¼ teaspoon baking powder
¼ cup toasted wheat germ
2 teaspoons apple pie spice
¼ teaspoon ground ginger
⅓ cup nonfat buttermilk
1 cup peeled, grated pear
Vegetable cooking spray
⅓ cup graham cracker crumbs
2 tablespoons brown sugar
2 tablespoons reduced-calorie margarine, softened

Combine first 4 ingredients in a large bowl; beat well at medium speed of an electric mixer.

Combine flour, baking soda, baking powder, wheat germ, apple pie spice, and ginger in a bowl; stir well. Add to brown sugar mixture alternately with buttermilk, beginning and ending with flour mixture. Mix well after each addition Stir in grated pear.

Pour gingerbread batter into an 8-inch square baking pan coated with cooking spray. Combine graham cracker crumbs and 2 tablespoons brown sugar; cut in 2 tablespoons margarine with a pastry blender until mixture resembles coarse meal. Sprinkle brown sugar mixture evenly over batter. Bake at 350° for 40 minutes or until a wooden pick inserted in center comes out clean. Let cool in pan 10 minutes. Serve gingerbread warm. Yield: 12 servings (162 calories per serving).

PROTEIN 3.0   FAT 5.0   CARBOHYDRATE 27.3   CHOLESTEROL 18
IRON 1.7   SODIUM 138   CALCIUM 48

CREAMY CHOCOLATE CHEESECAKE

Vegetable cooking spray
8 chocolate wafer cookies, crushed
1 (15-ounce) carton part-skim ricotta cheese, drained
1 (8-ounce) package Neufchâtel cheese, softened
½ cup frozen egg substitute, thawed
3 tablespoons skim milk
¼ cup unsweetened cocoa
2 tablespoons praline liqueur
1 tablespoon vanilla extract
1½ teaspoons grated orange rind
2 egg whites
¼ cup plus 2 tablespoons sugar
Chocolate curls (optional)

Coat a 9-inch springform pan with cooking spray. Dust bottom and sides of pan with crushed wafers.

Beat cheeses in a large bowl at medium speed of an electric mixer 2 to 3 minutes or until smooth. Add egg substitute and milk, beating well. Add cocoa and next 3 ingredients, beating well.

Beat egg whites (at room temperature) at high speed of electric mixer until soft peaks form. Gradually add sugar, 1 tablespoon at a time, beating until stiff peaks form. Fold egg whites into cheese mixture. Spoon over crushed wafers. Bake at 275° for 1 hour (center will be soft but will firm when chilled). Turn off oven, and leave cheesecake in oven for 30 minutes. Remove from oven, and let cool to room temperature; cover and chill at least 4 hours. Remove sides of pan. Garnish with chocolate curls, if desired. Yield: 12 servings (164 calories per serving).

PROTEIN 8.4   FAT 8.3   CARBOHYDRATE 13.9   CHOLESTEROL 28
IRON 0.8   SODIUM 160   CALCIUM 127

INDIVIDUAL APPLE-CHEDDAR CHEESECAKES

12 vanilla wafers
¾ cup 1% low-fat cottage cheese
¼ cup (1 ounce) shredded 40% less-fat Cheddar cheese
1 (8-ounce) package Neufchâtel cheese, softened
¼ cup plus 2 tablespoons sugar
½ cup frozen egg substitute, thawed
1 teaspoon vanilla extract
¾ cup finely chopped peeled apple
¼ teaspoon apple pie spice

Line 12 (2½-inch) muffin pans with paper baking cups. Place a vanilla wafer in each cup.

Combine cottage cheese and Cheddar cheese in container of an electric blender or food processor; top with cover, and process until smooth.

Combine cottage cheese mixture and Neufchâtel in a medium bowl; beat at medium speed of an electric mixer until smooth. Gradually add sugar, beating well. Add egg substitute and vanilla; beat until blended.

Combine apple and apple pie spice; toss to coat. Add apple mixture to cheese mixture; stir well. Spoon mixture evenly into prepared baking cups. Bake at 350° for 25 to 30 minutes or until almost set (do not overbake). Remove pan from oven, and let cool to room temperature on a wire rack. Remove cheesecakes from pans, and chill thoroughly. Yield: 12 cheesecakes (119 calories each).

PROTEIN 5.3   FAT 5.8   CARBOHYDRATE 11.5   CHOLESTEROL 16
IRON 0.4   SODIUM 177   CALCIUM 44

HONEY-ALMOND CHEWS

¼ cup plus 2 tablespoons margarine
3 tablespoons honey
½ cup firmly packed brown sugar
¼ cup plus 1 tablespoon all-purpose flour
3 tablespoons finely chopped almonds
2 tablespoons amaretto
¼ teaspoon salt

Combine margarine and honey in a small saucepan. Cook over medium heat until margarine melts, stirring constantly. Remove from heat; stir in brown sugar and remaining ingredients.

Drop mixture by teaspoonfuls, 3 inches apart, onto parchment paper-lined cookie sheets, making 4 cookies at a time; spread mixture to 2½-inch circles. Bake at 350° for 5 minutes. (Cookies will spread during baking.) Remove from oven, and let cool slightly (about 1 minute).

When cookies are cool enough to hold their shape, lift them quickly with a wide spatula. Flip cookies over, and roll each around the handle of a wooden spoon or other cylindrical object. Let cool on wire rack. When each cookie has cooled and is set, slide off wooden spoon. Repeat with remaining batter. If necessary, keep batter warm over very low heat. Store cooled cookies in an airtight container. Yield: 40 cookies (39 calories each).

PROTEIN 0.3　FAT 2.1　CARBOHYDRATE 5.2　CHOLESTEROL 0
IRON 0.2　SODIUM 36　CALCIUM 5

CHEWY CHOCOLATE-OATMEAL COOKIES

½ cup reduced-calorie margarine,
　softened
½ cup firmly packed brown sugar
2 egg whites
¼ cup plus 1 tablespoon unsweetened
　orange juice
1 teaspoon vanilla extract
1¼ cups all-purpose flour
2½ tablespoons unsweetened cocoa
1 teaspoon baking soda
¼ teaspoon salt
1¾ cups regular oats, uncooked
¼ cup toasted wheat germ
Vegetable cooking spray

Cream margarine; gradually add brown sugar, beating at medium speed of an electric mixer until light and fluffy. Add egg whites, orange juice, and vanilla; beat well.

Combine flour and next 3 ingredients, stirring well. Gradually add flour mixture to creamed mixture, mixing well. Stir in oats and wheat germ.

Drop dough by level tablespoonfuls, 2 inches apart, onto cookie sheets coated with cooking spray. Bake at 350° for 10 minutes. Cool slightly on cookie sheets. Cool completely on wire racks. Yield: 3 dozen (62 calories each).

PROTEIN 1.4　FAT 2.1　CARBOHYDRATE 9.7　CHOLESTEROL 0
IRON 0.6　SODIUM 65　CALCIUM 11

ORANGE CAPPUCCINO BON BONS

¼ cup plus 2 tablespoons unsalted margarine
¼ cup plus 2 tablespoons unsweetened cocoa
1½ tablespoons instant coffee granules
⅔ cup sugar
2 eggs, lightly beaten
1 teaspoon grated orange rind
½ teaspoon vanilla extract
3 tablespoons Grand Marnier or other
　orange-flavored liqueur
½ cup all-purpose flour
1 teaspoon ground cinnamon
½ teaspoon baking powder
¼ teaspoon salt
28 (2-inch) foil muffin liners

Combine margarine, cocoa, and coffee granules in a medium saucepan. Cook over low heat until margarine melts, stirring constantly. Remove from heat; let cool slightly. Add sugar and next 3 ingredients; stir well to combine. Stir in liqueur.

Combine flour, cinnamon, baking powder, and salt in a small bowl; add to cocoa mixture, stirring well to combine.

Place muffin liners on a baking sheet; spoon 1 tablespoon batter into each liner. Bake at 375° for 12 minutes or until a wooden pick inserted in center comes out clean. Cool completely on a wire rack. Yield: 28 cookies (59 calories each).

PROTEIN 1.0　FAT 3.0　CARBOHYDRATE 7.0　CHOLESTEROL 15
IRON 0.4　SODIUM 32　CALCIUM 9

Cooking Light 1992 Menu Plans

This plan for seven days of calorie-controlled meals provides a healthful approach to weight loss. Follow the plan precisely, or use it as a model for planning your own balanced meals by substituting foods of comparable calories and nutrients. Refer to the Calorie/Nutrient Chart on pages 250—261 for these values. The menu items marked with an asterisk are included in the menu or recipe sections and can be located in the Index. When planning your own menus, remember that of the total calories provided, at least 50 percent of the calories should be from carbohydrate, 20 percent from protein, and less than 30 percent from fat.

Most women can safely lose weight while eating 1,200 calories per day and most men can lose while eating 1,600. Once weight is lost, modify the menu plan according to the calories needed to maintain your ideal weight. If you feel you are losing weight too slowly, keep in mind that eating fewer calories to speed up weight loss may rob you of the nutrients your body needs to stay healthy. Also, your metabolism may slow down to accommodate a limited food supply. Exercise is the key to speedier weight loss.

1200 calories		Day 1	1600 calories	
		BREAKFAST		
1 (8-ounce) carton	127	Plain Nonfat Yogurt	1 (8-ounce) carton	127
2 tablespoons	44	Wheat Germ	3 tablespoons	66
½ cup	41	Fresh Blueberries	½ cup	41
	212			234
		LUNCH		
1 serving	141	*Herbed Tomato Sandwich	1 serving	141
—		*Cheesy Potato Chowder	1 cup	167
1 cup	121	*Toss and Serve Wild Rice Salad	1 cup	121
1 cup	86	Skim Milk	1 cup	86
2 cookies	94	*Scented Sugar Cookies	3 cookies	141
	442			656
		DINNER		
1 serving	183	*Mushroom-Stuffed Beef Tenderloin	1 serving	183
½ cup	103	Cooked Rice	½ cup	103
1 serving	51	*Maple-Glazed Carrots	1 serving	51
—		*Easy Green Salad	1 cup	20
—		Whole Wheat Roll	1 roll	72
1 serving	140	*Spiced Chocolate Cake Roll	1 serving	140
	477			569
		SNACK		
1 serving	72	*Pineapple-Neufchâtel Snack	2 servings	144
	Total 1203			Total 1603

1200 calories		Day 2	1600 calories	
		BREAKFAST		
1 each	113	*Fig-Orange Muffins	1 each	113
—		Reduced-Calorie Margarine	1 teaspoon	20
1 cup	86	Skim Milk	1 cup	86
½ cup	37	Sliced Peaches	½ cup	37
	236			256
		LUNCH		
1 serving	274	*Vegetable Cheese Burrito	1 serving	274
1 cup	85	*Summer Fruit Salad in Lemonade Glaze	1 cup	85
1 serving	112	*Mocha Angel Food Cake	1 serving	112
—		*Cantaloupe Cooler	1 cup	86
	471			557
		DINNER		
1 serving	205	*Chicken Paprika	1 serving	205
—		*Hot Sesame Noodles	½ cup	177
1 serving	48	*Lemon Asparagus Spears	1 serving	48
—		*Parsley-Dijon French Bread	1-inch slice	101
1 serving	187	*Ambrosia Compote	1 serving	187
	440			718
		SNACK		
2 cups	46	Air-Popped Popcorn	3 cups	69
	Total 1193			Total 1600

1200 calories		Day 3	1600 calories	
		BREAKFAST		
1 each	100	*Fruited Yogurt Pancakes	1 each	100
—		Reduced-Calorie Maple Syrup	1 tablespoon	6
1 cup	86	Skim Milk	1 cup	86
1 cup	45	Fresh Strawberries	1 cup	45
	231			237
		LUNCH		
1 serving	254	*Tex-Mex Patties	1 serving	254
½ cup	58	*Black Bean Slaw	½ cup	58
—		Hard Roll	1 roll	88
½ cup	159	*Strawberry Mousse Parfaits	½ cup	159
—		*California Lemonade	1 cup	135
	471			694
		DINNER		
1 cup	144	*Easy Brunswick Stew	1 cup	144
—		Cooked Rice	½ cup	103
½-inch slice	140	*Swiss Herb Loaf	½-inch slice	140
1 serving	159	*Tropical Fruit Crisp	1 serving	159
	443			546
		SNACK		
½ cup	57	*Peach Frappé	1 cup	114
	Total 1202			Total 1591

1200 calories		Day 4	1600 calories	
		BREAKFAST		
½ cup	119	*Sunny Orange Grits	½ cup	119
1 each	75	Poached Egg	1 each	75
1 slice	40	Reduced-Calorie Bread	1 slice	40
—		Skim Milk	1 cup	86
	234			320
		LUNCH		
1 serving	208	*Open-Faced Tuna Melt	1 serving	208
—		*Seasoned Corn-on-the-Cob	1 serving	102
½ cup	110	*Minted Peas in Lettuce Cups	½ cup	110
1 serving	162	*Crumb-Topped Gingerbread	1 serving	162
	480			582
		DINNER		
1 serving	220	*Apple-Glazed Pork Loin Roast	1 serving	220
½ cup	103	Baked Sweet Potato	½ cup	103
—		*Summer Squash Ring	1 serving	79
1 serving	56	*Striped Salad Platter	1 serving	56
1 serving	86	*Spiced Pear Kisses	1 serving	86
	465			544
		SNACK		
½ cup	28	Fresh Cantaloupe	1 cup	56
—		*Onion Crackers	3 crackers	105
	Total 1207			Total 1607

1200 calories		Day 6	1600 calories	
		BREAKFAST		
1 roll	141	*Overnight Sour Cream-Cinnamon Rolls	1 roll	141
1 cup	86	Skim Milk	1 cup	86
½ cup	57	Fruit Cocktail	½ cup	57
	284			284
		LUNCH		
1 serving	230	*Morrocan Pork Salad	1 serving	230
1 biscuit	47	*East Indian Spice Biscuits	2 biscuits	94
2 cookies	124	*Chewy Chocolate-Oatmeal Cookies	3 cookies	186
—		*Pear Brie Soup	½ cup	117
	401			627
		DINNER		
1 serving	170	*Sliced Turkey with Pumpkin Chutney	1 serving	170
½ cup	89	*Country-Style Brown Rice	½ cup	89
—		*Confetti Cabbage Casserole	1 serving	83
1 serving	195	*Maple Streusel Apples	1 serving	195
	454			537
		SNACK		
1 serving	66	*Quick After-School Pizzas	1 serving	66
—		Skim Milk	1 cup	86
	Total 1205			Total 1600

1200 calories		Day 5	1600 calories	
		BREAKFAST		
½ cup	73	Oatmeal	½ cup	73
1 cup	86	Skim Milk	1 cup	86
1 ounce	45	Canadian Bacon	1 ounce	45
—		Raisin Bread	1 slice	66
	204			270
		LUNCH		
1 serving	168	*Shrimp Vegetable Pita Pockets	1 serving	168
1 serving	46	*Marinated Tomato and Jicama	1 serving	46
—		*Toasted Herb Sticks	6 sticks	84
1 serving	187	*Orange Parfaits	1 serving	187
	401			485
		DINNER		
—		*Fresh Salsa with Pita Chips	1 serving	100
1 cup	255	*Mexican Meatball Stew	1 cup	255
4 crackers	48	Unsalted Crackers	6 crackers	72
½ cup	58	*Black Bean Slaw	½ cup	58
3 cookies	117	*Honey-Almond Chews	3 cookies	117
	478			602
		SNACK		
1 pretzel	102	*Hard Spicy Pretzels	1 pretzel	102
—		*Berry Cider Fizz	1 cup	139
	Total 1185			Total 1598

1200 calories		Day 7	1600 calories	
		BREAKFAST		
1 each	106	*Cornmeal-Cheddar English Muffins	1 each	106
1 tablespoon	16	*Plum-Pineapple Butter	1 tablespoon	16
—		Orange Juice	½ cup	56
1 cup	86	Skim Milk	1 cup	86
	208			264
		LUNCH		
1 serving	223	*Oven-Fried Catfish Fillets	1 serving	223
½ cup	12	Steamed Broccoli	½ cup	12
—		*Tangy Horseradish Coleslaw	1 cup	95
1-inch slice	57	*Whole Wheat French Bread	1-inch slice	57
1 serving	100	*Red Berries and Cream	1 serving	100
	392			487
		DINNER		
1 serving	257	*Spicy Vegetable Ragoût	1 serving	257
—		*Celery Oriental	½ cup	36
—		*Kiwifruit-Blueberry Salad	1 serving	97
½-inch slice	116	*Pumpernickel Quick Bread	½-inch slice	116
—		*Lemon Chablis Cooler	1 cup	109
1 serving	165	*Peanut Butter Ice Milk Sandwiches	1 serving	165
	538			780
		SNACK		
½ cup	70	*Raspberry-Banana Frosty	½ cup	70
	Total 1208			Total 1601

Calorie/Nutrient Chart

FOOD	APPROXIMATE MEASURE	FOOD ENERGY (CALORIES)	PROTEIN (GRAMS)	FAT (GRAMS)	CARBOHYDRATES (GRAMS)	CHOLESTEROL (MILLIGRAMS)	IRON (MILLIGRAMS)	SODIUM (MILLIGRAMS)	CALCIUM (MILLIGRAMS)
Apple									
Fresh, with skin	1 medium	81	0.2	0.5	21.0	0	0.2	0	10
Juice, unsweetened	½ cup	58	0.1	0.1	14.5	0	0.5	4	9
Applesauce, unsweetened	½ cup	52	0.2	0.1	13.8	0	0.1	2	4
Apricot									
Fresh	1 each	18	0.4	0.1	4.1	0	0.2	0	5
Canned, in juice	½ cup	58	0.8	0.0	15.0	0	0.4	5	15
Canned, in light syrup	½ cup	75	0.7	0.1	19.0	—	0.3	1	12
Canned, peeled, in water	½ cup	25	0.8	0.0	6.2	0	0.6	12	9
Dried, uncooked	1 each	17	0.3	0.0	4.3	0	0.3	1	3
Nectar	½ cup	70	0.5	0.1	18.0	0	0.5	4	9
Artichoke									
Fresh, cooked	1 each	53	2.6	0.2	12.4	0	1.6	79	47
Hearts, cooked	½ cup	37	1.8	0.1	8.7	0	1.1	55	33
Asparagus, fresh, cooked	½ cup	23	2.3	0.3	4.0	0	0.6	4	22
Arugula	3 ounces	21	2.2	0.5	3.1	0	—	23	136
Avocado	1 medium	322	3.9	30.6	14.8	0	2.0	20	22
Bacon									
Canadian-style	1 ounce	45	5.8	2.0	0.5	14	0.2	399	2
Cured, broiled	1 slice	43	2.3	3.7	0.0	6	0.1	120	1
Bamboo shoots, cooked	½ cup	7	0.9	0.1	1.1	0	0.1	2	7
Banana									
Mashed	½ cup	101	1.1	0.5	25.8	0	0.3	1	7
Whole	1 medium	109	1.2	0.5	27.6	0	0.4	1	7
Barley, dry	½ cup	352	9.9	1.2	77.7	0	2.5	9	29
Basil, fresh, raw	¼ cup	1	0.1	0.0	0.1	0	0.1	0	3
Bean sprouts, raw	½ cup	16	1.6	0.1	3.1	0	0.5	3	7
Beans, cooked and drained									
Black	½ cup	114	7.6	0.5	20.4	0	1.8	1	23
Cannellini, canned	½ cup	96	5.5	0.5	16.1	—	1.8	—	21
Garbanzo	½ cup	134	7.3	2.1	22.5	0	2.4	6	40
Great Northern	½ cup	132	9.3	0.5	23.7	0	2.4	2	76
Green, fresh	½ cup	22	1.2	0.2	4.9	0	0.8	2	29
Green, canned, regular pack	½ cup	18	1.0	0.1	4.2	0	1.0	442	29
Kidney or red	½ cup	112	7.7	0.4	20.2	0	2.6	2	25
Lima, frozen, baby	½ cup	94	6.0	0.3	17.5	0	1.8	26	25
Pinto	½ cup	117	7.0	0.4	21.9	0	2.2	2	41
Wax, canned	½ cup	14	0.8	0.1	3.1	0	0.5	171	18
White	½ cup	127	8.0	0.6	23.2	0	2.5	2	65
Beef, trimmed of fat									
Flank steak, broiled	3 ounces	207	21.6	12.7	0.0	60	2.2	71	5
Ground, extra-lean, broiled	3 ounces	218	21.5	13.9	0.0	71	2.0	60	6
Liver, braised	3 ounces	137	20.7	4.2	2.9	331	5.7	60	6
Roast, roasted	3 ounces	204	23.1	11.7	0.0	69	2.2	63	9
Round, bottom, braised	3 ounces	189	26.9	8.2	0.0	82	2.9	43	4
Round, eye of, cooked	3 ounces	156	24.7	5.5	0.0	59	1.7	53	4
Round, top, lean, broiled	3 ounces	162	27.0	5.3	0.0	71	2.4	52	5
Sirloin, broiled	3 ounces	177	25.8	7.4	0.0	76	2.9	56	9
Beets									
Fresh, diced, cooked	½ cup	26	0.9	0.4	5.7	0	0.5	42	9
Canned, regular pack	½ cup	30	0.8	0.1	7.2	—	0.5	209	15

Dash(—) indicates insufficient data available

FOOD	APPROXIMATE MEASURE	FOOD ENERGY (CALORIES)	PROTEIN (GRAMS)	FAT (GRAMS)	CARBOHYDRATES (GRAMS)	CHOLESTEROL (MILLIGRAMS)	IRON (MILLIGRAMS)	SODIUM (MILLIGRAMS)	CALCIUM (MILLIGRAMS)
Beverages									
Beer	12 fluid ounces	146	1.1	0.0	13.1	0	0.1	18	18
Beer, light	12 fluid ounces	95	0.7	0.0	4.4	0	0.1	10	17
Brandy, bourbon, gin, rum, vodka, or whiskey, 80 proof	1 fluid ounce	65	0.0	0.0	0.0	0	0.0	0	0
Champagne	6 fluid ounces	129	0.5	0.0	2.0	0	0.9	7	5
Club soda	8 ounces	0	0.0	0.0	0.0	0	—	48	11
Coffee, black	1 cup	5	0.2	0.0	0.9	0	1.0	5	5
Coffee liqueur	1 fluid ounce	99	0.0	0.1	13.9	0	0.0	2	0
Cognac brandy	1 fluid ounce	69	—	—	—	0	—	—	—
Crème de menthe liqueur	1 tablespoon	105	0.0	0.1	11.8	0	0.0	1	0
Sherry, sweet	1 fluid ounce	39	0.1	0.0	2.0	0	0.1	4	2
Vermouth, dry	1 fluid ounce	35	0.0	0.0	1.6	0	0.1	5	2
Vermouth, sweet	1 fluid ounce	45	0.0	0.0	4.7	0	0.1	8	2
Wine, port	6 fluid ounces	279	0.2	0.0	21.3	0	0.7	7	7
Wine, red	6 fluid ounces	121	0.4	0.0	0.5	0	1.4	18	12
Wine, white, dry	6 fluid ounces	112	0.2	0.0	1.0	0	0.9	7	15
Blackberries, fresh	½ cup	37	0.5	0.3	9.2	0	0.4	0	23
Blueberries, fresh	½ cup	41	0.5	0.3	10.2	0	0.1	4	4
Bouillon, dry									
Beef-flavored cubes	1 cube	3	0.1	0.0	0.2	—	—	400	—
Beef-flavored granules	1 teaspoon	10	0.0	1.0	0.0	—	—	945	—
Chicken-flavored cubes	1 cube	7	0.2	0.1	0.5	—	—	800	—
Chicken-flavored granules	1 teaspoon	10	0.5	1.0	0.5	—	0.0	819	—
Bran									
Oat, dry, uncooked	½ cup	153	8.0	3.0	23.5	0	2.6	1	31
Wheat, crude	½ cup	65	4.7	1.3	19.4	0	3.2	1	22
Bread									
Bagel, plain	1 each	161	5.9	1.5	30.5	—	1.4	196	23
Biscuit, homemade	1 each	127	2.3	6.4	14.9	2	0.6	224	65
Bun, hamburger or hot dog	1 each	136	3.2	3.4	22.4	13	0.8	112	19
Cornbread	2-ounce square	154	3.5	6.0	21.1	56	0.7	273	96
English muffin	1 each	182	5.9	3.6	30.9	32	1.5	234	41
French	1 slice	73	2.3	0.5	13.9	1	0.6	145	11
Light, wheatberry or 7-grain	1 slice	40	2.0	1.0	7.0	5	0.7	11	20
Pita, whole wheat	1 medium	122	2.4	0.9	23.5	0	1.4	—	39
Pumpernickel	1 slice	76	2.8	0.4	16.4	0	0.7	176	26
Raisin	1 slice	66	1.6	0.7	13.4	1	0.3	91	18
Rye	1 slice	61	2.3	0.3	13.0	0	0.4	139	19
White	1 slice	67	2.2	0.8	12.6	1	0.6	127	18
Whole wheat	1 slice	61	2.6	0.8	11.9	1	0.6	132	25
Breadcrumbs									
Fine, dry	½ cup	196	6.3	2.2	36.7	2	1.7	368	61
Seasoned	½ cup	214	8.4	1.5	41.5	—	1.9	1590	59
Bread stick, plain	1 each	17	0.4	0.5	2.7	—	0.2	20	1
Broccoli, fresh, chopped, cooked	½ cup	12	1.3	0.1	2.3	0	0.6	12	21
Broth									
Beef, canned, diluted	1 cup	32	4.8	0.6	2.6	24	0.4	782	0
Chicken, low-sodium	1 cup	22	0.4	0.0	2.0	0	0.0	4	0
Chicken, no-salt-added	1 cup	16	1.0	1.0	0.0	—	—	67	—
Brussels sprouts, fresh, cooked	½ cup	30	2.0	0.4	6.8	0	0.9	16	28
Bulgur, uncooked	½ cup	239	8.6	0.9	53.1	0	1.7	12	25
Butter									
Regular	1 tablespoon	102	0.1	11.5	0.0	31	0.0	117	3
Whipped	1 tablespoon	68	0.1	7.7	0.0	21	0.0	78	2
Cabbage									
Bok choy	1 cup	9	1.0	0.1	1.5	0	0.6	45	73
Common varieties, raw, shredded	½ cup	8	0.4	0.1	1.9	0	0.2	6	16

FOOD	APPROXIMATE MEASURE	FOOD ENERGY (CALORIES)	PROTEIN (GRAMS)	FAT (GRAMS)	CARBOHYDRATES (GRAMS)	CHOLESTEROL (MILLIGRAMS)	IRON (MILLIGRAMS)	SODIUM (MILLIGRAMS)	CALCIUM (MILLIGRAMS)
Cake, without frosting									
Angel food	2-ounce slice	147	3.2	0.1	33.7	—	0.2	83	54
Pound	1-ounce slice	305	3.6	17.5	33.7	134	0.5	245	27
Sponge, cut into 12 slices	1 slice	183	3.6	5.0	30.8	221	0.8	99	44
Yellow, cut into 12 slices	1 slice	190	2.8	7.5	28.0	40	0.2	157	79
Candy									
Fudge, chocolate	1 ounce	113	0.8	3.4	21.3	0	0.3	54	22
Gumdrops	1 ounce	98	0.0	0.2	24.8	0	0.1	10	2
Hard	1 each	27	0.0	0.0	6.8	0	0.1	2	1
Jelly beans	1 ounce	104	0.0	0.1	26.4	0	0.3	3	3
Milk chocolate	1 ounce	156	2.1	9.1	16.1	—	0.5	26	54
Cantaloupe, raw, diced	½ cup	28	0.7	0.2	6.7	0	0.2	7	9
Capers	1 tablespoon	4	0.4	0.0	0.6	0	—	670	—
Carambola (starfruit)	1 medium	42	0.7	0.4	9.9	0	0.3	3	5
Carrot									
Raw	1 medium	31	0.7	0.1	7.3	0	0.4	25	19
Cooked, sliced	½ cup	33	0.8	0.1	7.6	0	0.4	48	22
Juice, canned	½ cup	66	1.6	0.2	15.3	0	0.8	48	40
Catsup									
Regular	1 tablespoon	18	0.3	0.1	4.3	0	0.1	178	4
No-salt-added	1 tablespoon	15	0.0	0.0	4.0	—	—	6	—
Reduced-calorie	1 tablespoon	7	0.0	0.0	1.2	—	0.0	3	0
Cauliflower									
Raw, flowerets	½ cup	12	1.0	0.1	2.5	0	0.3	7	14
Cooked, flowerets	½ cup	15	1.2	0.1	2.8	0	0.2	4	17
Caviar	1 tablespoon	40	3.9	2.8	0.6	94	—	240	—
Celeriac, raw, shredded	½ cup	30	1.2	0.2	7.2	0	0.5	78	34
Celery, raw, diced	½ cup	10	0.4	0.1	2.2	0	0.3	53	23
Cereal									
Bran flakes	½ cup	64	2.5	0.4	15.3	0	5.6	182	10
Bran, whole	½ cup	104	6.0	1.5	32.7	0	6.7	387	30
Corn flakes	½ cup	44	0.9	0.0	9.8	0	0.7	140	0
Crispy rice	½ cup	55	0.9	0.1	12.4	0	0.3	103	3
Granola	½ cup	242	5.8	8.9	34.7	0	1.8	66	29
Puffed wheat	½ cup	22	0.9	0.1	4.8	0	0.3	0	2
Raisin bran	½ cup	77	2.7	0.5	18.6	0	3.0	179	9
Shredded wheat miniatures	½ cup	76	2.3	0.5	17.0	0	0.9	2	8
Toasted oat	½ cup	44	1.7	0.7	7.8	0	1.8	123	19
Whole-grain wheat flakes	½ cup	72	2.0	0.0	15.7	—	0.2	1	—
Cheese									
American, processed	1 ounce	106	6.3	8.9	0.5	27	0.1	405	175
American, processed, light	1 ounce	50	6.9	2.0	1.0	—	—	407	198
American, processed, skim	1 ounce	69	6.0	5.0	1.0	10	—	—	149
Blue	1 ounce	100	6.0	8.1	0.7	21	0.1	395	150
Brie	1 ounce	95	5.9	7.8	0.1	28	0.1	178	52
Camembert	1 ounce	85	5.6	6.9	0.1	20	0.1	239	110
Cheddar	1 ounce	114	7.0	9.4	0.3	30	0.2	176	204
Cheddar, 40% less-fat	1 ounce	71	5.0	4.1	6.0	15	0.1	150	192
Cheddar, light, processed	1 ounce	50	6.9	2.0	1.0	15	—	442	198
Cottage, dry curd, no-salt-added	½ cup	62	12.5	0.3	1.3	5	0.2	9	23
Cottage, low-fat (1% milk-fat)	½ cup	81	14.0	1.1	3.1	5	0.2	459	69
Cottage, low-fat (2% milk-fat)	½ cup	102	15.5	2.2	4.1	9	0.2	459	77
Cottage (4% milk-fat)	½ cup	108	13.1	4.7	2.8	16	0.1	425	63
Cream, light	1 ounce	62	2.9	4.8	1.8	16	0.0	160	38
Farmer	1 ounce	40	4.0	3.0	1.0	—	—	—	30
Feta	1 ounce	75	4.0	6.0	1.2	25	0.2	316	139
Fontina	1 ounce	110	7.3	8.8	0.4	33	0.1	—	156

Dash(—) indicates insufficient data available

FOOD	APPROXIMATE MEASURE	FOOD ENERGY (CALORIES)	PROTEIN (GRAMS)	FAT (GRAMS)	CARBOHYDRATES (GRAMS)	CHOLESTEROL (MILLIGRAMS)	IRON (MILLIGRAMS)	SODIUM (MILLIGRAMS)	CALCIUM (MILLIGRAMS)
Cheese *(continued)*									
Gouda	1 ounce	101	7.1	7.8	0.6	32	0.1	232	198
Gruyère	1 ounce	117	8.4	9.2	0.1	31	—	95	287
Monterey Jack	1 ounce	106	6.9	8.6	0.2	22	0.2	152	211
Monterey Jack, reduced-fat	1 ounce	83	8.4	5.4	0.5	19	0.1	181	227
Mozzarella, part-skim	1 ounce	72	6.9	4.5	0.8	16	0.1	132	183
Mozzarella, whole milk	1 ounce	80	5.5	6.1	0.6	22	0.0	106	147
Muenster	1 ounce	104	6.6	8.5	0.3	27	0.1	178	203
Neufchâtel	1 ounce	74	2.8	6.6	0.8	22	0.1	113	21
Parmesan, grated	1 ounce	111	10.1	7.3	0.9	19	0.2	454	336
Provolone	1 ounce	100	7.2	7.5	0.6	20	0.1	248	214
Ricotta, part-skim	1 ounce	39	3.2	2.2	1.5	9	0.1	35	77
Romano, grated	1 ounce	110	9.0	7.6	1.0	29	—	340	302
Swiss	1 ounce	107	8.1	7.8	1.0	26	0.0	74	272
Swiss, reduced-fat	1 ounce	85	9.6	5.0	0.5	18	0.1	44	334
Cherries									
Fresh, sweet	½ cup	52	0.9	0.7	12.0	0	0.3	0	11
Sour, in light syrup	½ cup	94	0.9	0.1	24.3	0	1.7	9	13
Sour, unsweetened	½ cup	39	0.8	0.2	9.4	0	0.2	2	12
Chicken, skinned, boned, and roasted									
White meat	3 ounces	147	26.1	3.8	0.0	72	0.9	65	13
Dark meat	3 ounces	163	22.1	7.6	0.0	75	1.2	63	12
Liver	3 ounces	134	20.7	4.6	0.7	537	7.2	43	12
Chili sauce	1 tablespoon	18	0.4	0.1	4.2	0	0.1	228	3
Chives, raw, chopped	1 tablespoon	1	0.1	0.0	0.1	0	0.0	0	2
Chocolate									
Chips, semisweet	¼ cup	215	1.7	15.2	24.2	0	1.1	1	13
Sweet	1 ounce	150	1.2	9.9	16.4	0	0.4	9	27
Syrup, fudge	1 tablespoon	64	0.9	2.5	9.6	—	0.2	22	19
Unsweetened, baking	1 ounce	141	3.1	14.7	8.5	0	2.0	1	23
Chutney, apple	1 tablespoon	41	0.2	0.0	10.5	—	0.2	34	5
Cilantro, fresh, minced	1 tablespoon	1	0.1	0.0	0.3	0	0.2	1	5
Clams									
Raw	½ cup	92	15.8	1.2	3.2	42	17.3	69	57
Canned, drained	½ cup	118	20.4	1.6	4.1	54	22.4	90	74
Cocoa powder, unsweetened	1 tablespoon	24	1.6	0.7	2.6	—	0.9	0	8
Coconut									
Fresh, grated	1 cup	460	4.3	43.5	19.8	0	3.2	26	18
Dried, sweetened, shredded	1 cup	463	2.7	32.8	44.0	0	1.8	242	14
Dried, unsweetened, shredded	1 cup	526	5.5	51.4	18.8	0	2.6	30	21
Cookies									
Brownie	2-ounce bar	243	2.7	10.1	39.0	10	1.3	153	25
Chocolate	1 each	72	1.0	3.4	9.4	13	0.4	61	18
Chocolate chip, homemade	1 each	69	0.9	4.6	6.8	7	0.3	30	7
Fortune	1 each	23	0.3	0.2	5.0	—	0.1	—	1
Gingersnaps	1 each	36	0.5	1.3	5.4	3	0.4	11	14
Oatmeal, plain	1 each	57	0.9	2.7	7.2	9	0.3	46	13
Sandwich, with creme	1 each	40	0.3	1.7	6.0	—	0.2	41	2
Sugar	1 each	50	0.3	2.7	6.6	—	0.1	38	2
Vanilla wafers	1 each	13	0.3	0.4	2.3	—	0.1	10	2
Corn									
Fresh, kernels, cooked	½ cup	89	2.6	1.0	20.6	0	0.5	14	2
Cream-style, regular pack	½ cup	92	2.2	0.5	23.2	0	0.5	365	4
Cornmeal									
Enriched, dry	1 cup	442	9.9	4.4	93.8	0	4.2	43	7
Self-rising	1 cup	407	10.1	4.1	85.7	0	7.0	1521	440
Cornstarch	1 tablespoon	31	0.0	0.0	7.3	0	0.0	1	0
Couscous, cooked	½ cup	98	3.5	0.0	20.6	—	0.5	—	10

FOOD	APPROXIMATE MEASURE	FOOD ENERGY (CALORIES)	PROTEIN (GRAMS)	FAT (GRAMS)	CARBOHYDRATES (GRAMS)	CHOLESTEROL (MILLIGRAMS)	IRON (MILLIGRAMS)	SODIUM (MILLIGRAMS)	CALCIUM (MILLIGRAMS)
Crab									
Blue, cooked	3 ounces	87	17.2	1.5	0.0	85	0.8	237	88
Imitation	3 ounces	76	10.2	0.0	8.5	—	0.5	—	255
King, cooked	3 ounces	82	16.5	1.3	0.0	45	0.6	912	50
Crackers									
Butter	1 each	17	0.0	1.0	2.0	—	0.1	32	4
Graham, plain	1 square	27	0.6	0.7	5.2	0	0.1	47	3
Melba rounds, plain	1 each	11	0.4	0.2	2.0	—	0.1	26	—
Saltine	1 each	13	0.3	0.3	2.0	—	0.1	43	5
Whole wheat	1 each	27	0.5	1.0	3.5	—	0.1	50	0
Cranberry									
Fresh, whole	½ cup	23	0.2	0.1	6.0	0	0.1	0	3
Juice cocktail, reduced-calorie	½ cup	24	0.0	0.0	5.9	—	2.8	4	7
Juice cocktail, regular	½ cup	75	0.0	0.1	19.2	0	0.2	5	4
Sauce, sweetened	¼ cup	105	0.1	0.1	26.9	0	0.1	20	3
Cream									
Half-and-half	1 tablespoon	20	0.5	1.7	0.7	6	0.0	6	16
Sour	1 tablespoon	31	0.5	3.0	0.6	6	0.0	8	17
Sour, reduced-calorie	1 tablespoon	20	0.4	1.8	0.6	6	0.0	6	16
Whipping, unwhipped	1 tablespoon	51	0.3	5.5	0.4	20	0.0	6	10
Creamer, non-dairy, powder	1 teaspoon	11	0.1	0.7	1.1	0	0.0	4	16
Croutons, seasoned	1 ounce	139	3.0	5.0	18.9	—	0.3	—	20
Cucumbers, raw, whole	1 medium	32	1.3	0.3	7.1	0	0.7	5	34
Currants	1 tablespoon	25	0.3	0.2	6.7	—	0.3	1	8
Dandelion greens, raw	3 ounces	38	2.3	0.6	7.8	0	2.6	65	159
Dates, pitted, unsweetened	5 each	114	0.8	0.2	30.5	0	0.5	1	13
Doughnut									
Cake type	1 each	156	1.8	7.4	20.6	24	0.5	200	16
Plain, yeast	1 each	166	2.5	10.7	15.1	10	0.6	94	15
Egg									
White	1 each	16	3.2	0.0	0.4	0	0.0	49	4
Whole	1 each	75	6.4	5.1	0.6	213	1.0	69	28
Yolk	1 each	59	2.8	5.1	0.0	213	0.9	8	26
Substitute	¼ cup	30	6.0	0.0	1.0	0	1.1	90	20
Eggplant, cooked without salt	½ cup	13	0.4	0.1	3.2	0	0.2	1	3
Extract, vanilla	1 teaspoon	12	—	—	—	—	—	—	—
Fennel, leaves, raw	½ cup	13	1.2	0.2	2.3	0	1.2	4	45
Figs									
Fresh	1 medium	37	0.4	0.2	9.9	0	0.2	1	18
Dried	1 each	48	0.6	0.2	12.2	0	0.4	2	27
Fish, cooked									
Catfish, farm-raised	3 ounces	195	15.4	11.3	6.8	69	1.2	238	37
Cod	3 ounces	89	19.4	0.7	0.0	47	0.4	66	12
Flounder	3 ounces	100	20.5	1.3	0.0	58	0.3	89	15
Grouper	3 ounces	100	21.1	1.1	0.0	40	1.0	45	18
Haddock	3 ounces	95	20.6	0.8	0.0	63	1.1	74	36
Halibut	3 ounces	119	22.7	2.5	0.0	35	0.9	59	51
Mackerel	3 ounces	134	20.1	5.4	0.0	62	0.6	56	11
Perch	3 ounces	100	21.1	1.0	0.0	98	1.0	67	87
Pollock	3 ounces	96	20.0	1.0	0.0	82	0.2	99	5
Pompano	3 ounces	179	20.1	10.3	0.0	54	0.6	65	37
Salmon	3 ounces	184	23.2	9.3	0.0	74	0.5	56	6
Scrod	3 ounces	89	19.4	0.7	0.0	47	0.4	66	12
Snapper	3 ounces	109	22.4	1.5	0.0	40	0.2	48	34

Dash(—) indicates insufficient data available

FOOD	APPROXIMATE MEASURE	FOOD ENERGY (CALORIES)	PROTEIN (GRAMS)	FAT (GRAMS)	CARBOHYDRATES (GRAMS)	CHOLESTEROL (MILLIGRAMS)	IRON (MILLIGRAMS)	SODIUM (MILLIGRAMS)	CALCIUM (MILLIGRAMS)
Fish *(continued)*									
Sole	3 ounces	100	20.5	1.3	0.0	58	0.3	89	15
Swordfish	3 ounces	132	21.6	4.4	0.0	43	0.9	98	5
Trout	3 ounces	128	22.4	3.7	0.0	62	2.1	29	73
Tuna, canned in oil	6½ ounces	343	48.9	14.9	0.0	57	1.2	730	7
Tuna, canned in water	3 ounces	116	22.7	2.1	0.0	36	0.5	333	—
Flour									
All-purpose, unsifted	1 cup	455	12.9	1.2	95.4	0	5.8	3	19
Bread, sifted	1 cup	495	16.4	2.3	99.4	0	6.0	3	21
Cake, sifted	1 cup	395	8.9	0.9	85.1	0	8.0	2	15
Rye, light, sifted	1 cup	374	8.6	1.4	81.8	0	1.8	2	21
Whole wheat, unsifted	1 cup	401	12.0	1.0	86.3	0	4.5	5	0
Frankfurter									
All-meat	1 each	130	5.8	11.2	1.1	29	0.8	484	3
Chicken	1 each	113	5.7	8.6	3.0	44	0.9	603	42
Turkey	1 each	99	6.3	7.8	0.7	47	0.8	627	47
Fruit bits, dried	1 ounce	93	1.3	0.0	20.0	0	0.5	24	—
Fruit cocktail, canned, packed in juice	½ cup	57	0.6	0.0	14.6	0	0.2	5	10
Garlic, raw	1 clove	4	0.2	0.0	1.0	0	0.1	1	5
Gelatin									
Flavored, prepared with water	½ cup	61	1.4	0.0	14.4	0	0.0	52	2
Unflavored	1 teaspoon	10	2.6	0.0	0.0	—	—	3	—
Ginger									
Fresh, grated	1 teaspoon	1	0.0	0.0	0.3	0	0.0	0	0
Crystallized	1 ounce	96	0.1	0.1	24.7	0	6.0	17	65
Grape juice, concord	½ cup	77	0.7	0.1	18.9	0	0.3	4	11
Grapefruit									
Fresh	1 medium	77	1.5	0.2	19.3	0	0.2	0	29
Juice, unsweetened	½ cup	47	0.6	0.1	11.1	0	2.5	1	9
Grapes, green, seedless	1 cup	114	1.1	0.9	28.4	0	0.4	3	18
Grits, cooked	½ cup	73	1.7	0.2	15.7	0	0.8	0	0
Ham, cured, roasted, extra-lean	3 ounces	123	17.8	4.7	1.3	45	1.3	1023	7
Hominy									
Golden	½ cup	80	1.5	0.5	17.1	0	0.6	—	—
White	½ cup	58	1.2	0.7	11.4	0	0.5	168	8
Honey	1 tablespoon	64	0.1	0.0	17.5	0	0.1	1	1
Honeydew, raw, diced	1 cup	59	0.8	0.2	15.6	0	0.1	17	10
Horseradish, prepared	1 tablespoon	6	0.2	0.0	1.4	0	0.1	14	9
Hot sauce, bottled	¼ teaspoon	0	0.0	0.0	0.0	0	0.0	9	0
Ice cream									
Vanilla, regular	½ cup	134	2.3	7.2	15.9	30	0.0	58	88
Vanilla, gourmet	½ cup	175	2.0	11.8	16.0	44	0.1	54	75
Ice milk, vanilla	½ cup	92	2.6	2.8	14.5	9	0.1	52	88
Ice, cherry	½ cup	82	0.2	0.0	10.3	—	—	0	—
Jams and Jellies									
Regular	1 tablespoon	54	0.1	0.0	14.0	0	0.2	2	4
Reduced-calorie	1 tablespoon	29	0.1	0.0	7.4	0	0.0	16	1
Jicama	1 cup	49	1.6	0.2	10.5	0	0.7	7	18
Kiwifruit	1 each	44	1.0	0.5	8.9	0	0.4	0	20
Kumquat	1 each	12	0.2	0.0	3.1	0	0.1	1	8
Lamb									
Ground, cooked	3 ounces	241	21.0	16.7	0.0	82	1.5	69	19
Leg, roasted	3 ounces	162	24.1	6.6	0.0	76	1.8	58	7
Loin or chop, broiled	3 ounces	184	25.5	8.3	0.0	81	1.7	71	16

FOOD	APPROXIMATE MEASURE	FOOD ENERGY (CALORIES)	PROTEIN (GRAMS)	FAT (GRAMS)	CARBOHYDRATES (GRAMS)	CHOLESTEROL (MILLIGRAMS)	IRON (MILLIGRAMS)	SODIUM (MILLIGRAMS)	CALCIUM (MILLIGRAMS)
Lard	1 tablespoon	116	0.0	12.8	0.0	12	0.0	0	0
Leeks, bulb, raw	½ cup	32	0.8	0.2	7.3	0	1.0	10	31
Lemon									
Fresh	1 each	22	1.3	0.3	11.4	0	0.6	3	66
Juice	1 tablespoon	4	0.1	0.0	1.3	0	0.0	0	1
Lemonade, sweetened	1 cup	99	0.2	0.0	26.0	0	0.4	7	7
Lentils, cooked	½ cup	115	8.9	0.4	19.9	0	3.3	2	19
Lettuce									
Belgian endive	1 cup	14	0.9	0.1	2.9	0	0.5	6	—
Boston or Bibb, shredded	1 cup	7	0.7	0.1	1.3	0	0.2	3	—
Curly endive or escarole	1 cup	8	0.6	0.1	1.7	0	0.4	11	26
Iceberg, chopped	1 cup	7	0.5	0.1	1.1	0	0.3	5	10
Radicchio, raw	1 ounce	7	0.4	0.1	1.3	0	—	6	6
Romaine, chopped	1 cup	9	0.9	0.1	1.3	0	0.6	4	20
Lime									
Fresh	1 each	20	0.4	0.1	6.8	0	0.4	1	21
Juice	1 tablespoon	4	0.1	0.0	1.4	0	0.0	0	1
Lobster, cooked, meat only	3 ounces	83	17.4	0.5	1.1	61	0.3	323	52
Luncheon meats									
Bologna, all meat	1 slice	90	3.3	8.0	0.8	16	0.4	289	3
Deviled ham	1 ounce	78	4.3	6.7	0.0	—	0.3	—	1
Salami	1 ounce	71	3.9	5.7	0.6	18	0.7	302	4
Turkey ham	1 ounce	35	5.6	1.4	0.0	16	0.8	196	3
Turkey pastrami	1 ounce	40	5.2	1.8	0.5	—	0.5	296	3
Lychees, raw	1 each	6	0.1	0.0	1.6	0	0.0	0	0
Mango, raw	½ cup	54	0.4	0.2	14.0	0	0.1	2	8
Margarine									
Regular	1 tablespoon	101	0.1	11.4	0.1	0	0.0	133	4
Reduced-calorie, stick	1 tablespoon	60	0.0	7.3	0.0	0	0.0	110	0
Marshmallows, miniature	½ cup	73	0.5	0.0	18.5	0	0.4	9	4
Mayonnaise									
Regular	1 tablespoon	99	0.2	10.9	0.4	8	0.1	78	2
Reduced-calorie	1 tablespoon	40	0.0	4.0	1.0	5	—	85	—
Milk									
Buttermilk, low-fat	1 cup	120	9.0	4.0	12.1	—	—	126	301
Buttermilk, nonfat	1 cup	90	9.0	1.0	12.0	—	—	255	285
Chocolate, low-fat 2%	1 cup	180	8.0	5.0	25.8	18	0.6	150	285
Condensed, sweetened	1 cup	982	24.2	26.3	166.5	104	0.5	389	869
Evaporated, skim, canned	1 cup	200	19.3	0.5	29.1	10	0.7	294	742
Low-fat, 1% fat	1 cup	102	8.0	2.5	11.6	10	0.1	122	300
Low-fat, 2% fat	1 cup	122	8.1	4.7	11.7	20	0.1	122	298
Nonfat dry	⅓ cup	143	14.3	0.3	20.6	8	0.1	212	498
Powder, malted	1 tablespoon	35	1.0	0.6	6.2	—	0.1	43	26
Skim	1 cup	86	8.3	0.4	11.9	5	0.1	127	301
Whole	1 cup	149	8.0	8.1	11.3	34	0.1	120	290
Millet, cooked	½ cup	143	4.2	1.2	28.4	0	0.8	2	4
Mint	¼ cup	1	0.1	0.1	0.1	0	0.1	0	4
Molasses, cane, light	1 tablespoon	52	0.0	0.0	13.3	0	0.9	3	34
Mushrooms									
Fresh	½ cup	9	0.7	0.1	1.6	0	0.4	1	2
Canned	½ cup	19	1.5	0.2	3.9	0	0.6	—	—
Shiitake, dried	1 each	14	0.3	0.0	2.6	0	0.1	0	0
Mussels, blue, cooked	3 ounces	146	20.2	3.8	6.3	48	5.7	314	28
Mustard									
Dijon	1 tablespoon	18	0.0	1.0	1.0	0	—	446	—
Prepared, yellow	1 tablespoon	12	0.7	0.7	1.0	0	0.3	196	13

Dash(—) indicates insufficient data available

FOOD	APPROXIMATE MEASURE	FOOD ENERGY (CALORIES)	PROTEIN (GRAMS)	FAT (GRAMS)	CARBOHYDRATES (GRAMS)	CHOLESTEROL (MILLIGRAMS)	IRON (MILLIGRAMS)	SODIUM (MILLIGRAMS)	CALCIUM (MILLIGRAMS)
Nectarine, fresh	1 each	67	1.3	0.6	16.1	0	0.2	0	7
Nuts									
Almonds, chopped	1 tablespoon	48	1.6	4.2	1.7	0	0.3	1	22
Cashews, dry roasted	1 tablespoon	49	1.3	4.0	2.8	0	0.5	1	4
Hazelnuts, chopped	1 tablespoon	45	0.9	4.5	1.1	0	0.2	0	14
Macadamia, roasted, unsalted	1 tablespoon	60	0.6	6.4	1.1	0	0.1	1	4
Peanuts, roasted, unsalted	1 tablespoon	53	2.4	4.5	1.7	0	0.2	1	8
Pecans, chopped	1 tablespoon	50	0.6	5.0	1.4	0	0.2	0	3
Pine	1 tablespoon	52	2.4	5.1	1.4	0	0.9	0	3
Pistachio nuts	1 tablespoon	46	1.6	3.9	2.0	0	0.5	0	11
Walnuts, black	1 tablespoon	47	1.9	4.4	0.9	0	0.2	0	5
Oats									
Cooked	1 cup	145	6.1	2.3	25.3	0	1.6	374	19
Rolled, dry	½ cup	156	6.5	2.6	27.1	0	1.7	2	21
Oil									
Canola (rapeseed)	1 tablespoon	117	0.0	13.6	0.0	0	0.0	0	0
Olive or peanut	1 tablespoon	119	0.0	13.5	0.0	0	0.0	0	0
Vegetable or sesame	1 tablespoon	121	0.0	13.6	0.0	0	0.0	0	0
Okra, cooked	½ cup	26	1.5	0.1	5.8	0	0.3	4	50
Olives									
Green, stuffed	1 each	4	0.0	0.4	0.1	—	—	290	—
Ripe	1 medium	5	0.0	0.4	0.3	0	0.1	35	4
Onions									
Green	1 tablespoon	2	0.1	0.0	0.3	0	0.1	0	4
Raw, chopped	½ cup	29	1.0	0.2	6.2	0	0.3	2	21
Cooked, yellow or white	½ cup	15	0.4	0.1	3.3	0	0.1	4	14
Orange									
Fresh	1 medium	62	1.2	0.2	15.4	0	0.1	0	52
Juice	½ cup	56	0.8	0.1	13.4	0	0.1	1	11
Mandarin, canned, packed in juice	½ cup	46	0.7	0.0	12.0	0	0.4	6	14
Mandarin, canned, packed in light syrup	½ cup	79	0.0	0.0	19.7	0	0.3	7	—
Mandarin, canned, packed in water	½ cup	37	0.0	0.0	8.4	—	0.4	11	—
Oysters, raw	3 ounces	59	6.0	2.1	3.3	47	5.7	95	38
Papaya									
Fresh, cubed	½ cup	27	0.4	0.1	6.9	0	0.1	2	17
Nectar, canned	½ cup	71	0.3	0.3	18.1	0	0.4	6	13
Parsley, raw	1 tablespoon	1	0.1	0.0	0.3	0	0.2	1	5
Parsnips, cooked, diced	½ cup	63	1.0	0.2	15.1	0	0.4	8	29
Passion fruit	1 medium	17	0.4	0.1	4.2	0	0.3	5	2
Pasta, cooked									
Macaroni or lasagna noodles	½ cup	99	3.3	0.5	19.8	0	1.0	1	5
Medium egg noodles	½ cup	106	3.8	1.2	19.9	26	1.3	6	10
Rice noodles	½ cup	138	3.1	1.3	28.6	0	2.2	—	40
Spaghetti or fettuccine	½ cup	99	3.3	0.5	19.8	0	1.0	1	5
Spinach noodles	½ cup	100	3.8	1.0	18.9	0	1.8	22	46
Whole wheat	½ cup	100	3.7	1.4	19.8	0	1.0	1	12
Peaches									
Fresh	1 medium	37	0.6	0.1	9.7	0	0.1	0	4
Canned, packed in juice	½ cup	55	0.8	0.0	14.3	0	0.3	5	7
Canned, packed in light syrup	½ cup	69	0.6	0.0	18.6	0	0.5	6	4
Canned, packed in water	½ cup	29	0.5	0.1	7.5	0	0.4	4	2
Peanut butter									
Regular	1 tablespoon	95	4.6	8.3	2.6	0	0.3	79	5
No-salt-added	1 tablespoon	95	4.6	8.3	2.6	0	0.3	3	5
Pear									
Fresh	1 medium	97	0.6	0.7	24.9	0	0.4	0	18

FOOD	APPROXIMATE MEASURE	FOOD ENERGY (CALORIES)	PROTEIN (GRAMS)	FAT (GRAMS)	CARBOHYDRATES (GRAMS)	CHOLESTEROL (MILLIGRAMS)	IRON (MILLIGRAMS)	SODIUM (MILLIGRAMS)	CALCIUM (MILLIGRAMS)
Pear *(continued)*									
Canned, packed in juice	½ cup	62	0.4	0.1	16.0	0	0.3	5	11
Canned, packed in light syrup	½ cup	71	0.2	0.0	19.6	0	0.3	6	6
Juice	½ cup	57	0.0	0.0	13.6	—	—	6	—
Nectar, canned	½ cup	64	0.4	0.2	16.1	—	0.1	1	4
Peas									
Black-eyed, cooked	½ cup	90	6.7	0.7	15.0	0	1.2	3	23
English, cooked	½ cup	62	4.1	0.2	11.4	0	1.2	70	19
Snow pea pods	½ cup	34	2.6	0.2	5.6	0	1.6	3	34
Split, cooked	½ cup	116	8.2	0.4	20.7	0	1.3	2	14
Peppers									
Chile, hot, green, chopped	1 tablespoon	4	0.2	0.0	0.9	0	0.1	1	2
Jalapeño, green	1 each	4	0.2	0.0	0.8	0	0.1	1	2
Sweet, raw, green, red, or yellow	1 medium	19	0.6	0.4	3.9	0	0.9	2	4
Phyllo strudel dough, raw	1 each	63	2.1	0.2	13.3	—	0.5	—	—
Pickle									
Dill, sliced	¼ cup	4	0.2	0.1	0.9	0	0.4	553	10
Relish, chopped, sour	1 tablespoon	3	0.1	0.1	0.4	0	0.2	207	4
Sweet, sliced	¼ cup	57	0.2	0.2	14.1	0	0.5	276	5
Pie, baked, 9-inch diameter, cut into 8 slices									
Apple, fresh	1 slice	409	3.3	15.3	67.7	12	0.8	229	37
Chocolate meringue	1 slice	354	6.8	13.4	53.8	109	1.2	307	130
Egg custard	1 slice	248	7.3	11.6	28.6	149	0.9	229	129
Peach	1 slice	327	3.2	11.0	55.1	0	1.0	339	35
Pecan	1 slice	478	5.8	20.3	71.1	141	2.4	324	51
Pumpkin	1 slice	181	4.0	6.8	27.0	61	1.1	210	78
Pimiento, diced	1 tablespoon	5	0.2	0.1	1.1	0	0.3	5	1
Pineapple									
Fresh, diced	½ cup	38	0.3	0.3	9.6	0	0.3	1	5
Canned, packed in juice	½ cup	75	0.5	0.1	19.6	0	0.4	1	18
Canned, packed in light syrup	½ cup	66	0.5	0.2	16.9	0	0.5	1	18
Juice, unsweetened	½ cup	70	0.4	0.1	17.2	0	0.3	1	21
Plum, fresh	1 medium	35	0.5	0.4	8.3	0	0.1	0	3
Popcorn, hot-air popped	1 cup	23	0.8	0.3	4.6	0	0.2	0	1
Poppy seeds	1 tablespoon	47	1.6	3.9	2.1	0	0.8	2	127
Pork, cooked									
Chop, center-loin	3 ounces	204	24.2	11.1	0.0	77	0.9	59	5
Roast	3 ounces	204	22.7	11.7	0.0	77	1.0	59	8
Sausage link or patty	1 ounce	105	5.6	8.8	0.3	24	0.3	367	9
Spareribs	3 ounces	338	24.7	25.7	0.0	103	1.5	79	40
Tenderloin	3 ounces	141	24.5	4.1	0.0	79	1.3	57	8
Potatoes									
Baked, with skin	1 each	218	4.4	0.2	50.4	0	2.7	16	20
Boiled, diced	½ cup	67	1.3	0.1	15.6	0	0.2	4	6
Potato chips									
Regular	10 each	105	1.3	7.1	10.4	0	0.2	94	5
No-salt-added	10 each	105	1.3	7.1	10.4	0	0.2	2	5
Pretzel sticks, thin	10 each	25	0.5	0.5	4.4	—	0.3	83	4
Prunes									
Dried, pitted	1 each	20	0.2	0.0	5.3	0	0.2	0	4
Juice	½ cup	91	0.8	0.0	22.3	0	1.5	5	15
Pumpkin									
Canned	½ cup	42	1.3	0.3	9.9	0	1.7	6	32
Seeds, dry	1 ounce	153	7.0	13.0	5.0	0	4.2	5	12

Dash(—) indicates insufficient data available

FOOD	APPROXIMATE MEASURE	FOOD ENERGY (CALORIES)	PROTEIN (GRAMS)	FAT (GRAMS)	CARBOHYDRATES (GRAMS)	CHOLESTEROL (MILLIGRAMS)	IRON (MILLIGRAMS)	SODIUM (MILLIGRAMS)	CALCIUM (MILLIGRAMS)
Radish, fresh, sliced	½ cup	10	0.3	0.3	2.1	0	0.2	14	12
Raisins	1 tablespoon	27	0.3	0.0	7.2	0	0.2	1	4
Raisins, golden	1 tablespoon	31	0.4	0.1	8.2	0	0.2	1	5
Raspberries									
Black, fresh	½ cup	33	0.6	0.4	7.7	0	0.4	0	15
Red, fresh	½ cup	30	0.6	0.3	7.1	0	0.3	0	14
Rhubarb									
Raw, diced	½ cup	13	0.5	0.1	2.8	0	0.1	2	52
Cooked, with sugar	½ cup	157	0.5	0.1	42.1	0	0.3	1	196
Rice cake, plain	1 each	36	0.7	0.2	7.7	0	0.2	1	1
Rice, cooked without salt or fat									
Brown	½ cup	108	2.5	0.9	22.4	0	0.4	5	10
White, long-grain	½ cup	100	2.0	0.2	21.6	0	1.0	3	17
Wild	½ cup	84	2.3	0.6	17.1	—	1.2	12	8
Roll									
Croissant	1 each	272	4.6	17.3	24.6	47	1.1	384	32
Hard	1 each	156	4.9	1.6	29.8	2	1.1	313	24
Kaiser, small	1 each	92	3.0	1.8	16.0	—	1.3	192	7
Plain, brown-and-serve	1 each	82	2.2	2.0	13.7	2	0.5	141	13
Whole wheat	1 each	72	2.3	1.8	12.0	9	0.5	149	16
Rutabaga, cooked, cubed	½ cup	29	0.9	0.2	6.6	0	0.4	15	36
Salad dressing									
Blue cheese	1 tablespoon	84	0.4	9.2	0.3	0	0.0	216	3
Blue cheese, low-calorie	1 tablespoon	14	0.7	1.1	1.0	3	0.0	307	18
French	1 tablespoon	96	0.3	9.4	2.9	8	0.1	205	6
French, low-calorie	1 tablespoon	22	0.0	0.9	3.5	1	0.1	128	2
Italian	1 tablespoon	84	0.1	9.1	0.6	0	0.0	172	1
Italian, no-oil, low-calorie	1 tablespoon	8	0.1	0.0	1.8	0	0.0	161	1
Thousand Island	1 tablespoon	59	0.1	5.6	2.4	—	0.1	109	2
Thousand Island, low-calorie	1 tablespoon	24	0.1	1.6	2.5	2	0.1	153	2
Salsa, commercial	1 tablespoon	4	0.2	0.0	0.8	0	0.1	1	2
Salt, iodized	1 teaspoon	0	0.0	0.0	0.0	0	0.0	2343	15
Sauerkraut, canned	½ cup	13	0.7	0.1	3.2	—	0.4	560	27
Scallops, raw, large	3 ounces	75	14.3	0.6	2.0	28	0.2	137	20
Sesame seeds, dry, whole	1 teaspoon	17	0.5	1.5	0.7	0	0.4	0	29
Sherbet									
Lime or raspberry	½ cup	104	0.9	0.9	23.8	0	0.0	67	39
Orange	½ cup	135	1.1	1.9	29.3	7	0.1	44	52
Shortening	1 tablespoon	94	0.0	10.6	0.0	—	—	—	—
Shrimp									
Fresh, peeled and deveined	½ pound	240	46.1	3.9	2.1	345	5.5	336	118
Canned, drained	3 ounces	102	19.6	1.7	0.9	147	2.3	144	50
Soup, condensed, made with water									
Beef broth	1 cup	31	4.8	0.7	2.6	24	0.5	782	0
Chicken noodle	1 cup	75	4.0	2.4	9.3	7	0.7	1106	17
Chili, beef	1 cup	168	18.4	7.9	6.1	59	3.9	606	36
Cream of chicken	1 cup	117	2.9	7.3	9.0	10	0.6	986	34
Cream of mushroom	1 cup	129	2.3	9.0	9.0	2	0.5	1032	46
Cream of potato	1 cup	73	1.7	2.3	11.0	5	0.5	1000	20
Onion	1 cup	58	3.7	1.7	8.2	0	0.7	1053	27
Tomato	1 cup	85	2.0	1.9	16.6	0	1.7	871	12
Vegetable, beef	1 cup	78	5.4	2.0	9.8	5	1.2	956	17
Soy sauce									
Regular	1 tablespoon	8	0.8	0.0	1.2	0	0.3	829	2
Low-sodium	1 tablespoon	6	0.0	0.0	0.0	—	—	390	—
Reduced-sodium	1 tablespoon	8	0.8	0.0	1.2	0	0.3	484	2
Spinach									
Fresh	1 cup	12	1.6	0.2	2.0	0	1.5	44	55

FOOD	APPROXIMATE MEASURE	FOOD ENERGY (CALORIES)	PROTEIN (GRAMS)	FAT (GRAMS)	CARBOHYDRATES (GRAMS)	CHOLESTEROL (MILLIGRAMS)	IRON (MILLIGRAMS)	SODIUM (MILLIGRAMS)	CALCIUM (MILLIGRAMS)
Spinach *(continued)*									
Canned, regular pack	½ cup	27	3.0	0.7	3.9	—	2.8	381	132
Cooked	½ cup	21	2.7	0.2	3.4	0	3.2	63	122
Squash, cooked									
Acorn	½ cup	57	1.1	0.1	14.9	0	1.0	4	45
Butternut	½ cup	41	0.8	0.1	10.7	0	0.6	4	42
Spaghetti	½ cup	22	0.5	0.2	5.0	0	0.3	14	16
Summer	½ cup	21	1.0	0.3	4.5	0	0.4	1	28
Squid, raw	4 ounces	104	17.7	1.6	3.5	264	0.8	50	36
Strawberries, fresh	1 cup	45	0.9	0.6	10.5	0	0.6	1	21
Sugar									
Granulated	1 tablespoon	48	0.0	0.0	12.4	0	0.0	0	0
Brown, packed	1 tablespoon	51	0.0	0.0	13.3	0	0.5	4	12
Powdered	1 tablespoon	29	0.0	0.0	7.5	0	0.0	0	0
Sunflower kernels	¼ cup	205	8.2	17.8	6.8	0	2.4	1	42
Sweet potatoes									
Whole, baked	½ cup	103	1.7	0.1	24.3	0	0.4	10	28
Mashed	½ cup	172	2.7	0.5	39.8	0	0.9	21	34
Syrup									
Chocolate-flavored	1 tablespoon	49	0.6	0.2	11.0	—	0.3	13	3
Corn, dark or light	1 tablespoon	60	0.0	0.0	15.4	0	0.8	14	9
Maple, reduced-calorie	1 tablespoon	6	0.0	0.0	2.0	0	—	4	—
Pancake	1 tablespoon	50	0.0	0.0	12.8	0	0.2	2	20
Taco shell	1 each	52	0.7	2.8	5.9	—	0.4	62	—
Tangerine									
Fresh	1 medium	38	0.5	0.1	9.6	0	0.1	1	12
Juice, unsweetened	½ cup	53	0.6	0.2	12.5	0	0.2	1	22
Tapioca, dry	1 tablespoon	32	0.1	0.0	7.8	0	0.0	0	1
Tofu									
Firm	4 ounces	164	17.9	9.9	4.9	—	11.9	16	232
Soft	4 ounces	65	6.0	4.0	2.0	—	1.4	2	193
Tomato									
Fresh	1 medium	23	1.1	0.2	5.3	0	0.6	10	9
Cooked	½ cup	30	1.3	0.3	6.8	0	0.7	13	10
Juice, regular	1 cup	41	1.8	0.1	10.3	0	1.4	881	22
Juice, no-salt-added	1 cup	49	2.4	0.0	12.1	—	—	27	—
Paste, regular	1 tablespoon	14	0.6	0.1	3.1	0	0.5	129	6
Paste, no-salt-added	1 tablespoon	11	0.5	0.0	2.6	0	0.2	6	4
Sauce, regular	½ cup	37	1.6	0.2	8.8	0	0.9	741	17
Sauce, no-salt-added	½ cup	42	1.2	0.0	9.7	—	—	27	—
Stewed, canned, no-salt-added	½ cup	32	1.3	0.0	7.5	—	0.7	20	33
Whole, canned, peeled	½ cup	22	0.9	0.0	5.2	—	0.5	424	38
Whole, canned, no-salt-added	½ cup	22	0.9	0.0	5.2	—	0.5	15	38
Tortilla									
Chips, plain	10 each	135	2.1	7.3	16.0	0	0.7	24	3
Corn, 6" diameter	1 each	67	2.1	1.1	12.8	0	1.4	53	42
Flour, 6" diameter	1 each	111	2.4	2.3	22.2	0	0.8	0	27
Turkey, skinned, boned, and roasted									
White meat	3 ounces	115	25.6	0.6	0.0	71	1.3	44	10
Dark meat	3 ounces	159	24.3	6.1	0.0	72	2.0	67	27
Smoked	3 ounces	126	20.4	4.9	0.0	48	2.3	506	9
Turnip greens, cooked	½ cup	14	0.8	0.2	3.1	0	0.6	21	99
Turnips, cooked, cubed	½ cup	14	0.6	0.1	3.8	0	0.2	39	17
Veal, loin, cooked	3 ounces	149	22.4	5.9	0.0	90	0.7	82	18

Dash(—) indicates insufficient data available

FOOD	APPROXIMATE MEASURE	FOOD ENERGY (CALORIES)	PROTEIN (GRAMS)	FAT (GRAMS)	CARBOHYDRATES (GRAMS)	CHOLESTEROL (MILLIGRAMS)	IRON (MILLIGRAMS)	SODIUM (MILLIGRAMS)	CALCIUM (MILLIGRAMS)
Vegetable juice cocktail									
Regular	1 cup	46	1.5	0.2	11.0	0	1.0	883	27
Low-sodium	1 cup	48	2.4	0.2	9.7	—	1.7	48	34
Venison, raw	4 ounces	136	26.0	2.7	0.0	96	3.9	58	6
Vinegar, distilled	1 tablespoon	2	0.0	0.0	0.8	0	0.0	0	0
Water chestnuts, canned, sliced	½ cup	35	0.6	0.0	8.7	0	0.6	6	3
Watercress, fresh	½ cup	2	0.4	0.0	0.2	0	0.0	7	20
Watermelon, raw, diced	1 cup	51	1.0	0.7	11.5	0	0.3	3	13
Wheat bran, crude	1 tablespoon	8	0.6	0.2	2.4	0	0.4	0	3
Wheat germ	1 tablespoon	26	1.7	0.7	3.7	0	0.5	1	3
Whipped cream	1 tablespoon	26	0.2	2.8	0.2	10	0.0	3	5
Whipped topping, non-dairy, frozen	1 tablespoon	15	0.1	1.2	1.1	0	0.0	1	0
Wonton wrappers	1 each	6	0.2	0.1	0.9	5	0.1	12	1
Worcestershire sauce									
Regular	1 tablespoon	12	0.3	0.0	2.7	0	0.0	147	15
Low-sodium	1 tablespoon	12	0.0	0.0	3.0	0	—	57	—
Yeast, active, dry	1 package	20	2.6	0.1	2.7	0	1.1	4	3
Yogurt									
Coffee and vanilla, low-fat	1 cup	193	11.2	2.8	31.3	11	0.2	150	388
Frozen	½ cup	124	3.1	2.1	23.7	—	—	51	—
Fruit varieties, low-fat	1 cup	225	9.0	2.6	42.3	9	0.1	120	313
Plain, low-fat	1 cup	143	11.9	3.5	16.0	14	0.2	159	415
Plain, nonfat	1 cup	127	13.0	0.4	17.4	5	0.2	173	452
Zucchini									
Raw	½ cup	9	0.7	0.1	1.9	0	0.3	2	10
Cooked	½ cup	9	0.7	0.1	1.9	0	0.3	2	10

Source of Data:

Computrition, Inc., Chatsworth, California. Primarily comprised of *The Composition of Foods: Raw, Processed, Prepared.* Handbooks - 8 series. United States Department of Agriculture, Human Nutrition Information Service, 1976-1989.

Recipe Index

Subject Index

Acknowledgments and Credits

Oxmoor House wishes to thank the following individuals and merchants:

J. William Abercrombie, Birmingham, AL
Alpine Life Sports, Suffolk, VA
Barbara Ashford, Birmingham, AL
Bromberg's, Birmingham, AL
Holly Buffington, Birmingham, AL
California Tropics, Carpinteria, CA
Cassis & Co., New York, NY
Dansk International Designs Ltd., Mt. Kisco, NY
Delchamps, Vestavia Hills, AL
Fitz and Floyd, Dallas, TX
Fioriware, Zanesville, OH
Fresh World Produce, Birmingham, AL
Gien, New York, NY
Goldsmith/Corot, Inc., New York, NY
Gorham, Providence, RI
J.R. Brooks and Son, Inc., Homestead, FL
Macy's, Birmingham, AL
Maralyn Wilson Gallery, Birmingham, AL
Mesa International, Elkins, NH
Monroe Salt Works, Monroe, ME
New Day Distributors, Los Angeles, CA
Nordic Fitness Products of Alabama,
   Birmingham, AL
Over-the-Mountain Outfitters, Birmingham, AL
Rich's, Birmingham, AL
Sasaki, New York, NY
Sportslife, Birmingham, AL
Simon Pearce, New York, NY
Weasy Smith, Birmingham, AL
Stone Fish Pottery, Providence, RI
Taitu, Dallas, TX
Vietri, Hillsborough, NC

Photographers

Ralph Anderson: back cover, pages 6, 17, 24, 25, 26, 27, 31, 32, 34, 36, 38, 41, 44, 46, 50, 56, 58, 60, 66, 69, 70, 73, 76, 82, 89, 93, 98, 104, 109, 123, 128, 132, 136, 152, 161, 199, 200, 207, 209, 215, 221, 227, 230, 238, 241

Jim Bathie: front cover, pages 2, 12, 13, 20, 29, 43, 48, 53, 55, 63, 79, 87, 101, 113, 116, 120, 125, 135, 141, 145, 147, 149, 157, 163, 167, 169, 172, 173, 177, 179, 184, 186, 189, 194, 197, 204, 205, 217, 224, 232

Photo Stylists

Kay Clarke: front cover, pages 1, 2, 6, 12, 13, 29, 43, 48, 55, 63, 66, 69, 79, 87, 89, 93, 98, 101, 104, 109, 123, 132, 135, 141, 145, 147, 149, 157, 161, 163, 167, 169, 172, 175, 177, 179, 184, 186, 189, 194, 197, 204, 217, 224, 232

Virginia Cravens: back cover, pages 17, 24, 26, 27, 31, 32, 34, 36, 38, 41, 44, 46, 50, 53, 56, 58, 60, 70, 73, 76, 82, 113, 116, 120, 125, 136, 152, 199, 200, 207, 209, 215, 221, 227, 230, 238, 241